THE TIMES

Holida
Handbook

The Essential
Trip-Planning Guide

G000093845

Cath Urquhart

navigator guides

www.navigatorguides.com

Contents

Published by Navigator Guides

The Old Post Office, Swanton Novers,

Melton Constable, Norfolk NR24 2AJ, UK

www.navigatorguides.com

info@navigatorguides.com

Copyright © Cath Urquhart 2006

"THE TIMES" is a registered trade mark of Times Newspapers Ltd

ISBN 1-903872-17-0

ISBN 13: 978-1-903872-17-8

Reprinted 2006

Publisher: Rupert Wheeler

Managing Editor: Antonia Cunningham

Editor: Susannah Wight

Indexer: Isobel Mclean

Cover Design: Horacio Monteverde

Cover photos: © The Travel Library/Navigator Guides

Text design: Paul Webster

Typeset in Rotis Sans Serif

Printed in Malta by The Progress Press Ltd

Acknowledgements

In researching and writing this book, I had the help of many people who generously gave me their time, advice, and the benefit of their wisdom. At *The Times*, my colleagues on the travel desk have been endlessly supportive and good-humoured, while Robert Thomson, Editor of *The Times*, and George Brock, Saturday Editor, gave me the opportunity and freedom to write the book. At Navigator Guides, publisher Rupert Wheeler and editor Antonia Cunningham led me by the hand up the sharp publishing learning curve, and Bill Bryson gave me generous encouragement far beyond the hopes of any first-time author. And I couldn't have finished the book whilst staying (relatively) sane without the support and love of my wonderful family and friends.

I'd particularly like to thank the following for their help:

Jane Ashton, Tricia Barnett, Ian Belcher, Steve J Benbow, Keith Betton, Sue Biggs, Chloë Bryan-Brown, Simon Calder, Sophie Campbell, Barbara Catchpole, Paul Charles, Tom Chesshyre, David Clover, Jennifer Cox, Jill Crawshaw, Richard Dawood, Glen Donovan, Tony Douglas, Victoria Eld, Mark Ellingham, Carol Farley, Sinead Finn, Debbie Flynn, Justin Francis, Mark Frary, James Fremantle, Mary Gold, the late Bronwyn Gold Blyth, Harold Goodwin, Paul Goodyer, Mike Gooley, Tom Griffiths, Richard Hammond, Maria Harding, John Hatt, Anoushka Healy, Caroline Hendrie, Will Hide, Charlotte Hindle, Debbie Hindle, Sue Hurdle, Robin Hutson, Jeannette Hyde, Pippa Isbell, Tim Jeans, Noel Josephides, Steve Keenan, Jane Knight, Robert Lyle, Brian MacArthur, Molly Maher, Anna Martin, Chris Mason, Nigel Massey, Victoria Mather, Ken McCulloch, Maureen McDonagh, Doug McKinlay, Alex McWhirter, David Moesli, Jo Morris, Sue Ockwell, Andy Phillipps, Kate Quill, Alison Rice, Keith Richards, Roy Riley, Ann Sadler, Alan Saggerson, Sally Shalam, Paul Sizeland, Mark Smith, Hugh Stacey, Andrew Steed, Malcolm Tarling, Sean Tipton, Frances Tuke, Lucia van der Post, Tony Wheeler, Peter Wilson, Patricia Yates

Introduction

For more than 20 years, ever since I spent my gap year in India and Nepal, I have been passionate about travelling. Since 1997 I have edited the travel pages of *The Times*, and writing this book after nearly a decade in the job has made me appreciate just how much our travelling lives have changed.

The internet, and the growth of budget airlines, have been the key catalysts for change, and so fast has been the pace of developments that it can be hard to keep on top of the best advice. That's why readers of *Times Travel* regularly write in to us with sensible, straightforward questions, such as how to book a wonderful villa, how to find travel insurance for older people, or how to find a bargain family trip during the school holidays.

But while we answer these individual queries each week in the travel pages of *The Times*, nowhere could I find a reliable reference book to point readers to that would answer all these important questions, and more. The shelves are full of excellent guides to cruise holidays, backpacking trips or ski breaks – but there didn't seem to be a guide for the reader who, like so many of us today, takes a variety of holidays all year round – perhaps a villa break with friends or family in summer, a ski trip in winter, a couple of short breaks throughout the year and the occasional long-haul adventure.

So I've had a stab at writing it myself. This book takes you chronologically through the holiday process, starting with how to research and plan your trip and the ethical issues to consider. Then I look at whether you should book the trip yourself online, or use a travel company, and I give detailed information on travel's "red tape" – essentials such as how to renew your passport, whether you need a visa for the USA, how to find the best travel insurance policy and smart ways to manage your money overseas.

After that, there's a guide to what to pack, getting through the airport, travelling overseas by train, ferry or car, dealing with problems that arise on holiday, and the most important travel health issues. There is masses for families throughout the book, from finding the best school-holiday deals to coping with flights and foreign food. Finally, in chapter 11, the Directory, I've listed hundreds of tour operators and airlines – such a comprehensive list has never before, to my knowledge, been collected together in one publication.

Researching this book has made me realise how fundamentally the internet has wrested power from the travel agents and the airlines and given it to us, the travelling public. I believe anyone who does not have internet access is now in serious danger of becoming a second-class citizen when it comes to organising their travels.

I don't just mean that you can find deals on the internet that are not available elsewhere, though certainly this is often the case. It's not just how we book travel that's changed – it's how we actually travel. Perhaps the clearest example of this is online check-in: if you have a computer at home or work, you can check in for many flights and, in some cases, print your boarding card before the flight, then at the airport you simply go straight to security, avoiding the queues (see chapter 8). This raises the prospect that the traditional check-in queues will end up consisting of people who do not have access to a computer: not only must these passengers queue up, but once they reach the desk, they may well find that the best seats have already been taken by those logging on to their home computers that morning.

Accessing insider information about travel has become far easier thanks to the web, too. Sites such as www.flyertalk.com, www.hotelchatter.com, www.family-travel.co.uk and www.holidaysuncovered.co.uk make it easy to swap travel tips and horror stories with others, while many excellent travel companies (such as www.i-escape.com and www.responsibletravel.com) have never published conventional paper brochures.

For technophobes, the news is not all bad. Horror stories from the internet frontline – emails not received, bookings unconfirmed, intransigent budget airlines, misleading photos of villas to rent – are once again making us appreciate the value of a good, old-fashioned travel agent. He or she will have access to deals that we travellers cannot find independently, and can also help you avoid the pitfalls – which may be as simple as ensuring you do not go to Parma when you want Palma, or Girona when you want Genoa.

There is another marked trend that has not been so widely observed by the travelling public. Because we so often put together our own trips now by booking separate elements, such as flight, villa and hire car, over the internet, we are increasingly travelling without the financial protection that a package holiday offers. If everything works out fine, that doesn't matter. But when things go wrong, you may have no one to turn to for help, and you may lose your money, or find yourself stranded abroad.

In this book I have attempted to outline these risks, what you can do about them, and how you can find and book good-value holidays worldwide, whether you want a city break in Europe, a round-the-world adventure or a luxurious villa holiday in the Caribbean.

I hope you find it useful, and I look forward to hearing your feedback – please contact me at holidayhandbook@thetimes.co.uk. Today, the world is genuinely our oyster. Travel has rarely been better value, and the world has rarely been so wide open to us. Enjoy your travels!

Cath Urquhart
Autumn 2006

My all-time top ten travel tips

- Don't over-plan your trip – stay flexible and enjoy what comes along.

- Always take out travel insurance.

- A good travel agent can save you money, especially for long-haul trips.

- When booking a trip, if in doubt, get it in writing.

- Take the same care of your personal safety as you do at home.

- If you see something you really want to buy, snap it up there and then – I find you rarely go back to a shop.

- Be a generous tipper.

- Use sunscreen.

- If you see a clean lavatory, use it – you never know when the next one's coming along.

- Take time to talk to local people – it will enrich your visit.

CHAPTER ONE
Choosing your destination

Introduction

I t is one of the travel industry's best—kept secrets, but if you want to find the latest cool destination, get ahead of the pack and venture off the beaten track – ask a bird—watcher. Twitchers lead the way when it comes to exploring unusual corners of the earth. If a rare creature's been spotted, serious bird—watchers care not a jot for the wars, revolutions, insurrections or acts of God that may stand between them and the slaty—tailed trogon, rufous marmot or ground—dwelling great tinamou (all to be found in Panama, I'm told).

Keith Betton is often on TV and radio in his role as spokesman for the Association of British Travel Agents, but he's also an enthusiastic bird—watcher, having so far seen more than 4,300 of the 9,800—odd bird species to be found in the world. Recent trips have taken him to Kazakhstan, where he found the Himalayan snowcock, a native of that region, and Uganda; Angola's now in his sights.

"There is an elite group of bird—watchers, that includes me, that are obsessed with seeing birds that are found in one country and nowhere else," he said. "I've never gone anywhere dangerous – I'm not going to put my life at risk to see a bird – but Iraq is the next place I'm hoping to go, once it's safe, to see the 'Iraq babbler', which is found all along the Euphrates river."

Because of this enthusiasm, bird—watchers have been known to "pioneer" destinations – such as parts of Central America or Central Asia – that mainstream holidaymakers discover much later. But for most of us, holiday plans are usually based on more mundane considerations such as, what's the weather like? is it expensive? are the beaches good? are children welcome? can I drink the water?

Planning a trip should be part of the fun of the holiday, not a chore to plough through (or worse, a stage to skip entirely), so in this chapter I'll look at the sources you can use to plan a trip, such as guidebooks, websites, travel magazines, newspaper travel sections, and clubs for travel enthusiasts.

CHOOSING YOUR DESTINATION

Country guides

Wherever you are thinking of going, you'll want basic information such as what the local currency is, which days are public holidays and what language people speak there. A useful book that pulls all this together is *A to Z of Countries of the World* by Peter Stalker (Oxford University Press, £8.99), which gives the vital statistics of every country and is regularly updated. Another excellent starting point is the **Foreign & Commonwealth Office**'s website (**www.fco.gov.uk**), which reflects the British government's world view. Its Country Profiles are in the Policy part of the site – these give a general overview of a country, such as its recent history and political developments. For more specific trip planning, click on Travel Advice (**www.fco.gov.uk/travel**), which covers more than 200 countries, considering issues such as personal safety, dangers and scams, driving conditions, local festivals and entry requirements. It also has emergency contact numbers for British embassies, consulates and high commissions. You can register for email alerts, so that if the advice on a country you are interested in visiting changes, you are informed electronically. If you don't have internet access you can call 0845 850 2829 for travel advice, or write to: Travel Advice Unit, Consular Directorate, Foreign & Commonwealth Office, Old Admiralty Building, London SW1A 2PA.

- Its useful "Know Before You Go" campaign, also on this website, is valuable reading at this stage, offering safety advice and a trip-planning checklist (**www.fco.gov.uk/knowbeforeyougo**). For more on personal safety while you're travelling, and what the Foreign Office can and cannot do for travellers, *see* chapter 9.

- You can also check out the official advice from Australia (**www.smarttraveller.gov.au**), the USA (**http://travel.state.gov**) and Canada (**www.voyage.gc.ca**).

- Other comprehensive sites for country information include **www.gazeteer.com**, **www.bootsnall.com**, **www.world–guides. com**, **www.cities.com** and the CIA World Factbook at **www.cia.gov/ cia/publications/factbook/index.html**, originally published for US government staff. The World Travel Guide site **www.travel–guides. com** is good, too.

- For an unusual sneak preview of a destination you're considering, download **Google Earth (http://earth.google.com)**, which uses satellite photography to give you a view of the resort or city you're interested in – which could be useful if it reveals that it's miles from the beach, or next to a big construction site.

Weather

What will the weather be like? is for many of us one of the most important considerations. Many of the sites listed in the "country guides" section, above, have weather information, as do guidebooks. For the up-to-the-minute situation, a host of websites (**such as www.weatheronline.co.uk** or **www.metcheck.com**) offer five-day forecasts, as does *The Times* (**www.timesonline.co.uk**). The site **www.weather2travel.com** gives year-round charts showing sunshine, temperature and rainfall. But for more detailed information, the book *Weather to Travel – the Traveller's Guide to the World's Weather*, by Maria Harding (Tomorrow's Red Books, £8.99) is useful. As well as typical temperature and rainfall information, there's a page about each country, suggesting packing tips and explaining regional weather variations.

Even in the rainy season, many tropical countries can be delightful. The rain often pelts down for an hour or so, then clears up and the rest of the day is sunny. Travelling at this time can mean reduced prices from tour operators, too. This sort of detailed weather information is not always clear from bald temperature and rainfall charts, so talk to a tour operator or travel agent who really knows the destination, to see if you will enjoy a visit in this season.

Festivals

It's important to find out when local festivals and carnivals take place – whether you want to join in, or to avoid them. Carnival time can mean a scarcity of hotel rooms, high prices, but plenty of fun if you're in the mood to party. But some religious festivals such as Christmas or Yom Kippur may be less good times to travel, as the emphasis is on families getting together, and local businesses may close and it may be hard to book public transport.

One month-long festival that can seriously affect your travels is Ramadan, the ninth month of the Muslim year. During this time, Muslims do not eat, drink or smoke during daylight hours, ending their fast with a meal at sunset. Tourists are not expected to fast, but you may find more shops and businesses than usual are closed at this time, and so you're forced to eat in hotels all the time. You may also only be allowed to drink alcohol discreetly in your hotel, not in public places, and it may be harder to organise money changing or use public transport at this time.

You will find Ramadan observed across the Arabian peninsula (including Dubai and the rest of the United Arab Emirates, Oman and Yemen), and in countries such as Indonesia, Malaysia and north African countries including Morocco and Egypt. Ramadan starts around 23 September in 2006 and 12 September in 2007 – it moves forward by about 11 days each year, always dependent on sightings of the moon – and it ends with the festival of Eid al-Fitr (around 22 October in 2006, 11 October in 2007), a festival that can be a welcoming experience for visitors, as locals celebrate the end of a month of hardship.

Livelier festivals can generally be found in spring, as Mardi Gras is celebrated noisily, particularly in Venice, New Orleans, Rio de Janeiro and Sydney. Easter is also a celebratory time, especially in Spain and Greece (which celebrates Easter a few weeks later), and there are several spring festivals where you run serious risk of being bombarded with water, such as Songkran in Thailand and Holi in India (where you may get coloured powder thrown at you too). I've been in both countries during these festivals and foreigners always prove a favourite target – but as the weather's so hot then, it can be rather refreshing to have water chucked over you.

Sites to check include:

www.whatsonwhen.com

www.bugbog.com

http://worldparty.roughguides.com/

Tourist boards

I have long believed that tourist boards reflect their country's national characteristics. Thus those run by Germans, Scandinavians, Austrians and Swiss, for example, are pretty organised, responding promptly to requests for information. The French insist you ring them on an expensive inquiries number but it is at least answered by a person, rather than a machine.

Things start to take on a "mañana" aspect when it comes to dealing with the Italians, Greeks and Spaniards, in my experience, and, astonishingly, the USA doesn't even have a proper tourist board in the UK, though links are grouped on the website **www.visitusa.org.uk**. Further afield, certain tourist boards, such as Egypt's and Thailand's, have always impressed me with their efforts to attract visitors, especially after disasters (such as the Luxor massacre or the Asian tsunami) have struck them.

The useful website of the **Association of National Tourist Office Representatives**, known as Antor (0870 241 9084**, www.antor.com**), can put you in touch with around 70 tourist offices based in the UK. Also check **www.officialtravelguide.com** or the **Tourism Offices Worldwide Directory** at **www.towd.com**.

Some tourist boards can be contacted in the UK on freephone 0800 numbers, suggesting they are genuinely keen for you to visit their country. Others, such as Canada, Cyprus, the Czech Republic, France and New Zealand, use expensive 0906 numbers typically costing us 60p a minute.

Here are some of the most commonly requested tourist board details:

Australia, 0191 501 4646, **www.australia.com**

Caribbean, 020 8948 0057, **www.caribbean.co.uk**

Croatia, 020 8563 7979, **http://gb.croatia.hr**

Dubai, 020 7839 0580, **www.dubaitourism.ae**

Egypt, 020 7493 5283**, www.gotoegypt.org**

France, 0906 824 4123, **www.franceguide.com/uk**

Germany, 020 7317 0908, **www.germany–tourism.co.uk**

Greece, 020 7495 9300, **www.gnto.gr**

Hungary, 00800 3600 0000, **www.gotohungary.co.uk**

India, 020 7437 3677, **www.incredibleindia.org**

Ireland, 0800 039 7000, **www.tourismireland.com**

Italy, 00800 0048 2542, **www.enit.it**

Portugal, 0845 355 1212, **www.visitportugal.com**

Spain, 020 7486 8077, **www.tourspain.co.uk**

Sri Lanka, 020 7930 2627, **www.srilankatourism.org**

Sweden, 00800 3080 3080, **www.visitsweden.com**

Thailand, 0870 900 2007, **www.thaismile.co.uk**

Turkey, 020 7839 7778, www.gototurkey.co.uk

USA, 0870 777 2213, www.visitusa.org.uk; also see www.seeamerica.org.uk

Tour operators

In the Directory (chapter 11), you'll find a comprehensive list of holiday companies, arranged according to destination and type of holiday; most will send you their brochure on request. Also contact:

- **The Association of Independent Tour Operators (Aito)** (020 8744 9280, **www.aito.co.uk**) whose 150–plus members are smaller, specialist companies, usually run by experts in their particular destinations.

Two websites, **www.brochurebank.co.uk** and **www.holidaywizard.co.uk**, will process your request for a selection of brochures and send them out to you.

If you want to view a selection of different companies' brochures online in PDF format rather than have them posted to you, visit **www.onlinetravelbrochures.com**.

The **Association of British Tour Operators to France** provides a valuable resource for planning a French holiday at **www.holidayfrance.org. uk**; also see the **Association of British Travel Organisers to Italy** (**www. italiantouristboard.co.uk/abtoi.html**), the **African Travel and Tourism Association** (www.atta.co.uk) and the **Latin American Travel Association** (020 8715 2913, **www.lata.org**).

Travel planning on the internet

Websites and newsletters

The internet has proved so popular with the travelling community, and there are so many sites out there, that my choice of favourites is bound to be both limited and personal. But I think it's helpful, nonetheless, to select sites that I regularly visit for a mix of information and inspiration. Unsurprisingly, savvy publishers have found a way to harness the net, and the books *Travel Online* (Rough Guides, £6.99) and *The Traveller's Internet Guide* (Wexas, £5.95) will point you to thousands more sites to help you plan and book a trip. The websites **www.surf2travel.com** and **www.travel–lists.co.uk** are portals to a wide source of travel and destination websites covering everything from essential tasks such as renewing your passport to choosing a golf or beach holiday.

For "inspiration", here are some of my favourites:

- **I-escape (www.i-escape.com)** is a delight – founders Nikki Tinto and Laila Ram constantly come up with stylish, boutique places before the rest of us spot them. They are not travel agents but put you in touch with the hotel to book.

- **Lonely Planet (www.lonelyplanet.com)** – the guidebook giant has succeeded in creating a real sense of community among the travellers who visit its Thorn Tree message board and discussion forums.

- **Frommer's (www.frommers.com)** and **National Geographic (www.nationalgeographic.com)** are two more guidebook publishers with great email newsletters.

- **Responsible Travel (www.responsibletravel.com)** is an innovative online travel agency featuring holidays that "give the world a break"– trips that support, rather than damage, the host community and environment while still giving you a memorable holiday.

- **Travel Intelligence (www.travelintelligence.net)** combines travel writing by some of the best journalists, hotel reviews and a booking service.

- **World Heritage Sites (http://whc.unesco.org)** – this site lists the cultural and natural wonders on Unesco's World Heritage list. There are currently 830 (more are added each year), from the archaeological remains at Jam in Afghanistan to the Matobo Hills in Zimbabwe.

- **Hip Guide (www.hipguide.com)** offers the latest "in" places in nine cities, including New York, London and Paris. **Grid Skipper (www.gridskipper.com)** calls itself an "urban travel guide" with entries on dozens of cities worldwide.

- **Craigslist (www.craigslist.org)** is a phenomenon that has grown from its humble 1995 beginnings as a small what's-on site in San Francisco to carrying small and personal ads for cities in 35 countries worldwide. The sites can give a fascinating insight into the daily lives and cultural mores of a city, and are used by travellers to post and answer questions about cities they are planning to visit.

Blogs and podcasts

Posting a "blog", or "weblog", chronicling your journeys or offering an opinion, has become hugely popular. To get a feel for what's out there, try **www.travelblog.org**, **http://blog.travelpost.com/**, **www.world66.com** or **www.gadling.com**. To create your own, head for **www.blogger.com** to get started. And the travel section of *The Times*'s website (**www.travel. timesonline.co.uk**) has blogs from correspondents on the road.

There are literally millions of blogs out there and new ones appearing daily – the challenge is to find someone whose stories you feel in tune with. Take the advice and information offered in blogs with a certain degree of caution, as you cannot be sure of the agenda or motivation of the blogger. Creating your own blog, which you update daily on the road, may be one of the best ways to let family and friends know what you're up to on your travels (for more on this, and other ways to keep in touch while you're travelling, *see* chapter 9).

Podcasts are broadcasts on the internet, which you can download on to a computer or portable MP3 player, such as an iPod – and they are really starting to catch on in the travel field. Publishers **Lonely Planet (www.lonelyplanet. com)** and **Rough Guides (www.roughguides.com/podscrolls)** have recently launched podcasts on travel-related subjects, and **Heart Beat Guides (www. heartbeatguides.com)** launched in 2006 offering podcast guides to some 200 destinations. The site **www.expodition.com** offers podcast guides to parts of Britain. How long can it be before enterprising museums provide guided tours that you can download to your iPod when you arrive?

Podcasting is not the only use of technology in this field; long-haul specialist operator Kuoni is one of several tour operators putting videos on its website to give a flavour of the destination (*see* **www.broadband–travel.co.uk**).

Warts–and–all reviews

The internet is the ideal medium for travellers to publish their own reviews of holidays and hotels, and a host of sites now do just that. Their reviews can be eye-wateringly honest, and thus make compulsive reading.

Andrew Burton set up **Holidays Uncovered** in 1999 as a hobby after he went on holiday and was disappointed that the place he booked wasn't what he'd expected. On his site, holidaymakers post their reviews of holiday hotels and apartments, mostly across the popular Mediterranean resorts. But although there are some corking moans, many reports are positive.

"We want folk to tell everyone about the wonderful places they've been to so others can try them, too," said Burton. "We've been threatened by a couple of hotels and small tour operators, but we've worked out the best way to deal with such bullying. We always try to be very fair. If a hotel complains about a review and the review is totally inconsistent with every other review submitted, then we have been known to remove the odd one. We also keep an eye out for bulk submissions of positive reviews!"

Always take these websites' offerings with a pinch of salt. It is not unknown for proprietors of hotels to log on as customers and praise their properties while denigrating a rival's. Sites to try include:

> **www.holidaysuncovered.co.uk**
>
> **www.trivago.co.uk**
>
> **www.holidaywatchdog.com**
>
> **www.holiday–truth.com** for reports on mainstream package holiday destinations
>
> **www.tripadvisor.co.uk** for hotel reviews.

Luxury travel guides

> • Andrew Harper's **Hideaway Report** (001 512 340 7850, **www.andrewharper.com**) has been produced for 26 years. "Andrew Harper" (a pseudonym) and his fellow reviewer "Ian Harper" travel the world anonymously to produce a monthly newsletter for subscribers about the world's best hotels. US–based, it has a bias towards US hotels and those favoured by older, wealthy American travellers. Subscriptions from US$99pa.

> • The **Gallivanter's Guide** (**www.gallivantersguide.com**) is a UK–based monthly eight-page newsletter that also focuses on upmarket hotels, for travellers who know that "an inaccessible resort is not inaccessible if you have your own jet". Quirky and personal; £119 pa.

> • US–based luxury travel site **LuxuryLink** (**www.luxurylink.com**) profiles the world's best hotels and auctions holiday packages to them.

> • **Nota Bene** (0870 240 4089, **www.nbreview.com**): its sometimes acerbic reviews go into huge detail about the smallest issues, and cover relatively little ground, sticking to five–star hotels and

restaurants in each destination. But if you care whether your hotel room boasts Saarinen chairs and Gio Ponti lamps, this is for you. For £275pa you receive ten A5, hardbound destination guides, access to back numbers online, a members' online forum and a personal travel service – you can call up for suggestions of places to stay, eat or visit in any of the 30-plus destinations Nota Bene has previously covered. These include Italy's Aeolian Islands, St Moritz, Miami and Milan. Non-subscribers can sometimes find individual Nota Bene guides on sale in good travel bookshops.

• Top-end traveller Mary Gostelow produces a free online luxury travel magazine, *WOWtravel*, and a monthly email newsletter, *WOWconfidential*, available through the Canada-based hotel marketing group **Kiwi Collection** (**www.kiwicollection.com**), which offers information and a booking service for 3,000 luxury hotels worldwide.

Travel shows

If you can spare a day, it's worth heading to one of these city-based travel fairs for a dose of information and inspiration. Exhibitors include tour operators, specialist activity companies, airlines, guidebook publishers and suppliers of relevant gear – from camping stoves to caravans, snowboards to sailing boats. There are also demonstrations, talks from experts, videos, photography shows and exhibitions, so you'll acquire plenty of fresh ideas for your next big trip. Buying tickets in advance is cheaper than buying them on the door.

The first show to mark in your diary is **Destinations – The Holiday and Travel Show**, which since 2006 has been sponsored by *The Times*. In the February 2006 show, there were more than 300 travel companies and tourist boards, talks on subjects such as becoming a travel writer or taking a career break to travel, and speakers such as BBC World Affairs Editor John Simpson and Nick Middleton, who recently presented *Going to Extremes: the Silk Routes* on Channel 4.

• **Destinations**, the Holiday and Travel Show presented by *The Times* (0870 120 0332, **www.destinationsshow.com**) is at London's Earls Court in February 2007 and Birmingham NEC in March 2007, and again in early February and March 2008.

- **The Holiday & Travel Show,** a separate consumer show, is at Manchester's G-Mex Centre and Glasgow's SECC in January. Details: **www.holidayshows.com.**

- **The Global Adventure Sports + Travel Show** is at Birmingham NEC in November (0871 230 5449, **www.globalsnowshows.co.uk**).

- **The Northern Ski & Snowboard Show**, from the same organisers, is at Manchester's G-Mex Centre in October.

- **The Daily Mail Ski and Snowboard Show** is at Olympia, London, in October (0870 590 0090, **www.dailymailskishow.co.uk**).

- **The Daily Telegraph Adventure Travel and Sports Show** (0870 161 2122, **www.adventureshow.co.uk**) is at Olympia in January.

- **The Ordnance Survey Outdoors Show** is at Birmingham NEC in March (0870 010 9086, **www.theoutdoorsshow.co.uk**).

- **Dive shows** are held at London's Excel in April and Birmingham's NEC in October (**www.diveshows.co.uk**).

- **The Cycle Show** (0870 126 1795, **www.cycleshow.co.uk**) is at Excel in London in October.

- **The Spa Show**, about spa holidays, is held at London's Olympia in November 2006 (0870 060 6090, **www.spashow.co.uk**).

- **One Life Live** (0870 272 0001, **www.onelifelive.co.uk**), in March 2007, also at Olympia, tackles taking a career break.

- **The Accessible Holiday Show**, the first dedicated show for disabled travellers, took place in 2005 and more are planned (**www.accessibleholidayshow.co.uk**).

- **The Luxury Travel Fair** is in June at London's Olympia (0870 060 6090, **www.luxurytravelfair.com**).

Travel clubs

Travellers are naturally convivial creatures so it's hardly surprising that we want to get together and exchange stories – and not just online. Some clubs, such as the Royal Geographical Society and The Travellers' Club, have membership criteria based on achievement (and, in the latter case, gender), while others are open to anyone prepared to pay the joining fee.

• Globetrotters (www.globetrotters.co.uk) is an informal club for independent travellers that has regular London meetings, newsletters and provides a forum for exchanging advice and finding travelling companions. Membership is £15pa.

• **The Royal Geographical Society** (020 7591 3000, **www.rgs.org**), based at wonderful premises opposite Hyde Park in London, was formed in 1830 to promote geographical knowledge and understanding, and its 14,000 members still pursue those aims today, whether by undertaking field research, expeditions, teaching or otherwise being involved in geography and related areas. Membership starts at £78pa.

• The **South American Explorers' Club (www.saexplorers.org)** is worth joining if you're planning an independent trip to that continent. For your US$50 annual membership fee, as well as accessing masses of information and receiving a quarterly magazine, you'll be able to use the clubhouses, located in Quito, Lima, Cusco, Buenos Aires and New York.

• **The Travellers Club** in London's Pall Mall (020 7930 8688, **www.thetravellersclub.org.uk**) is a very different kettle of fish – an old-fashioned gentleman's club, all mahogany furniture and brass light fittings, with a beautiful library of classic travel editions. Rather tediously, women are still not admitted as full members. The club's original purpose, when it was dreamt up by Lord Castlereagh in the 19th century following the Napoleonic Wars, was as a place that diplomats, explorers and the like could meet. To join you must be proposed and seconded by members; from £900pa.

• **Wexas** (020 7589 3315, **www.wexas.com**) is a commercial club, offering members deals and discounts on flights, insurance, airport car parking and the like. Its magazine *Traveller*, which is included in your membership, is excellent. You can buy both the magazine and Wexas's useful reference work *The Traveller's Handbook* (£16.95) in bookshops, without being a member. Membership costs £59pa for the basic (blue) level, £130pa for gold.

Guidebooks and maps

Where do guidebooks go from here?

Strolling through the bazaar near the River Ganges in Varanasi, India, a few years ago, I saw a banner across the road proclaiming: "Yogi Lodge! Recommended by Lonely Planet!" A little further on, I saw another sign, with an arrow pointing to a different scruffy hostel, announcing that it, too, was the Yogi Lodge "As Featured In Lonely Planet". Soon I noticed that almost every backpackers' flophouse in the bazaar seemed to be called Yogi-something, and to have its own ringing endorsement from the guidebook.

The mystery was quickly solved by consulting my Lonely Planet guide to the city. "Its [the Yogi Lodge's] success has spawned the Jogi Lodge, the Old Yogi Lodge, Gold Yogi Lodge, New Yogi Lodge and Yogi Guest House, some of which are inferior copies..."

The Lonely Planet author ascribes the situation to the success of the original guest house, which has long been popular with budget travellers – but he coyly overlooks the effect that a favourable mention in his own guidebook can have. Not for nothing do legions of backpackers refer to Lonely Planet as "the Bible", and often seem reluctant to step off the trails it describes. Hoteliers also quickly realise its power, as numerous Varanasi lodge owners would testify: a favourable mention in a Lonely Planet guide can save you a small fortune in advertising. The publisher admits as much on its website, where it states: "Secluded beaches or fragile tribal areas may be purposely omitted: after all, travel is still about making your own discoveries and we don't ever want to change that."

Such has been the success of this global publishing empire – Lonely Planet claims to cover every country in the world, and publishes more than 600 titles – and so rapidly have other guidebook publishers expanded too, that it can seem hard to recall a time when we travelled without a guidebook, or used them more sparingly. Yet when I first travelled to India, spending most of a year there in 1984–5, it did not even occur to me to pack a guidebook. Partly this was due to my inexperience as a traveller, and the fact that guidebook culture was far less established two decades ago than it is now, but I managed to traverse the continent perfectly happily without a guidebook and, arguably, had the more interesting experiences for it.

Would I travel without a guidebook today? Of course not – and nor should you. Reading about a country will help you make the most of your trip, see the best sights, avoid inadvertently causing offence or falling victim to the local scams. But my early India experiences taught me that you don't need to be guidebook-dependent to have a great trip. When you're on holiday, try putting your guidebook away and following your nose for a day or two, going to the restaurants, parks and markets that the locals favour instead of the theme parks, busy beaches or tourist shops frequented by holidaymakers. It could well be the most rewarding part of your holiday.

Guidebooks make good slaves but bad masters. Lonely Planet and other guidebook publishers tacitly acknowledge this, pointing out that prices may rise or restaurants close between the time the books are researched and the date of publication, so the information given should be treated with a sensible dollop of caution. Guidebooks should offer suggestions, ideas, sketch out scenarios – not dictate every step of your itinerary. The question is, which one is right for your trip?

Whether you're planning a dirty weekend in Brighton, a business trip to Saudi Arabia or a six-month backpacking trip through southeast Asia, there will be a guidebook to help you, quite possibly with integral CD-rom, fold-out laminated map, discounted phonecard, free sunblock and website with downloadable information for your PDA. There's been a huge explosion in guidebook publishing (and the gimmicks used to sell them) over the past decade, partly reflecting the fact that we're all taking so many more trips since the introduction of budget airlines. Guidebook sales took a dive after the terrorist attacks of September 11, 2001, as we temporarily stopped travelling, but they are now back on track. Rough Guides has even acknowledged the changed political climate by publishing, in 2005, its first *Travel Survival* book, tapping in to the increased sense of traveller unease over issues such as bombings and other terrorist attacks in tourist destinations.

This shows how publishers cannily pick up on the key trends in travel today. The growth of interest in Eastern Europe (helped by all those new budget flights), the fact that we're taking so many more short breaks (ditto), and the rapid rise of the "adult gap year" are all creating mini publishing phenomena. "Our staff get asked for books on Croatia more than anywhere else," said Andrew Steed, who has been purchasing manager for Stanfords travel bookshop in London since 1995. So popular has Eastern Europe become, and so great the number of new books published on that region, that the Eastern Europe section at Stanfords has expanded out of the ground floor Europe section into its own space on the first floor.

"Short breaks have certainly been the flavour of the past couple of years," said Mark Ellingham, who in 1982 founded Rough Guides, now owned by

Penguin. "And it has to be said, people are a lot more demanding of everything in the travel market, guidebooks included, than when we started, with a rather amateur ethos."

Several guidebook series, such as Purple Guides and A Hedonist's Guide to..., have sprung up explicitly to cater for this short-breaks market, and are well aware of the desires of these more demanding travellers. They are as clear on what they do not cover as on what they do. Purple Guides, which cover regions of Italy including Tuscany, Venice and Rome, does not review accommodation, for example. Robin Bell, editor and publisher, explained: "Other guidebooks do this, plus you are not likely to want to change hotels if you are only staying for a short break, so why include that information?" Instead, his guides focus on restaurants, food and shopping, perceived to be their readers' main interests. "People want to eat well, and dine out on this when they get home, too," he said.

While Purple Guides are explicity not for night owls, A Hedonist's Guide to..., as the title suggests, are. "The idea behind the books was to encourage relaxing weekends away, in stylish surroundings, without the pressure of educationally furthering oneself," said the MD, Tremayne Carew Pole. "No other travel guides concern themselves with the more decadent and Epicurean principles of eating, drinking and over-indulging."

The stylish, black-covered guides concentrate on cities popular with the short-break crowd, but which are under-represented in the guidebook field, such as Marrakesh, Moscow, Beirut and Tallinn. "Ten years ago, you went for culture – for example, in Paris you saw the Louvre or the Musée d'Orsay – but I went to Paris recently and didn't see a single museum," said Carew Pole. "We eat and shop our way around."

The big publishers are increasingly looking to exploit niches, too: Rough Guides has long been canny at spotting the coming thing, with its guide to the internet now in its 11th edition, and the publisher Bradt is usually first out of the starting block when it comes to covering a country that is just recovering from war or unrest, such as Iraq or Rwanda, or simply somewhere you'd never thought of going, such as Turkmenistan or Benin.

Lonely Planet has perhaps gone the furthest, with its recent Guide to Experimental Travel. This is a sort of "anti-travel" craze, with suggestions for trips including creating a route from the first street to the last in a city's A to Z; photographing the building opposite every famous landmark; and visiting a city at the same time as, but separately from, your partner and trying to find each other without using your phone. It's interesting to see that the company that has sent so many backpackers to the same tourist sites the world over is, with this volume, trying to get them to think a little outside the box.

And it's ironic that, while the Guide to Experimental Travel promotes the sort of trips you will never find in a guidebook, Lonely Planet has brought out a guidebook to teach you how to do it. With inventiveness like that, I don't have too many fears for the future of our guidebook industry.

A guide to the guides

Which guidebook is right for my trip?

Over the past 20 years of travelling I have compiled a personal list of favourite guidebooks (see box, page 29), and while I try to test as many as possible, I still find myself turning to a particular series for certain types of trip or destination. In Asia, I tend towards Lonely Planet, in Africa I like Rough Guides and Bradt, for South America I pick Footprint first, and in the USA I'll often try an American series, such as Moon or Fodor's. Time Out is excellent on European cities, and in Central Asia you part me from my Trailblazer guides at your peril. But there are so many guidebook series published now that you should be able to find something to suit every type of trip and traveller.

- **The AA** (**www.theaa.com/bookshop**) is the biggest travel publisher in the UK, with its guidebook series, driving maps, walking guides and hotel guides. Its best known guidebooks are the slender Citypacks, which have a separate map at the back, and its comprehensive Explorer country or regional guides, which also come with a map. **Best for**: short breaks.

- **Alastair Sawday's** Special Places to Stay (**www.alastairsawday. co.uk**). This interesting and opinionated publisher now offers 22 titles detailing places to stay in countries including Britain, France, Morocco and India. It tends towards owner–run, comfortable hostelries where the emphasis is on warm hospitality, not whether there's a trouser press provided (chances are, there won't be). It takes payment from the properties it features, but inspects them all and applies strict criteria for inclusion. In 2006 it is publishing *Green Places to Stay*, looking at hotels worldwide run on environmental principles. **Best for**: weekends in charming, quirky properties.

- **Berlitz** (**www.berlitzpublishing.com**) is best known for its Pocket Guides – which offer a basic introduction to a city or region – and its

language teaching books, including phrasebooks, and several aimed at teaching children a foreign language. Berlitz also publishes the classic cruise guide *Ocean Cruising and Cruise Ships*, annually updated by the *eminence grise* of the cruising world, Douglas Ward.
Best for: short breaks and cruising.

• Blue Guides (**www.blueguides.com**), originally started during the First World War and long known for their erudition but dull presentation, were taken over in 2004 by Somerset Books, which aims to pep them up. "We felt the time was right to bring them back to life and make them look a little more contemporary," said editor-in-chief Annabel Barber. "They were dreary to look at – black and white, and dense." Colour photographs and a cleaner layout have been used for the revised editions, and greater attention is being paid to hotels and restaurants, though Blue Guides remain highbrow companions for those who enjoy culture, art, architecture and history. The series is strong on European cities and the Middle East.
Best for: European culture.

• Bradt Guides (**www.bradtguides.com**). Founder Hilary Bradt started this eclectic publishing house in the 1970s with volumes on Peru and other South American destinations. Bradt now publishes guides to more than 100 destinations, specialising in countries recovering from civil war or political upheaval – Mozambique, Iraq, Armenia and Tibet – or those under-represented by other series, such as Cameroon, Gabon or the Faroe Islands. Its guide to Rwanda literally kick-started tourism there. **Best for**: adventurers, aid workers, journalists.

• Bugbooks (**www.bugbooks.com**) is a small series for budget travellers, offering guides to backpacker hostels in Australia, New Zealand, Britain and Ireland. **Best for**: budget travellers.

• Cadogan Guides (**www.cadoganguides.com**) cover more than 100 destinations, and are particularly strong on regions of Europe, such as the Rhône-Alpes in France or the Italian Riviera and Piemonte. Reflecting our growing interest in short breaks, it has a nifty "Flying Visits..." series aimed at weekend-break visitors to destinations throughout Europe. Its travellers' health book, *Bugs, Bites & Bowels*, is excellent. **Best for**: sensible families.

• **Culture Smart Guides (www.culturesmartguides.co.uk)**, formerly known as Culture Shock guides, are pocket-sized books that focus heavily on customs and etiquette, but do not offer practical information about hotels or attractions. Business travellers, expatriates or those planning longer stays will find them most useful. **Best for**: expats and business travellers.

• **Dorling Kindersley (http://uk.dk.com)** specialises in glossy, heavily pictorial, beautifully illustrated volumes that can be rather heavy to carry around. Its key series is the Eyewitness Travel Guides, while its Top Ten series offers easily digestible guides to popular city break destinations. Its new e-guides, to London, New York, Paris and Rome, give you access to a password-protected website which helps keep them up to date. It also produces great atlases. **Best for**: impressing your girlfriend.

• **The Economist (www.economist.com)** has guides to 24 cities on its website, in a clear, accessible format. **Best for**: business travellers.

• **Fodor's (www.fodors.com)**. This American group's key series is its Gold Guides, comprehensive coverage of countries or regions, often written by in-country authors. Its other series include Exploring guides, city guides and maps, a series on travelling with children, and a useful website. **Best for**: upmarket breaks.

• **Footprint (www.footprintguides.com)** started in 1924 when its South American Handbook was first published, but it now encompasses much of the world, although it has relatively few guides to Europe and North America. "We try to take people a little bit away from the crowds and off the beaten track, and try to get people to travel in context – the cultural background and history are very important," said MD Patrick Dawson. It has a new Backpacker series aimed at travellers with limited time who are happy to stay in modest accommodation but spend plenty on activities. **Best for**: "flashpackers", backpackers on a two-week trip.

• **Frommer's (www.frommers.com)** is an American publisher with a strong catalogue of guides to North America, and its authoritative "Complete" guides to destinations worldwide, updated annually. Its best selling guide (at 100,000 copies a year!) is *The Unofficial Guide to Walt Disney World*. It also publishes the less saccharine Irreverent

Tony Wheeler's vision for the future

Tony Wheeler, who with his wife Maureen founded Lonely Planet in 1973, is something of a legend in the travelling community. He enjoys telling stories of how rumours swirl around the internet about him, including various stories commiserating over his untimely demise. What always impresses me about Tony is that, despite having millions in the bank, he travels a lot of the time like the rest of us – dressed down, backpack over his shoulder, heading off into the night to catch the nearest tube or bus back to his hotel.

Recently I asked him how he saw the future. What does a guidebook company do once it's covered almost every country on the planet?

"The guidebook of the future? I've been saying for years, "here it is, I've got it already," and holding up my GPS, my PDA and my mobile phone. Now all we have to do is weld the three together. Quite apart from the location and communication functions of this 'new age' guidebook, we could also have far greater information capacity. If we can condense a shelf full of CDs and a CD player into an iPod, why do we put up with bulky guidebooks?

"For example, a couple of months ago I went to Tunisia (and took our Tunisia guidebook) and contemplated making a short side trip into Algeria but didn't want to tote our Africa guide along as well. So I simply loaded the PDFs of the Algeria chapter on to my laptop and took that. I could easily have PDFs of our entire range on my laptop on that 'just in case' basis. But at the moment, who would possibly want to look at a guidebook on a laptop? It takes several minutes for my laptop to wake up and start thinking; a guidebook you can flick open instantaneously.

"What I do see happening one day is having that GPS–PDA–mobile phone–and–camera all–in–one device which also has instant updating capability. Perhaps you'll plug it in to an ATM-like docking device at the airport, swipe your credit card and download this hour's guidebook update. Perhaps you'll do the same thing via an internet connection. My new Mini [car] is already part way there – the satellite navigation system incorporates some guidebook–like information capabilities, and that is bound to increase."

guides, Dummies series (basic introductions to a country), a series on travel with children to certain US cities, driving tours, walking holidays and "unofficial" guides for independent travellers. **Best for**: surviving Walt Disney World.

• **A Hedonist's Guide to... (www.ahedonistsguideto.com)**. These black-covered, pocketbook-sized volumes offer stylish guides to cities that are sometimes overlooked by major guidebook publishers, such as Tallinn, Moscow, Beirut and Marrakesh. Aimed squarely at the weekend-break brigade who want funky hotels, the best restaurants, the latest nightclubs and the merest smattering of culture. **Best for**: hedonists, of course.

• **In Your Pocket** guides (**www.inyourpocket.com**) cover eastern Europe and the Baltic states (and, somewhat randomly, the Isle of Man), and are particularly strong on city information. Great, up-to-date website, with free, downloadable short city guides. **Best for**: hens and stags.

• **Insight Guides** (**www.insightguides.com**) started with a Bali guide in 1970 and since then has become one of the world's biggest guidebook publishers. The 200-plus destination guides have more photographs than most: while this makes them attractive to armchair travellers, they can be rather heavy. Perhaps conscious of this, Insight has added smaller city guides, laminated fleximaps, and compact guides for short visits. Insight also publishes the useful *Asia's Best Hotels*. **Best for**: armchair travel.

• **Let's Go** (**www.letsgo.com**) is a budget travel series aimed at backpackers, put together exclusively by Harvard students, with most guides updated annually. Its Europe book is a classic. A feature on its website offers the following advice: "Forget what your mom told you about hygiene: you do not need showers every day (or even week, really)... Don't waste your precious backpack room taking extra changes of clothes and excessive toiletries. Be simple; be smelly." If this is you, you've just found your ideal guidebook. Its sister site, **www.beyondtourism.com**, promotes sustainable tourism projects. **Best for**: backpackers on a budget.

• **Lonely Planet** (**www.lonelyplanet.com**). For many travellers this is less a guidebook series, more a way of life. "The difference between us and other publishers is authority – we cover every country in the world – we're the only publisher to do that," a spokeswoman told me firmly. Despite starting in the 1970s as the "backpacker's Bible", Lonely Planet has more recently aimed at a more monied readership, conscious that many of its customers have grown up and want to stay on the top floor of the Mandarin Oriental, not the actual floor of a railway station waiting room. **Best for**: round–the–world travellers.

• **Luxe City Guides** (www.luxecityguides.com) cover 16 Asian countries or cities, including Hanoi, Chiang Mai, Sri Lanka and Melbourne, updated twice yearly to include the most happening shops, hotels, bars and restaurants. **Best for**: upmarket travellers to Asia.

• **Michelin** (**www.michelin.com**) produces its famous Red guides, which rate upmarket hotels and restaurants and award the famous stars for *haute cuisine*, and Green guides, which have more emphasis on other attractions in the region. **Best for**: touring holidays in Europe.

• **Moon Handbooks** (**www.moon.com**), like Insight Guides, also started with an Indonesia volume produced in the early 1970s by its founder, Bill Dalton. This US publisher now covers more than 110 destinations, specialising in guides to North, Central and South America. Moon also produces Metro guides to 18 US and European cities, with detailed fold–out maps. **Best for**: USA and Mexico.

• **National Geographic** (**www.nationalgeographic.com**): this American publisher, which has published the magazine *National Geographic* since 1888, also puts out guidebooks to destinations worldwide in its Traveller series. These are strong on photography, history, geography and culture rather than hotels and restaurants, though these are listed. National Geographic also produces atlases and has a rather good website with regular email updates and news stories on natural history and environmental topics.
Best for: inspiration and education.

• **Navigator Guides** (**www.navigatorguides.com**) publishes a useful series on visiting popular cities using only the underground system – Paris and London titles will soon be joined by Berlin and New York. Essential sights are listed based on walking distance from the metro exit. **Best for**: city visitors planning to use public transport.

• **Purple Guides** (www.thepurpleguide.com): a small series, focusing on regions of Italy and concentrating on culture, eating out and good food. Aimed at the older traveller on a short break who is not interested in the latest bar or nightclub. Does not review hotels. **Best for**: foodies.

• **Rough Guides** (www.roughguides.com): in 1982 Mark Ellingham put together the first Rough Guide, to Greece; nearly 25 years later his empire is owned by Penguin and responsible for more than 200 destination titles and an inventive website. Like Lonely Planet, it has steered away from its backpacker roots and moved firmly mainstream, bolstering destination titles with zeitgeisty guides to everything from the internet and world music to Shakespeare and pregnancy. It also offers maps, both printed and digital. Its website has travellers' forums, a free newsletter, a thrice-yearly magazine – and most of the guidebooks' content. **Best for**: independent travellers.

• **Thomas Cook Publishing** (www.thomascookpublishing.com) may be best known for the *European Rail Timetable* and the *Overseas Timetable*, essential for planning rail trips, and the excellent *Greek Island Hopping*, but it also publishes a range of guides to mainstream destinations, the "spots" series to popular cities, beach and ski resorts, driving guides for touring holidays, and Out Around, a series for gay holidaymakers. **Best for**: train- and ferry-spotters.

• **Time Out** (www.timeout.com): its city guides, in my experience, are often the best, and it also produces imaginative books such as *Weekend Breaks in Great Britain and Ireland* – suggesting hotels, restaurants and activities to fill a short trip – and several cheap, magazine-style guides to, for example, European cities, sunshine resorts served by budget airlines, or cheap places to eat in London. **Best for**: weekenders.

• **Trailblazer** (www.trailblazer-guides.com), founded by Bryn Thomas in 1991 with the *Trans-Siberian Handbook*, this company produces informed guides to some out-of-the-way places (such as Azerbaijan), trekking guides to regions such as the Pyrenees and the Himalayas, and guides to classic overland routes, whether you're travelling by train, bicycle, motorbike or Jeep. **Best for**: adventurers.

- **Vacation Work Publications** (**www.vacationwork.co.uk**) publishes various guides to working abroad, whether for a few months or a few years, and to organising an "adult gap year", plus under the Travel Survival Kit series it offers conventional guidebooks to a range of destinations including Cuba, Lebanon and the USA. Its website has a noticeboard for people seeking work overseas.
Best for: grown-up gappers.

Walking guides

Many of the guidebook series listed above – particularly the AA, Lonely Planet and Trailblazer – publish walking guides, but there are also specialists in the field for enthusiastic hikers. Also *see* chapter 5 – Holidays in the UK.

- **Cicerone** (**www.cicerone.co.uk**) publishes nearly 300 titles to the walking and trekking regions of the UK, Europe and a few further-flung destinations such as Bhutan and Kilimanjaro; plus climbing, mountaineering and biking guides, all with maps.

- **Discovery Guides** (**www.walking.demon.co.uk**) specialises in walking guides to Spain, Portugal and their islands – the Canaries, Balearics and Madeira, plus Malta and Gozo. It also publishes walking guides to regions of Britain, particularly National Parks such as the Peak District or Dartmoor.

- **Rother** (**www.rother.de**), a German outfit, publishes walking guides (in English) to destinations across Europe.

- **Sunflower** (**www.sunflowerbooks.co.uk**) publishes the distinctive blue-backed Landscapes guides to popular walking destinations across Europe, with its long-standing Madeira guide one of its best-sellers. It has just launched the "Walk and Eat" series aimed at people on short breaks who want good restaurant recommendations.

It's also worth tracking down *The Backpacker's Handbook* by Chris Townsend (McGraw-Hill, £11.99; **www.mcgraw-hill.co.uk**) which is, despite its title, aimed at expedition participants and outdoor adventurers rather than 18-year-olds wanting to explore the fleshpots of Phuket, and *The Mountain Traveller's Handbook* by Paul Deegan (£13 from the British Mountaineering Council; **www.thebmc.co.uk**) which has good advice for trekkers, climbers and anyone travelling to altitude.

Travel literature

- **Armchair Traveller** is a new imprint from Haus Publishing (**www.hauspublishing.co.uk**) which offers thoughtful travelogues to destinations including Damascus, Morocco and Italy.

- **Eland** (**www.travelbooks.co.uk**) reproduces classic works of travel literature by such luminaries as Norman Lewis, Mungo Park and Martha Gellhorn.

Tracking down your book

Specialist travel bookstores

All major bookshops have travel sections, but a specialist travel bookshop should carry a wider stock and have more knowledgeable staff.

- **Daunt Books**, 83 Marylebone High Street, London W1U (020 7224 2295, **www.dauntbooks.co.uk**). A beautiful, galleried Edwardian bookshop with large skylights; the books – guides, literature, history, cookery, art – are organised by country rather than subject. It was opened by James Daunt in 1990, who told me: "We take a large general bookshop and flip it – anything that can be arranged by country, we do. It makes life very much easier. Otherwise, finding novels about Goa, for example, is impossible unless you know what you're looking for."

- **Stanfords Map and Travel Bookshop** (**www.stanfords.co.uk**) carries a huge stock, and is particularly strong on maps. I start every trip here. It has three branches: 12–14 Long Acre, Covent Garden, London WC2E (020 7836 1321); 29 Corn Street, Bristol BS1 (0117 929 9966), 39 Spring Gardens, Manchester M2 (0161 831 0250).

- **The Travel Bookshop**, 13–5 Blenheim Gate, London W11 (020 7229 5260, **www.thetravelbookshop.co.uk**) was opened by writer Sarah Anderson in 1979 and moved to its present base in Notting Hill in 1982, where it was famously used as a setting in the film *Notting Hill* – it's where Hugh Grant's character worked. Anderson, who in 2004 sold the shop, is the author of the excellent *Anderson's Travel Companion* (out of print, but available on Amazon), a guide, by destination, to the best non–fiction and fiction about each country. She has also written her first regional guide: *Sarah Anderson's Travel*

Companion: Africa and the Middle East (Portobello Publishing, £14.99) and hopes to produce further volumes.

• **Oriental and African Books** in Shrewsbury (01743 352575, **www.africana.co.uk**) specialises in rare, antiquarian and out-of-print books on Africa, the Middle East and Asia.

Specialist websites

If you're having trouble tracking down a book, you may well be able to find it for sale (possibly second hand) through **Amazon** (**www.amazon.co.uk**), **Abebooks** (**www.abebooks.com**) or **Book Finder** (**www.bookfinder.com**).

For forthcoming titles, visit **Booktrust** at **www.bookinformation.co.uk**. You can also order books, often at a discount, from *The Times* BooksFirst (0870 160 8080, **www.timesonline.co.uk/booksfirst**).

Maps

Driving around Crete on holiday once, I made an uncomfortable discovery: the map I was using appeared to show the roads the Greeks would like to have, rather than those they actually had.

Since then, whenever I hire a car overseas, I make a real effort to get a decent map before I set off, rather than try to buy one once I'm there. Because funnily enough, the best maps of foreign countries can usually be bought right here at home.

Maps are something the British do very well. I don't just mean producing them – although the Ordnance Survey maps are things of wondrous beauty and usefulness. Sourcing maps of the world's most obscure corners is also something we're good at. As Martin Brown, manager of **Maps Worldwide**, told me: "People from all over the world order maps from us. For example, Spanish people cannot get good maps of Spain in Spain, so they order them from us. And the British and American military buy lots of maps from us, especially of Iraq and Afghanistan. We always know something's going on before it breaks in the news – Fort Knox sometimes orders several hundred maps of Afghanistan suddenly."

Andrew Steed, purchasing manager at Stanfords travel bookshop, which has a large maps section, said the ease of obtaining maps to a particular region depends on the political situation in the country. "There's a misconception that anywhere is available. That never has been the case – in some areas it's gone backwards." He cites the example of former French possessions in Africa; maps of Niger and Chad dating from 1961 are still the best that Stanfords can find to sell.

Contacts

- **British Cartographic Society** (www.cartography.org.uk) is an association that celebrates and promotes mapmaking.

- **Greaves & Thomas** (01983 568555, **www.globemakers.com**) is the last globemaker left in the UK.

- **Harvey Maps** (01786 841202, **www.harveymaps.co.uk**) are waterproof maps for walkers to destinations worldwide.

- **Latitude Maps and Globes** (01707 663090, **www.latitudemapsandglobes.co.uk**) is a map and globe specialist.

- **Maps International** (0800 038 6277, **www.mapsinternational.co.uk**) sells a wide range of maps.

- **Maps Worldwide** (0845 122 0559, **www.mapsworldwide.com**) sells street, walking and roadmaps.

- **National Map Centre** (020 7222 2466, **www.mapsnmc.co.uk**) has worldwide driving and walking maps on sale at its shop at 22-24 Caxton St, London SW1H, or through **www.mapstore.co.uk**.

- **Ordnance Survey** (0845 200 2712, **www.ordnancesurvey.co.uk**) has masses of information on its website – including free downloadable guides to map-reading – and details of its OS Explorer maps (1:25,000 scale) and OS Landranger series (1:50,000).

- **Ramblers' Association** (020 7339 8500, **www.ramblers.org.uk/ navigation**) offers lots of information about maps and navigation in the UK.

- **Rough Guides** (www.roughguides.com) has produced rip-proof maps to some 40 countries and regions since 2003, working with the World Mapping Project, a consortium of German cartographers.

- **Stanfords** (020 7836 1321, **www.stanfords.co.uk**) has one of the best map sections of any travel bookshop.

Newspapers and magazines

All national newspapers in Britain now have a travel section; these have expanded hugely over the past decade.

• *The Times* publishes a separate travel section of up to 60 pages, in the new compact format, every Saturday, backed by an excellent (and substantially different) website, **www.travel.timesonline.co.uk** which, as well as carrying material from the newspaper, features its own stories, blogs from correspondents on the road, plus micro-sites on subjects such as green travel, spas and railway-based holidays.

• *The Sunday Times*, its sister paper, publishes not only a weekly newspaper section but also a glossy monthly magazine, *Sunday Times Travel* (**www.sundaytimestravel.co.uk**); both are known for their thorough, up-to-the-minute guides to popular holiday destinations.

• *The International Herald Tribune* (**www.iht.com**) and the *New York Times* (**www.nytimes.com**) also have excellent, free travel content on their websites.

Magazines

• *Wanderlust* (**www.wanderlust.co.uk**) is a glossy monthly travel magazine which is aimed at independent travellers who might take the odd package trip (my 73-year-old uncle is a huge fan) but will be happiest when exploring on their own. Lively guides to lesser-known destinations (come in Guyana, Laos, Krygyzstan) combine with European city breaks, travel advice, and lots of reader interaction through competitions, feedback, tips and its website.

• *Geographical* magazine, published since 1935 by the Royal Geographical Society, also suits those interested in adventure travel and the environment (**www.geographical.co.uk**).

• The excellent *The Traveller* magazine (**www.travelleronline.com**) is for those of a more adventurous bent, attracting big name writers such as Jan Morris or Paul Theroux.

• *Condé Nast Traveller* (**www.cntraveller.com**) has plenty of suggestions for stylish hotels and luxury villas.

• Design magazine *Wallpaper**, also upmarket but much less family oriented (**www.wallpaper.com**), has quirky travel features and each month profiles a slightly left-field city (Seoul, Kolkata, Montevideo). In late 2006, the magazine is set to publish a series of guides to the world's great cities.

My top ten travel guides

The Tropical Traveller by **John Hatt** (Penguin, out of print) – fantastically useful for anyone heading to any country where you can't drink the water. It is dated – it lists no websites, for example – but it's a mine of useful advice. Hunt for it on Amazon.

The Traveller's Handbook (Wexas, £16.95) is a hefty guide to every type of travel (and disaster) you could imagine – travelling by camel, buying discounted air tickets, surviving a kidnapping, crewing a boat – plus guides to countries worldwide.

India (Lonely Planet, £17.99) – despite failing to take a guidebook the first time I went to India, copies of this brick-like volume have accompanied me on subsequent trips. Just one look at the hand-drawn maps of the earlier editions and I can hear the cries of "chai! a-chai!" as another overnight train pulls away from the station.

Libya Handbook (Footprint, £14.99) by **James Azema**:

sometimes I am struck by the enthusiasm of the author for a destination and I found this excellent guide to a complex country to be a good example of that.

The World's Most Dangerous Places by **Robert Young Pelton** (HarperCollins, US$22.95 on Amazon; also see **www.comebackalive. com**) – you've got to love a book with chapter headings that include "Making the Best of Nasty Situations", "Tourists: Fodder for Fiends", and "Kidnap, Rescue and Extortion Insurance".

Trans-Siberian Handbook by **Bryn Thomas** (Trailblazer, £12.99) – I found it an invaluable guide to making sense of this week-long train journey; Thomas uses the kilometre markers alongside the railway to tell you what you can see from the train, plus gives clear information on how to undertake the journey.

Hip Hotels: Italy by **Herbert Ypma** (Thames & Hudson, £18.95). When this book on Italy's stylish hotels came

out I went to Florence to interview Ypma, who writes the copy and takes all the photographs. He turned out to be handsome, witty and a multi-million-selling author to boot – some writers have all the luck. He's also spot on about hotels – his favourite (Villa Feltrinelli on Lake Garda) has also become one of mine.

Bugs, Bites & Bowels by **Dr Jane Wilson-Howarth** (Cadogan, £9.99) is a well-written dollop of common sense that explains what health precautions travellers should take and assuages your fears about most of the illnesses that you are likely to pick up.

The Survivor's Guide to Business Travel by **Roger Collis** (Kogan Page, £12.99) is a collection of Collis's knowledgeable and accessible columns from the *International Herald Tribune.*

The Backpacker's Bible by **Suzanne King** and **Elaine Robertson** (Robson Books, £8.99) is a great introduction to budget travel.

- UK glossy monthlies *Harper's Bazaar* (**www.harpersandqueen. co.uk**), *Tatler* (**www.tatler.co.uk**) and *Vanity Fair* (**www.vanityfair. co.uk**) have good travel sections; the latter two produce annual travel guides; *Tatler* in January and *Vanity Fair* in April.

- *Food and Travel* magazine (**info@foodandtravel.com**) is good on mainstream, uncomplicated destinations (with plenty on Europe).

- *Real Travel* (**www.realtravelmag.com**) launched in 2006 and is aimed at gap year travellers and those taking a career break.

- Outdoor enthusiasts have plenty of magazines to cater for their interests: try *The Great Outdoors* (**www.tgomagazine.co.uk**) and *Outdoor Enthusiast* (**www.oe-mag.com**). I also enjoy *Far Flung* (**www.farflungmagazine.com**), an online travel magazine on adventure travel.

- In airline lounges around the world I'm pleased when I find a copy of *CNN Traveller* (**www.cnntraveller.com**), which carries travel news- and issue-led reports, and I love the venerable, yellow-bound *National Geographic* magazine (**www.nationalgeographic.com**).

- Regional magazines can inspire if you want to narrow your search – try the quarterly *Travel Africa* magazine (**www.travelafricamag. com**), the new magazine *Steppe*, which covers Central Asia (**www.steppemagazine.com**), *Asia and Away* (**www.asiaandaway. com**) and *Action Asia* (**www.actionasia.com**).

- Of the many airline in-flight magazines I've encountered, the only one I'd pay for is British Airways' *High Life* magazine (**www.ba.com**), which carries a stylish mix of travel features, news and interviews. Its sister magazine on European flights, *Business Life*, and the independent *Business Traveller* magazine (**www.businesstraveller. com**), both manage to interest the general reader as well as the corporate road warrior. *Business Traveller* carries previously published content free on its useful website.

- Finally, if you are interested in the nuts and bolts of consumer travel issues, plus want reliable guides to mainstream holiday destinations, the quarterly *Holiday Which?* (**www.which.co.uk**) is essential reading.

CHAPTER TWO
Travel and the environment

Introduction

I was sitting in the bar at Soneva Fushi in the Maldives, chatting with an accountant from Fulham who was on his honeymoon. Soneva Fushi is one of my favourite resorts: its laid-back, no-shoes philosophy might sound a little hippy, but its beautiful, private villas, peerless food and spot-on service are anything but. However, my companion was aghast at one aspect of the resort's service. "There's a sign that we have to leave on the bed if we want them to wash our sheets and towels each day!" he lamented. "Of course we want our sheets and towels washed each day. We can use dirty towels any time we like at home. Laundry is one of the things we're paying for."

Was he right to insist on the daily laundry service? Shouldn't we be trying to travel in as environmentally friendly a way as possible, and if that means putting up with three-day-old towels if we're saving fresh water in places like the Maldives, so be it? Well – yes and no. It's no longer that simple. There is no denying that it's good that places such as Soneva Fushi take their environmental obligations seriously – for example, the resort aims to run entirely on renewable energy by 2010 (see www.sixsenses.com/corporate/environment.php). And, undoubtedly, reusing sheets and towels saves both water and money (the US-based Green Hotels Association (www.greenhotels.com) calculates that hotels save $6.50 (about £3.60) per room per day when guests request that laundry is not done), but the "towel test" is becoming an outdated motif. In some places you can even stand it on its head. Take the case of the Green Hotel in Mysore, India. Its policy is to employ as many people as possible, often the very poor, who find it hard to get work, so the hotel's laundry is all done by hand. Here, insisting on fresh towels daily would mean you are keeping the local *dhobis* gainfully employed. Not such a bad thing after all.

Justin Francis, MD of online travel agency responsibletravel.com, agrees that the issue of towel washing has become an unhelpful totem. "It's like a millstone round our necks," he said. "People say, 'I have heard of responsible tourism, it's the towel thing, isn't it?' But it's really not a very good description of what we mean by responsible tourism!"

What is "Responsible Tourism"?

So what is "responsible tourism"? I think if you take a "responsible" holiday it means you will have fun by connecting with local people and learning about their lives, and you will have more dignified encounters with them than if you simply lie on the nearest beach and expect them to bring you drinks. Responsible tourism suits curious travellers who want their trip to have a beneficial impact on the people they meet. Responsible tourism should give us opportunities to find out more about foreign lands and peoples than we can glean from the swim-up bar at the resort, and so enable us to have holidays that are genuinely memorable and, in some cases, life-changing. They are about having respect for other people's homes, and about recognising that our visits can help our hosts to have a better quality of life than if we had not visited. So, no pressure there, Justin!

But I like the swim-up bar at the resort

Well, yes, so do I. Sometimes we all need holidays that simply allow us to recharge and relax, and at such times we don't want to feel obliged to pop off and watch some tribal dancing or shuffle round a museum, thanks very much. Goodness knows, Dubai has made a huge success of offering fabulous hotels and shops in a pretty much culture-free desert, where the only tribal dancing I saw was the tradesman's two-step as he stuffed the fake Louis Vuitton handbags out of sight when a customs officer was approaching.

But I don't want anyone to think that "responsible tourism" is somehow a niche product, the sort of holiday you might choose *instead* of a lazy beach trip, a ski holiday or a cruise. In this chapter I want to show that "responsible tourism" is a concept that can be – and I think should be – applied to every type of holiday we might take. If you want to visit a resort with a swim-up bar, holiday companies with good responsible tourism credentials can organise that. If you are worried about the damage flying does to the environment, there are ways you can compensate for that damage, and also alternative ways to travel. Even if you want to go skiing, go on a cruise, take a golf holiday – all of which are towards the dodgier end of this particular spectrum – there are ways that avoid or minimise the potentially harmful environmental and social effects of those holidays.

If responsible tourism is so important, how come I haven't heard of it?

Even if you have not heard the phrase before, the practice of responsible tourism is becoming widely accepted. The big holiday companies (such as First Choice and Thomas Cook) are seeing which way the wind is blowing, and trimming their sails accordingly.

Of the big tour operators, **First Choice** leads the way. In 2005, it became the first major British tour operator to publish a corporate social responsibility (CSR) report, and has debuted on the FTSE4GOOD index, which recognises companies with corporate responsibility standards. It's worth asking why this is such a big deal. To put it into context, when a mining or oil company goes into a new country, it has to carry out numerous surveys and produce reports explaining how it will leave the country in, if anything, a better shape when it pulls out than when it moved in.

Holiday companies have never been required to do this. It is simply assumed that their wish to offer holidays overseas is, in itself, a good thing, and environmental or social responsibility reports have not, to my knowledge, been requested by any host country. Yet a tour operator can do huge, if unintentional, damage in the way it affects the local communities it moves in to: encouraging the growth of large hotels at the expense of small, locally owned enterprises, for example, or creating conditions – by introducing so many new visitors – in which pristine beaches are overused, palm trees cut down, nesting turtles disturbed and wildlife sites trampled on, and a host of other negative consequences.

Justin Francis of **responsibletravel.com** says the impact a tour operator can have on a destination can produce a downward spiral in that environment. "For example, Thomson and First Choice dropped one of the Spanish costas in 2005, stating it had become a degraded destination," he said. "The operators claimed that tourism income had not been re-invested into improving the destination, but at the same time they had been battering down prices, leaving precious little money to re-invest. Either way, the resorts are now left with ageing hotels, fewer tourists and seemingly no way to invert the downward spiral."

It was earlier concerns about these sorts of issues that led to the launch of the **Travel Foundation** in 2003. This charity works on projects that protect popular tourist destinations, improving life for the locals and providing a better experience for tourists. For example, in the Yucatan peninsula in Mexico, it is educating tourism workers about the *cenotes*, the limestone sinkholes that are part of the underground river system which provides the region's only source of fresh water, but which are at risk of pollution from hotels' waste water leaching into them, and from tourists' non-biodegradable sunscreen as they swim in the *cenotes*. And in Tobago, it's running an "adopt-a-farmer" scheme to encourage hoteliers to use fresh, local produce rather than flying it in from Florida.

Crucially, the Travel Foundation was set up with, and continues to attract, support from the big tour companies such as First Choice, Thomas Cook and Sunvil Holidays. Some of these companies have schemes whereby holidaymakers are asked to donate a small fee, such as 50p, to the foundation when booking a holiday. "This is the first initiative of its kind in the world – it shows the UK's leadership in changing the way the world travels," said the foundation's director, Sue Hurdle.

But it has taken time for our collective consciousness to be raised. Over the past decade there have been promising responsible tourism initiatives that have not had much impact. One of the best-known failures was the "eco tax" that was introduced in the Spanish Balearic islands – Majorca, Minorca, Ibiza and Formentera – in 2002. This added one euro, about 60p, per person per day to the cost of most holidays, with the money going to environmental improvements. Having visited Majorca several times, I had seen the unlovely tourist ghettos of Magaluf and Palma Nova, and had written approvingly of how Calvia Council, which administers this part of the island, had taken big steps to improve matters, such as buying up and then blowing up some of the tackier hotels, and turning the sites into public parks.

So the eco tax seemed to me a bold, brave move by a destination that realised it had to look after, and improve, its tourist product or risk losing holidaymakers to cheaper destinations, such as Turkey and Croatia. Even holidaymakers did not seem to mind the tax much, especially as many hoteliers effectively refunded the tax through extra drinks vouchers. The number of British visitors to the Balearics rose during the time the eco tax was imposed.

But the levy did not apply if you stayed in a private apartment, which angered the islands' hoteliers, and the big tour operators were furious, too, claiming it would damage their businesses. Pressure from these groups resulted in the electorate voting out the tax in 2003.

But just because it was a badly thought out piece of legislation does not mean that levying a tourist tax is in itself a bad idea. In West Africa, The Gambia continues to do so without attracting protests: at Banjul airport the tourist board collects £5 from each arriving passenger, which goes towards improving the tourist infrastructure. That country has perhaps learned from its failed initiative in the 1990s when the tourist authorities tried to tackle one of the green traveller's biggest taboos: the all-inclusive holiday.

All-inclusive resorts: free drinks all day! What's not to like?

When I visited The Gambia in the 1990s, I realised the problem of "us and them" was particularly acute here. Tourists hid away in the all-inclusive resorts, rarely even venturing on to the beautiful beaches, because every time they stepped outside the hotel they were pursued by a pack of would-be guides, hustlers (known as "bumsters" here), craft sellers and others. These local people were frustrated because they felt excluded by the big hotels from being able to make money by selling services to tourists. But from the tourists' point of view, the hassle was exhausting, relentless and unpleasant.

The authorities first tried a blunt approach: they banned the sale of all-inclusive holidays, so that tourists would be encouraged to leave their hotel for lunch and dinner, thus bringing money into the wider economy. But it soon became apparent that this was putting the cart before the horse. Before holidaymakers would feel comfortable about leaving their hotels, they needed to know that measures were being taken to reduce the hassle.

The Gambia has since dropped its ban on all-inclusives, but has come up with some really imaginative ways of tackling the problem. One clever initiative was very simple. Women fruit sellers on the beach were fed up with chasing tourists across the sand to get them to buy their pineapples or mangoes. The tourists were fed up with being chased. Then someone had the bright idea of knocking a few planks of wood together to create a market stall. The women felt more dignified standing behind a stall to sell fruit, and the tourists were happy to come and buy, knowing they would not be chased. Profits shot up. Everyone was happy.

Another positive move has come from **Brighter Futures** (**www.brighterfutures.biz**), which helps craftspeople in The Gambia to tap into the tourist market by selling their handicrafts in shops, hotels and galleries frequented by tourists.

Today, The Gambia's first spa is due to open, eco lodges are doing good business in the interior, and classy restaurants have opened. The hassle has not stopped entirely, but local people are now much more easily able to access legitimate work in the tourism industry.

In The Gambia and elsewhere, all-inclusive hotels have often been held up as a symbol of all that is wrong with mass tourism: the arguments go that they stop tourists from venturing out and spending money in local shops and restaurants; the money spent on holidays in these hotels generally returns to the parent company in Europe or North America; they foster an "us and them" mentality – sometimes, unscrupulous staff even suggest it is "dangerous" for visitors to venture outside the hotel, as though it was in some sort of war zone.

All of this is sometimes true of all-inclusives – and not only at the cheaper end of the spectrum. When I stayed at the five-star Amankila resort on Bali, staff did everything except block the drive to stop me leaving when I mentioned I was venturing out to the nearby (safe, friendly, clean) village restaurant for supper one night.

But, just like the towel issue, the question of all-inclusives is not entirely clear cut. Dr Harold Goodwin, director of the **International Centre for Responsible Tourism** at the University of Greenwich, says: "The argument is not that all all-inclusives are bad, but that some are better than you think, and some are better than what was there before." He cites the example of the resort of Varadero in Cuba, where most of the food and alcohol that is included in the "all-inclusive" price is locally sourced, and the hotel entertainers are locals, all of which puts money into the hands of Cubans.

It is hotels at the upper end of the market that tend to offer international brands of gin or whisky, and fly in fancy food from around the world: but by drinking local, rather than imported, rum or beer you are not just reducing carbon emissions from planes flying in the luxury provisions, but you are helping to ensure local people keep jobs in the breweries. So yes, free drinks all day: when you look at it this way, what's not to like?

But if you do stay in an all-inclusive, try to get out to see what's beyond the compound walls. It's really not that scary. We're the nation that produced daredevil explorers and adventurers such as Cook, Livingstone and Shackleton and you're telling me you cannot even wander out into a nearby village to buy handicrafts?

I'm worried that "responsible tourism" is all hair shirts and camping...

I promise, you can have an extremely luxurious, indulgent holiday and still have the satisfaction of knowing that you have bought a holiday that has supported local people, rather than trampled all over them.

For a start, check out **www.responsibletravel.com**, which works with 160 holiday companies to offer more than 1,300 holidays. All tour operators and hotels on its site have responsible tourism policies and each holiday

Should I go to an all-inclusive?

Ask the hotel (or your tour operator):

- Do they employ staff year round, even if the destination is a seasonal one?
- Do they offer career development opportunities, insurance and properly paid overtime to their staff?
- Do they allow local craft sellers and entertainers in to the hotel?
- Do they use local food and drink, or import most of it from overseas?

Ask yourself:

- Do you feel uncomfortable about wearing a wristband that shows you are staying in this resort? (Wristbands are the accepted indicator that you are entitled to free drinks, etc.) If so, why is that?
- Do you feel uncomfortable about being cut off from local people by eating all your meals in the hotel?
- Will you get bored with seven or 14 nights eating in the same restaurant and drinking in the same bar?

description includes details of "how this holiday makes a difference" to the host community. Its offerings might be as modest as a B&B in Wales providing great organic meals, but if money is no object, you can spend nearly £3,000pp on a private vehicle safari in Botswana with Expert Africa, which takes you to breathtaking scenery and benefits the local communities you visit. Or for £3,050pp you can go on a two-week tour of Madagascar with Discovery Initiatives, or you could even spend £4,300pp on a 19-day tour of Ecuador and the Galapagos Islands through Audley Travel.

Contacts

Responsibletravel.com, 0870 005 2836, **www.responsibletravel.com**

Travelroots, 020 8341 2262, **www.travelroots.com**

Ethical Escape, 01244 570336, **www.ethicalescape.co.uk**

Natural Discovery, 0845 458 2799, **www.naturaldiscovery.co.uk**

Ecoclub, **www.ecoclub.com**

Booking a "green" hotel

If you are staying in a small hut on a tropical beach, with no running water or electricity, your accommodation is probably not having too harmful an impact on the local environment. But most of us find ourselves in bigger resort or city centre hotels when we travel, which inevitably have a bigger environmental "footprint".

Energy considerations

Richard Hammond, author of the new *Green Places to Stay* (Alastair Sawday, £13.99) and a writer on eco-friendly holidays, says there are four areas to ask your hotel staff about. "The key issues are waste, energy, water and guest education," he said. "Do they provide recycling facilities, such as a separate bin for paper, in the bedroom? Do they explain how to switch off all the lights and air conditioning when you leave the room? Often that's surprisingly difficult – it's best if you have a key card that is slotted into the master switch by the door.

"Do they use low-energy lightbulbs? Do they have a sign saying they will only wash sheets and towels on request? Finally, do they have information in your room about how you can do your bit for the environment – for example, about how to conserve water locally?"

I dislike using air conditioning: not only does it dehydrate me, but I like to sleep with fresh air coming in through the window if possible. I recently stayed at the posh Ritz-Carlton hotel in Shanghai, and was dismayed to find myself on the 41st floor of a skyscraper with windows that, for safety reasons, did not open, so I was forced to rely on air conditioning to keep cool.

But Claire Baker, editor of the magazine *greenhotelier*, which encourages the hotel industry to adopt environmentally friendly policies, says we should not automatically see air conditioning as bad. "It is not realistic to expect a 1970s tower block hotel to be using natural ventilation and solar louvres," she said. "Much more important is whether they have invested in energy-efficient equipment, and metering and monitoring equipment."

Looking after the staff

Another important question to raise is how hotels treat their staff. In many countries hotels can be little more than sweatshops, where staff have no job security, are expected to do overtime without being paid, and may also be victims of sex discrimination, according to Tricia Barnett, director of the charity **Tourism Concern**. She urges holidaymakers to talk to the staff in their hotels: "They are amazed that someone is interested in talking to the chambermaid or going to her home, but it's very eye-opening; finding out how people live, and forming relationships with them." Tourism Concern runs a campaign, "Sun, Sea, Sand and Sweatshops", which aims to pressurise UK tour operators to audit and improve labour conditions in the hotels they contract (details: **www.tourismconcern.org.uk/campaigns/ssss.html**). Other practical steps you can take include asking your tour operator about the issue, praising good staff to the hotel manager, and leaving tips in your room. (Unfortunately one of the problems is that many local staff are forced to rely on tips to make up their wages.)

Other questions you may wish to ask your tour operator or hotel – perhaps by emailing them before booking – could be about how much food they source locally; how many of the hotel's key staff are local and how many are western managers parachuted in to the top jobs; and whether, if it is a beach resort, they allow locals to access the beach as well as hotel guests (beaches in most countries are public, but hotels sometimes illegally appropriate them for their exclusive use).

Many of the hotels that meet high ethical and environmental standards are small, privately owned enterprises where the hotelier is able to dictate how the property is run. But that's not to say that big hotel groups ignore ethical or environmental criteria. Increasingly, these are rising up their agenda. For example, the Radisson SAS Airport Hotel in Oslo, Norway, has two "ecological" rooms where guests can measure their energy consumption during their stay, and work out how to reduce it by their use of heat, water and air conditioning. Its parent group, Rezidor SAS Hospitality, has a benchmarking scheme that helps reduce waste and energy consumption in its hotels. Hilton UK & Ireland received a "highly commended" award in the 2004 Responsible Tourism Awards for its staff training programme and is hot on using recycled building materials.

However, even the most environmentally friendly hotel can disappoint if other things are not right. I once stayed at a hotel in Jamaica that has won awards for its commitment to the environment. Unfortunately the owners' six large dogs were allowed to roam the property, so all the public rooms ponged unpleasantly of damp dog.

Booking with a holiday company

If you plan to book with a tour operator, check whether it has a responsible tourism policy. This is the company's commitment to treat its suppliers and staff fairly, to ensure that the environmental impact of its activities is as limited as possible, and to try to ensure that the host community benefits from holidaymakers' visits rather than suffers because of them.

It's not just the members of Aito (see page 7) that have these policies. Many big operators are now starting to make some effort here and their policies are usually posted on their websites in the "about us" or "corporate" areas of the site. If you find a tour operator that does not have a responsible tourism policy, when so many now do, you may want to question why they do not, and consider spending your money elsewhere. Making tour operators realise there is a financial benefit to considering responsible tourism issues – hitting them in the pocket, where it hurts – is a crude yet effective way to get them to prioritise these issues.

Of course, sticking a worthy-sounding policy on your website is one thing – adhering to it is another. If you think your operator or its staff are behaving in a way that contradicts its responsible tourism policy, write to both the operator and, if it is a member, an organisation such as Aito, Responsibletravel.com or the Travel Foundation.

On the other hand, if you come across a company, hotel or other travel organisation that you think worthy of praise for its environmental initiatives, you can nominate it for an award. Given what we have just heard about First Choice, it may be no surprise to hear that they are now the headline sponsor of the **Responsible Tourism Awards**, which are, in 2006, in their third year and recognise the achievements of tour operators, hotels, visitor attractions and other parts of the industry in addressing responsible tourism issues. *The Times* is the awards' media partner and details are on the website **www.travel.timesonline.co.uk/greentravel**. Typically the awards are launched in summer each year, and prizes awarded in winter.

The cost of flying

You know it's serious when Lonely Planet and Rough Guides, two of the biggest guidebook publishers, drop their rivalry to promote a single message.

In March 2006 the publishers issued a joint statement to boost awareness of climate change, to which air travel is a contributory factor. Both publishers now include information on climate change on their websites and in every book they publish, explaining the issues and suggesting ways readers can tackle the problem.

As Rough Guides' founder Mark Ellingham said: "We have a responsibility to limit our personal impact on global warming, and that means giving thought to how often we fly, and what we can do to redress the harm that our trips create."

Strong stuff, a guidebook publisher suggesting we question whether every air trip is necessary. But Tony Wheeler, co-founder of Lonely Planet, was even more succinct. "Every time I jump on a plane I think, 'oh no, I'm doing it again'," he said.

Offsetting your emissions

Over the past couple of years, the issue of global warming and the aviation industry's contribution to it has become a major topic of conversation among travellers. When we drive our cars, take a flight or heat our homes, we produce "greenhouse gases" – of which the biggest is carbon dioxide (CO_2) – which attack the ozone layer, encouraging global warming and altering the world's climate.

For example, if you fly from London to New York or Florida and back, your plane produces up to two tonnes of carbon dioxide per passenger, according to the organisation Climate Care, which is about the same as the emissions produced by a driver over a year's typical car use.

An increasingly popular way for holidaymakers to respond to this is to "offset emissions" by paying a fee to organisations such as Climate Care or the CarbonNeutral Company to compensate for the damage your flights are causing the environment. **Climate Care** (01865 207000, **www.climatecare.org**) puts 80 per cent of the money it receives into sustainable energy, and projects such as providing energy-efficient cooking stoves in Bangladesh and Honduras, and installing energy-efficient lighting in South Africa. The other 20 per cent goes to a reforestation project in Uganda, reflecting the consensus that 20 per cent of carbon emissions worldwide are considered to come from deforestation. Since summer 2005, *The Times* has paid Climate Care the fees for all its travel writers' flights. **The CarbonNeutral Company** (0870 199 9988, **www.carbonneutral.com**) was known as Future Forests, but changed its name in 2005 to emphasise that its work, like Climate Care's, is about more than simply planting trees. Some of the projects in which it invests include switching boilers from oil to woodchip fuel in Scotland, and installing solar-powered lights in India and Sri Lanka.

"In the past year, we have nearly doubled the amount of CO_2 we're offsetting," said Nicola Scholfield of Climate Care. "Awareness of climate change is growing, helped by the Government offsetting emissions for G8." Not only did the British government offset the CO_2 emissions created by the G8 summit at Gleneagles, Scotland, in July 2005, but from April 2006, all Whitehall departments have been offsetting the emissions from flights that their staff take on business trips. However, the government has also been criticised for backing plans for new runways at airports in the south east.

Since September 2005, British Airways has invited its passengers to pay a fee to Climate Care to offset their emissions when they buy a plane ticket. A growing number of tour operators offer this when you book, too.

It's unrealistic to suggest that we should all stop flying. For one thing, our travels can bring huge benefits overseas in areas such as poverty reduction and conservation. For another, the continued growth of budget airlines and the cheap flights they offer – which are usually far cheaper than taking the train – is continuing to create a new market for flying that simply did not exist a decade ago.

You just have to listen to Michael O'Leary, the provocative chief executive of budget airline Ryanair, who has no truck with concerns over climate change, to see that the carbon-neutral lobby has a fight on its hands. Announcing record profits in November 2005, he said: "We will double our [carbon] emissions in the next five years because we are doubling our traffic. But if preserving the environment means stopping poor people flying so only the rich can fly, then screw it. People are enjoying low-cost air travel and it creates jobs and tourism, which allows environmentalists to keep their highly paid jobs so they can spend their spare time whingeing about the environment."

But as we understand more about the damage that aviation does to the environment, we as responsible travellers should think about our decision to fly, and consider whether it would be possible to take another form of transport (or, in a business context, to use video conferencing instead of sending executives around the world). Rough Guides' Mark Ellingham said: "It worries me that we are treating planes like buses, as the Americans do. I would rather we travel less often, for longer." He has already reduced the number of flights he takes each year, and he added that he thought that the growing awareness of this issue would see more Britons taking holidays in the UK.

Government measures

Should the government be stepping in to this debate? Tricia Barnett, director of Tourism Concern, thinks it should. "I feel governments have to work much harder on this," she said. "It's a global issue and has to be dealt with globally. Much as I respect organisations such as Climate Care for raising awareness of the issue, simply offsetting your emissions is not the solution."

Environmental groups such as Friends of the Earth have called for moves such as the introduction of a tax on aviation fuel (it is currently untaxed, which FoE maintains is effectively a subsidy to the airline industry). No doubt this would be passed on to passengers in higher ticket prices – airlines such as BA are already happy to slap on a "fuel surcharge" when the price of oil rises – but I don't think it would put many of us off flying. Travellers have already absorbed fuel surcharges and the addition of Air Passenger Duty, yet air travel continues to increase.

Another solution may be to force airlines to join the EU Emissions Trading Scheme, which already operates in Europe in some non-aviation industries, with companies and organisations trading carbon allowances between themselves. If airlines were to join, they would be given an annual limit on their carbon emissions, and if they exceeded them they would have to buy carbon credits from other industries, such as power stations, which would then reduce their emissions by an equivalent amount.

The EU is currently looking into extending this scheme to the aviation industry but it will face strong opposition from some airlines concerned that it will force up ticket prices. However, such a system has much to recommend it: it would force airlines to put concerns over carbon emissions at the heart of their business model, rather than reducing the issue to a PR-friendly option to be added to the airline's website, with responsibility given to the customer to decide whether or not to offset their emissions.

What can I do?

- Question whether your stag or hen party really needs to be in Prague or Zagreb, when you could take the train to a UK city.

- Choose airlines with newer, more fuel-efficient planes – Ryanair and easyJet have some of the most modern fleets in Europe.

- Choose direct flights rather than those that touch down somewhere *en route*.

- Offset your emissions using one of the schemes listed below.

- Take holidays in the UK.

- Use trains to reach your destination, then hire bikes instead of a car.

- Ask for local dishes rather than imported food that has been flown around the world.

- Switch off lights and air conditioning in your room when you go out.

Contacts

- **Climate Care**, 01865 207000, **www.climatecare.org**

- **The CarbonNeutral Company**, 0870 199 9988, **www.carbonneutral.com**

- **My Climate**, www.myclimate.co.uk

- **CO2 Balance**, www.co2balance.com

- **Carbon Planet**, www.carbonplanet.com

- **Atmosfair**, www.atmosfair.de

- **Choose Climate**, http://chooseclimate.org/flying

- **TerraPass**, www.terrapass.com

- **EU Emissions Trading Scheme**, www.uketg.com

- Groups that campaign on this issue include **Friends of the Earth** (0808 800 1111, **www.foe.co.uk**) and **Greenpeace** (020 7865 8100, **www.greenpeace.org.uk**).

- Protest groups such as **Airport Watch (www.airportwatch.org.uk)** campaign against airport expansion, and urge you to sign the **Pledge Against Airport Expansions (www.airportpledge.org.uk)**.

- A new group, **Stop Climate Chaos**, formed in September 2005, also campaigns on climate change issues (020 7324 4750, **www.stopclimatechaos.org**).

- **Flight Pledge (www.flightpledge.org.uk)** asks you to reduce the number of times you fly.

Travel's moral dilemmas

We are increasingly aware that there's an ethical dimension to travelling. Deciding whether to leave your towels washed or offset your carbon emissions is important, but there are some destinations and activities that raise more fundamental questions about whether you should visit in the first place.

Popular holiday options that raise particular ethical dilemmas are cruise holidays, ski holidays and golfing holidays, which we'll look at below. But perhaps the most widely discussed issues are whether or not to travel to destinations such as Burma (Myanmar), Tibet, the Maldives, Zimbabwe or northern Cyprus. The argument is broadly balanced between those who feel that visiting these countries is to be avoided because it legitimises the governing powers and thus helps to prolong the rule of a regime that may be regarded as illegal or known to abuse human rights, and those who feel that only by visiting, talking to local people, and coming home and telling their stories can the people's voices be heard and thus the real picture of a country start to emerge. Before travelling to any such destination, you can research the issues using guidebooks, the Foreign Office and organisations such as Amnesty International (*see* Contacts, page 48).

Should I go to Burma?

Most countries are guilty of human rights abuses of some kind, but Burma (Myanmar) is up there at the top of the class. It is run by a military junta that keeps the democratically elected leader and Nobel peace prize winner, Aung San Suu Kyi, under house arrest. There are well-documented cases of human rights abuse of numerous kinds – the use of slave labour for road construction and tourism projects being one of the best known. The judicial system is harsh and prison sentences long, and prison conditions are particularly grim.

But I do not agree with the tourist boycott of Burma, as called for by **The Burma Campaign UK**, based on Aung San Suu Kyi's plea that tourists stay away. I understand the reasons for the boycott call, but I think tourism should be about breaking down barriers between peoples rather than building them up, as a boycott does, and a tourist boycott, which is of little concern to the regime – which cares nothing for western opinion, and, anyway, has powerful regional allies such as China – seems to me unhelpful.

The boycott has limited the number of visitors to the country, but it hasn't altered the behaviour of the appalling government in any notable way. And while it may have succeeded in deterring some British visitors from travelling to the country, many other European, American and Asia-based expat tourists, and lots of regional (Asian) visitors go there, and few that I spoke to had even heard of the boycott.

Few of the Burmese I spoke to had heard of it either, such as my hotelier in Mandalay. "We support Aung San Suu Kyi all the way," she said, anxiously. "But we have mixed feelings [about the boycott]. After all, we have to live. If you stay at private guesthouses, and use private trishaws to get around, your money does not go to the government." Pro-democracy activist and former political prisoner Ma Thanegi, who used to work for Aung San Suu Kyi, also argues that a boycott is unhelpful. "Sanctions have increased tensions with the government and cost jobs. But they haven't accomplished anything positive," she writes in Lonely Planet's guide to the country.

When I visited Burma, I went on a private holiday rather than on assignment, as I was not sure whether or not I would write about my trip. One evening in Mandalay, I went to see a performance by the Moustache Brothers, a troupe of satirical comedians, one of whom had recently been released from jail after serving a lengthy sentence for telling an anti-government joke. After the show, one of the performers, Lu Maw, told me: "We want tourists to come and spread the word. Take our photograph and put it on the internet! Foreigners are our protection." Lu Maw's plea swung my decision to write about Burma in *The Times*.

Other commentators support informed tourism. For example, the travel writer Rory Maclean, in his 1998 travelogue *Under the Dragon*, says: "The people of Burma wish their horrific circumstances to be known, while their unelected leaders want the reality to be hidden." And James Mawdsley, the pro-democracy campaigner who has been imprisoned in Burma several times, encourages visitors to come with open eyes: "Those who would learn more, those who are sensitive to the suffering, they should definitely come," he writes in his book *The Heart Must Break*. "If they spend their money wisely the junta need not see any of it; it can go directly to the people."

Burma is a beautiful country and it is heart-breaking to see ugly developments such as the new concrete "viewing platform" at the marvellous temples of Pagan. But it's better, in my opinion, to visit with open eyes and see the problems and come home and make a fuss about them than to ignore the country. You could write to UNESCO, for example (**http://whc.unesco. org**), to urge it to put pressure on the Burmese government to allow Pagan to be listed as a World Heritage Site, which status would offer it far more protection than a tourist boycott ever will.

My views are not shared by some campaigning groups such as **Tourism Concern**, whose director, Tricia Barnett, told me: "We feel the campaign [for a tourist boycott] has been won. The number of visitors going to Burma is minute, there are no direct flights from the UK, the British government is opposed to trading with Burma and many tour operators have pulled out. Many of the insignificant number of visitors who do go from the UK are visiting friends and family. The campaign has raised the issues and that's what we wanted to do."

On that, we can agree: few visitors now go to Burma without considering the political situation, and that has been a welcome result of the tourist boycott.

Contacts

Amnesty International, 020 7033 1500, **www.amnesty.org.uk**

The Burma Campaign UK, 020 7324 4710, **www.burmacampaign.org.uk**

The Free Burma Coalition, **www.freeburmacoalition.org**

Tourism Concern, 020 7133 3330, **www.tourismconcern.org.uk**

Lonely Planet, **www.lonelyplanet.com**

Tour operators to Burma (Myanmar)

Tour operators to Burma include Andrew Brock Travel, Audley Travel, Bales Worldwide, Orient-Express, Peregrine Adventures, Pettitts, Steppes East, TransIndus and the Ultimate Travel Company (see contact details in the Directory, chapter 11).

However, some of them ignore the nature of the regime in Burma and the tourist boycott, just giving us the usual "unspoilt land/beautiful temples" guff in their brochures and on their websites. This really isn't good enough with such a controversial destination.

Andrew Brock Travel, Audley Travel, Bales and TransIndus do tackle this issue. Orient-Express and Steppes East hint at the problems, but I could not find any mention of the issues on the websites of Peregrine, Pettitts or the Ultimate Travel Company.

Other destinations

The Maldives

In *The Times* we have recently reported on the call by the pressure group **Friends** of **Maldives** to boycott 23 resorts which, it claims, have links to President Maumoon Abdul Gayoom, who heads a regime guilty of human rights abuses. Tourists staying on these paradise islands rarely see the repression that takes place on the little-visited capital, Male. For more information, contact **Friends of Maldives** (01722 504330, **www.friendsofmaldives.org**).

Tibet

Likewise there is an argument over visiting Tibet, with some commentators saying that tourists can endanger locals by speaking to them, and their visits will prop up the Chinese regime. Alison Reynolds of the **Free Tibet Campaign** said it does not advocate a boycott, but urges visitors to tread carefully. "We encourage people to consider the pros and cons of making a trip to Tibet and to reach their own conclusion," she said. "If they decide to go, we encourage them not to join an organised tour, so that they will have more freedom to determine who gets their business, and – like the Dalai Lama does – we would urge anyone visiting Tibet to put their experiences to good use on their return by supporting the Tibet movement." For more information, contact **The Free Tibet Campaign** (020 7324 4605, **www.freetibet.org**).

North Cyprus and Zimbabwe

Other destinations where your visit can be controversial include north Cyprus and Zimbabwe, where some observers also see tourist visits as propping up what they consider to be an unpalatable or illegal regime.

Golf, cruise and ski holidays

The golf, cruise and ski industries all face criticisms from environmental campaigners. For travellers wanting to minimise the impact of their trips, here are some suggestions.

Golf holidays

Widespread concerns have been aired, especially in Asia, that the creation of golf courses has led to such problems as the forced removal of local people from their land, diversion of water supplies, deforestation and use of harmful pesticides.

But water is not a problem everywhere – such as Scotland – so golfers should consider whether playing golf somewhere hot, where the greens need plenty of watering, is advisable. (Or, for that matter, desirable – my golfing friends often rise at 5am to play in hot countries, as the temperature is unbearable by mid morning. Is that really a holiday?) Golf courses can be a refuge for rare plant species, and can be an important source of local employment.

The forum **Golf Environment Europe** (01620 850659, **www. golfenvironmenteurope.org**) runs the **Committed to Green** programme which sets environmental standards and awards recognition to European golf courses that meet those standards – 500 are currently on this programme, with 19 having met the criteria.

The **Scottish Golf Course Wildlife Group** works to conserve the environment of golf courses in Scotland (**www.scottishgolf.com/environment**) and **English Heritage** is studying ways of managing the impact of golf courses on the environment (**www.english-heritage.org.uk/parksandgardens**).

Cruises

Cruising is not all bad news for the environment. To start with, if you do not fly to your embarkation port (for example, you sail from Southampton or Dover), your cruise has far less environmental impact than if you had taken a holiday involving a flight.

But one area where cruise ships have a hugely polluting effect is in the waste that the less scrupulous operators dump at sea. In the USA, the environmental group **Bluewater Network** (**www.bluewaternetwork.org**) campaigns for tighter controls in this area, and claims credit for helping to sponsor successful bills in California that prevent cruise ships dumping sewage and wastewater in those waters. Yet, claims Bluewater, a typical one-week cruise will generate 50 tons of rubbish, a million gallons of "greywater" from sinks and showers, and 210,000 gallons of sewage – much of which is still being dumped at sea, despite cruise ships' claims to be cleaning up their act. A list of fines dished out to polluting cruise lines is posted on the website **www.cruisejunkie.com**.

What you can do

One area where individual cruise passengers can have a direct, positive impact on the places they visit is in what they choose to do when a ship arrives in port. If you pre-book excursions, much of that money may end up back with the cruise operator. But with a little research, or simply by heading off on your own once you reach the port, you can buy excursions, eat in local restaurants and use local taxi firms which ensures the money you spend on shore stays in local hands.

The **Heritas project** in St Lucia in the Caribbean is a good example of this. It's a community-owned scheme that sells tours on the quayside to cruise passengers and its success has helped the island earn EC$10 million (£2,131,665) a year from visiting cruise passengers (001 758 458 1454, **heritas@candw.lc**).

When you choose a cruise, it's worth considering the size of the ship and its impact on a port. For example, Royal Caribbean International's largest ships, such as *Explorer of the Seas*, carry not far short of 4,000 passengers and 1,200 crew, and even larger ships are under construction. Smaller ports quickly become swamped, making it hard for visitors to see much of the "real" destination. You can also spend a long time waiting to disembark from a large ship, which is no fun for you, and not much use to the locals.

Ski trips

It is hard to see skiing as environmentally friendly, as *The Times*'s ski correspondent, Mark Frary, freely admits. "The cutting of the pistes, which destroys wildlife, the artificial snowmakers that suck up alpine river supplies and litter that pollutes the soil and rivers mean skiers have a lot to account for," he said. Dr Harold Goodwin, director of the International Centre for Responsible Tourism at the University of Greenwich, agrees, saying that skiing is "the most difficult" holiday to do responsibly. "Downhill skiing is difficult, but North America has some sustainable resorts, where your impact is less because the ski field is bigger," he said. "Also, there the snow is deeper."

- Try cross-country skiing, which has hardly any of the negative impact that downhill slopes have on the mountain.

- Travel to the Alps by train, rather than plane – see **www.raileurope. com** and **www.eurostar.com**.

- Pick a holiday from the **Association of Independent Tour Operators**' ski directory (020 8744 9280, **www.aitoskiholidays.co.uk**) as all their members have signed up to a responsible tourism policy.

- Check the new *Green Resort Guide* from the **Ski Club of Great Britain** at **www.skiclub.co.uk/skiclub/resorts/greenresorts/**, which outlines what environmental measures resorts are taking.

- In the USA, check the resort has signed up to the Sustainable Slopes Campaign run by the **National Ski Areas Association (www.nsaa. org/nsaa/environment/sustainable_slopes/)**. Aspen is considered particularly hot on environmental issues – though it is one of the most expensive resorts.

- Don't drop litter from the ski lift. It might get hidden by the snow below but it will still be there when the snow melts.

- Avoid lower-lying resorts that use fake snow, as snowmaking machines can draw water from lakes and rivers, potentially causing supply problems for people downstream.

• Turn off the heating in your chalet when you are out during the day.

Treatment of porters

I find lifting a 20kg suitcase pretty hard going, so you won't catch me with a 60kg pack on my back – and you certainly won't find me charging up a mountainside at high altitude in flip-flops with one. Yet that is what many porters routinely do in popular tourist destinations such as the Everest base camp area in Nepal, the Inca Trail in Peru and on Mount Kilimanjaro in Tanzania. And a growing problem with the treatment of porters is being reported in Papua New Guinea as it opens up to tourism.

Porters are employed by tour companies to support the treks that we book, and they not only carry our heavy packs, but also tents, food and cooking equipment for our expeditions. In Nepal I've even seen them carrying deckchairs strapped to their backs, scurrying along, bent double, some wearing shoes made from cut-up tyres.

Porters are certainly fit compared with most of us over-fed, under-exercised westerners, but no one carrying such an enormous load, often while wearing flimsy clothes and poor footwear, will escape health problems. Many of them are just as prone to altitude sickness as you or I, and many also suffer at the hands of unscrupulous tour companies or foremen who deny them proper food, shelter and medical care.

In 1997, the **International Porter Protection Group** (IPPG) (**www.ippg. net**) was formed after a young Nepali porter became ill with altitude sickness. Instead of being accompanied down the mountain by a fit colleague who could look after him, he was paid off and sent down on his own: within 30 hours he was dead. Sadly this case is not unique, and the IPPG has a five-point plan to try to prevent such tragedies recurring.

If you're planning a trekking trip, ask your tour operator if they actively support the IPPG's aims. If not, why not? The IPPG's website has lots of suggestions for questions to raise with a trekking company before booking, and useful links to other groups concerned with porter welfare and health at high altitudes.

A campaign by **Tourism Concern**, "Trekking Wrongs Porters Rights", has also had considerable success in persuading UK tour operators to create policies to safeguard porters' rights and guarantee good working conditions.

The charity has worked with local pressure groups in mountain regions, and supported the formation of the **Kilimanjaro Union of Porters** in 2004 to raise awareness of this issue. Details: **www.tourismconcern.org.uk/ campaigns/porters-trecking.html**.

It's important to give porters work, as often many people in an extended family depend on their income. But in some countries, such as Bhutan, donkeys are used to transport trekkers' gear – and, occasionally, a tired trekker.

Animal welfare

Swimming with dolphins off the coast of New Zealand, spotting rare wild dogs on a walking safari in Zimbabwe and having penguins peck my boots in Antarctica are some of my most cherished travelling memories.

I feel pretty confident that the encounters I had with these animals were well regulated by the tour operators I travelled with. For example in Antarctica, staff from our company, Peregrine, told us not to go within five metres of a penguin, so I sat on the snow to watch them from a distance. But no one tells the penguins the rules, so they waddle over inquisitively to check you out. It's incredibly endearing.

Unfortunately not all holiday companies are so assiduous in making sure that tourists do not disrupt the animals' lives. In 2005, tourism charity the **Travel Foundation** issued a report that highlighted bad practice in a bid to encourage tour operators to tighten their guidelines.

Some of the worst offenders are at the cheaper end of the African safari market. "Cheetahs in Amboseli National Park in Kenya suffer significant disturbance. As many as 30 vehicles can crowd around a single group of cheetahs," said the report. I've been on safari in Tsavo East national park in Kenya, and felt extremely uncomfortable as our minibus and 12 others gathered in a circle within 10 yards of a lion. Tourists are unhappy about this practice too, not least because all their photos of an animal have other minibuses and tourists in the background.

You don't need to travel far to see animals in distressing circumstances. In many Spanish seaside resorts you'll often see men with monkeys on their shoulder, trying to persuade you to pay them to have your photograph taken with the animal. Do resist, and don't support performances by "dancing" bears in northern Greece or eastern Europe either.

And think long and hard before you swim with dolphins in an aquarium. It is possible to be injured by them, or to injure them with your jewellery or sunscreen. When I snorkelled with dolphins in the sea, we were given a dramatic warning about how they sometimes playfully pull swimmers deep under water. Suddenly we all paid great attention to the safety briefing about sticking together in the water. But the excitement of swimming with several thousand dolphins was memorable and strangely moving.

What you can do

- Try to book with guides and companies that are accredited by, or have links to, wildlife organisations.

- Ask questions – for example, if you are on safari, will you be near other vehicles?

- Listen to the briefings before the trip – staff are concerned with your safety as well as the animals'.

- Never feed animals, or drop litter near them.

- Ask other tourists to behave if they are breaking the rules.

- Do not buy products made from endangered species (see chapter 7).

- Have realistic expectations. If you do not see the tiger you have travelled so far for, will your entire holiday be a disaster?

- Report abuse through Born Free's Travellers' Alert scheme.

Contacts

Born Free, 01403 240170, www.bornfree.org.uk

Friends of Conservation, 020 7603 5024, www.foc-uk.com

International Fund for Animal Welfare, 020 7587 6700, www.ifaw.org

The Travel Foundation, 0117 927 3049, www.thetravelfoundation.org.uk

Travel Operators for Tigers, 01285 643333, www.toftiger.org

Whale and Dolphin Conservation Society, 0870 870 0027, www.wdcs.org

World Wide Fund for Nature, 01483 426444, www.wwf-uk.org

When charity begins abroad

Fund-raising trips

For several years, there's been a huge enthusiasm among the travelling public for joining overseas fund-raising trips. Typically these are active trips to exotic destinations, such as hiking the Inca Trail in Peru, cycling across Cuba or trekking through Jordan, organised by some of our biggest charities, such as Breakthrough Breast Cancer, Barnardo's and the Anthony Nolan Trust. Those taking part raise money for the charity before they go, or simply pay the required minimum fee (typically, £2,000 to £3,000) themselves. Many major charities in the UK offer these trips and they can be a great way to raise money for charity while enjoying yourself overseas. The adventure travel company **Charity Challenge** (020 8557 0000, **www.charitychallenge.com**) organises fundraising expeditions on behalf of many UK charities, as does **Discover Adventure** (01722 718444, **www.discoveradventure.com**).

A word of warning: at *The Times* we reported that some charities allow participants in these fund-raising trips to pay for their own travel arrangements using sponsorship money they had collected from their friends and colleagues. If you are asked to sponsor someone on one of these trips, it's reasonable to ask whether your money goes directly to the charity, or is a way of giving your friend a subsidised holiday.

Voluntourism

More recently, another altruistic strand has become apparent in the travel industry, given a large boost by the Asian tsunami of December 2004. This shocking disaster prompted many holidaymakers to drop everything and head for the disaster zone to help. Charities and NGOs were at times overwhelmed, but the generosity displayed by travellers is now finding new outlets as a growing number of "voluntourism" organisations emerge.

These offer holidaymakers the chance to take "volunteer holidays", trips that literally give something back – you might find yourself teaching, building a school, repairing tsunami damage – but you can go for, in some cases, as little as a week, which means these trips are now opening up to holidaymakers as much as to the gap-year traveller with time on their hands.

Indeed, older travellers taking a short break are just what this sector is looking for, according to Chris Simmonds of **Saga** (**www.saga.co.uk**), the organisation for the over-50s, which has recently launched "voluntourism" trips. Saga's first projects are in South Africa and involve teaching, training counsellors to deal with the HIV crisis, and mentoring students at Cape Town University. "We need people who have something to give back," said Simmonds. "While these sorts of trips are great experiences for youngsters, if they have not got the skills to pass on, are they really contributing? We are not looking for manual labour."

Saga's partner is the new web-based venture **People and Places (www.travel–peopleandplaces.co.uk)** which launched in late 2005 to send volunteers to projects in South Africa and Swaziland. Projects in Pakistan, India, Morocco and The Gambia are at the planning stage. The company's founder, Sallie Grayson, had heard horror stories about volunteers' trips that weren't properly planned – such as the IT specialist sent to a village in Nigeria that had no electricity. So she has put checks in place to ensure that the volunteer's work is useful, and that they also enjoy the placement.

Questions to ask before booking a volunteering holiday:

- Is the work you will do clearly explained before you set out?

- Can the company you're travelling with demonstrate the value of the project, perhaps by showing you research they have undertaken? If not, you should be wary of signing up.

- Are locals involved in running the project? If they have had no input into the scheme, it may not be something they need, and your contribution may even be resented.

- What sort of accommodation and food can you expect?

- Is there someone in charge to whom you can turn if difficulties arise? If you are paying an agency to place you on a project they should ensure you have proper support.

- Do you really want to spend a holiday doing hard physical work?

- What is the insurance position? Standard travel insurance policies are unlikely to cover you for accidents sustained if you are undertaking manual work, so check with the organisation to ensure you're protected.

Contacts

The Adventure Company, 0870 794 1009,
www.adventurecompany.co.uk

Biosphere Expeditions, 0870 446 0801,
www.biosphere-expeditions.org

British Trust for Conservation Volunteers, 01302 572244,
www.btcv.org.uk

Coral Cay Conservation, 0870 750 0668, www.coralcay.org

The Different Travel Company, 02380 669903,
www.different-travel.com

The Earthwatch Institute, 01865 318838, www.earthwatch.org

Global Vision International, 0870 608 8898, www.gvi.co.uk

Go Differently, 01799 521950, www.godifferently.com

Hands Up Holidays, 0800 783 3554, www.handsupholidays.com

i-to-i, 0800 011 1156, www.i-to-i.com

Imaginative Traveller, 0800 316 2717, www.imaginative-traveller.com

National Trust Working Holidays, 0870 429 2429,
www.nationaltrust.org.uk/volunteering

People and Places, 01795 535718, www.travel-peopleandplaces.co.uk

Saga, 0800 096 0084, www.saga.co.uk

Scientific Exploration Society, 01747 853353, www.ses-explore.org

VSO, 020 8780 7200, www.vso.org.uk

When you're there

Travelling responsibly is about good manners. It's about treating the people around us with respect, whether they are the airline crew, local people, taxi drivers, hotel staff, guides, market traders, porters, fellow holidaymakers or beggars. If we treat the people we meet with dignity, curiosity, equality and friendship, we're going to have a far better holiday, and those in the host community will gain far more from our visit, than if we go around armed with pre-conceived prejudices and looking for the worst in everyone.

Back in the early 1990s, when eco-tourism, as it was then known, was starting to catch on, the traveller's mantra was "take only photographs, leave only footprints". But if you think about it, that's a rather selfish philosophy that ignores the concept of giving something back to the local community. Perhaps today's responsible tourist will adopt a new slogan? It's not as snappy, but "take only photographs, leave only money" is a better way to sum up this new thinking.

However you choose to travel, there are a few guidelines that apply worldwide:

- Try to ensure your trip leaves as much money as possible in the local community.

- Learn something of the local language.

- Dress in a way that will not offend local people or give off inappropriate signals.

- Think before you take a photograph – it may be better to engage in conversation with people rather than simply pointing a camera at them.

- Ask your holiday company if there are any appropriate small gifts that you can take to a developing country.

- Ask your tour operator and hotelier about responsible tourism and try to spend money with companies that have policies in place.

- Think about your "carbon footprint" and consider paying to offset the emissions from your flights.

- Carry a water bottle to avoid buying endless plastic bottles, which in many places cannot be recycled.

Haggling and beggars

Two issues that holidaymakers often cite as causing them difficulty in tourist resorts are haggling, and how to deal with beggars. Responsible holidaymakers are often reluctant to haggle too hard, perhaps because they are uncomfortable with the practice. Rest assured, it's rare that a trader will allow the price to drop so low that they will not make a profit – if haggling is the way business is done, you should enter into the spirit of it and enjoy the banter. Don't, however, start to haggle unless you genuinely want to buy, as this can cause offence; on the other hand, if you are a committed shopper, don't feel guilty if the carpet seller or tailor starts pulling out carpets and bolts of cloth and throwing them elaborately over the shop to demonstrate their quality – it's the way business is done.

Of course you will end up paying more than a local would – that's the way of the world, and there's no point getting wound up about it. If you are happy to pay a certain price for an item, then it's the right price.

Begging can cause a little more heart-searching, because the state of some of the street urchins or disabled people you sometimes see begging can be pitiful. But if you give them money, won't they spend it on drink or drugs, or come after you for more?

It can be helpful to gauge what local people are doing and follow suit – even in poor countries I often see locals give money, particularly to elderly beggars or those with disabilities, or to the beggars who congregate outside temples or churches. But what of the groups of street children who can follow you, tugging on your jacket, with some persistence? Often giving money to one will create a mini feeding frenzy and you may find yourself besieged. Yet it's clear that they are desperately poor and their needs are real.

In Delhi once, after a particularly trying morning being pursued by begging children around Connaught Place, I asked an Anglican vicar who lived there how he dealt with the problem. He told me he gave money to charities that helped street children. But there are no hard and fast rules, and if you meet a deserving case and your conscience is pricked, then give money.

Finally, don't let anxieties over things like haggling or begging mar your trip. Enjoy your holiday! I hope that being aware of the issues raised in this chapter will help you to choose a holiday that is much more rewarding than one you may otherwise have chosen.

Contacts and resources

• **The Association of Independent Tour Operators** (Aito) (020 8744 9280, **www.aito.co.uk**) is a group of 150 tour operators with a sister organisation of specialist travel agents (020 8744 9271, **www.aitoagents.co.uk**). Every Aito member must adopt Aito's responsible tourism policy. Contact Aito for a free brochure.

• **Blue Flag beaches** (**www.blueflag.org**) is an international award scheme for clean beaches; for more on this, and other marine awards in the UK, see chapter 5.

- **Discovery Initiatives** (01285 643333, **www.discoveryinitiatives.co.uk**) runs nature holidays with conservation organisations; it has contributed £600,000 to conservation projects.

- **EcoEscapes** (**www.ecoescapes.co.uk**) is an online eco-travel magazine.

- **Ecotravel** (**www.ecotravel.com**) is a US-based directory of eco-friendly holidays and a web-based magazine.

- **Exodus** (0870 240 5550, **www.exodus.co.uk**) won the best tour operator category, and was joint overall winner, in the 2004 Responsible Tourism Awards for its commitment to sustainable tourism in the 90 countries in which it operates.

- **Explore** (0870 333 4001, **www.explore.co.uk**) runs small group adventure tours worldwide and is working with Tourism Concern to develop a labour standards code of practice for suppliers.

- **Fair Trade in Tourism South Africa** (**www.fairtourismsa.org.za**) encourages and publicises fair and responsible business practices by South African tourism establishments through the FTTSA trademark, an independent symbol of fairness in the tourism industry. You can find FTTSA-recommended companies on its site.

- **First Choice** (**www.firstchoice.co.uk**), the tour operator, published its first Environment and People Report in October 2005. It can be read at **www.fcenvironmentandpeople.com**.

- **The Foreign & Commonwealth Office** (0845 850 2829, **www.fco.gov.uk/knowbeforeyougo**) has advice for travellers on respecting local culture and protecting the environment.

- **Friends of Conservation** (020 7603 5024, **www.foc–uk.com**) works with communities worldwide to find ways that local people can live in harmony with their wildlife and ecosystems. Membership costs £25pa.

- **Green Globe** (**www.greenglobe.org**) advises on sustainable tourism, and also runs a certification system for travel companies and hotels, which can then display the Green Globe logo.

- **Green Tourism Business Scheme** (01738 632162, **www.green–business.co.uk**) benchmarks tourism-related business in the UK and Europe.

• **Greenstop** (**www.greenstop.net**) offers a directory of tourism businesses with environmental policies.

• **Guerba** (01373 826611, **www.guerba.co.uk**) runs trekking, overland, discovery and adventure tours and has a good track record of supporting local projects.

• **The Independent Traveller** (01628 522772, **www.independenttraveller.com**) runs small group or tailor-made "fair trade" trips worldwide; it also runs some trips for women only.

• **The International Centre for Responsible Tourism** (**www.icrtourism.org**) is a post-graduate research and training centre based at the University of Greenwich, run by Dr Harold Goodwin.

• **The International Ecotourism Society** (001 202 347 9203, **www.ecotourism.org**), based in Washington DC, works to promote responsible tourism by bringing together experts, tourist businesses and travellers.

• **The International Tourism Partnership** (020 7467 3620, **www.internationaltourismpartnership.org**) is part of the International Business Leaders Forum (**www.iblf.org**), a charity established by the Prince of Wales to promote sustainable international development.

• **North South Travel** (01245 608291, **www.northsouthtravel.co.uk**) is a travel agency that donates the profits it makes from the sale of air tickets to grass-roots charities worldwide, such as Street Child Africa, which works with homeless children.

• **The Responsible Tourism Partnership** (**www.responsibletourismpartnership.org**) brings together tourism businesses and people in holiday destinations to try to improve the destination for the people who live there.

• **Responsibletravel.com** (0870 005 2836, **www.responsibletravel.com**) is an online marketplace for 160 travel companies that offer holidays, from modest to luxurious, that benefit the host community as well as the traveller.

• **Rough Guides** has produced the *Rough Guide to a Better World* in conjuction with the Department for International Development; it has a section on ethical tourism. It's now only available online at **www.roughguide-betterworld.com**.

• **Sustainable Travel International** (**www.sustainable travelinternational.org**) is a US-based organisation that educates travellers, for example listing eco-travel benchmarking schemes and other resources.

• **Sustrans** (0845 113 0065, **www.sustrans.org.uk**) is the leading sustainable transport charity in the UK; for more information, *see* chapter 5.

• **Tourism Concern** (020 7133 3330, **www.tourismconcern.org.uk**) is a charity that works with local communities to reduce the problems that tourism can cause them, and with UK-based tour operators to find ways that their holidays can benefit local people.

• **Traidcraft Meet the People Tours** (0191 265 1110, **www.traidcraft-tours.com**) offers small group tours to countries where you can meet the suppliers who produce the goods this fair-trade operator sells.

• **The Travel Foundation** (0117 927 3049, **www.thetravelfoundation.org.uk**) works on sustainable tourism projects in some of the most popular destinations for British tourists, with the support and involvement of many of the UK's biggest holiday companies.

• **Tribes Travel** (01728 685971, **www.tribes.co.uk**), the overall winner of the 2005 First Choice Responsible Tourism Awards, offers mostly tailor-made, "fair-trade" trips to 14 countries.

• **The World Travel and Tourism Council** (0870 727 9882, **www.wttc.org**), a forum for business leaders in the tourism industry, has information on responsible tourism initiatives on its website.

• **The World Tourism Organization** (**www.world-tourism.org**), an agency of the United Nations, has put together a Global Code of Ethics for Tourism: *see* **www.world-tourism.org/code_ethics/eng.html**.

CHAPTER THREE

Growth of the 'DIY' traveller:
buying flights and booking hotels
using the internet

Introduction

When I first took a long-haul flight, to India in 1984, I bought my ticket after phoning around the "bucket shops" listed in the back of the Sunday newspapers. These travel agencies sold air tickets that the airlines could not get rid of and so offered the cheapest fares, although the tickets usually came with restrictions that meant you could not, for example, change the date of travel. I paid £380 to fly to Delhi with the now defunct airline Pan Am: it was a lot of money for an impoverished student at the time.

Skip two decades, and how much more choice do we have! Now if I wish to buy a flight, I can simply log on to the internet. Within seconds I have a list of fares, routes and airlines to my chosen destination. A few mouse clicks later, and I can secure the booking. And greater competition means prices are keen. A quick search on the website www.cheapflights.co.uk, for example, offers flights to Delhi for even less than I paid 20 years ago – £369 if I fly with Turkish Airlines via Istanbul, for example.

The same has happened to the way we book hotel rooms, cruises, car rental, travel insurance and almost every element of a trip. No longer do we have to go to a high-street travel agency and be sold a tour operator's package by a callow 19-year-old who has never been to the resort in question. No longer do we have to book a set seven or 14-night package because that's what the tour operator finds most convenient to sell us. No longer do we have to pay a fortune to a scheduled airline for weekend flights that they probably wouldn't have sold anyway, or feel bludgeoned into buying a travel agent's over-priced travel insurance.

In short, the internet has freed us up to become our own travel agents from the comfort of our own homes. In this chapter I will explore how to book flights and hotels in safety, using the internet, and explain how to make the most of the online revolution that has brought us lower fares and greater choice.

Is your money protected?

The internet makes a good slave, but a bad master. The computer will only give you the information you ask it for: it will not point out, for example, that the day you are flying into Barbados is a national holiday and the car rental office will close at midday, or that the hotel in Bali will be full of families with young children when you expected adult company, or that if you book that French villa for a holiday that starts two days later than you were thinking of, the price will drop substantially.

These are not the only potential pitfalls of being your own travel agent. You may also find that the trip you put together yourself is not financially protected. In many cases, when everything works out fine, this will not matter. But if something goes wrong – the airline goes bust, the hotel is a building site, you miss a train connection – lack of financial protection means you may have no one to help you out of the fix. You may be stranded abroad (as many of EUjet's passengers were when that airline collapsed in 2005), you may lose a substantial amount of money and time out of your holiday to sort out the problem, or if you are yet to travel you may simply lose your money.

In the mid 1990s, some 98 per cent of leisure travellers were financially protected under the Air Travel Organisers' Licence (Atol) scheme when they took a holiday involving a flight. By 2006, according to the Civil Aviation Authority (CAA), this figure had dropped to 61 per cent. David Moesli of the CAA's Consumer Protection Group told me: "We have nothing against people buying seats direct from airlines and picking up accommodation elsewhere, but people do not realise they have lost their financial protection. Our great fear is if one of these low-cost carriers fail – we think it's only a matter of time before we have a major airline failure in the UK and we think a lot of people will have a lot of trouble returning home."

When you put together your own holiday by buying a flight, hotel and hiring a car from different companies, you do not have the same level of financial protection as you do if you buy a package holiday from a travel agent or tour operator. Sometimes, you have no financial protection at all. You might think you've effectively created your own package holiday, for example by buying flights on one website, hotel rooms on another and car hire direct from the agency, but in law this does not constitute a package.

So before you book any type of travel, it's wise to ask if your trip is financially protected. A good clue is to look for the Atol, Abta or Aito symbols on a company's brochure or website, which indicates they hold a financial bond.

There's nothing wrong or illegal about buying (or selling) an unbonded travel product – on the contrary, it's very common practice – and some observers say the risk of things going wrong is miniscule. But what's important, and what this chapter and the next are all about, is that you know what level of protection, if any, you have before you buy. Then you can decide whether, if there is no financial protection, the risk is an acceptable one to you.

It's also wise to pay for your travels with a credit card, because this gives you another layer of protection. In March 2006, the Office of Fair Trading (OFT) won an important victory for consumers at the Court of Appeal, where judges agreed with the OFT that the 1974 Consumer Credit Act should apply to credit card purchases made overseas, as well as to those made in the UK. This means that if you buy something that is faulty, or pay for a service that is not provided, anywhere in the world, you can apply for a refund to the card company, if the purchase was between £100 and £30,000. For example, if you buy flights with a foreign airline or book an overseas hotel through a website and something goes wrong, you can now take it up with your credit card company, though you should try to sort it out with the vendor first. Details: **www.oft.gov.uk**.

Booking tips

- Always ask if your trip is financially protected. Check for Atol, Abta or Aito symbols.

- Pay for your travels by credit card.

Buying a flight direct from the airline

In the pre-internet days, travellers rarely bought a ticket direct from the airline – the bargains were to be found at the travel agents. A decade ago, scheduled airlines did not yet fear competition from budget airlines and the established aviation industry was complacent, with high ticket prices, silly restrictions on the cheaper tickets (such as insisting you stayed over a Saturday night, which was meant to stop business travellers buying the cheap tickets), and a sneering attitude towards the then-tiny budget carriers – such as easyJet, which was launched in 1995. Many national airlines were propped up financially by their governments (some, such as Air France, still are).

Today things are very different. Ryanair, easyJet and their ilk have really shaken up the market because they base their business model around having low prices. To keep prices as low as possible, they make sure their best deals

Who flies where?

It's all very well being your own travel agent, but how do you find out which airlines fly to which city? Several websites can help.

- Start with **www.whichbudget.com** to find out routes involving budget and charter airlines.

- The new site **www.flycheapo.com** is excellent – it lists 50 budget airlines across Europe, enabling you to pick a city and find out which airlines fly to it, plus it has links to the website of each airline and airport listed. It offers email news updates about the budget sector, too.

- The site **www.dohop.com** searches 660 airlines to find the connections that fit your journey. The sites **www.jetnav.co.uk** and **www.jumblefly.com** are also useful.

- Another useful tool is **www.flightmapping.com** which lists pretty much every worldwide airline and the routes they operate in to and out of the UK.

- The site **www.skyscanner.net** shows a map for scheduled and charter airline routes across Europe.

- The **Official Airlines Guide (www.oag.com)** is a subscription-based service offering data such as frequently updated timetables of thousands of airlines and airports; it's particularly useful for business travellers. For a guide to the punctuality of airlines using UK airports, see **www. flightontime.info**.

are available on their own websites, and do not sell through travel agents as scheduled and charter airlines do. They charge higher ticket prices if you book by phone, or they force you to use an expensive phone number – for example, easyJet charges you £1 a minute if you phone up for help with making a booking, rather than doing everything yourself online. Their phenomenal popularity has led to such rapid growth in the budget airline sector that in summer 2005, for example, there were 1,000 no-frills flights a week between the UK and Spain and the Balearic islands.

Eventually the traditional carriers, such as British Airways and British Midland, realised they had to play the budget airlines at their own game.

BA launched Go, which it eventually sold to easyJet for what many commentators believe was too low a price (under easyJet's ownership the Go brand disappeared). British Midland created its budget arm, bmibaby. They also created websites where you could book online, made pricing clearer, and started offering the cheapest fares to those who booked furthest ahead.

More recently BA has once again launched what is effectively a budget airline, by replacing its CitiExpress service with BA Connect in March 2006. BA Connect offers routes from six regional UK airports to European destinations, and following the budget airline model, it has no business class seats, you can buy one-way tickets, and you must pay for snacks on board. But unlike most budget airlines it offers pre-bookable seats and frequent flyer points.

Scheduled, budget and charter airlines

Scheduled airlines

These are the traditional, often long-established airlines such as British Airways, Air France or United Airlines. You may see them referred to as a country's "flag carrier" or "national" airline.

- Typically, scheduled airlines offer "frills" – a meal service, in-flight entertainment, a magazine and a frequent flyer scheme.

- They tend to fly to major capitals and other cities where their business customers wish to travel, rather than routes aimed primarily at holidaymakers.

- Many scheduled airlines are members of global alliances, such as oneworld or the Star Alliance, and if you book with one alliance member you may find yourself on a plane belonging to another. See "code-sharing", below (*see* page 90).

Budget airlines

These are, strictly speaking, scheduled airlines too. Also described as "no-frills" airlines, the best known are Ryanair and easyJet. Typically these airlines strip out the features you expect on a scheduled airline, such as assigned seating, free food and drinks and in-flight entertainment, to keep costs low.

- They are sometimes called "low-cost" airlines, but this is misleading, as sometimes ticket prices can be high, depending on demand.

- Budget airlines often travel to unusual destinations (for example,

Ryanair offers eight cities in Poland) where there is no other competition on the route, and they may use "alternative" airports that are miles from the city centre, requiring a lengthy bus transfer to the final destination. They also offer lots of summer sun destinations across the Mediterranean.

• Budget carriers rarely offer long-haul flights as their business model is based on their planes making lots of short flights each day.

Charter airlines

Many big holiday companies have their own airline (such as Thomsonfly, Thomas Cook Airlines or MyTravel Airways). Other familiar charter airline names include Excel Airways and Monarch Airlines, which are also part of larger groups.

• Holiday companies sell seats on charter planes as part of a package holiday, which means charter flights are rarely overbooked, because if a passenger does not turn up for their flight, they miss their entire holiday.

• Charter airlines often charge extra for items such as headphones (to watch the in-flight film), meals, and adjacent seats for members of the same party.

• Charter airlines also offer "seat-only" sales, meaning you can buy flights on charter airlines that are not part of a package holiday.

• They tend to offer more regional departures than scheduled airlines, and offer lots of direct routes to summer and winter sun destinations (such as in the Mediterranean or the Caribbean) that scheduled airlines ignore.

• Somewhat confusingly, many of these airlines now also operate as scheduled airlines, too, usually adopting the budget airline model, and selling tickets direct to the public through their websites. This is a growing area of the market.

* For a list of scheduled, budget and charter airlines, with their phone numbers and websites, see the Directory, chapter 11.

How safe are budget airlines?

The colourful chief executive of Ryanair, Michael O'Leary, is famed for such antics as telling staff to bring their own pens to work and for refusing to let them charge their mobile phones on company electricity. But while such parsimony may add a few euros to Ryanair's swelling coffers, it does nothing to allay the perfectly reasonable concerns of many travellers, who often wonder how an airline that offers tickets for silly fares, such as 1p plus taxes, can possibly make money. Surely it cannot be making enough to pay for essential maintenance and safety checks? Don't they cut corners?

Yes, budget airlines cut corners – on everything *except* safety. Boarding passes, free sandwiches, in-flight magazines – these are the "corners" that are cut. But budget airlines know that, such is the public perception they encounter, they must do everything they can to convince travellers of their high safety standards. As the old airline industry saw goes: "If you think safety is expensive, try having an accident."

"An accident on a low-fare operator would have a very damaging effect on the whole market," said Tim Jeans, MD of Monarch Scheduled. "Even if it was not a maintenance-related issue the implication would be drawn that it was." And their safety standards are excellent. No budget airline in Europe has had a fatal accident. And it's clear they can make money in spades: Ryanair, for example, announced a record €237m (£159m) half-year profit in November 2005. So how do they do it?

Ryanair sells 98 per cent of its tickets online, whereas BA only sells about 30 per cent in this way. Selling tickets over the internet saves money on staffing a call centre; budget airlines also do not pay commission to travel agents. You are not given a printed ticket or individual boarding pass on most budget airlines, and there is not usually pre-assigned seating. The airlines claim that not giving out seat numbers in advance means people get on the planes more quickly – they rush to be first to secure the seat they want.

And time is of the essence when you run a budget airline. The longer your planes are in the air each day, the more money you make. Hence Ryanair's famous 25-minute turn-around time, made possible largely by its choice of small, out-of-the-way airports where there is unlikely to be any other traffic to cause hold-ups. "We have better aircraft utilisation than most short-haul carriers because others are using congested airports, which means taxi times are longer," said Peter Sherrard, head of communications for Ryanair. Typically the airline's planes make eight short hops each day, of one hour and ten minutes on average, which, Ryanair claims, is more than its competitors.

Over to easyJet, which tends to use bigger, more central airports than Ryanair. "We fly to main city airports so we are competing against full-service airlines," said Samantha Day, spokeswoman for easyJet. "While it costs more to fly to these airports, we can earn more money per passenger."

Usually airlines pay fees to airports for being allowed to land, but Ryanair in particular turns this on its head by deliberately hunting out obscure airports across Europe that are so thrilled with the business the airline brings to the local economy that they pay Ryanair to fly there. The flipside can be that you may find yourself at an airport miles from the city you were hoping to fly to. Perhaps the most notorious example of this is Ryanair's flight to Frankfurt, which lands at Hahn, a 1hr, 45min bus journey from Frankfurt.

On board you encounter other money-saving tricks. Ryanair, which is perhaps the best at paring back on unnecessary "extras", has fixed all its seats so they cannot be pushed back – it reckons to save about £1 million a year in seat maintenance costs. Budget airlines charge you for snacks and drinks. Ryanair operates only one type of aircraft, the Boeing 737-800, which streamlines maintenance operations and means any crew member can work on any plane.

And Ryanair snapped up huge numbers of planes – it bought 70 and optioned a further 70 – when prices were at rock bottom after September 11, 2001. "That gives us the lowest cost per seat of any airline in Europe," said Ryanair's Sherrard. EasyJet has both Boeings and Airbuses in its fleet but is moving toward an all-Airbus fleet for similar operational reasons.

Then they make pots of money through tie-ups with hotel, car hire and insurance providers. And in 2006, Ryanair and Flybe started to charge passengers who had bags to check in to the hold (see chapter 7, page 243), creating another income stream.

Finally, let's blow away the myth that "budget" airlines are also "low-cost" airlines. The real key to a budget airline's financial success is in the arcane world of "yield management", the computer system that works out how fast seats are selling, and when to put up prices.

"All flights start with at least 10 per cent of the seats available at the lowest fares," said easyJet's Day. "The yield management system then monitors every flight and sees how quickly it is selling. If, for example, 30 people book, the computer thinks it's a popular flight so the fares need to be higher." Occasionally, prices are lowered to stimulate demand, but it happens less often these days: the airlines know how unpopular it is with a web-savvy travelling public. EasyJet and BA even promise to refund the difference if you buy a ticket and later find the price on that flight has tumbled.

How to book flights on the internet

Online security

First, a word of warning. When paying for something over the internet, check that you are dealing with a secure server – the beginning of the name of the site you are on should change from http:// to https:// when you are on the payment part of the site. A small locked padlock will probably appear at the bottom of the screen. Never send your credit card details in an email, to anyone – only fill them in on the secure payment page. Note any booking reference number you are given and print out the confirmation page. Be wary of any website that does not list its address and phone number.

E-ticketing

The days when you would receive a traditional airline ticket printed on flimsy paper with carbon copies are rapidly disappearing. These were first replaced by shiny card tickets, like those issued by many train companies, but now the buzzword is e-tickets.

Your e-ticket is a reference number that you are sent by email once you have completed an online booking. When you check in, it's wise to bring a print-out of the e-ticket, but your passport and the flight number should be enough for the check-in person or machine to find your booking and print your boarding card.

E-ticketing is now very common in Britain, but if you buy an airline ticket in a developing country, you are still likely to be given the paper type.

Booking a flight using an airline's own website

Let's say I fancy a week in late July in Puglia, southern Italy. I feel sure that Ryanair, with its numerous routes, must fly to somewhere in that region, so I log on to **www.ryanair.com** and up pops one of the least sophisticated-looking websites on the net. But although its garish blue and yellow colours and flashing panels are fairly headache-inducing, the site is well thought out and it's simple to use.

Special offers – sometimes advertised at just a few pence per flight – take up the centre of the screen. I see that the airline flies from Stansted to both Bari and Brindisi, either of which suits me. I want to go for a week or so in late July, leaving in just 10 days' time.

I put in some sample dates, travelling from Friday to Friday to Bari, and am given one-way fares of £79.99 on each day. Clicking on the "next day" tab on each fare, I find that travelling the following day, Saturday to Saturday, costs £119.99 going out but only £59.99 coming back. Clicking on the "prev day" button takes me to Thursday's fares, which are £59.99 each way – the cheapest so far. I check the Brindisi route, but fares are more expensive, so, to accept the Thursday flights to Bari, I click in the small dot next to the words "reg fare", then click on "select and continue".

This shows me the total cost including taxes – in this example, taxes added come to £14.68 for the outward journey and £9.15 for the return, making a total flight price of £143.81. If I book now, this is the price I pay. However, if I return to the booking later, perhaps even the same afternoon, the price may well have risen.

Before I buy, I remember reading that British Airways has started a service to Bari for the summer, so I log on to **www.ba.com** to check BA's prices on this route. The airline does not fly daily, as Ryanair does, but flying on the same dates, Thursday to Thursday, comes to £226.60 once taxes are added.

So British Airways is more expensive – £226 compared with £143. But Ryanair's flight to Bari leaves Stansted airport at 7.05am. In theory this means I must check in at 5.05am, although it is possible to check in as little as 40 minutes before departure.

By comparison, BA's flight leaves Gatwick airport at 11.40am, meaning I must arrive at the airport by around 9.40am to check in. I can easily take the Underground to Victoria station, then the Gatwick Express to the airport, which costs £14. Both Ryanair's and BA's return flights land in the afternoon, meaning getting home is equally easy.

Weighing up these options, the BA flight now seems more attractive. I do not have to get out of bed at the crack of dawn and endure a stressful race against time on the train or bus, a long drive, an expensive taxi ride or an overnight stay at Stansted. Plus British Airways offers "frills" such as meals and drinks on board. So although the Ryanair flight is cheaper, the cost of reaching the airport is much higher, so I plump for British Airways on this occasion. I think it will be a less stressful journey – which is important at the start of a holiday.

This example is a good illustration of the factors you must weigh up when booking flights. How far is the arrival airport from where you really want to go? How will you travel between the airport and your ultimate destination, and what will that cost? The cheapest flights are often at unsociable times of day, so you must factor in the ease and cost of transport to or from the airport at those times.

Finishing the booking process on BA's website is straightforward. Once I have accepted the flights I want, I am taken to a secure area of the site and asked for personal details including my credit card number. I am then given the number of my "e-ticket" – the reference number I quote when I check in. I also have the option of printing out my ticket reference number, which I choose to do.

Within a few minutes I am sent a confirmation email of my booking from the airline to the email address I've given them. Finally, it is good practice to log out of the website completely after making a credit card booking over the internet and to close down the browser, if you are using a shared computer – this is especially important if you are in an internet café.

Talking flying – websites that go behind the scenes

- **www.airwise.com** – vibrant consumer discussion forum, plus airport and airline information

- **www.pprune.org** – pilots and cabin crew let off steam and discuss in-flight incidents and problems

- **www.flyertalk.com** – a discussion board on a wide number of travel topics

- **www.airsafe.com** – lots of safety information; not one for the nervous flyer

- **www.aviationpics.de** – weird, scary and funny photographs of airline incidents

Booking a flight using an online travel agent

We have seen how straightforward it is to book a flight on the internet, if you know where you want to go and are not trying to put together a complex itinerary. But should you rely on an airline's website to give you the best deals on every occasion? Of course not. It also makes sense to tap your request into some of the huge number of online travel agents to see if you can get a better deal.

These websites can save you time and often money by scouring the sites of lots of different airlines in just a few seconds, which will probably throw up carriers you had not even thought of using. In the example above, when I searched for flights to southern Italy, I only checked with Ryanair and British Airways. But Expedia reveals that I could also have chosen to fly with Alitalia or SN Brussels Airlines, albeit involving a change of plane.

But puzzlingly, Expedia does not tell me that I could have flown to southern Italy on Ryanair. Why not? The answer lies in the way that many online travel agents work.

In the late 1990s emerged the now familiar travel agents, such as **www.expedia.co.uk**, **www.ebookers.co.uk** and **www.lastminute.co.uk**. These sites were revolutionary because, in effect, they put on to the internet, for all of us to see and book, what had previously been the secrets of the travel agents' computers.

As well as selling flights, the online travel agents sell other travel products, too, such as hotel rooms, car hire and travel insurance, and you can also now book a complete package holiday through many of them. (*See* chapter 4, "Create your own package holiday online", page 134).

These online agents use a traditional form of booking travel products called a global distribution system (GDS), which compares lots of different airlines', travel agents' and tour operators' prices. Lastminute is even owned by a big GDS company, Sabre. GDS technology is rather like a private internet for the travel industry. It's offered by companies with racy names such as Amadeus, Galileo, Pegasus and Worldspan, and it allows airlines, hotels and car hire companies to spread information about price and availability. GDS technology is what high-street travel agents and scheduled and charter airlines have used for years to book your trip.

However, some budget airlines use the internet as their method of distribution, rather than a GDS. EasyJet has never bothered with a GDS, as it set itself up in 1995 as a phone and internet booking airline from the start. Ryanair stopped using a GDS in the late 1990s, to howls of protest from the travel agents who booked flights using it (and took the commission this gave them). That's why you cannot find prices for budget carriers such as Ryanair on sites such as Expedia or Opodo – because the two types of technology, internet and GDS, cannot talk to each other.

Spotting a gap in the market, in came the latest wave of online travel companies. These are known as price comparison websites (PCWs) and include **www.skyscanner.net**, **www.traveljungle.co.uk**, **www.travelfusion.com** and **www.travelsupermarket.com**. These sites use a different type of technology from GDS. They do what's called "screen-scraping" or "spidering", meaning they go into the websites of the big online travel agents, plus airlines' own websites, to find the widest choice of flight deals possible. So they can include fares from budget airlines such as Ryanair and easyJet. Lastminute has now started to use this "spidering" technology, offering its customers flights on some 40 European budget airlines alongside scheduled and charter airlines, but many online travel agents still do not offer this.

If you use a PCW, you will find yourself booking with a third party – the PCW is simply a shop window, not a travel agency itself. And because PCWs are effectively feeding off online travel agents' and airlines' websites, their prices may not be quite up to date. Some established online agents such as Expedia actively dislike the PCWs. "Screen-scraping is basically duping the customer into thinking they are booking with them when they are booking with someone else," said Robin Sutherland, director of retail for Expedia.

So you should always shop around. Deals can change on an hourly basis. Scouring half a dozen sites before you book should give you a good overview of what's on the market and what sort of price is fair. For sites to check when looking for a flight, *see* the Directory, page 420.

Tips for booking flights online

- Book as far ahead as possible to get the lowest fares.

- Sign up for airlines' and travel agents' email newsletters which alert you to special offers.

- Check prices a day or two either side of your intended dates to see if that produces cheaper deals.

- Tuesdays and Wednesdays are traditionally the cheapest days to travel; Fridays and Sundays tend to be the most expensive.

- Check for other nearby airports – if you're hiring a car they may be just as convenient. Expedia has a useful function that throws up the nearest alternatives to the airport you have searched on.

- Consider whether it's worth paying more for a direct flight to avoid the hassle of changing planes on a cheaper, less direct route.

- Ensure the names you put on the booking form are in exactly the same format as the names on your passports.

- Check if the website adds travel insurance to the cost – some do automatically, but if you already have insurance you can uncheck this box.

• Read the small print about cancellation charges, or charges to change the name on the ticket or to swap to another flight – these can vary wildly, and sometimes such changes are not allowed.

• Check to see if the company you are buying from holds an Atol to protect your money. If it does not, it's still OK to book, but if the airline goes bust you won't get any help.

Airline jargon – what does it mean?

• **APEX tickets, discounted or restricted tickets, and fully flexible tickets**: APEX stands for Advance Purchase Excursion fares – these are tickets that must be bought a certain number of days before the flight, and carry restrictions. "Discounted", "restricted" or "semi-flexible" tickets all have limits on them – for example you may not be able to cancel the ticket, or change the date of travel, route or passenger's name; or you may be able to do so but only on paying a fee. "Fully flexible" tickets are the most expensive, but allow any change, such as swapping to a later (or earlier) flight. You can also cancel fully flexible tickets and get your money back.

• **Direct flight**: in airline terms, a direct flight means you may stop *en route*, but you won't have to get off the plane. The faster option is a "non-stop" flight.

• **Lost tickets**: if you have an e-ticket you need not worry, as your details are in the computer, but if you lose an old-fashioned paper ticket airlines can refuse to replace it, although in practice they will usually reissue a ticket once they are satisfied you have genuinely lost it. Keep a photocopy of the ticket separately. Check your travel insurance for help with lost tickets, too.

• **Open jaw**: this is a return ticket that allows you to fly in to one city and out of another.

• **Overbooking**: sadly, this is a fact of life on popular routes on many scheduled airlines (though budget and charter airlines rarely overbook). The earlier you check in, the better the chance you have of avoiding this. For information on your rights, *see* below (page 86).

• **Reconfirmation**: you used to have to reconfirm that you intended to travel at least 72 hours before the flight's departure, unless it was the first flight on the ticket or you were on a stopover of less than 72 hours. Many airlines now say there is no need to reconfirm, but it doesn't hurt to do so, especially in developing countries. Your hotel concierge or holiday company rep can do this for you.

• **RTW**: a "round-the-world" ticket, popular with backpackers, usually involves a series of flights that must be taken within a year. For more details, *see* below (page 88).

• **Seat pitch**: this is the distance between the back of your seat, and the back of the seat in front of you. Most scheduled airlines offer a rather cramped 30 to 32in seat pitch in economy, though some (such as Air New Zealand, Malaysia Airlines and Thai Airways) have a more generous 34in. Further information from your airline, a good travel agent or from the website **www.airlinequality.com**.

• **Stopover**: this is a point on your flight where you are allowed to break your journey. If you're flying to Sydney in Australia, for example, and want to stop off on the way in a city such as Bangkok, you must check when buying the ticket that you will be allowed to do so as some tickets do not permit this.

• **Taxes and charges**: airlines slap on all sorts of "extras" that can easily add £40 or more to the cost of your flight. **Air Passenger Duty**, which airlines pass to the government, is levied on every ticket at a rate of £10 for a return flight in economy class within Europe (£20 long haul), and £20 for a return flight in Europe in business class (£40 long haul). **Fuel surcharges** can be heavy: by April 2006, in response to rising fuel prices, British Airways was charging passengers £16 extra per return flight within Europe and £70 extra long-haul. An **insurance and security** charge has been added by many airlines since the events of September 11, 2001, ostensibly to pay for better security measures and the airlines' higher insurance premiums. **Passenger Service Charge** is another cheeky "extra" – airlines have always had to pay this to airports for handling their customers, but since 1999 many airlines have separated it out as though it is a new tax foisted on them. Some airlines (such as Ryanair) charge a **credit card booking fee**, and Ryanair, uniquely and controversially, charges every passenger a **wheelchair levy** for providing assistance to disabled travellers.

Buying flights for children

Babies up to the age of two generally pay either nothing for their tickets, or a token sum of up to 10 per cent of the adult ticket price. Taxes and charges are added to this. However they do not get a seat, nor a baggage allowance, and you are expected to sit them on your knee during the flight, usually using a special seatbelt extension. On some flights, particularly long-haul, you can request a bassinet or skycot for your baby. You are also able to take the baby's pushchair as far as the aircraft gate and this does not count against the weight of your checked luggage. Some airlines allow car seats to be used on board to carry young children.

Once your child reaches the age of two, they are expected to pay for their own seat, and you do not always get much of a discount on the adult price. You're more likely to find a discount on long-haul than on short-haul flights. It's worth using a good travel agent such as **Trailfinders** (0845 058 5858, **www.trailfinders.com**), as they cut exclusive deals with individual airlines.

Unaccompanied minors

Once children are aged six or more, many airlines allow them to travel unaccompanied, but you must register them with the airline in advance so they can be met and looked after by airline staff. British Airways, for example, has the Skyflyer Solo service, charging £32 one way to accompany children. Other airlines that offer similar services include Cathay Pacific, bmi, Lufthansa, Flybe and Qantas. Airlines that do not carry unaccompanied children include Aer Lingus (even on flights it code-shares with BA), Ryanair, easyJet and Monarch Scheduled.

Flights: your rights

Your rights when buying a plane ticket

Buying a flight from a travel company

If you book a flight with a travel company (a tour operator or travel agent) that holds an **Air Travel Organisers' Licence** (Atol), and the tour operator or travel agent goes bust, you will be protected under the Atol scheme. If the company goes bust before you travel, you will get your money back. If the company goes bust while you are abroad, you will usually be able to finish your holiday, and then be flown home.

This is because the Civil Aviation Authority, which runs the Atol scheme, checks the finances of each Atol holder to reduce the risk of insolvency. Every Atol holder must arrange a bond, so that if it goes out of business, the CAA can use the bond money either to refund you or to fly you home.

It's a similar story if you buy an airline ticket through a tour operator or travel agent that holds an Atol and the *airline* goes bust. The Atol holder is responsible for its customers and so, as before, it must make alternative holiday arrangements for you, or refund your money.

You are protected by an Atol if you buy charter or scheduled flight tickets direct from companies such as Trailfinders, Gold Medal, Freedom Flights or Avro, which are all Atol holders. Likewise the big online travel retailers such as Expedia, Opodo, Travelocity and Lastminute hold Atols. The price comparison websites I referred to above, such as Skyscanner and TravelJungle, do not hold Atols, because they do not sell you the flight – instead, they link you either to travel agents that hold Atols, or direct to airlines, which do not, so you must work out who you are buying a ticket from before you can tell whether or not it is Atol protected.

The simplest way to tell if you are covered is to look for the Atol logo on the company's website and literature. To check that the Atol is up to date (and for further details about the Atol scheme), contact the **CAA** (020 7453 6430, **www.atol.org.uk**). But whether you buy your flight in a travel agency, over the phone or on the internet, make sure you get the Atol booking confirmation or receipt straight away – it should either be handed to you, or posted to you within 24 hours. If you are booking on a website, you are usually sent a confirmation email immediately too, which is effectively the same as the printed receipt, as it confirms who your contract is with.

During 2006, there have been moves within the travel industry to change or abandon the Atol scheme. Some holiday companies would prefer to see a £1 levy on every travel arrangement, whether it is sold by a travel agent, tour operator or an airline, to create a level playing field and to remove some of the confusion that surrounds consumer protection. But in March 2006 the House of Lords voted not to allow this proposal to be included within the Civil Aviation Bill currently going through Parliament.

The holiday company TUI, which owns brands including Thomson Holidays, and rival operator Thomas Cook, have now threatened to withdraw from the Atol scheme, perhaps as early as autumn 2006, if changes are not made. TUI spends around £8 million a year on Atol bonding and feels it is unfair that it has to do so, when airlines do not have to hold Atols. If TUI does withdraw from the scheme it says it will offer customers alternative guarantees.

Buying a flight direct from an airline

You are not financially protected if you buy your flight direct from an airline, or from a travel agent who hands over the ticket straight away or within 24 hours. By giving you the ticket immediately, the agent is effectively acting as an arm of the airline, so your contract is with the airline and it is irrelevant whether or not the agent is an Atol holder.

Airlines are not obliged to hold Atols for historical reasons. Back in 1973, the Atol scheme was introduced by the government, because some travel companies were going out of business and leaving people stranded or out of pocket. But in those days there wasn't much of a problem with airlines going bust – most airlines were state-owned, and governments were reluctant to let them collapse for reasons of national pride, if nothing else. So it was successfully argued that airlines need not hold Atols.

Thus if you buy a ticket direct from an airline and it goes bust when you are on holiday, you will not get any help from that airline, or your money back, and you will have to buy a ticket on another airline to get home (although sometimes other airlines step in to offer stranded passengers cheap tickets to get home). The 39,000 customers who were either travelling or booked to travel with EUjet in summer 2005 found this out the hard way, when the airline collapsed, leaving many of them stranded across Europe. They had to pay for new flights on other airlines to get home.

If you are yet to travel when your airline collapses, you will join a long list of creditors and it is unlikely that you will get your money back. You will also have to buy another ticket if you still want to take your holiday, and that is likely to cost you more than the original, because it will be closer to the departure date. And if you decide to scrap your holiday, you may lose money on any other bookings, such as car hire or hotel rooms, you have made. Your travel insurance will not usually cover you for airline insolvency, unless you have bought a policy that specifically includes it.

Government pride in an airline is no longer enough to protect you, it seems: since 2000, 19 airlines in Europe have failed, including the national carriers of Belgium (Sabena) and Switzerland (Swissair), which did not survive the turmoil created by the attacks of September 11, 2001.

If you are worried about financial protection, buy airline tickets from a travel company that holds an Atol; alternatively, take out airline insolvency insurance, either as part of your overall travel insurance policy (see chapter 6), or by buying it at the time you buy the tickets. Pay for your tickets by credit card if possible.

What happens if the airline changes the flight schedule?

Airlines sometimes change their flight schedules before your holiday, for example, if they are not getting the level of bookings that they need to make a particular route viable. They may combine two departures, substitute a smaller plane, or scrap the route altogether. It happens more often with charter airlines than with scheduled airlines, but can affect any flight, and it often happens around the end of March and again at the start of the winter season, when airlines switch between winter and summer timetables.

If you are told that there has been a major change to your flight – such as a difference of 12 hours in the flight time, or a change of departure airport – you are entitled to cancel and ask for a refund from the airline. This may not be ideal, because you must then find alternative flights for your holiday. You can also accept a major change and ask for compensation – for more on this, *see* chapter 4, page 112.

Your rights if you cannot fly

If you have to cancel your flight

If you have bought a fully flexible ticket – the most expensive type – you should be able to get your money back from the airline or travel agent.

If you bought a non-refundable ticket it is unlikely that the airline will help, and you will probably lose your money. But the budget airlines are leading the way in helping customers here. Although they do not offer refunds, airlines including easyJet, Ryanair, Flybe, Monarch, BA Connect and Jet2 allow customers to change things like the date, the passenger name and in some cases even the route. You'll have to pay a fee (typically £15–£30pp) and the difference in price if a ticket on the route you switch to is more expensive.

Other carriers, such as BA, may give you credit towards another flight on a discretionary basis. You will have to ask for this: it is not automatic.

If you have to cancel your flight, your travel insurance policy may pay out, depending on the circumstances. And you are morally entitled to a refund of the tax and airport charges you paid to the airline, because the airline only hands these over to the government and airport respectively if you actually fly. It is worth writing to request this refund, though most airlines will charge an "administration" fee that eats into or even exceeds it.

If you miss your flight

If you have a fully flexible ticket, you can simply book on to a later departure. If you have a non-refundable ticket you will probably have to buy another ticket for the next flight, although staff may be sympathetic if you have an excellent reason for running late. EasyJet, for example, allows passengers who miss a flight to take the next flight for a missed departure fee of £35, as long as you arrive at check-in within two hours of the original departure (unless the original delay is caused by another easyJet flight, in which case the transfer is free). You may also be covered by your travel insurance.

If you arrive at the airport short of time and there's a long queue to check in, ask a member of the airline staff if you need to be sent to the front of the queue and checked in quickly. If you only have hand luggage, you are more likely to be able to persuade the check-in staff to let you on the flight after the gate has officially closed, as they will not have to worry about your checked luggage making its way to the plane on time. These days, there are also alternative check-in methods – such as online check-in or using a self-service kiosk – which can save time. EasyJet also allows customers to switch, at no charge, from a later departure to an earlier one, if there are two or more flights per day on that route, and a seat is available on the earlier flight. For more on checking in, *see* chapter 8.

Your rights if the airline gets things wrong

In February 2005, new European Union rules came in to force that strengthened passengers' rights. Essentially the new rules mean that if your flight is delayed, you are entitled to refreshments, a hotel room if necessary and, ultimately, a refund of the ticket price, and if your flight is cancelled or you are bumped off your flight, you are entitled to all this plus compensation. (The rules don't apply if you are flying for free, or on deals that are not available to the public – so airline crew, the Queen and the Prime Minister are ineligible!) Details at **www.europa.eu.int/comm/transport**.

Outside the EU, you may not get financial compensation, but you should be looked after, with refreshments and accommodation if you are delayed overnight. Here are guidelines for the most common scenarios.

If your flight is cancelled

The European Union Denied Boarding Regulation, which was introduced in February 2005, strengthens passengers' rights. It applies to flights leaving from EU airports, or from other airports if the airline is based in the EU and you are flying into the EU, on condition that you have a confirmed reservation and have turned up on time for the flight.

The rules are slightly different depending on whether the flight is delayed – for example, while repairs are carried out, but you eventually leave on the flight you originally booked – or cancelled, in which case you find yourself on a flight with a different number from the original. In either case, you should be given printed information on your rights by the airline at the time.

"The real consumer benefit of the new denied boarding regime is that there are criminal sanctions for airlines failing to inform passengers of their denied boarding compensation rights," said barrister Alan Saggerson, who specialises in travel and tourism law. "The old regulations did not have any such sanctions. Now the airline has to tell you what your rights are, and if they do not, the CAA can bring them to book."

- If you are at the airport and your **outward flight is cancelled**, you should be offered either a refund of the full cost of the return ticket, or an alternative flight that departs either as soon as possible, or at a later date that you choose.

- If you are abroad and your **return flight is cancelled**, you are entitled to either a refund of the unused return portion of the ticket, or an alternative flight home. It is probably best to accept the alternative flight in this case, as the refund is unlikely to cover the cost of a new single ticket.

- If you are in the middle of a **more complicated journey** the rules are slightly different. Say you are flying from Dublin to Brussels via Heathrow, where you must change planes, and the Heathrow to Brussels flight is cancelled. This means you will miss the meeting you are going to in Brussels, so the rest of the journey is pointless. In this situation, you are entitled to a refund of the whole ticket, plus a free flight back to Dublin.

- In all cases, you are also entitled to **help at the airport**: meals and refreshments, a hotel room if you have to stay overnight, and two free phone calls, faxes or emails.

- You're also entitled to **financial compensation** if you arrive at your destination late because of a cancelled flight. Note that you are not entitled to this compensation if your flight was merely delayed, no matter how long you waited. The table opposite sets out what you are entitled to if your flight was cancelled.

Length of journey	Delay to destination	Compensation
Up to 1,500km	Up to 2 hours	€125
Up to 1,500km	More than 2 hours	€250
1,500km to 3,500km	Up to 3 hours	€200
1,500km to 3,500km	More than 3 hours	€400
More than 3,500km	Up to 4 hours	€300
More than 3,500km	More than 4 hours	€600

Source: the Air Transport Users' Council (**www.auc.org.uk**)

There is still confusion over these new rules. Airlines argue that they do not apply if the problem is due to bad weather, strikes or terrorist acts. Barrister Alan Saggerson said: "It is for the airline to demonstrate that exceptional circumstances have arisen, and they have to be unusual, such as very bad weather, or a breakdown that the airline can prove is very rare." If the airline can prove this, it will not have to pay compensation.

Another airline tactic is to claim that a cancellation is really only a delay, which also means they don't have to pay compensation. But a court ruling in early 2006 has strengthened passengers' rights in this respect. An airline passenger from Oxford won compensation from Thomas Cook Airlines when his flight to Vancouver was cancelled. Thomas Cook argued that the flight had merely been delayed, and used the same flight number for the flight that eventually took off, 24 hours later and from a different UK airport to the one the passenger had booked to travel from. But the district judge who heard the case at Oxford County Court said: "The fact that the same flight number was used has no bearing on the issue at all. The time differential of 24 hours is more indicative of a cancellation than of delay."

If the airline cancels the flight more than 14 days in advance, but offers you a re-routed flight instead, it is not obliged to pay compensation. If it cancels the flight less than 14 days beforehand, but will still get you there on another flight within a few hours of the original time, you won't get compensation either. So the most likely scenario in which compensation would be payable is if the problem is obviously the airline's fault, such as a technical problem with the plane.

If your flight is cancelled and appropriate financial compensation is not forthcoming, take the matter up first with the airline. If you are still not satisfied you can complain to the **Air Transport Users' Council** (AUC), the

UK's passenger watchdog body, at CAA House, 45-49 Kingsway, London WC2B 6TE (020 7240 6061, **www.auc.org.uk**).

If your flight is cancelled and you are outside the EU, and not using an EU carrier, these new EU rules do not apply. The **International Air Transport Association (www.iata.org)**, of which most airlines are members, suggests airlines should offer you refreshments and a hotel room, if necessary, plus either a refund, or transport to your final destination either on another flight or even by another means of transport.

But you do have rights under the Montreal Convention, which came into force in the UK in June 2004. In theory this provides for financial compensation if your flight is cancelled or delayed, but in practice, according to an AUC spokesman, the most you are likely to get is meals, refreshments and accommodation while the problem is sorted out. Airlines' conditions of carriage (the small print) generally exclude any liability for losses you incur as a result of a delay or cancellation (such as missing a subsequent flight).

If your flight is delayed

Under the EU Denied Boarding Regulations, you cannot claim financial compensation if you are delayed, but after a delay of two hours or more you now have a legal right to food, refreshments and a hotel room where necessary.

The point at which these rules kick in depends on how far you were travelling. They apply after a two-hour delay on flights of up to 1,500km, after three hours on flights of 1,500 to 3,500km, and after four hours on longer flights.

After five hours, if you decide not to continue with the journey, you are entitled to a refund of the ticket price. If you have already completed part of the journey, you are entitled to either a refund of the return part of the ticket, or to an alternative flight back, but not both.

If the delay comes part way through a more complicated journey – such as the Dublin–Heathrow–Brussels example I gave above – and the delay means the whole trip becomes pointless, you are entitled to a refund of the whole ticket price plus a flight back to the airport you started from, but not to any further compensation.

If you are "bumped" off the flight

Scheduled airlines routinely overbook flights because business travellers on flexible tickets may not show up, but sometimes the airline miscalculates and there are too many passengers for the plane. So some are "bumped", that is, not allowed to board the flight. They are literally "denied boarding".

Sometimes this can work to your advantage as airline staff will offer incentives such as money or free hotel stays to anyone willing to travel on a later flight. If you accept such an offer you are still entitled to be transported from A to B, but you cannot claim further compensation for being bumped.

But if you are bumped against your will, and you are flying from an airport within the EU, or into an EU airport on an EU-based carrier, you are entitled to Denied Boarding Compensation, so long as you hold a confirmed ticket and had turned up, sober, in time for the flight. This is the same amount of money as in the table above under "cancellation".

If you are not within the EU, or flying on an EU-based carrier into the EU, you are still likely to be offered benefits for being bumped. Ask airline staff for a letter detailing what you are entitled to, and if you are offered vouchers instead of cash, look closely at the small print. For example, if the voucher is for another flight on that airline, are you likely to make use of it? You're generally better off taking the cash, if it's on offer.

If the airline loses your luggage

See chapter 7 (page 251) for full details of what to do in this situation.

Problems with flights that are part of a package holiday

As well as the rules on cancellation and delay outlined above, you have further protection if you buy a package holiday, under the 1992 EU Package Travel Regulations. In a nutshell, these force holiday companies to ensure that all elements of a trip – flight, hotel and transfer, for example – are up to the required standard, and if not, to put things right. For more on this and the advantages of buying a package holiday, *see* chapter 4, and *see* chapter 9 for details of how to press a claim against a tour operator if your package holiday goes wrong.

Can travel insurance help?

Yes: most policies offer compensation if you are delayed, usually after a certain amount of time – at least eight hours, perhaps as much as 12 – though it is often only a small amount, such as £30–£50, designed to cover essentials. If you decide to abandon the trip your travel insurance may pay you a lump sum as compensation, although it will not repay the cost of the trip – you must negotiate with the travel company for that.

Airline troubles – action plan

- Pack your hand luggage with trouble in mind – take snacks and a book in case of delays, and a change of clothes in case your checked luggage is lost.

- When a delay is announced, ask airline staff for a written copy of your rights – they are obliged to provide it.

- Keep all paperwork and receipts for emergency items.

- Check that you have travel insurance that covers delays.

- Considering buying a policy that covers airline insolvency.

- Leave plenty of time for transfers when booking connecting flights, especially if using two different airlines.

- Check in on time even if you hear there's a delay – the situation may change quickly.

Round-the-world tickets

These can be a good way to organise air travel for a trip of up to one year, so they are ideal for backpackers. But there are so many variables that I urge you to use a travel agent to help you book the one that's right for you.

First, consider your route. East to west or vice versa? Do you want to fly every leg, or build in an overland stretch (for example, across the USA)? And can you say for sure how long you want to spend in each place? It's wise to buy a ticket that has a degree of flexibility, so you can change the date of flights without penalty. A travel agent can advise on this.

Sticking to popular RTW destinations (such as Bangkok, Sydney, Fiji and Los Angeles) will keep your costs down. Adding in South America or Africa tends to put prices up, as does trying to backtrack or build in less popular destinations. If, for example, you want to travel around Indochina, it might be wise to buy separate tickets out of Bangkok for this leg of your journey, rather than build a fiddly RTW itinerary: again, a good agent can advise. Tickets must be used within one calendar year.

Good starting points for buying RTW tickets include:

Airline Network, 0870 700 0543, **www.airline-network.co.uk**

Flight Centre, 0800 587 0058, **www.flightcentre.co.uk**

STA Travel, 0870 163 0026, **www.statravel.co.uk**

Tailor-Made Travel, 0845 456 8006, **www.tailor-made.co.uk**

Trailfinders, 0845 058 5858, **www.trailfinders.com**

Travelbag, 0800 082 5000, **www.travelbag.co.uk**

Travelmood, 0870 066 0004, **www.travelmood.com**

In the US, the specialist RTW agent Airtrek has a useful online planner (**www.airtreks.com**)

Frequent–flyer schemes

Most scheduled airlines offer membership schemes to their customers, who earn points when they buy a flight. These points can then be redeemed for further flights, upgrades, or other goods, such as hotel stays, car hire, wine or hot-air balloon trips. Hotel chains offer similar schemes for regular guests, and you can often spend the points accrued in one scheme on another – for example using airline miles to upgrade to a better hotel room.

The first frequent-flyer scheme was AAdvantage, launched by American Airlines in 1981 as a marketing ploy. Since then the industry has exploded, with around 130 airlines offering schemes, and some 10 trillion frequent-flyer miles now sitting in our accounts.

You can earn miles in a variety of ways besides buying flights. Using a credit card linked to a frequent-flyer programme is, worldwide, the biggest way to earn miles after actually flying. Store cards offer another route: for example, when I shop at Tesco's I earn AirMiles through my Tesco's loyalty card. **AirMiles** (0870 557 7722, **www.airmiles.co.uk**) is perhaps the best known points-collection scheme in the UK, and although it started life as British Airways' frequent-flyer programme it is now a fully fledged tour operator itself, offering holidays as well as flights on a wide range of airlines.

I think it's worth joining the scheme of any airline you fly with even if you're not a frequent flyer. Among the advantages: airlines often have special offers for customers in their loyalty scheme; presenting your card at check-in can add weight to your request for an upgrade or other special treatment; you can register preferences for a particular type of meal or aisle/window seat; presenting your card at a hotel reception desk may get you further benefits.

Frequent-traveller schemes become more interesting once you reach the second tier of membership, having earned a certain number of points: for example, at the second (silver) level of British Airways' Executive Club, you can use BA's airport lounges and check in at the Club World (business class) counter even if you are flying in economy.

An entire industry is dedicated to helping frequent travellers maximise their points. In America, Randy Petersen is an acknowledged expert: he edits and publishes *Inside Flyer* (see **www.insideflyer.com** and **www.webflyer.com**). Business travel expert Roger Collis is the author of *The Survivor's Guide to Business Travel* (Kogan Page, £12.99), which covers this subject and others. The consultancy **Global Flight** (**www.globalflight.net**) helps travellers to get the most out of their frequent-flyer schemes, for a fee of about £88.

Tips for using frequent-flyer schemes

- Check the expiry date of your points: sometimes they are valid for only a few years.

- Always ask when checking in at an airport, hotel or car hire desk if there are any deals for frequent travellers.

- Check the small print when booking using your miles – a common complaint is that you must travel at antisocial times, and that you cannot use miles to pay the taxes.

- Book early, as airlines typically only allow 10 per cent of seats on any flight to be paid for using miles.

- Be aware that airlines may impose "blackouts" over popular holidays, when you cannot travel using your miles, or will have to redeem them at twice the normal rate.

- Remember that you cannot usually earn miles on the cheapest tickets.

- Keep your boarding pass until you see your mileage credited to your frequent-flyer account – if it's not credited, you'll need the boarding pass to prove that you flew.

Airline alliances and code-sharing

Alliances are groupings of airlines that provide services to each other and favour each others' passengers. Not all airlines are in alliances, but it's worth finding out which airlines are in bed together if you want to maximise your frequent-traveller points.

- **Star Alliance** (**www.staralliance.com**) consists of 18 airlines, including Air New Zealand, bmi, Singapore Airlines, South African Airways and United.

- Oneworld (www.oneworld.com) has eight members, including American Airlines, British Airways, Cathay Pacific and Qantas.

- SkyTeam (www.skyteam.com) has nine members, including Continental, KLM, Alitalia and Delta.

By joining the frequent-flyer programme of one alliance member, you can generally earn and redeem points with any other airline in the same alliance.

The growth of alliances has mirrored the growth in code-sharing. This is a practice whereby two or more airlines within the same alliance use the same flight number. This can come as a surprise to travellers who, for example, think they are flying to Sydney with Qantas but find themselves on a British Airways plane.

When booking your flight ask:

- Which airline operates the flight?

- Do I have to change planes en route?

- Will my meal and seat requests be valid on each leg of the journey?

- Can I earn frequent-flyer points with both airlines in the code-share?

- How and with which airline do I check in?

Flying in comfort
Concorde

"It's the closest you'll ever get to space travel," said the man in the bar of the Sandpiper hotel in Barbados, as we discussed flying to the Caribbean island on Concorde. One of the real perks of my job as travel editor of *The Times* was occasionally flying on Concorde to Barbados or New York – the only two scheduled destinations for the supersonic service out of Heathrow. The man at the Sandpiper was right. On my first flight, I realised that the real thrill of Concorde, for the passengers, was not how fast it went, but how high.

After a steeper take-off than normal, you didn't really feel as if you were going faster than a normal plane, although a digital display in the cabin flashed up the speed as we raced towards Mach 2. But Concorde cruised at around 60,000ft – nearly twice as high as a normal jumbo – and if you peered out of one of the tiny windows, you could see a shimmering blue and gold rainbow – the earth's curvature. And you were higher than all the clouds, so if you looked up, all you saw was the deep purple of space. It was thrilling.

Funnily enough, things on board were relatively humdrum. Yes, of course there was Krug and lobster and caviar, but the cabin was tiny – just one aisle, 25 rows of four seats, and the seats were far less roomy than you get in business class on subsonic planes these days. The point of Concorde was not the in-flight service, but the sheer delight at flying in one of aviation's class acts. And the fact that you could leave London at 9.30am on a drizzly winter's day and arrive in Barbados four hours later – also, magically, at 9.30am, in brilliant sunshine. Concorde pilots would even fly down the island's "platinum" coast and dip a wing at the rich holidaymakers eating breakfast on the terraces of the island's best hotels.

So loved was Concorde that when *Times Travel* ran a competition to win a flight, we received 25,000 entries.

But enough nostalgia. In 2003 Concorde retired from service. The question now, for those with the money, is what can replace her? Today there are two choices: the front of the plane (business or first class), or a private jet.

Business and first class

Travelling in business or first class is delicious from the moment you are asked to turn left when you step on board. Right at the front of the plane, the extra perk of **first class** is really the space. As well as a generous seat/bed area, you'll have plenty of room to store your bags, toiletries and magazines. Some airlines even give customers pyjamas for overnight flights. Airlines compete for first-class passengers with the most glamorous extras. I once flew from Doha in Qatar to London in first class on Qatar Airways and was driven from Doha's terminal building in a private 7-series BMW to the steps of the plane, rather than having to suffer the indignity of the transfer bus. Somewhat mortifyingly, the passengers getting off the bus when I arrived were told to wait while I climbed the steps ahead of them. I'm not sure I'm really cut out to be a diva.

In **business class**, you can expect lots of personal attention, good, sometimes excellent meals served on china and often at a time of your choosing, a choice of dozens of movies to watch on your personal DVD player, free magazines and toiletries, even a massage or a manicure on Virgin Atlantic. And, increasingly these days, a bed. Seats that turn into fully flat beds are now common on the long-haul routes of most major airlines, so for a long flight, there's little reason to book business class on an airline that does not offer them.

These beds are truly revolutionary: even men of 6ft and more can stretch out flat and sleep well. **Qantas**'s Skybed, for example, is 6ft 6in long, and **Virgin Atlantic** claims its Upper Class Suite beds are the longest business-class beds in the air, at 6ft 7in. The panel of buttons you're presented with to move the seat into a bed brings out the teenage gadget-freak in most of us. Airlines are now adapting their services around the beds: for example, if you're flying overnight from New York to London with British Airways, you can eat dinner in the business-class lounge, hop on board and go straight to sleep, to maximise sleeping time on a six-hour flight. Virgin Atlantic offers a similar service on some overnight flights. Some travellers have told me that the new problem is people who snore loudly, as everyone now sleeps so well in the business-class beds.

Premium economy

If you cannot afford business class, but don't want to sit at the back of the plane, you might try "**premium economy**". Airlines including Virgin Atlantic, British Airways, bmi and Air New Zealand have introduced these cabins on long-haul flights as a half-way house between economy and business. You sit in front of the economy cabin, and have perks such as more legroom, better meals and a larger cabin baggage allowance. But you do not have a flat bed and cannot use the business lounge, two valuable perks for the business-class passenger. Typically these seats cost around £300–£400 more per person than the equivalent in economy.

Some charter airlines, including First Choice and Excel, also offer premium economy services, and although the leg room may not be as generous as with a scheduled airline, the prices are not as high either.

How to get the best business–class deals

More and more of us are choosing to buy **business–class** seats when we take a holiday. Executives who are used to travelling in business during their working lives don't like to return to economy once they retire, or when they are on holiday with the family. And more of us are choosing to upgrade to a roomier cabin to give a more relaxing start and finish to our trip.

But can you ever get a bargain in business class? Yes, says Alex McWhirter, airline fares expert at *Business Traveller* magazine, if you think a little outside the box.

"The home airlines or national carriers – in the UK, that's BA, bmi and Virgin – tend to offer the worst deals in business class," he said. "This is the case the world over. It's the foreign airlines that are more hungry for business." This means choosing airlines such as Lufthansa, Air France or KLM to fly from London to New York. You'll have to change planes in Frankfurt, Paris or Amsterdam, but as leisure travellers generally have more time than business travellers this isn't necessarily a problem.

The savings can be substantial – foreign airlines might charge little more than £1,000 for a business-class flight to New York, whereas BA can charge three or four times this much. New York is not the only route where you can successfully shop around for business-class deals. "Take Bangkok, for example," said McWhirter. "BA and Qantas stop there *en route* to Australia so they are not so interested in Bangkok-only traffic, but Taiwanese carrier EVA Air flies there from London. No one knows about EVA Air so they offer good fares through travel agents and it's a non-stop flight."

Other airlines to try include:

- For Los Angeles, Air New Zealand, which has daily flights and has just introduced beds in business class

- For Australia, Emirates, Malaysia Airlines and Singapore Airlines

- For Thailand, KLM, Air France, Qatar Airways or Emirates.

I put McWhirter's advice to the test and searched for business-class flights from London Heathrow to New York's JFK Airport, booking three months in advance and on the same dates in each case (all prices include taxes). The cheapest business-class return fare was on Kuwait Airways, which I found on **www.ebookers.com** at £872 (though Kuwait is a dry airline, so no free champagne). Next came Air India (**www.airindia.com**) at £942, another direct service. KLM (**www.klm.com**) was offering £1,165 via Amsterdam, Alitalia was available for £1,641 via Milan on Ebookers, and BA (**www.ba.com**) and Virgin (**www.virgin-atlantic.com**) both came in at exactly £1,978.

In late 2005, two new airlines launched on the Stansted to New York route, competing for business and first-class passengers. **Eos Airlines** (0800 019 6468, **www.eosairlines.com**) has just 48 first-class flat beds in a Boeing 757, which normally carries about 200 people, with returns from about £3,500, though it has been offering discounts. **MAXjet Airways** (0800 023 4300, **www.maxjet. com**) has 102 business-class seats (at 60in, they are roomy, but do not recline flat) on a Boeing 767 with prices from around £850 return. It also flies to Washington DC.

Business-class booking tips

- Try booking through a tour operator, as they often have good business-class fares with airlines they deal with a lot.

- Consider upgrading to business class for only one leg of the journey. For example, most flights from the UK to the Caribbean go out in the day but come back overnight – which is when you really want the flat bed.

- Shop around, not forgetting indirect routes via a third country.

- To pick the best seat before you book log on to **www.seatguru.com**, which has diagrams of the interiors of many of the major airlines' planes.

- Ask at the check-in desk if you can buy an upgrade to premium economy or business – there may be deals available if the flight is not full.

- Join the airline's frequent-flyer programme.

Private jets

A limo collects you from your home, drives you to a convenient, nearby airfield, and pulls up on the tarmac at the steps of your private jet. You and half a dozen pals step on board to be greeted by a stewardess offering you champagne, and caviar-topped canapés. Your favourite magazines are waiting for you, and an in-flight music playlist has been put together at your request. No detail is too small: Michael Winner, who regularly flies with private jet operator **Club328**, insists on bowls of Smarties being provided on his jet. Within two hours you're in the south of France, at Hyères airport – so much closer to St Tropez than Nice, where the commercial jets land – or perhaps you're touching down in St Moritz for a weekend's skiing. Commercial planes cannot land on this tiny airstrip, but instead must fly to Zurich, a two-and-a-half-hour drive away. But you can practically ski off from the airline steps.

Is this a fantasy that only the super-rich can afford? Not any longer. A dramatic growth in private-jet travel has seen increased competition and hence prices tumbling. Both the above trips can be arranged for as little as £800 to £1,000 per person.

"It's not just for the rich and famous any more," said Mike Bevens of **Jeffersons**, which organises holidays using private jets. "Private jets are much more frequently used by people for celebrations, such as silver weddings, as they no longer have Concorde for this purpose. And more people are concerned about the delays, inconvenience and hassle of commercial airlines, especially if they are travelling with children and lots of luggage."

Few travellers are using private jets to cross the Atlantic, as it's still eye-wateringly expensive. But groups of friends celebrating anniversaries, or bankers blowing their bonuses, are now copying celebrities such as Tim Henman or David and Victoria Beckham and hiring jets for shorter trips.

Travellers like the speedy check-in, no queueing for luggage, and the limo service at either end. **NetJets Europe**, for example, claims that a journey from central London to St Tropez takes 2hrs 59min door to door, compared with British Airways' service via Heathrow which, allowing time for check-in and luggage collection, takes 6hrs 44min.

Flexibility is another plus, because private jets can fly in to 500 airfields across Europe that are too small for commercial planes. Business travellers can build itineraries such as London-Cologne-Vienna-London in one day that would be nigh-on impossible using scheduled airlines. And security is a big consideration – you know exactly who your fellow passengers are.

Savvy travellers ask about "empty legs" – positioning flights which private jets must make to pick up a client, but on which there are rarely passengers. You may be able to pick up an "empty leg" with a broker such as **London Air Charter Centre** for a considerable discount on the published price.

Contacts

See The Directory, chapter 11, page 420.

Hotels
Choosing a hotel

I love staying in hotels. I love ordering a club sandwich and watching rubbish TV in bed; I love sitting in hotel bars getting the bartender to mix me a martini; I love wiping my make-up off on pristine white towels and knowing I don't have to wash them... hmm, do hotels turn all of us into slobs?!

Certainly, there's something incredibly liberating about the anonymity of a hotel. "We never say 'welcome back' to a regular guest," the general manager of one discreet London hotel told me. "We just say, 'hallo!'" She had learnt the hard way: she said "welcome back" to a guest she recognised, only for his wife to give her a stony look and declare: "We've never been here before." The wife might not have been, but he certainly had – with his mistress.

In more than a decade of travel writing I have stayed in literally hundreds of hotels, and inspected hundreds more. I've found a naked man asleep outside my door at a hotel in Belfast and woken up on two consecutive mornings to gunfire outside my window in Phnom Penh. I'm still cross about forgetting to retrieve the US$50 bill I shoved for safekeeping behind a lobster-shaped lampshade at a fleapit in Ho Chi Minh City when I realised I'd accidentally checked into a brothel. I've had rooms with a gun safe (Bogota), a minstrel's gallery (London), a hammock in the shower (Mexico City) and kitsch 1960s furniture (Kiev); I've stayed in hotels with views of Hong Kong harbour, the Grand Canal in Venice, the Taj Mahal, Machu Picchu...

So I've learnt a thing or two about what makes a good hotel. Unfortunately, what really counts, in my view, is something you cannot tell from a hotel booking website or brochure: service. A hotel with average facilities can be an excellent place to stay if the staff are charming and helpful, and the reverse is true too. Personal recommendations from friends and family can help, and also see reviews on **www.priceline.co.uk** and **www.tripadvisor.co.uk**. The addictive **www.hotelchatter.com** has tales of "hotel heaven", "hotel hell" and the latest gossip about where the stars are staying.

Service aside, there are other ways to assess whether a particular hotel will suit you:

- **Location**: try to find a hotel in the area you'll be spending your evenings, as taxis generally charge more after dark, and there's the safety issue to consider too. The areas near railway stations and ports are often run down and, therefore, dangerous parts of town, so are generally worth avoiding. Ask if the hotel offers any complimentary shuttle services, for example to and from the airport.

- **Aspect**: does your room look out on to a busy road, a car park, a building site, or is it next to the lift? You'll need to call the hotel to discuss these issues as most internet booking sites or travel agencies won't have this much detail.

- **Smoking room**? unless you're a hard-core smoker, just say no. If the hotel splits its rooms into smoking and non-smoking, the smoking rooms can really stink.

- **Creature comforts**: if you want a bath, request this, as many rooms only offer showers. Likewise, if full-length mirrors, tea and coffee and irons/ironing boards are important to you, ask if they are provided.

• **Work or pleasure**? if you're on a business trip, you'll value the desk, internet or wi-fi access, and widescreen plasma TV – but you may not wish to pay for these if you're on a romantic break.

• **Safety**: I dislike being on the ground floor in case of a break-in; equally I dislike being so high up that I could not jump out in case of fire (and so I really dislike hotels with windows that cannot be opened). For more on hotel safety *see* Chapter 9.

• **Price**: before you book through a website it can be worth calling the hotel direct. You may well be offered the "rack rate" – the published price – but the reservations manager will know exactly how full the hotel is and whether it's worth offering a better rate. Don't be afraid to haggle. Always ask: is that your best price? Can I upgrade to a better room in that price range? Do you have any special offers? Does that price include breakfast and tax? Do you have a club floor – a section of the hotel that only preferred guests can access, usually serving free drinks and snacks? (Ritz-Carlton and Pan Pacific are among hotel groups that offer these.) Read the travel press to find out about new hotels – they may offer low introductory rates in their first few months of operation (known as a hotel's "soft opening") before ratcheting prices up.

• **In an emergency**: if you're stuck somewhere and need a hotel in a hurry, phone the hotel, even if you're just around the corner, as it's easier to negotiate the price than if you simply walk in.

Online hotel guides

For more information some useful online hotel guides include:

Alastair Sawday's Special Places to Stay (www.alastairsawday.co.uk)

I-escape (www.i-escape.com)

Michelin (www.michelin.com)

Hip Hotels (www.hiphotels.com)

Mr and Mrs Smith (www.mrandmrssmith.com)

Travel Intelligence (www.travelintelligence.net)

For hotel booking sites, *see* the Directory, page 377.

Booking a hotel online
The pitfalls

In October 2005, there was unwelcome news for holidaymakers who had booked hotel rooms on the website TravelExtras.com – the company had gone bust. Some of its customers had come across TravelExtras when buying flights on budget airlines such as bmibaby and Flybe, on whose websites TravelExtras advertised. But if they thought they would get any help from either bmibaby, Flybe or TravelExtras, they were disappointed. A statement on the bmibaby and Flybe websites informed travellers:

"TravelExtras are advising all customers with unfulfilled reservations to contact their credit/debit card issuers for refunds and/or the hotel, car parking provider, or insurance company directly to make alternative arrangements to pay for the service."

A polite way of saying go away, in other words. The reason TravelExtras was not obliged to help its customers was because it did not hold a financial bond that protected the bookings. There's nothing illegal about this – but if an unbonded company goes bust, the only chance customers have of getting their money back is if they paid with a credit card (as most would), and the bill came to more than £100. The airlines were not obliged to help as they were not part of the same company as TravelExtras.

Booking accommodation over the internet can be risky. Earlier in this chapter we saw how you can be protected when buying flights if the seller holds an Atol. Companies selling elements of a trip such as hotel rooms, but not selling you a flight, may hold a bond from an organisation such as the **Association of British Travel Agents (www.abta.com)**, or the **Association of Independent Tour Operators (www.aito.co.uk)**. While many of the online hotel booking sites do hold financial bonds – such as Octopus Travel or Hotel Connect, which are both Abta-bonded – others do not. Even some sites set up by the big package holiday companies are not bonded: Hotelopia, for example, owned by First Choice, is not bonded, although its parent company is.

Does bonding matter? Any of TravelExtras' customers that were affected by the company's demise will tell you it does. Had the company held a bond, it would have been obliged to sort out alternative accommodation for customers in resort, or offer full refunds to customers yet to travel.

The situation gets even more complicated when you try to buy two or more elements of a holiday yourself over the internet. You may remember the airline Buzz, a subsidiary of Dutch carrier KLM, which was bought by Ryanair in 2003. Ryanair then cancelled some of Buzz's services, and quite properly refunded Buzz customers for these losses.

However, many of Buzz's customers had also made other arrangements, such as booking hotels and car hire, and they came up against real problems because, even though they had in many cases done this through websites linked to Buzz's, they had not technically bought a package, so they had no financial protection when one element (in this case, the flight) went wrong. They were faced with cancelling the other arrangements and paying any cancellation charges due, or rebooking flights with another airline, which probably involved a further overland journey as Ryanair had simply scrapped many Buzz routes.

This episode illustrates another confusing thing about booking separate components of a trip through what seems to be the same website. For example, if you book your flight on **www.ryanair.com**, and then click the panel on the right which offers accommodation, you'll find yourself on **www.ryanairhotels.com**. You could be forgiven for thinking that you were buying flights and hotel from the same company (Ryanair) and therefore you are financially protected because you are buying a package.

Wrong! At the top of the ryanairhotels web page it explains (in fairly small print) that this hotel booking site is provided by **www.needahotel.com**, a Dublin-based booking company that is entirely separate from Ryanair.

There is nothing illegal about this. On the contrary, it is a good example of online companies getting together to market their services, and Needahotel is a thriving, successful company. Indeed, Needahotel effectively has its own bond, as its bank happens to hold a fund of money which would be used if the company collapsed. However, this is not the same as having your entire holiday protected. In the scenario I've outlined here, if Ryanair collapsed, the fact that you had booked the hotel part of your trip through the **ryanairhotels.com** website would not help you one iota in getting any money back for the flight. You had not bought a package, so if you did not turn up to use the hotel, the hotel website would have no reason to refund you.

The same situation applies with easyJet, for example. Click on the hotels tab on **www.easyjet.com** and you find yourself on **www.easyjethotels.co.uk**. But this content is provided by Hotelopia, an unbonded part of First Choice. If you book a flight and a hotel from these two websites, neither is protected.

There is some good news for those of us who like to put our own holidays together on the internet. If you buy all the bits of your holiday through a sole agent that is bonded, such as Expedia or Lastminute, your trip will be financially protected even though you have not bought an off-the-shelf package but have picked the different elements of the trip (flight, hotel, etc) from the stock they offer. I go into more detail about creating your own package holidays online in chapter 4 (see page 134).

However, a lack of financial protection isn't the only potential pitfall when booking hotels online. The internet is completely unregulated, so anyone with a laptop can set themselves up as an accommodation booking site. How can you trust what you are being told?

If it's a hotel you're after, it's fairly easy to find more information about it. It will probably have its own website, it may be reviewed in guidebooks, and for warts-and-all reviews of thousands of hotels worldwide, try websites such as **www.tripadvisor.co.uk** or **www.priceline.co.uk**.

But if you want to rent a holiday villa or apartment, especially if you are dealing with one of the numerous small websites that offer holiday properties around the Med or in the USA, it's worth making further checks as you won't be able to look up these properties in guidebooks.

Hotel booking sites

As with buying a flight, research is the key to finding the best accommodation deals. Search on a selection of sites – I've listed some of the most impressive in the Directory, see page 377, but there are dozens more out there – and also visit the hotel's website, or email/phone the hotel to ask for their best rate. Establishing a personal contact this way also makes it easier to request a quiet room, an upgrade, late check-out or other extras. For a list of hotel chains and designer hotels, see the Directory, page 377.

Holiday hotels, villas and apartments

Over the past five years, the big tour operators, such as Thomson, First Choice and Cosmos, have woken up to fact that many of us now like to put our own holidays together, buying hotel, flight and car hire separately without being tied in to a tour operator's package. So they have all hopped on the accommodation-only bandwagon and started selling hotel rooms and villas without forcing us to buy their flights or other services too.

There are several pluses to booking accommodation through a big tour operator. Their buying power in the key summer sun resorts is huge, so you are likely to get good prices, and you will be able to access hotels that other online retailers cannot offer, because the big operators buy up all the rooms in some of the best summer sun hotels for an entire season. These are some of the major operators:

Cosmos, www.somewhere2stay.com

First Choice, www.hotelopia.co.uk

MyTravel, www.mytravel.com

Thomas Cook, www.thomascook.com

Thomson, www.thomsonhotelsandapartments.co.uk

* For more suggestions, see the Directory (page 377), and for more information about choosing and booking a villa, see chapter 4, page 147.

Hotel price comparison websites

Earlier in this chapter we came across price comparison websites (PCWs) that offer a wide selection of air fares, by searching through the websites of a variety of airlines, tour operators and travel agents. The same technology is now coming on stream for hotels. These sites compile hotel prices from a range of websites and hotel chains:

www.cheapaccommodation.com

www.hotelscomparison.com

www.kelkoo.co.uk

www.nextag.com

www.traveljungle.co.uk

www.tripadvisor.com

Can't pay, won't pay?

Enterprising travellers have started websites that hook you up with others who are prepared to offer a room, bed or sofa for free: it's just an organised way of kipping at a mate's. Needless to say, single women travellers should proceed with caution and only stay if they feel comfortable with their host.

Couchsurfing (www.couchsurfing.com),

Global Freeloaders (www.globalfreeloaders.com)

Sleeping in Airports (www.sleepinginairports.net)

CHAPTER FOUR
The package holiday

Introduction

Package holidays have acquired a bit of an image problem. Now that we are all travel agents, able to bore our friends at dinner parties with the fantastic bargains we found on the internet, it sounds rather last-century to admit you popped along to a travel agent and bought a package holiday. These days, package holidays seem to be described in terms of school-leavers getting drunk in Rhodes or Zakynthos, hen parties who want a last fling before settling down or resort reps behaving badly. Or – whisper it quietly – they're holidays for people who cannot use a computer.

But the package holiday is far from dead. In 1995, we bought 15.2 million overseas package holidays, according to the Association of British Travel Agents (Abta). By 2004, this figure had risen to 19.5 million.

These statistics support the argument by holiday companies that the growth of the "DIY" holiday, which we explored in chapter 3 (in which travellers put together their own trips by buying separate elements, often over the internet), has not had the negative impact on sales of package holidays that you might expect.

"Everyone is always quick to say that the package is coming undone," said Manny Fontenla-Novoa, chief executive of Thomas Cook UK and Ireland, "but that simply is not true. Our data shows that, far from dying a death, the package holiday is experiencing something of a renaissance. With all the recent natural disasters and also the international terrorism threat, people are really appreciating the key benefits of booking a package with a bonded travel company – namely, the reassurance that if anything goes wrong, the company will endeavour to get them home as quickly as possible."

Rather than shying away from package holidays, it seems we are simply taking more holidays by adding our own independent trips. "We're finding that low-cost carriers are not taking away from the package holiday but that people are travelling more," said Emma Waddell of First Choice.

The modern package holiday

Tour operators are bound to want to talk up the market, but they have a point. In 1995, a total of 27.8 million overseas holidays (both packages and independent trips) were taken by UK citizens, according to Abta; by 2000 this had risen to 36.7 million and by 2004 it had reached 42 million. Many of us are now squeezing in extra short breaks, often using budget airlines, pretty much on impulse in response to crazy ticket prices.

So what are all these package holidays that we're taking each year? The term "package" may sound a little dowdy, but it describes everything from the £199 beer-swilling fortnight on the Costa Ghastly to a £10,000 luxury Caribbean holiday with business-class flights, film-star villa with frangipani petals down the loo, and hot and cold running flunkies catering to your every whim.

A massive 85 per cent of all overseas package holidays in the UK are sold by the "big four" tour operators – Thomson, MyTravel, Thomas Cook and First Choice – and their subsidiaries, but that's not to say that a package holiday means two weeks on the beach in Spain. These days you can encounter polar bears in Canada, hike up Mount Kilimanjaro or explore the Roman ruins of Libya on a package holiday.

For "package" is a literal description: a package holiday is defined as any type of holiday, no matter how cheap or expensive, in which two or more elements of the holiday – for example, flight, hotel and resort transfer; or flight, hotel, car hire, services of a rep and travel insurance – have been packaged together by a holiday company. By buying a trip in this way, rather than putting it together yourself by buying separate elements from different companies, you are protected under the 1992 European Union Package Travel Regulations.

"When people belittle the package holiday, they are belittling the immense consumer protection they have," said Alan Saggerson, a barrister specialising in travel and tourism law. "By and large if you get into a scrape, tour operators will go the extra mile to help you."

The Package Travel Regulations force holiday companies to fix any problems that occur with your package holiday, whether or not they are their fault. And if they don't sort things out properly you can take them to court in this country, which is much easier than dealing with a Greek ferry company or a Spanish hotelier.

Your rights when buying a package holiday

Holidays involving flights have, since 1973, been protected by the **Air Travel Organisers' License** (Atol) scheme; an Atol is issued to the tour operator or travel agent by the Civil Aviation Authority (CAA). But although most package holidays from the UK involve a flight, Atol protection does not extend to package holidays that do not involve a flight but use another form of transport, such as rail, ferry or bus travel. So in 1992, European Union legislation was introduced to ensure that *all* package holidays were protected. The **EU Package Travel Directive** was adopted into UK law, and is rather grippingly known as the Package Travel, Package Holidays and Package Tours Regulations 1992. It's overseen by the Department for Trade and Industry, and local trading standards officers deal with complaints from the public.

Basically, the regulations say that all organisers of package holidays must protect their customers' money. This is done through the Atol scheme for holidays that involve a flight, while for holidays that don't involve a flight, the organiser could be a member of an organisation such as the Association of British Travel Agents, the Association of Independent Tour Operators, or hold a trust account or insurance to protect your money. The organiser is responsible for the smooth working of everything you have booked, whether that's the transport, hotel, car hire or other elements of the package.

If the company that has organised your travel goes out of business, you should get your money back or, if you are in a resort, be able to continue your holiday and return as normal, or be refunded for the costs you incur while completing your holiday and returning home. And if one element of the package goes wrong – for example, the airline or car hire firm goes bust, or a hurricane destroys the hotel – your tour operator is obliged to sort things out, by organising a suitable replacement holiday or by bringing you home early if necessary.

Package holidays that involve a flight

Look for the Atol logo on the website or literature of the tour operator when you book a package that involves a flight, and ensure you get a holiday confirmation or receipt with the Atol holder's details and Atol number printed on it. If you want to find out whether a company's Atol is still current, check with the **Civil Aviation Authority** (020 7453 6430, **www.caa.co.uk/atol**).

Many travel agents hold an Atol, too, because as well as selling the package holidays of tour operators, they may put together their own packages to sell to you, and to protect these they must hold an Atol. However, your package is still protected if you book a holiday with a travel agent that does not hold an Atol, as long as the agent books the trip for you with a tour operator that does hold an Atol, tells you who the Atol holder is, and gives you an Atol receipt on behalf of that company.

Package holidays that do not involve a flight

The Association of British Travel Agents (020 7307 1907, **www.abta.com**) is the best known association that offers financial protection for package holidays that don't include a flight, but there are others that do so too, listed below.

Abta has traditionally insisted that its members, which are both travel agents and tour operators, provide financial protection against insolvency. Members offering package holidays involving flights must hold an Atol, and members offering package holidays that do not include a flight must hold another form of financial protection such as a bond with Abta.

However in 2006, Abta loosened this protection. Now, if an Abta travel agent sells you a single item that's not a flight – for example, hotel accommodation – and that agent goes bust, you will not get your money back. This applies largely to the online accommodation-only suppliers. Abta argues that because it is not a legal requirement for providers of a single item (rather than a package) to be financially protected, it will no longer force its members to offer protection for these sales. However, the agent must make the lack of protection clear to you, and may offer you the option of buying insurance against the failure of a non-bonded company.

Abta also argues that the public is now so confident in booking accommodation in this way, and does it so often, that this change will barely cause a murmur of protest. "If it was something we felt customers really cared about, we would probably not have made this change," said Abta spokesman Keith Betton. However this move will contribute to a further fall in the number of holidays that are financially protected.

Abta has also recently introduced another rule change. If you book with an Abta travel agent that goes out of business before it has made firm bookings with the supplier of your holiday (such as a tour operator), you will not be protected. The change has been brought in to protect Abta from the activities of a few fraudulent agents who take customers' cash but do not then buy the holidays from the suppliers, and Abta's Keith Betton tells me it will only affect a handful of customers, as the vast majority of agents are bona fide.

Bruce Treloar, the trading standards lead officer for the holiday and travel industry, said this move puts a far greater onus on the customer to get the right paperwork. "If you book a package holiday from a travel agent, make sure you have the documents in your hand, or a letter on headed paper saying that they will be issued nearer the departure date," he said. "Consumers must be much more canny about picking up their documentation." In summer 2006, Abta produced new leaflets explaining these changes (available from 020 7637 2444, **www.abta.com**).

Abta also offers an arbitration scheme for holidaymakers who booked with an Abta member and whose trips went wrong – see chapter 9.

Aito, the Association of Independent Tour Operators (020 8744 9280, **www.aito.co.uk**), insists that its members hold Atols to protect holidays involving flights, and it provides its own bonding system, the Aito Trust, to protect non-air holidays.

Financial protection for non-air holidays may also be organised through the **Passenger Shipping Association** (020 7436 2449, **www.the-psa.co.uk**), which represents cruise lines and ferries, **Bonded Coach Holidays** (020 7240 3131, **www.bondedcoachholidays.co.uk**), the **Travel Trust Association** (0870 889 0577, **www.traveltrust.co.uk**), the **Association of Bonded Travel Organisers Trust (www.abtot.com)** or the **Federation of Tour Operators (www.fto.co.uk)**.

If the travel company you're dealing with doesn't have a bond with any of these organisations, ask if it has insurance or another means of financially protecting your trip.

The future of financial protection

The current system is extremely confusing. Under the Package Travel Regulations there are two parallel systems – the Atol scheme for packages involving flights, and other forms of protection such as the Abta bond for holidays that don't involve flights – but increasingly, many holidays are not protected at all, as we found in chapter 3. And the Air Travel Trust Fund, an independent fund that provides additional money to the CAA if bonds are insufficient to meet all the costs of protection, is currently £10 million in the red and needs topping up.

In preparation for the Civil Aviation Bill that came before Parliament in autumn 2005, the CAA presented a report to the government recommending a £1 levy on every ticket sold on every flight out of the UK, to replace the Atol scheme. This would have protected every passenger, whether or not they were travelling as part of a package, and the plan was supported by Abta. However, under pressure from the airlines, the government rejected the £1 levy proposal.

In summer 2006, as this book went to press, there was continuing uncertainty about how consumer protection would work in future, given that increasing numbers of people are now travelling outside the protection of the Package Travel Regulations and the Atol scheme. It is likely that the CAA will soon be proposing new ways of reforming the system.

Tips for protecting your money

- Look for the Atol, Abta, Aito or other relevant symbol on websites and literature to see if the company holds a bond.

- If you cannot tell if a company has financial protection, ask.

- If a company does not hold a bond, it's not doing anything wrong, but it may mean your holiday is not protected.

- Book with a credit card for any purchases over £100.

- Make sure your receipt shows the name of the company providing the holiday, and it is the same as the name of the company you are paying. Keep all paperwork.

- A few insurers will cover you for the failure of a scheduled airline, but this is not included in most travel insurance policies so you must request it.

For what to do if things go wrong on holiday: see chapter 9.

Your responsibilities

I'm sorry to come over all Tony Blair-ish, but holidaymakers have responsibilities as well as rights! When you buy a package holiday you enter into a contract with the travel company, and that means you have certain obligations. Mostly they are the obvious things such as paying the bill on time, but you're also obliged to tell the company as soon as possible if you need to make any changes to the trip – cancel it, or change the name of a party member, for example.

You are also obliged to bring any problems during your holiday to the attention of the company – typically via the rep – as soon as they arise, so the company has a chance to fix things on the spot. If you don't do this, but complain later, you may find your complaint is rejected.

The package holiday grows up

Ten years ago, buying a package holiday was pretty much like choosing a brand of teabags or shampoo. Yes, there were different brand names on the high street – Thomson, Airtours, First Choice – but the holidays were mostly variations on a set theme. Seven or 14 days, half board or full board, use the tour operator's airline, depart at 5am but pay a supplement because it's a regional airport – hey, that's how the industry works, and there's no alternative.

The boot is on the other foot now. Tour operators have realised that to compete with the growing number of online travel agents, and harness our new-found enthusiasm for booking our own trips, they have to become more flexible and offer us much more of what we want. James Watts, a spokesman for tour operator Thomson, said: "We have had to acknowledge that people want to be able to fly at a time that suits them and have reacted to it, for example by offering a huge increase in regional departures, and launching our own low-cost airline, Thomsonfly. Now the passenger holds all the cards, whereas in the 1970s and 1980s it was a case of, 'you travel when we tell you to.'"

So tour operators are now offering holidays for three, 10 or however many days you want, with flights at more convenient times and from a wider range of airports across the UK, such as Doncaster, Southampton and Liverpool. They are trying to offer more daytime, rather than the less popular night-time, flights, and are sharpening up their act regarding hotels, too, by reducing the number of holidays offered to unnamed accommodation, which are usually cheap, last-minute deals and tend to generate more complaints than holidays where the customer chooses the hotel.

Who owns what

The four giants of the UK package holiday market – Thomson, MyTravel, Thomas Cook and First Choice – all own a mixture of tour operators, travel agencies and even cruise lines. Here's a guide to their best-known brands.

> • **TUI** – this German company owns Thomson Holidays, the biggest tour operator in the UK, as well as familiar names including Austravel, Crystal, Jetsave, Simply Travel, Skytours, Headwater and Tropical

Places. Its airline is Thomsonfly, its cruise division is Thomson Cruises and its main travel agency chain is Thomson Shops. Details: **www. thomson.co.uk**.

• **MyTravel**'s best-known tour operating division is Airtours Holidays. It also owns Bridge Travel, Cresta Holidays, Tradewinds, Panorama Holidays and Manos Holidays, and its main travel agency chain is called Going Places. It also sells packages online through Direct Holidays (**www.directholidays.co.uk**). Its airline is MyTravel Airways. It used to run Sun Cruises but no longer has a cruise division. Details: **www.mytravel.com**.

• **First Choice** owns the tour operator First Choice Holidays, the travel agencies First Choice Travel Shops and First Choice Holiday Hypermarkets, and many specialist operators including Unijet, 2wentys, Sovereign, Hayes & Jarvis, Meon Villas, Longshot Golf, Citalia, Sunsail, Crown Blue Line, Exodus, Peregrine, The Adventure Company, Waymark, Trips Worldwide, Magic of the Orient, Imaginative Traveller, Flexiski and Trek America. Its airline is First Choice Airways and it runs Island Cruises with Royal Caribbean. Details: **www.firstchoice.co.uk**.

• **Thomas Cook**, also German-owned, owns the eponymous travel agency chain, airline and tour operation. Its other operators include JMC, Neilson, Club 18–30, Sunset and Thomas Cook Signature. Details: **www.thomascook.com**.

• The **Federation of Tour Operators** groups together the big four plus another eight of the major package holiday companies in the UK. Follow this link to find a list of members, with direct links to their own websites: **www.fto.co.uk/resources/fto-members/**.

See the Directory (chapter 11) for listings of hundreds of tour operators, from the package giants to the small specialists.

What's included in your package?

Transport

There is such a wide choice of **flight and ferry departures** for most popular holiday destinations that you should be able to find travel times that suit you. Opting for an early or late departure at an antisocial hour may reduce the cost of the holiday, but you may have to pay for a hotel near the airport or ferry terminal the night before you depart. You may also be charged a **flight supplement** for flying from certain airports, particularly those in the north of England and Scotland. Operators say this is to cover the fuel costs as it is farther to fly to the Mediterranean from there. Typically these supplements might be £50 per person.

It is possible that the flight or ferry times will change between the date you book and the date of your holiday. If this happens, you may be entitled to compensation. If it is a "**significant change**", you should be offered the option of accepting the change and receiving compensation, switching to another holiday from the same company, or cancelling the trip and receiving a refund of everything you've paid, plus compensation in some cases.

So what is a "significant change"? Typically this means if a flight time moves by more than 12 hours, or your departure or arrival airport changes, or you are offered a lower grade of accommodation than the one you have booked. For example, First Choice Holidays sets out what it considers to be significant changes pretty clearly (although it takes a bit of hunting to find this on its website):

"Major Change includes (but is not limited to) the following:

- A change to your UK departure airport
- A significant change of resort
- A change of accommodation to one with an officially lower rating
- A change of more than 12 hours to your scheduled time of departure or return
- A change from a day to a night flight involving a difference of more than 4 hours in your departure time
- A significant increase in the price of your holiday

Any change in the airline or the type of aircraft from that stated on the website or on your ticket does not count as a Major Change."

You should be offered compensation if there is a major change to your trip, whether you cancel or go ahead with the new arrangements. However, this is not terribly generous. Typically you'll get nothing at all if you were notified more than 56 days before departure, rising on a sliding scale to £40 per person if you were notified within two weeks of departure. Which is a bit unfair, given that if you cancelled the trip within two weeks of departure, you'd probably forfeit most of the cost.

And holiday companies often try to wriggle out of coughing up anything if they can cite "force majeure". Basically this get-out clause covers pretty much everything they can think of – war, insurrection, riots, terrorism, hurricanes, airport closures, plagues of locusts, England losing at home, you name it.

Extra flight charges

You and I may think it's obvious that when we go on holiday together as a family or group of friends, we will want to sit together on the plane. Sadly, the big tour operators take a different view. In the late 1990s they realised that this was a potential income stream and, for many of the mainstream package holidays on sale, you will now find many operators charge an extra fee to guarantee that you will sit together on a charter flight. Thomson and First Choice Holidays, for example, both charge £10 per adult and £5 per child for you to sit together on a short-haul flight, and £17/£7 on a long-haul trip. MyTravel charges £12 short haul, and £24 long haul, while Thomas Cook charges adults £20 return on a short-haul flight and £30 on long-haul flights, and children £10 on any flight, to guarantee seats together.

I've always thought these charges are scandalous. Of course a family will expect to sit together if they are going on holiday together. These charges are not usually levied if your package holiday involves a scheduled airline, and generally the scheduled airlines organise their seating pretty effectively so families are together, so I don't see why tour operators using charter airlines should charge for this "service".

Most smaller holiday companies do not levy these charges. Sunvil, for example, which has a big programme to the Mediterranean, especially Cyprus and Greece, does not charge extra for things like sitting together, fuel surcharges or meals on planes. Sunvil MD Noel Josephides said: "We think it's unethical. Everything is included in our prices."

The scalping doesn't end there. With the big tour operators, you are also likely to be charged £10 per return trip for a hot meal and as much as £60 each for seats with extra legroom.

Surcharges are also unwelcome news. Sometimes a holiday company slaps on a surcharge, in other words puts up the price of the holiday, after you have booked it. Usually this is because the cost of fuel has risen, which forces up the price of the flight. If the cost of the holiday rises by up to 2 per cent, the tour operator must absorb the increase, but if it rises above this the tour operator may charge you an extra fee to cover it. If the surcharge adds more than 10 per cent to the cost of your trip, you are usually given the option of cancelling and receiving a full refund. Recently there has been a tendency on the part of tour operators not to penalise customers who have already bought a holiday, but to charge new customers higher prices.

Transfers

The "transfer" refers to your transport from the airport to the hotel on arrival, and back to the airport on the day you depart. Traditionally, transfers would be included in a package holiday, but now many operators separate the charge of the airport transfer – typically around £15 per person – so it's easy to opt out of it, for example if you know the destination well or will be met by a friend.

Transfers on most mainstream package holidays are made by coach, and invariably the Law of Sod dictates that your hotel is always the last drop-off point on any transfer, and the first collection point on the way back to the airport, giving you the dubious benefit of an hour or more's drive around the resort dropping off or collecting other passengers.

In the past few years several web-based companies such as **www. holidaytaxis.com**, **www.shuttledirect.com** and **www.lowcosttaxis.com** have started to offer pre-bookable transfer services at most popular sun and ski resorts. If you book a transfer this way, check the small print to find out what happens if your flight is delayed (will you be charged waiting time?), and how many people and how much luggage the taxi can carry.

Accommodation

Ten years ago I took a package holiday on the Greek island of Rhodes with holiday company Airtours. The hotel was delightfully situated between the airport and a power station, and we gained useful health benefits from walking up five flights of stairs (the lift was out of order). The staff and fellow guests were so friendly that there was no need to lock the door (the lock was broken) and the cooling sea breeze made the air-conditioning redundant (no, that didn't work either).

Fortunately for the staff, we weren't able to ring down to reception to complain because the phone was out of order, too.

We've all experienced, or know someone who has experienced, a terrible resort hotel. So how do you avoid the real horrors when you book? First, scour the brochure and cross-examine the travel agent on issues like these:

- Some hotels will charge more for a **sea view**. If this is the case it may be worth paying for. In my experience the alternative is usually described as a "garden" view, and it surprises me how often hoteliers seem to keep cars, rubbish bins and delivery vans in their "gardens".

• If you're a keen swimmer ask if the **pool** is big enough to do lengths, or if there's a roped-off area, set times when it is child-free, or even a separate pool for adults.

• Is the **disco** pounding out all night?

• Is there a choice of **restaurants** in the hotel?

• Are you in a resort or in the **middle of nowhere**? If the hotel is miles out of town you may have to take a cab if you want to eat out. For example, most of the expensive resorts on the east coast of Mauritius are miles from any other hotel or restaurant, meaning a pricey cab ride if you want to eat elsewhere.

• If you're booking a **ski resort**, you will want to know how far it is to the slopes.

If you feel you're not getting the full story from the brochure or travel agent, ask to consult the *OAG Gazetteer*, which is the travel agents' "Bible" that they keep hidden behind their desks. It runs to half a dozen printed volumes, like a phone directory (although new editions are online), and gives warts-and-all descriptions of hotels and apartments across the major resorts worldwide. Its descriptions are down-to-earth. Of hotels in the resort of Alcudia, Majorca, it says: "The majority were built in the 1960s and 1970s and belong to the blockhouse school of architecture." It also carries comments from holidaymakers, who don't pull their punches: "Faliraki was quite simply the seediest, dirtiest, most expensive, violent and most uncomfortable resort that I have visited," writes one unimpressed visitor. You can see an edited version of the Gazetteer online at **www.virgin.net/travel/resortfinder**.

Room occupancy

When it comes to working out the package price, many holiday companies complicate matters further by putting stringent conditions on how many people must share a hotel room to qualify for the per-person price in the brochure – and if you're travelling with children, things can get even more complicated.

Hotel rooms and apartments are priced by tour operators at a level that assumes a certain number of people will be sharing them. Clearly, the more people that share the room, the more the price per person can be reduced, while still making a profit for the holiday company. So some deals that seem particularly tempting – often in ski resorts – may be cheap because, for example, four people are expected to share a one-bedroom apartment. Two of you will have to sleep on a sofa bed in the living area. For some travellers, keen to be out on the beach or ski slopes all day, that doesn't much matter. For anyone who values space, peace and calm on holiday, it's about as appealing as living through an episode of *The Young Ones*.

If two people book the apartment instead of four, you will have to pay an under-occupancy supplement which can dramatically increase the price of the trip. So ask your holiday company how many people are supposed to share the room to get the price advertised.

Paying for the children

Babies up to the age of two are generally charged either nothing, or a token sum for the holiday (perhaps 10 per cent) – though they will not be given a seat on the plane, or a baggage allowance; you will have to keep them on your lap. For more information on buying childrens' seats on a flight, see chapter 3 (*see* page 79). The definition of "child" depends on which holiday company you are dealing with, but the cut-off point at which they start paying adult fares is generally between ages 12 and 16. Children will normally qualify for the child price in a holiday brochure if they travel with two adults, and share their room. The reduced price for children reflects the fact that essentially you are paying for only their flight, as they are sharing your hotel room.

"Free" or "reduced-price" child places are among the gimmicks the big tour operators use to encourage us to book our holidays early. Certainly there can be savings if you are prepared to commit to your holiday when the deals are available – typically, up to and over the busy New Year booking period when we're thinking about the following summer's holidays. But, as with child prices, the "free" or "reduced-price" child holidays only apply to children sharing their parents' room – and there must be two full-fare-paying adults in the room already for this deal to apply.

Usually, children do not count towards the occupancy level of a room (though how anyone would get through a week without noticing they're there is one of the great travel industry mysteries). So if your family consists of two adults and two children and you wish to share an apartment designed for four adults, you will still be expected to pay an under-occupancy supplement, because there are not four adults sharing.

Even if you do qualify for a "free" child place, you will still face some charges – for example the meal on the plane if your child wants one, airport taxes and charges, and travel insurance.

Hotel jargon – what does it mean?

- **Room only**: the price you pay includes only the cost of the room; no meals are provided.

- **B&B**: your room plus breakfast.

- **Half board**: room plus breakfast and dinner.

- **Full board**: all meals are provided at the hotel, but not alcoholic drinks.

- **All-inclusive**: these hotels provide all meals, plus alcohol (usually local brands rather than more expensive international ones), and often ice creams and soft drinks too. Guests usually have to wear a wristband to prove they are entitled to this.

- **Accommodation on arrival**: on reaching the resort you are taken to whichever hotel in the tour operator's programme has a room available. It's a lottery – you may get a great deal, or nothing special – and I don't advise families to buy these deals as you may end up in a hotel that's unsuitable for children.

- **Under-occupancy supplement**: if the apartment or hotel room sleeps four adults and there are only two or three adults sharing it, you must each pay this daily per-person charge, which can add substantially to the cost of a package; children do not count when working out the occupancy level.

Services of a rep

A good rep can really make a difference to your holiday. I once went to Crete for a week's flop on the beach, booking with Simply Travel, an upmarket holiday company. My rep, Alison, was really knowledgeable about the places to see, spoke Greek, pointed me to the best bars and restaurants and invited me to go out with a group of her friends one evening. Her knowledge and enthusiasm greatly added to my enjoyment of the week.

But the role of the resort rep is changing. Previously you could expect a rep to dance attendance on you throughout your package holiday, escorting you from the airport to your hotel, holding a welcome meeting on the first morning to tell you about the resort (and to sell excursions, on which they make commission), and popping in to the hotel most days to hand out help and advice.

Now some operators are cutting their services back. Lee Ormesher, operations director at package giant Thomson, said: "Many resorts, particularly in Spain, are well known by our customers. People are confident travelling there and lots of guests have visited these resorts numerous times. For many people, it's simply not necessary to have the rep visiting the hotel on a daily basis."

Hence in summer 2005 Thomson dramatically reduced the rep service in some of its most popular Mediterranean resorts, particularly in Spain. Customers were instead given the phone number of a roving "super-rep" and a promise that they were on call 24 hours a day. In summer 2006, it introduced Thomson Travel Buddy, a free service for its customers offering information by text. However in less familiar destinations such as Egypt or Mexico the full rep service remains.

By contrast, First Choice tells me it's stepping up its rep service, putting all its reps who are on seasonal contracts on to year-round ones and encouraging staff to stay put and really build up their local knowledge. Steve Barker, operations director at First Choice, said: "We're increasingly trying to take on "career reps", people who know which beach in Ibiza will be empty even in August.

"The fundamental reason to have them is to differentiate ourselves from the people who choose to 'DIY'," he said. "They can help with any sort of problem solving, for example if you have lost a passport or your hire car has not turned up, and that gives the customer more free time."

Independent travellers who want the reassurance of a rep can now book one online. **Destination Care (www.destinationcare.com)** launched a pre-bookable rep service in popular destinations such as Majorca and Tenerife in early 2006, costing £10 per group per holiday. "This is an in-resort rep service for clients who feel they are exposed when away, or who want to get the best out of their holiday," said Paul Stanyer, the MD of Destination Care. "We're putting reps back in as tour operators take them out."

Insurance and advice

The tour operator or travel agent you are booking your holiday with should make sure you hold **travel insurance** – though there is no obligation to buy the insurance that they sell. For more information on buying travel insurance, see chapter 6. The holiday company should also ensure you are told if you need a **visa** and that you are given appropriate information about **safety** issues, such as the Foreign & Commonwealth Office's travel advice for that country, and **health** requirements. For more on these subjects, see chapters 9 and 10. And if you're planning to **hire a car** as part of your holiday, see chapter 8 for details of what to watch out for.

Should you book early or late?

Holiday companies love it when we book early – they keep our money for longer. But over the past decade we have started to book closer and closer to the departure date, and the big holiday companies are partly to blame. In the past they have greedily contracted too many hotels in some resorts, been unable to sell the holidays, and so flooded the market with cheap deals just weeks before the main summer holidays.

We've learned to look for these late deals and are increasingly reluctant to book months in advance. But while you will still find last-minute deals even for high summer, they may no longer be bargains. Tour operators have learnt their lesson and generally match supply and demand more accurately these days. The online agency Lastminute.com might get you away at short notice, but there's no guarantee it will be cheap – its customers spend an average of £650 per booking.

And there are lots of trips that you should book early. If you have school-age children and want a particular hotel, it's wise to book early. Child discounts are often only available to early bookers. Specialist, upmarket companies offering trips such as cultural tours or safaris are often booked up a year or so in advance. The best villas usually go early, especially in peak season in honeypot areas such as the Côte d'Azur.

But if you don't much mind where you go for early summer sun, and don't have school-age children, May and June can be the best months for a late bargain as tour operators desperately try to shift the last of their stock. And seat-only bargains on charter flights can often be found at the last minute (which is the opposite of the budget airlines, whose cheapest seats are usually found the further ahead you book).

Single travellers

More people than ever are single, yet many holiday companies seem stuck in a time-warp, as reluctant to accept your single status as a clucky mother. They seem to assume we always travel in pairs, joined at the hip.

It ain't so. Plus, many people who have a partner sometimes want to travel on their own, perhaps to indulge a particular enthusiasm that their partner doesn't share, such as skiing or scuba-diving. A Mintel survey for singles specialist **Just You** found that more than 4 million Britons took a holiday by themselves in 2004, and a third of them were in a relationship. But what do single travellers find? Often they face paying a single supplement – *and* have the indignity of being offered a "room" that's the pokiest broom cupboard by the lift shaft.

A single supplement is like the under-occupancy supplement we came across when travelling with children (above). Hoteliers usually price rooms on the basis that two adults will share them, so if only one person has the room they are expected to pay this supplement. The hoteliers claim that they lose out if there's only one person in the room as they spend less in the bar and restaurant than two people do. However, unless the hotel is full that argument doesn't stand up – having one person to stay is going to be more profitable than having an empty room. So I think it's more to do with greed, laziness and an unwillingness to adapt to a changing market.

There are a few tricks to try if you want to avoid single supplements. Travel off-peak, when hoteliers are more hungry for your business. Some tour operators give you the option of sharing a room with a fellow single traveller. Adventurous holidays may see you camping, or sleeping on the deck of a yacht, which can get around the problem. Smaller properties, such as B&Bs and hostels, are far better at catering for single travellers than big, impersonal hotels (and you're likely to meet pleasant travelling companions in them, too). Hotels in the USA are generally much better at charging per room than per person, which can be good for single travellers.

Most of my experience of travel on my own has been as a backpacker – and for backpackers, travelling solo is often the norm. I've always loved the challenge of finding a bed for the night in a strange town, finding the best café for local food, and making new friends among fellow travellers and picking their brains about the places to see and how to get around. Backpackers' hostels and small hotels are very well geared up for single travellers, offering cheap rooms, or even cheaper beds in dormitories.

Several tour operators have now woken up to the singles market. Their holidays vary from laid-back beach visits to full-on activity programmes, so questions to ask before you book include:

- Is there a single supplement, or are you expected to share a room?
- What is the typical range of ages, and the male/female split?

- Is the holiday very organised, with group activities, or are you left to your own devices?

- Evening mealtimes can be the loneliest for single travellers so find out what the arrangements are then.

I have listed companies that specialise in singles holidays in the Directory (chapter 11); operators that offer escorted cultural tours or activity holidays are usually good for singles, too.

The websites **www.holiday41.co.uk** and **www.singulartravel.co.uk** put you in touch with hundreds of holidays for singles from a wide range of operators.

A new service, launched in 2006, is offered by **www.someone2travelwith. com**, which aims to link like-minded travellers. It stresses it is not a dating agency. A longer established service is **www.companions2travel.co.uk**, aimed at single, divorced or widowed people who want to find travel companions. *Wanderlust* magazine (**www.wanderlust.co.uk**) has a Connections service, both through its magazine and online, putting solo travellers in touch with each other. Also worth trying are **www.travel–companion.net**, **www. travellersconnected.com** and **www.soulescape.com**.

The **Single Travellers Action Group** can supply further information and suggestions. Write to STAG, Church Lane, Sharnbrook, Bedford MK44 1HR or email **vivstag1@aol.com** (annual subscription, £12).

Booking a family holiday

Taking my nine-year-old cousin Rebecca to Disneyland Paris was an eye-opener. Not for her – she took the Big Thunder Mountain rollercoaster, the meetings with Mickey Mouse and the excitement of being away from home in her stride. No, I was the worried one, clutching her hand until her circulation nearly stopped, looking for unexpected dangers and dodgy characters at every turn, and barely letting the poor girl so much as visit the bathroom on her own.

For a non-parent, the sudden responsibility of having to look after another human being for every moment of the day is daunting, and the pressures can really mount when you go on holiday. I've had some lovely breaks with my delightful nieces, Emily and Ruby, but their parents have always been around to do the difficult stuff, while I've just done the fun aunt things. So when putting together advice on family travel I consulted some colleagues at the sharp end. Jane Knight, Jeannette Hyde, Chloë Bryan-Brown and Jill

Crawshaw are regular contributors to the travel pages of *The Times* – Jane's the deputy travel editor – and have children of various ages.

They all said that one of the biggest shocks, when travelling as a family after previously travelling without children, was dealing with changing expectations of their holidays. As a family, they had to travel at a far slower pace, in less flexible fashion, and often to destinations or hotels they would never have chosen before children arrived.

Throwing money at your holiday isn't always the answer. "Just because you've paid a fortune for a trip, it doesn't mean that your kids will like it," said Chloë. "This is especially true of skiing holidays and posh hotels with kids' clubs – your child might hate the snow or refuse to go in to the kids' club and there's not an awful lot you can do about it."

A package holiday is often an easy option for families – the big tour operators compete to offer the most family-friendly deals, including childcare and kids' activities, and I've listed a wide choice of operators in the Directory (chapter 11).

Independent travel and self-catering, whether you are simply flying and flopping at a villa near the beach, or sweeping the children off on an overland adventure, puts the onus much more heavily on the parents to be permanently on duty, without the brief respite of a few hours' childcare that big resort hotels may offer. Of course, for many parents that's the attraction of an independent trip – they don't want to pack the kids off to a club, and have come on holiday intending to do things as a family.

So how you can you plan a family holiday that suits everyone? The first decision to make is whether to book a hotel, or to go self-catering. "We try to go half-board in hotels, as that usually works well economically, and it is nice for us mums not to spend the holiday planning meals and cooking," said Jeannette. "Having said that, you have to be pretty rich to afford two hotel rooms, but otherwise you find yourselves cooped up for two weeks in one room with young kids. This means creeping around the room to get undressed after you have put them to bed at 7-8pm, and you can't have the light on to read. And forget trying to have sex!

"Self-catering provides much more privacy – often the kids have their own room – and you can make lunch the main meal of the day, perhaps eating out, and fill the fridge with lovely local hams, cheeses, salads and breads for evening tea times."

For new mum Jane, a big shock has been the amount of clobber you can end up carrying. "Babies bring with them the prospect of carting around huge volumes of luggage, which is quite a shock when, like me, you've always managed with a wheelie suitcase that can fit as hand luggage," she said.

Some holiday providers are trying to help new parents cut down on what they need to carry.

• **Tots to France** (020 8123 4511, **www.totstofrance.co.uk**) offers a small number of houses to rent in southwest France where you can pre-book items such as nappies of the correct size.

• The **Almyra Hotel** in Cyprus (**www.thanoshotels.com**) has a "Baby-Go-Lightly" programme which provides everything from swim nappies to buggies.

• **Tinytotsaway** (0800 279 4433, **www.tinytotsaway.com**) will deliver all the baby gear you need (nappies, Calpol, baby food, beach gear etc) to your holiday destination in a wide range of countries.

Some of the most common questions parents ask are about how to transport the buggy and the car seat if their holiday involves a flight. "The safest option is to take your own car seat or booster seat with you," said Jeannette. "You can use it for the journey to the airport, then check it in with your luggage – most airlines will not count it towards your luggage allowance. You then collect it off the carousel at the other end.

"If you have a baby under six months, in a car seat with a swing handle, you might want to use it to carry your baby through the airport, but the airline, very annoyingly, usually confiscates it at the gate and you must then wake the baby up and put them on your lap."

If you are hiring a car you'll be particularly glad of your own child seat as, even if you have pre-booked one, it's not unknown for car rental firms to run out, especially at the height of the season, or to offer you one that's the wrong size. Older children may like their car booster seat so they can see out of the window, which can help prevent them getting car sickness.

Pushchairs are carried in the hold of the plane but they do not count towards the weight of your checked luggage.

Buggies and car seats aside, Chloë, with two children, has learned to travel light. "In my experience children are much happier playing eye spy or counting red cars than playing with expensive travel toys. As long as you have something like colouring books for the plane you should be OK. But always take your own formula and medicine for babies, as you can't always get the stuff abroad that your child is used to."

Once children reach school age, holiday prices shoot up, as you are obliged to travel during school holidays, when tour operators hike their rates. You can, with the head teacher's permission, take your child out of school for a maximum of 10 school days per academic year, but if you travel without the head's permission, or keep your child away from school for longer than 10 days, you can be prosecuted. Head teachers are increasingly reluctant to grant this permission, meaning parents need to be prepared for peak-season prices (see tips box, opposite, on how to keep costs down).

With older children, setting a few boundaries is the way to make sure everyone enjoys the holidays, said Jill. "Have a daily pocket money budget for each child, or your money will go out like the tide on ice creams and Cokes." If you're in a hotel, beware of an open account and room service, which they think is absolutely fantastic and "free" (some parents even insist that the hotel empties the minibar in their room to avoid this temptation!).

"Don't overdose on museums and galleries," added Jill. "Before you go, get every member of the family to pick one thing they want to do, then stick to it. With two boisterous lads, our no-nos were remote French gîtes and elegant townhouse hotels, but things like skiing, safaris and watersports came into their own." It's worth looking for a hotel or apartment complex where older children can go off and do their own thing, such as enjoy watersports or go to the hotel disco, with other teens they meet on holiday, within the safe confines of the resort.

It's not all hard work, Jill stressed. "In many ways, these are the halcyon days of travelling with children. They can start to become your personal sherpa, instead of the other way round; they're curious, interested and, until their mid-teens anyway, not biased or prejudiced."

Chloë agreed. "Travelling with children can be a hassle, but they can really open your eyes as they are so curious about everything – and that can be infectious. My main tip is to alter your expectations. Peggy's [her daughter's] favourite ever trip was to Majorca when she was four. I hated it, but she just loved it and after a few days, because she was enjoying herself so much, I started to have a really good time too."

Sadly, some families are less fortunate and cannot afford any holidays. The **Family Holiday Association** (020 7436 3304, **www.familyholidayassociation. org.uk**) is a charity that specialises in providing holidays to disadvantaged children and their families. The FHA believes that taking holidays strengthens family relationships, helps poorer children fit in better at school, as they are able to share stories of their holidays, and by providing a restorative break, helps disadvantaged families to deal more successfully with the problems they face.

Booking tips for family holidays

- Book early – the best hotels, free child places and other deals get snapped up fast.

- Think of a different destination – countries such as Turkey and Bulgaria, outside the euro zone, can offer cheaper living costs.

- Register for email alerts from the airlines so you can book flights the moment they go on sale.

- Self-catering minimises the cost of eating at expensive restaurants.

- All-inclusive holidays mean your kids can enjoy drinks and ice creams without it busting the budget.

- For ski trips, consider the week immediately before Christmas or Easter when prices can be lower than the popular February half term.

- For summer sun, travel at the very end of August when prices start to drop.

- Consider smaller, specialist operators that do not market themselves specifically to families, as they may not hike prices so much in the school holidays.

Family holiday operators

Rare is the holiday company that doesn't offer family trips, so in the Directory (chapter 11), you'll find listings for all the big summer sun operators, and individual country specialists. The small selection of companies listed here have a particular emphasis on catering for families.

Powder Byrne (020 8246 5300, **www.powderbyrne.co.uk**) and **Scott Dunn** (020 8682 5010, **www.scottdunn.co.uk**) offer upmarket family holidays worldwide with top-notch extras – for example, all-day creches staffed by British-qualified nannies at some of the popular Mediterranean resorts.

The following popular operators specialise in club-based family activity holidays, usually focusing on watersports or skiing, with most meals and extensive childcare included in the price. (They also cater for couples and singles, and have some adults-only resorts.)

Club Med, 0845 367 6767, **www.clubmed.co.uk**

Mark Warner, 0870 770 4227, **www.markwarner.co.uk**

Sunsail, 0870 777 0313, **www.sunsail.com/clubs**

Neilson, 0870 333 3356, **www.neilson.com**

Esprit (01252 618300, **www.esprit-holidays.co.uk**) specialises in family ski holidays, plus active holidays in the Alps in summer.

The travel agent **Quo Vadis?** (01279 639600, **www.quovadistravel. co.uk**) specialises in organising luxury family holidays worldwide.

Daredevil families

Many of today's parents are yesterday's backpackers, used to travelling to exotic destinations, and don't see why having children should limit them. Luckily for them, many of the adventure tour companies, such as Dragoman and Explore, are run by travellers in the same boat, who have created "soft adventures" for families with children even as young as one, though most trips start at age five.

The upside of these trips is that you can satisfy your urge to visit exotic destinations – Africa and the Middle East are favourites due to their relatively short flying times and limited time differences – while giving your children a memorable holiday. The potential downside is that many of these holidays are group trips, so you will have to put up with Other People's Children, who are, of course, never as well behaved as your little angels.

Try these companies:

The Adventure Company, 0870 794 1009, **www.adventurecompany.co.uk**

Cox & Kings, 020 7873 5000, **www.coxandkings.co.uk**

Dragoman, 01728 861133, **www.dragoman.com**

Exodus, 0870 240 5550, **www.exodus.co.uk**

Explore, 0870 333 4001, **www.explore.co.uk**

Imaginative Traveller, 0800 316 2717, **www.imaginative-family.com**

Walks Worldwide, 01524 242000, **www.walksworldwide.com**

Family travel advice elsewhere in this book...

- Free child places and other family package deals – chapter 4, page 116

- Getting their passport and European Health Insurance Card – chapter 6

- At the airport and on the plane – chapter 8

- Dealing with holiday dangers – chapter 9

- Travelling while pregnant – chapter 10, page 366

- Childrens' health abroad – chapter 10, page 367

Advice on the web

The excellent websites **www.babygoes2.com**, **www.takethefamily.com**, **www.kidsintow.co.uk** and **www.family-travel.co.uk** have masses of information for parents, including advice on destinations, links to family holiday booking sites, and forums for parents to exchange tips and advice.

The site **www.parentscentre.gov.uk** explains the government's rules on taking children out of school and suggests ways of finding good-value holidays outside the school term. Also see **www.smallworldmagazine.co.uk**.

Activity holidays for children

"Parents Get Lost!" has long been the popular acronym for PGL, the activity holiday provider which caters for both families and unaccompanied children (though its name actually comes from the initials of its founder, Peter Gordon Lawrence).

Today there are hundreds of activity companies and centres in the UK, offering everything from abseiling to windsurfing. Unfortunately there is no compulsory code of safety standards, so parents should ask questions before they book. Ask about staff training, what happens in emergencies, the track record of the centre and how activities are supervised.

The **British Activity Holiday Association** (020 8842 1292, **www.baha.org. uk**) lists operators of activity holidays in UK and offers safety advice and an inspection regime for members; the **Adventure Activities Licensing Authority** (02920 755715, **www.aala.org.uk**) checks that safety standards for the riskier activities such as pot-holing or sailing are being observed.

Operators include:

Acorn Adventure, 0870 121 9950, **www.acornadventure.co.uk**

Camp Beaumont, 0870 499 8787, **www.campbeaumont.co.uk**

EAC Activity Camps, 0845 113 0022, **www.activitycamps.com**

PGL Adventure, 0870 055 1551, **www.pgl.co.uk**

Wickedly Wonderful, 07941 231168, **www.wickedlywonderful.com**

Child safety tips

• Teach "stranger danger".

• Make sure they know the name of their hotel; give them an identifying wristband (available from **IdentiKids**, 0845 125 9539, **www.identifyme.co.uk**) or pin a note of the hotel's name and your phone number inside a pocket.

• Teach them to use child seats and seat belts.

• Carry a full-face photograph of your child with you.

• Never leave a child alone to watch luggage or keep a place in a queue.

• Do not leave children or babies in a car in warm weather, even if the window is open.

Single-parent holidaymakers

Tempting offers emblazoned across holiday brochures – such as "free kids!" and "free child places!" – can leave a bitter taste in the mouth if you're a single parent. The mainstream tour operators' use of photographs in their brochures explains why: there's mum, dad and two (usually blond) children. The perfect family.

But life's not like that, and thousands of single parents each year trawl the brochures to find something suitable for one adult and one or more children. Although the big tour operators say they reserve some rooms for single-parent families, these can be very limited in number, or even, shockingly, only available during term time.

"There are tour operators that claim to do special deals for single parents but when you do the sums you find that either there were only a handful of places, or that the figures do not look quite as enticing when you've added in everything you need to," said Kate Calvert, editor of the website **Family Travel (www.family-travel.co.uk)**. "I concentrate on specialist companies because I have been so frustrated with mainstream companies. I do not think they offer much of a service to single parents."

The first problem with mainstream holiday companies is that if an adult and a child share a hotel room, they are usually charged an under-occupancy supplement as the price is based on two adults sharing the room. "Some even pay a single supplement on top of that!" said Jackie Lewis of Mango, a small tour operator that caters for single parents. "We've heard of cases where a single parent and child paid as much as a family of four." Either way, the supplement is likely to wipe out any benefit gained by a "free" child place.

The second problem is that, while children quickly make new friends, it can be lonely for single parents in the evenings. Solutions to these dilemmas include:

- Pairing up with another single-parent family.

- Picking self-catering rather than hotel accommodation, as it tends to be sold in a more flexible manner.

- Joining a group adventure tour where you all eat together (eg with Explore or Dragoman).

- Camping – campsite operators are used to single parents and often offer plenty of on-site activities.

- Using a destination specialist instead of a large tour operator.

- Using an upmarket company that offers really good childcare, albeit at a price (eg Powder Byrne, Scott Dunn).

Contacts

Mango, 01902 373410, **www.mangoholidays.co.uk**

Small Families, 01767 650312, **www.smallfamilies.co.uk**

Gingerbread, 0800 018 4318, **www.gingerbread.org.uk**

Single Parent Travel Club, 0870 241 6210

One Parent Families, 0800 018 5026

Holiday Endeavour for Lone Parents, 01302 728791 **www.helphols.co.uk**

Useful websites include **www.family-travel.co.uk** and **www.takethefamily.com**

Disabled travellers

Many holiday companies and hotels seem happy to wilfully ignore the business they could gain from a substantial, often monied, section of the population: people with a disability. The Disability Rights Commission says that one in seven of the UK population has some sort of disability, yet many holiday companies still seem unwilling or unable to cater for this market. Disabled travellers say that the mainstream holiday companies, while they may be willing to help, do not have the systems in place to ensure that, for example, a hotel room or transfer bus really is suitable for someone who uses a wheelchair.

In the UK it seems there is room for improvement, even though the Disability Discrimination Act came into force in 2004, making it a legal requirement that businesses, including hotels and restaurants, make appropriate provision for disabled people. Tony Reeve, MD of tour operator **Assistance Travel Service**, said he could think of only four hotels within 15 miles of Heathrow airport that have suitable roll-in showers for wheelchair users. In general, he added, the cheaper hotel chains – such as Novotel, Ibis and Travelodge – are better, possibly because they are often in new buildings, rather than older ones that are harder to adapt.

Many travellers with a disability do not want special treatment. Provision of relatively simply "extras" such as handrails, flashing fire alarms or vibrating pillows, and staff trained to offer appropriate help such as reading out a menu to someone with a visual impairment, enable many disabled people to use the same accommodation as the able-bodied.

A handful of tour operators cater for those with more restrictive disabilities, such as wheelchair users, whose needs mean greater planning is required to make their holidays a success. These holiday companies, which are often run by disabled people, make it their business to inspect personally the accommodation they offer, to ensure that, whatever the hotel says, the roll-in showers really are big enough for a wheelchair user, and staff are appropriately trained – hence their brochures often carry photographs of the lavatory alongside those of the hotel bedroom. But again the watchword is integration. Philip Scott, MD of tour operator **Can Be Done**, said that his customers wanted to stay in the same places as able-bodied holidaymakers. "Disabled travellers do not want to go somewhere with a hospital atmosphere."

Holiday companies offering overseas packages say that mainland Spain, the Balearics, the Canaries and Florida are among their most popular destinations (as they are for the able-bodied traveller). Spain and the USA are particularly praised for their efforts in offering suitable accommodation and services: in America, legislation ensures standards are high.

Northern European countries generally cater well for disabled travellers. France, however, is often found wanting. "It's about the worst," said Philip Scott of Can Be Done. "They just do not want to recognise disability. And Charles de Gaulle airport is absolutely appalling for disabled travellers." Greece, Italy and Cyprus are slowly improving. But it's quite possible to visit more adventurous destinations with specialist tour operators, including Turkey, Egypt, India and Thailand.

For a list of tour operators that specialise in holidays for disabled travellers, see the Directory, page 401.

Information

Door to Door, www.dptac.gov.uk/door-to-door

Holiday Access Direct, www.holidayaccessdirect.com

Holidays for All, 01865 432877, www.holidaysforall.org.uk

Royal Association for Disability and Rehabilitation (Radar), 020 7250 3222, www.radar.org.uk

Tourism for All, 0845 124 9974, www.tourismforall.org.uk

The website www.allgohere.com lists hotels in the UK that cater for disabled guests, and has an airline section that outlines the facilities for the disabled on some of the world's major carriers. The site www.everybody.co.uk/airline lists access arrangements on the major airlines. In the USA, the Open Doors Organization (www.opendoorsnfp.org) has useful advice for disabled travellers to America.

Many tour operators say cruise holidays are well geared up for disabled travellers, with American cruise companies thought to be particularly helpful. For contact details, see "cruises" in the Directory, chapter 11.

Tips for disabled travellers

- Tell the tour operator everything about your disability when booking. Tony Reeve of Assistance Travel Service said: "Sometimes they decide not to tell us something in case we will not take them, but in most countries we can organise flights, specialist aids or nursing care."

- Likewise, be frank with your travel insurance company to ensure you are fully covered. There are specialist insurers for travellers with particular illnesses or disabilities. Contact the national organisation that supports your condition to ask for their recommended brokers, and see chapter 6 for further suggestions.

- You must tell the airline if you need to carry an oxygen bottle on board; some have started to charge for this service. Tour operators specialising in holidays for disabled travellers tell me some airlines, including Ryanair and flyglobespan, are particularly unhelpful; conversely, British Airways, easyJet, Virgin, Monarch and South African Airlines were variously commended for their helpful attitude.

- Ask your tour operator or the airline about whether the lavatories on planes have disabled access. Some, particularly newer planes, do but older ones do not. For further holiday ideas, contact the national charity or organisation that campaigns and informs about your condition.

How travel agents can help

There's a purposeful buzz in the air inside **Trailfinders'** (0845 058 5858, **www.trailfinders.com**) flagship store on Kensington High Street in London. Agents wearing headsets are dealing with calls underneath an electronic display showing the number of people that are waiting, while others speak to customers who've popped in. The air is thick with talk of Antarctica, Nepal, round-the-world tickets and getting visas for Vietnam.

Mike Gooley spent the 1960s in the SAS before setting up Trailfinders in 1970, which has grown to 18 shops across the country. His army background shows through in his military bearing and imposing presence (he's 70 but looks much younger) and paternalistic outlook towards his staff, for whom he funds lunch every day (although they have only 25 minutes to eat it). Cigar-chomping Gooley is one of the travel industry's characters. Although Trailfinders has a website, he refuses to allow online booking – you can book only by phoning a consultant or visiting its shops, because he thinks the customer will get a better deal, more tailored to their needs, that way.

"If everyone booked on the internet, no one would have any buying power," he said. "But we have leverage because we deal with the travel companies. When there's a seat famine we are very good at finding a way of getting people somewhere on a particular day. We can sometimes dig down a bit deeper into the system. Airlines release certain seats that ordinary punters cannot access but we can be proactive and go after them." Trailfinders has its own unique software and staff must undergo five weeks of training before being allowed to deal with customers.

Across London, Philip Davies is doing something similar, albeit on a smaller scale. He was a teacher for 15 years before he set up **Real Holidays** (020 7359 3938, **www.realholidays.co.uk**), an independent travel agent in Islington, north London – and it shows. He still likes to keep his staff on their toes with daily tests to make sure they are keeping up with what's happening in the industry. "We're selling knowledge," he said, explaining that his customers tend to read about the latest hotels in glossy magazines, so he and his team have to stay one step ahead.

"We have to be knowledgeable because it's terribly easy to book on the internet, but we know, for example, which hotel in Kovalam, India, is better than another. We think we know why a hotel is right for particular people."

A good travel agent can save you time and money compared with putting your own trip together. Not only should they have expert knowledge, but they will have access to rates and deals that members of the public cannot obtain and, crucially, the package holiday you buy will be financially protected. Mike Greenacre, chief operating officer for the **Cooperative Travel Trading Group**, with 625 travel agencies across the country, said: "That might not seem important at the time, but it can become a very important element if, for example, you encounter something like Hurricane Wilma." When that hurricane tore into Cancun in October 2005, holidaymakers whose trips were financially protected were helped to get home, whereas independent travellers had to fend for themselves.

Travel agents can also sell you an "inclusive tour" (or IT) package, which is something you cannot organise independently. IT packages are formed when an airline finds it has spare seats that it cannot sell. It offloads these to a travel agent at a bargain price, and the agent bundles in a few nights in a hotel too – yet the overall package can still cost less than the published economy plane fare would be on its own.

Nevertheless travel agents are aware that they are losing ground to the web. Going Places, part of the MyTravel group, closed 110 of its 610 branches in late 2005, citing a growth in internet bookings as the reason for the closures. Some small agents have started to charge a fee for a consultation, redeemable against a booking, to deter those who pick their brains, then go home and book direct, online.

How to find a travel agent

Some 130 independent agents are members of the **Aito Specialist Travel Agents** group (020 8744 9271, **www.aitoagents.co.uk**), which specialises in selling the holidays of Aito members (*see* page 7), though they will also sell the big tour operators' holidays.

For mainstream package holidays you should get good deals through the big high-street chains, **Thomson**, **Going Places** (part of MyTravel), **Thomas Cook Travel Shops** and **First Choice Travel Shops**. These are owned by the big tour operators and they may push the products of their parent company before those of other operators. (To find out who owns what, *see* page 110, above.) For specialists in long-haul flights and complex itineraries, *see* the Directory, page 409.

The following agents specialise in helping students and the under-26 age group, though they can sell tickets to anyone: **STA Travel** (0870 163 0026, **www.statravel.co.uk**) and **Student Flights** (01782 715215, **www.studentflights. co.uk**). Ask about youth deals if you are under 26 or have an International Student Identity Card (**www.isic.org**), wherever you book.

Create your own package holiday online

Booking a simple return flight or a hotel room on the internet is fairly straightforward, as we've seen in chapter 3. But we've also learned about the drawbacks of doing this – in particular, the risk that you may have no financial protection, and thus no one to help you out if things go wrong.

But a new way of using travel websites is emerging, which allows you to combine hotel, flight and other elements, such as car hire, and bundle them into a "DIY package". Generally these holidays are financially protected, particularly if they include a flight. In the industry jargon, this way of booking is known as "dynamic packaging", but it's better described as a way of creating your own tailor-made holiday, using the internet.

Well-known online agents such as **Expedia** and **Lastminute** have been gradually introducing this "build your own package" technology. It is often called "flight + hotel" or "create your holiday" on websites. Typically you start by searching for flights. Once you've chosen the flights you want, you move to the hotels part of the website and pick accommodation. You're then offered the chance to buy extras such as insurance, car hire or tickets for attractions before you book and pay for the lot. Expedia and co are now being joined by the traditional tour operators, such as **Thomas Cook** (whose site is www.flexibletrips.com), and new operators such as **www.freshholidays. com**, which are using the "screen-scraping" or "spidering" technology we discovered in chapter 3 to hunt for the best deals from scheduled, charter and budget airlines.

Using these "build your own package" websites has both advantages and disadvantages. The good news is that you can generally create highly flexible deals – say a five-night break instead of the standard seven nights offered by many tour operators. You can play around with different combinations of flights and hotels in the comfort of your own home, at a time that suits you. You make only one credit card payment rather than dealing with lots of different suppliers. And you may find some real bargains, with genuine savings over high-street prices.

And the holiday will usually be financially protected, that is, if any of the companies involved goes out of business, you will either get your money back, or be helped if you are already on holiday. "We thought it was crucial when we went into dynamic packaging that we were bonded," said Robin Sutherland, director of retail at Expedia. "Our research showed that one of the main reasons people were coming to us was because of the Atol bonding."

The downsides are that you do not get the advice of a travel agent – who may have heard bad reports about a hotel, or who may know of a more convenient air route offered by another airline. Some of the sites (such as Expedia or Opodo) do not include results from budget airlines such as Ryanair, for example. It can be difficult or impossible to organise complex, multi-hotel, touring itineraries in this way. And the hotels offered on some sites can be more city-based instead of the beach resorts or villas you want for a summer break.

A final word of warning. It is not a legal requirement that a travel agent or tour operator who sells you separate components of a holiday must bond this as a package. Agents such as Expedia, Lastminute, flexibletrips.com, freshholidays.com and the like, which hold Atols, do protect the holidays that you put together from the elements on their websites, but if you simply ask a travel company (whether in the high street on or the web) to supply you with a flight and hotel room from separate sources, it probably will not be bonded, because they have not technically sold you a package.

An example of how you can fall through this particular net occurred when the city-break operator Travelscene went bust in August 2004. Anyone who had booked accommodation only with the company's subsidiary Citybedz was *not* protected – but those who had booked a package, combining flights and hotel, with Travelscene *were* protected. In this case, Abta stepped in to bail everyone out – Travelscene's boss was at that time Abta's president, embarrassingly for the trade association.

The rules are highly confusing – so the trick is always to ask, before you book, whether or not you have financial protection for the trip you are planning. There's nothing to stop you booking a trip that has no financial protection, but if something goes wrong you may be left high and dry.

Tips for booking your own holiday

- Book early to get the best deals.

- Check several sites before making a decision.

- Back up your research by using guidebooks and reading hotel reviews on sites such **as www.priceline.co.uk** or **www.tripadvisor.co.uk**.

- Play around with flight dates in case the price drops either side of your ideal dates.

- Check that your holiday is financially protected, if this is a concern.

- Use price comparison websites that compare package holidays online: you don't buy the holiday from these sites but click through to the provider. Try **www.cheapshortbreaks.co.uk** and **www.cheapholidaydeals.co.uk**.

Booking the perfect villa holiday

Hiring a private villa is the Rolls-Royce option for anyone planning a self-catering holiday – and it need not cost a fortune, especially if you avoid high summer. But before you decide on things like whether you want to be near the beach, who will do the cooking or what the house rules will be, the most important question is, how can you find the right villa for your group?

Pop the words "villa holiday" into the Google search engine and you'll be given 22 million pages of results. Yet "Googling" a holiday is exactly what many of us do now, and nowhere is the trend to online booking more marked than in the villa holiday scene.

Five years ago, 52 per cent of villa holidaymakers bought a package through a travel agent, according to the 2005-06 UK Villa Market report by specialist holiday company CV Travel. By 2004, that figure had dropped to 23 per cent. Another 15 per cent booked a villa holiday through a tour operator

– meaning more than 60 per cent of villas are booked independently, many of them online.

Partly this is a result of rising prosperity and the fact that so many of us now own properties overseas. We're quite happy to book flights online and then stay in a friend's villa, in a way that hardly happened a decade ago.

But if you don't have your own private bolthole, and feel daunted at the prospect of Google's 22 million suggestions, where do you start? Should you risk booking from a website? Or is a specialist villa company the answer?

"I would never book a villa over the internet, unless it was part of a bonded holiday company. Otherwise there's nobody to complain to," said Glen Donovan, who runs exclusive travel agency Earth. "I would risk a hotel, because at least you can check it out on Tripadvisor, but not a villa." This uncertainty is the major drawback to booking villas that you have tracked down over the internet. There are no recognised grading schemes for villas, as there are for hotels. There are no easy ways to read anecdotal opinions of particular villas online, as there are with hotels. The only, rather unscientific, way that villas are graded is by whether or not they are included in tour operators' brochures. I've even heard of holidaymakers who will devote a day of their holiday to inspecting prospective villas for next year's break, as they refuse to rely on pictures on the internet or other people's opinions.

Indeed, the anonymity of the internet means that the villa you book may look wonderful in that tiny picture on your computer, but in reality it may turn out to be a cockroach-infested, badly wired dump, with a murky swimming pool and the local sewage plant next door. And once you get there you may find there is nobody around to sort out your problems.

Paul Cleary, MD of Caribbean specialist **Caribtours**, said: "Our customers research their villas on the internet – they are very well informed when they phone us up – but they like the security of booking through a big tour operator. For example, if there's a hurricane we help you out at no extra cost, whereas people who have booked direct are left to their own devices."

Deborah Roach of upmarket villa specialists **A&K Villas** agreed. "In a few years' time the internet will be even more saturated with direct owners and it will be mind-boggling for anyone trying to find a villa – you will have no idea who owns them, and there are no guarantees. I think people will revert to tour operators. If you are spending that kind of money, you want to know who you are paying."

The glut of accommodation on the villa rental market now means that tour operators are able to pick and choose the very best villas to offer in their brochures. But the flipside of this is that in the mainstream destinations popular with British second-home owners, such as France, Spain and Cyprus, there is such fierce competition from small internet-based rental firms that some of the big villa operators are scaling back in these destinations. **Meon Villas**, for example, dropped France in 2005 and moved further into the eastern Mediterranean, offering villas in places such as Turkey where we are still less confident about booking a "DIY" holiday. And tour operator **Sunvil** has had a similar problem in its heartland, Cyprus, although it is still operating there.

"What's happening in Cyprus is that a retired couple sits on their veranda with a laptop and inputs 10 or 11 villas nearby that other Brits have bought, puts them on a website, and does a deal with the local taxi and car hire firms," said Sunvil's MD, Noel Josephides. "We've been noticing this for the last three or four years. People working in this way are now moving more people than we are as tour operators."

To compete, he has not increased prices in Cyprus and Greece, though this means he no longer has the money to invest in building swimming pools in villas. But he is adamant that the customer who books through his company is far better served than anyone booking through a DIY internet operation. Thanks to the protection of the EU Package Travel Regulations, if there's a problem such as building work next to your villa, for example, a tour operator will move you – but if you have booked direct, you have to try to thrash things out with the villa owner.

As to what we want in a villa, swimming pools are widely becoming standard now, although they may not suit families with young children, who must be eternally vigilant. Even in France, where, by law, pools must have gates or covers, parents must be alert in case their child falls in.

Villa-goers also want alternatives to the shopping and cooking – many companies can organise a large welcome hamper for your arrival and put you in touch with a local cook or catering firm who will send someone in to prepare your meals. I once stayed in a **CV Travel** villa on Majorca where this worked brilliantly. While we were relaxing on a boat trip off the north coast spotting dolphins, a cook was dispatched to our villa to prepare a delicious supper of salads, tarts and roast suckling pig for us to enjoy on our veranda overlooking Pollensa that evening.

At the top end, daily maid service and a cook come as standard with villa rental. You can also expect air conditioning, broadband internet access (often wi-fi), and sometimes a tennis court, the option of helicopter transfer from the airport, and, if you're on a beach or island somewhere like the Caribbean, toys such as a small powerboat or wet bikes.

Justin Stanton, who has worked for a Turkey and Greece villa specialist, reckons there are two groups of people who rent villas. "There are those who want DVDs, air con, Jacuzzis and gadgets, and those who deliberately do not want that, but want something very rustic and characterful – people who are willing to sacrifice comfort for character." If you plan to share your villa with a big group, it's important to work out what camp you all fall into, so you can find a villa to suit everyone.

Indeed, the group dynamics of a villa holiday can be tricky, as *Times* journalist Mary Gold, who with her husband has built and rents out a villa on Cephalonia, has discovered. "For sanity's sake, we have house rules for when we are there," she said. "No CD players around the pool (it's not fair on our neighbours), political discussions are off-limits (Princess Diana was not murdered and that's that), and if you want to get up at 7.30am just remember that others are asleep, having been up playing poker until the early hours."

Things are even more complicated if you are two families with children. What happens if one set of parents has a strict bedtime for their kids, and the others don't? What about a curfew for teenagers? How do you divide food bills, who does the washing up and who unloads the dishwasher? It's important to have a discussion about the ground rules before the holiday begins.

Robert Lyle, co-founder of luxury travel PR firm ZFL, has a dramatic solution. He thinks villa ground rules should be more fundamental – starting with who picks up the tab.

"If you can afford it, never share the cost of a villa holiday," he said. "Sharing villas is like paying for dinner. Once you get to the age of about 40, one person picks up the tab, and next time the other person pays. Because then, one person is in charge. If they order the wine, they are happy about the price. But if you share the cost of a villa everyone has very different ideas of what they want to do – one is out every night, another wants to entertain other people at the villa... when everyone thinks they are team captain, no one goes anywhere."

The person who's paying can also set ground rules – such as that everyone tips the maid a certain amount per day. "It's far better to have people to stay in a cheaper villa and pay the whole bill yourself," said Lyle. "Then your experience will be defined by your enjoyment of the people there, rather than how big the villa's pool is."

Upmarket villa holidays are now becoming increasingly popular in farther-flung destinations – not just the Caribbean, where they have long been popular, but Bali, Thailand, Malaysia, South Africa, Mauritius and Kenya are now getting in on the act, as is Morocco, which has some spectacular properties, particularly in the Palmeraie area of Marrakesh. Picking long-haul destinations can help on price – the Caribbean in summer can be extremely good value compared with the best Mediterranean villas in July and August, and the weather can be good too, though the hurricane season starts at the end of summer.

To avoid potential rows over catering and cleaning arrangements, many families are finding that villas within the grounds of a hotel are the way forward. Often these are found at very high-end properties in the Caribbean, such as the One & Only Ocean Club in the Bahamas, Sandy Lane on Barbados and Parrot Cay in the Turks & Caicos islands, where you can even rent Bruce Willis's villa (sadly, without Bruce). Others popular with families include Windjammer Landing on St Lucia, the St James Club on Antigua, Long Bay on Tortola and Otley's Plantation on St Kitts.

Hotels on Mauritius are also starting to offer these villas, such as at One & Only Le Touessrok, though you have a less typical villa experience on that island as many holiday properties are nowhere near shops or towns, making it harder to self-cater and throwing you back on the facilities of the hotel.

The fancy extras you can find at the world's best villas are as impressive as anything you'll find in a hotel – for example, at Baraka Point on Virgin Gorda in the British Virgin Islands, bookable through **Wimco**, you can have spa treatments in your own "wellness and relaxation rooms" set above a wonderful sea view (**www.barakapoint.com**).

Tips for surviving your villa holiday

- If you are in a mixed group, build in some time away from the others – eating lunch and dinner with the same people for a week can be hard work.

- Start a kitty for daily essentials.

- Don't feel obliged to do everything together.

- Decide from the start how many people will be put on the car hire agreement so you can share the driving fairly.

- Use unbreakable glasses around the pool.

Questions to ask when booking a villa

- How far is it from the airport?

- How near is the closest grocery store and town?

- Is a welcome pack provided, and is it included in the price?

- Do you have to pay a security deposit against breakages?

- What kitchen equipment is provided?

- Do they provide beach towels?

- Is there maid or chef service? If so, how often, and what work will they do?

- Do you have to share the swimming pool with other people?

Booking a villa on the internet

If you book direct with a villa owner over the internet, you do not have the same financial protection as you have when you book with a tour operator, so it's wise to make these checks before you hand over your money.

First, ensure that the company you book with has a contact phone number and address on its website. Ask them for letters of recommendation from former customers. Ask if they have visited the property themselves; if they have not, ask if you can speak to someone who has.

Be wary of relying on photos on a website as they may be close-cropped and leave off the power station looming in the background – ask if there are other photos you can see. Ask what size the pool is and exactly how far the villa is from other buildings.

Following this discussion with the villa owner or rental agent, email a clear summary of what was discussed and agreed to them, and get them to send you back an acknowledgement – having everything in writing will help if there is a problem.

Add in all the extra costs for linen, maid service, etc, and work out if this really is the bargain it first seemed. If you decide to book, pay with a credit card. If anything goes wrong with the booking, you can take it up with your credit card company.

Further information: For a list of villa companies, check out the Directory on page 379 and also consult listings for individual countries.

Luxury travel

What is luxury travel? Until recently it might have been something as straightforward as a business-class seat on the plane, a suite in a five-star hotel and a limousine to take you from one to the other.

These days, with airports horribly crowded, and certain resorts suffering from over-exposure in downmarket newspapers and magazines, the definition of luxury has moved on. For many travellers, real luxury is a swift, hassle-free journey through the airport, a stay in a discreet bolthole that's not usually on the rental market, and the services of an expert guide who can gain you access to a private art collection, or a knowledgeable concierge who can book you the best table in the best restaurant. Privacy, simplicity and access are the new watchwords.

Reaching your destination with the minimum of stress is your first hurdle. Using small, regional airports and flying mid-week are good tactics for avoiding the crowds, but an upmarket travel agent or tour operator can organise concierge services to ensure you are whisked past any queues. Luxury specialist **ITC Classics**, for example, has a Platinum service in which you are met kerbside as you arrive at the airport, your bags are carried for you and you are fast-tracked through check-in. On arrival you are met by an ITC rep who speeds you through immigration and customs, often getting you past the queues – which can be a real bonus after a long flight.

Many top-end companies offer these sorts of services – I've experienced this with **Abercrombie & Kent** in Cairo, for example – but any specialist operator with good ground handlers should be able to pull tricks for their customers overseas. The knowledgeable ground staff of South America specialist **Journey Latin America** once helped me to bypass a horrendous queue at Cusco airport in Peru because they knew the right people at the airport.

Airlines will also pamper their best customers with time-saving services. **Virgin Atlantic** offers limo collection and drive-through check-in for its Upper Class passengers, and in Barbados **British Airways** offers a similar service for its premium customers. There's something marvellously decadent about checking in without having to get out of your air-conditioned limo. **Lufthansa** has gone a step further, with dedicated first-class terminals at Frankfurt and Munich and limo transfer direct to the steps of the plane, while **Malaysia Airlines** offers complimentary helicopter transfers to Heathrow, Paris Charles de Gaulle or Nice airports.

Following the demise of Concorde, we've seen well-heeled travellers turning to private jets (see chapter 3), but it's *how* you use them that counts, not just the fact that you can afford it. "Smart travellers travel like they dress," said Robert Lyle, of luxury travel PR firm ZFL. "For example, five years ago, rich Russians wore Versace – they had lots of cash and wanted to spend the maximum they could. But the American or French tycoon might wear Armani jeans, a plain white T-shirt, a good jacket and shoes – he does not feel that every bit of his dress has to be expensive to validate him. It's a sophisticated luxury.

"I went to a wedding in Italy recently. Some people came on easyJet, despite owning their own yacht, because it was very easy and cheap and it went to the right place. EasyJet is like that white T-shirt. It's not that they could not afford a private jet, or were not generous – but there was no point in not taking that easyJet flight."

When it comes to picking your hotel, there's more to it than simply going for the one that's had rave reviews in the glossy mags. Using an experienced travel consultant means you'll be given the best room in that hotel, too. Mark Robinson, MD of **The Private Travel Company**, which arranges luxurious holidays, said he can cut deals direct with hotels where he knows which are the best rooms for his customers. "The "best" room is not always the most expensive," he said. "For example, a hotel might boast it has a four-bedroom suite, but that's of no interest to a couple." He cited the example of the Datai Resort Hotel Langkawi, in Malaysia, where it can be better to have a top-floor corner suite with a wonderful view over the surrounding rainforest than a ground-floor suite with a pool.

For many holidaymakers, the hotel has now become the destination – we increasingly book holidays because we want to stay in a hotel with a fabulous spa, or eat in the hotel's restaurant because a Michelin-starred chef is running it – so it has never been more important to make the right choice.

Barbara Catchpole, who co-founded the luxury tour operator **Elegant Resorts** in 1988, has seen such vast growth in the number of five-star hotels around the world since then that her company has recently launched **Contempo**, a web-based booking service focusing on stylish hotel breaks. "When we started, we only had 20 hotels in the Caribbean brochure – and they were not all what I would call five-star, but they were the best of what was around," she said. "There were the great city hotels, such as the Oriental in Bangkok or the Peninsula in Hong Kong, but the rest of the hotels around the world were mostly geared to business travel. And the Maldives were basic,

Robinson Crusoe islands 20 years ago – now they have some of the best hotels in the world."

But while the number of hotels claiming five-star facilities has sky-rocketed, her definition of what makes a great hotel includes high service standards, something that's harder to benchmark. It's not sufficient to offer a beautiful pool and fine restaurant if service is slow, rude or unimaginative. Like many observers of the international luxury scene, Catchpole believes that the Caribbean has lost ground in this respect to the hotels of the Indian Ocean, the Middle East and the Far East.

I agree. I recall a wonderful moment at a supposedly five-star hotel in Antigua when I asked my waitress at breakfast whether it was likely to rain that day. "Sorry ma'am, ah ain't slept with the weatherman," she replied, eyes rolling, before wandering off to patronise another guest. Contrast that with the Ritz-Carlton in Dubai, where a member of staff went off in her lunch hour, unasked, to buy a bit of sports kit for my travelling companion who wanted to use the gym but had not brought the right gear. Good travel consultants keep an eye on things like senior staff changes in hotels and advise their clients accordingly – they may refrain from recommending a once-good hotel until they have heard satisfactory reports of a new general manager, for example, and they track where the best chefs are working.

The hotel group **Amanresorts** is often cited as having a huge impact on what we expect luxury hotels to offer. Formed in the late 1980s, this boutique group of 18 resorts, mostly in Asia, set new standards of privacy and discreet luxury with its small properties where the emphasis is on cooking with local produce, employing local staff and designing the building in sympathy with the surrounding environment. That might have been ground-breaking stuff at the time, but it's now very much in tune with the way environmentally responsible tourists want to travel, as we've seen in chapter 2.

So it's a logical extension of that desire for peace, space and privacy that means agents such as **Earth** and **The Private Travel Company** are now using their contacts to rent villas and houses for their clients that are not usually made available to the public. But true luxury travel means you will come home rested and relaxed, not harried and hassled from the rigours of an uncomfortable journey home that spoils the memory of the wonderful experiences you've enjoyed.

Further information: for a list of luxury tour operators, travel agents, airlines and concierge services, *see* the Directory, pages 402 and 416.

CHAPTER FIVE
Holidays in the UK

Introduction

Hiking in Scotland, romantic weekends at country house hotels, childhood summers on the beaches of West Sussex, exploring the castles of Wales, grown-up getaways in north Norfolk: some of my best holidays have been taken here in the UK. Our crowded little island can still boast empty, often wild, scenery – take a hike up Kinder Scout in Derbyshire, or along the windswept beach at Dornoch in Scotland, and you may well have it to yourself. And when you want to unwind in a lovely hotel or superb restaurant, the news from the hospitality frontline these days is good, going on great.

Over the past decade I've noticed a determination on the part of the UK tourist industry to sharpen up its act and drive up standards. Fresh impetus for change followed the disastrous events of 2001: the foot and mouth outbreak, which closed large parts of the UK's countryside to walkers and cyclists just as summer was getting under way, and the terror attacks of September 11, which scared many American tourists into staying at home, depriving UK tourist businesses of valuable income.

Since then, helped by a dose of 2001-inspired patriotism, the fantastically hot summers of 2003 and 2006, and no doubt a certain amount of unease about terrorist atrocities overseas, many of us have decided to take holidays at home, and the tourist industry here has been making some serious improvements.

Common sense has finally been injected into the UK's hotel gradings scheme, for example. In 2006, the confusing schemes – awarding stars, diamonds and other gongs – are being simplified to make life easier for visitors (see www.qualityintourism.com). Boutique hotel fever – inspired by the likes of the Hotel du Vin and Malmaison groups (see pages 151–153) – has spread across the land, with power showers, freshly brewed coffee and thick, fluffy bathrobes starting to see off trouser presses, pots of UHT milk and scummy bathrooms, thank goodness – though there's still some way to go.

New-look Britain

We're seeing parts of the country in a new light. **Cornwall** has for some time now been on the map thanks in part to restaurateurs and hoteliers such as Rick Stein and Olga Polizzi, but it goes from strength to strength as more of us than ever head down there to learn to surf or enjoy the coastal walks, and the popular chef Jamie Oliver adds his mark with the opening of **Fifteen Cornwall** in Newquay in summer 2006 (01637 861000, **www.fifteencornwall. co.uk**). The **Isle of Wight**, once considered of interest only to yachties or pensioners, has had a huge injection of money and style, no doubt helped by the fabulous, recently revived June rock festival; there are now so many funky hotels and wonderful brasseries opening that Isle of Wight specialist **Red Funnel Holidays** has created a new group to market them (**Chic Treats**, 0870 458 6392, **www.chictreats.co.uk**).

Liverpool is beautifying itself, with stylish hotels opening and interesting arts and heritage projects, including the Kings Waterfront development, under way as it prepares to become European City of Culture in 2008 (**www.liverpool08.com**, **www.visitliverpool.com**). Meanwhile resorts on the **south coast**, such as Hastings, Camber Sands and Sandwich, which until recently weren't even on the radar of anyone planning a weekend break, are finding fresh life as stylish new hotels inject money and bring in visitors.

We still have some way to go: transport around the UK can be slow and expensive, and too many hotels and guest houses still need updating, both in appearance and service. But a holiday in the UK, whether it's a quick weekend away or your main summer break, has plenty going for it and in this chapter I'll put a few ideas under your nose.

Tourist boards

England: 0845 456 3456, **www.enjoyengland.com** (this site also links you to the 560 tourist information centres in England)

Scotland: 0845 225 5121, **www.visitscotland.com**

Wales: 0870 830 0301, **www.visitwales.com**

Northern Ireland: 02890 246609, **www.discovernorthernireland.com**

Public transport in the UK

• **Travel Line** (0870 608 2608, **www.traveline.org.uk**) will plan any UK journey by bus and train.

- **Transport Direct** (**www.transportdirect.com**) offers information about public transport across the country, and will also give routes for car journeys.

- **The National Rail** website, **www.nationalrail.co.uk**, is an excellent resource for rail information: it has links to all the train companies, giving details of their contact numbers, complaints lines, disabled facilities and whether and when they will carry bikes, plus it gives up-to-the-minute information about engineering works. For telephone enquiries, ring 0845 748 4950.

- **The Train Line** (**www.thetrainline.com**) and **Q Jump** (**www.qjump. co.uk**) are both useful for booking tickets.

- **Train Taxi** (**www.traintaxi.co.uk**) lists taxi firms that serve railway stations nationwide.

- **National Express** (0870 580 8080, **www.nationalexpress.com**) and **Megabus** (0900 160 0900, premium rate, **www.megabus.com**) offer inter-city coach services.

Hotels

Country house hotels

At **Hambleton Hall** in Rutland, the car park was full of ancient estate cars with dog blankets and muddy wellies on the back seat. At **The Grove**, near Watford, we would have needed an Aston Martin to turn heads in a car park full of Porsches. At **Cowley Manor** in Gloucestershire, I had trouble finding space among the Minis lined up for a promotional event. And at **Babington House** in Somerset, my boyfriend's rusty old Rover was whisked away by staff without so much as a raised eyebrow. (Sadly, we got it back the next day.)

You can tell a great deal about a country house hotel by its car park, I have decided: old money, new money, media-friendly, service with a smile... Hambleton's old money – a classic English country house that would send an American film director into raptures. Originally a Victorian hunting lodge, Hambleton is as remarkable for what it does not have – there's no spa, creche or screening room – as for what it does, which includes beautiful views over Rutland Water from its well-tended gardens, and a Michelin-starred chef producing exquisite meals. Sipping tea on the terrace outside my cottage, the Croquet Pavilion, all I could hear were church bells and lapping water.

At The Grove near Watford, you're more likely to hear the mwah! of air-kisses, the clash of bling jewellery and, in the background, the faint hum of the M25. It's great fun, but it couldn't be more different from Hambleton. It's big (227 bedrooms; Hambleton has just 15), with an 18-hole golf course, fabulous spa with an enormous, slate-lined pool and several restaurants. The gulf between it and Hambleton shows just how wide the vague label "country house hotel" has now been stretched.

A generation ago, most country houses were just that – someone's home, where a lucky few friends might be invited to stay. The country house hotel as commercial enterprise really started to emerge in the late 1970s and early 1980s; the booming economy of the mid-1980s ensured a ready supply of wealthy paying guests. Today, we have become used to spending weekends in the country – and we have also become used to jumping on a budget flight and whizzing off to Europe for the weekend. So the proprietors of country house hotels have had to raise their game, diversify, offer us new temptations. These days you can expect to find fantastic spas, round-the-clock childcare and the latest high-tech gadgets as well as excellent restaurants. Here's a quick guide to get you started.

- **Gastronomes** love the old-fashioned, slightly chintzy, classic country house hotel, which probably comes with a Michelin star and is often run by an owner-proprietor. Try **Hambleton Hall** in Rutland (01572 756991, **www.hambletonhall.com**), **Chewton Glen** in Hampshire (01425 275341, **www.chewtonglen.com**), **Gravetye Manor** in West Sussex (01342 810567, **www.gravetyemanor.co.uk**) and **Le Manoir aux Quat' Saisons** in Oxfordshire (01844 278881, **www.manoir.com**).

- **Urbanites** are metropolitan media types who fancy "countryside lite" – they like the idea of being in the country more than the reality. They want their hotels to offer all-day breakfasts, nursery food such as fishcakes and fry-ups, a bar where the staff stay up as late as you like, a great spa, a pool table, mobile phone reception and wi-fi. Try **Babington House** in Somerset (01373 812266, **www.babingtonhouse.co.uk**), **Barnsley House** in Gloucestershire (01285 740000, **www.barnsleyhouse.com**) and **Cowley Manor**, Gloucestershire (01242 870900, **www.cowleymanor.com**). The more grown up may graduate to **Whatley Manor** in Wiltshire (01666 822888, **www.whatleymanor.com**), which has an excellent spa.

• **Romantics** are splashing out for a special occasion – a proposal, a 40th birthday, a wedding anniversary – and they want the classic, full service, afternoon-tea-and-dressing-for-dinner experience, ideally in a hotel with a little history attached. Try **Cliveden** in Berkshire (01628 668561, **www.clivedenhouse.co.uk**), **Amberley Castle** in West Sussex (01798 831992, **www.amberleycastle.co.uk**), **Charlton House** in Somerset (01749 342008, **www.charltonhouse.com**) and **Hotel Endsleigh** in Devon (01822 870000, **www.hotelendsleigh.com**).

• **Parents** want plenty to occupy the kids – and preferably someone else to oversee their activities, so they can swan around in dressing gowns recapturing that long-lost pre-children sensation. Baby monitors, Ofsted-registered creches and 5pm kids' teas are top of their shopping lists. Try **The Ickworth Hotel** in Suffolk (01284 735350, **www.ickworthhotel.com**), **The Grove** in Hertfordshire (01923 807807, **www.thegrove.co.uk**), **Calcot Manor** in Gloucestershire (01666 890391, **www.calcotmanor.co.uk**) and **Bovey Castle** in Devon (01647 445016, **www.boveycastle.com**).

There are dozens more wonderful country house hotels across the country. Keep an eye on the rapidly expanding **Von Essen** hotel group (01761 240121, **www.vonessenhotels.co.uk**), which now owns 21 hotels in England and Scotland, including the four popular members of the Luxury Family Hotels group: Ickworth in Suffolk, Fowey Hall in Cornwall, Moonfleet Manor in Dorset and Woolley Grange in Wiltshire.

In **Scotland**, you'll find the grand country hotels are often very outdoorsy, with visitors who go for seriously good golf, or pursuits such as shooting and fishing – for example at **Gleneagles** in Perthshire (0800 389 3737, **www.gleneagles.com**), the **Westin Turnberry Resort** in Ayrshire (01655 331000, **www.turnberry.co.uk**), or the **Old Course Hotel, Golf Resort and Spa** in St Andrews, Fife (01334 474371, **www.oldcoursehotel.co.uk**). Likewise in the Republic of Ireland, there are many fine country houses, castles, and fishing estates.

Contacts

Bridgehouse Hotels, 020 7495 8801, **www.bridgehousehotels.com**

Elite Hotels, **www.elitehotels.co.uk**

Exclusive Hotels, **www.exclusivehotels.co.uk**

Hand Picked Hotels, 0845 458 0901, **www.handpicked.co.uk**

Historic House Hotels, **www.historichousehotels.com**

Paramount Hotels, 0870 168 8833, **www.paramount-hotels.com**

Pride of Britain Hotels (0800 089 3929, **www.prideofbritainhotels.com**) is a marketing consortium, many of whose members are country house hotels.

Ireland's Blue Book (00 353 1 676 9914, **www.irelands-blue-book.ie** is a consortium which markets some 40 Irish hotels and properties.

Manor House Hotels (00 353 1 295 8900, **www.manorhousehotels.com**) is a collection of Irish country houses and castles.

For additional information on hotel groups, *see* the Directory, page 426, and for recommended reading, *see* page 430.

Townhouse transformation

The party went on until 3am, with a swing band in the lobby encouraging the unlikely mix of guests – including a pneumatic beauty queen, the athlete Linford Christie and the movers and shakers of the Yorkshire town of Harrogate – to boogie on down. The launch party for the new **Hotel du Vin** in Harrogate in late 2003 was a typically jolly, lavishly catered affair, as I'd come to expect whenever a new member of this boutique hotel chain opens.

Next morning, nursing hangovers, some of us gathered for breakfast in the bistro. After hosting a party for 700 that finished only hours ago, the exhausted staff, few of whom had managed any sleep, were run off their feet, so Robin Hutson, Hotel du Vin's co-founder, pitched in to help serve the restorative plates of bacon and eggs.

A decade ago, few hoteliers in Britain would have rolled up their sleeves and joined in like that. But Hutson has been at the forefront of a quiet revolution in British hotels since the mid 1990s. He believes we should not have to feel grateful that, booted and suited, we are allowed to enter the hallowed portals of a hotel, as we might have felt a generation ago. These days, informality, comfort and good service are the watchwords – at least, in Hutson's world.

"I've stayed in rubbish hotels in almost every town in the country," he told me. "Even today, you are more likely to have a horrid experience than a decent one for £100 a night. But if a town or city can support a mediocre £100-a-night hotel, then it can probably support a decent one." It was this philosophy that prompted him to leave his job as general manager at Chewton Glen, the award-winning, five-star country house hotel in Hampshire, in 1994 and to open, with his partner, Chewton Glen's head sommelier Gerard Basset, the first Hotel du Vin, in Winchester.

Rave reviews quickly followed. The bistro served simple, seasonal dishes; the staff were chosen for their unstuffy attitude and friendliness; the rooms had fabulously comfortable beds and shower heads the size of saucepan lids that deliver a powerful 35 litres of water per minute. There's a real *joie de vivre* at a Hotel du Vin: guests are invited to pinch the toiletries from the bathroom, encouraged to smoke (there's a legendary cigar list) and, of course, to explore the well chosen, reasonably priced wine list. "We cannot do room service at these prices, or turn-down, or shoe cleaning," said Hutson, "but there's no reason that a waiter cannot help you if he's around. That approach was a massive shift in the hoteliers' psyche."

For customers such as me and my friends, it was perfect. I would much rather a hotel spent money on top-quality steak for the restaurant than on fancy tablecloths or chocolates on the pillow, and that's exactly what happens at a Hotel du Vin. My generation no longer sees staying in a hotel as a once-a-year treat, or eating in one the sort of thing you only do for a special occasion – we expect to stay in hotels for weekend breaks throughout the year, and we eat out in them regularly. Drinking in a hotel's lobby bar is now a commonplace alternative to the pub in many towns and cities. So Hutson cleverly captured a changing mood in our approach to hotels and dining out.

There are now seven hotels in the group, with others in York and Cambridge set to open in 2007. But Hutson is no longer in charge – in late 2004 he sold the company to Marylebone Warwick Balfour (MWB) for a tidy £66 million. MWB is the parent company of the successful boutique hotel group **Malmaison**. This also started in 1994 under another visionary hotelier, Ken McCulloch, kicking off with an Edinburgh hotel that was quickly praised for its sumptuous interiors, which have become a standard across the group – dark velvet fabrics, superb beds and strikingly modern furniture – and its good-value brasserie.

McCulloch, who is now no longer involved with Malmaison, told me how the success of his first Glasgow hotel, the upmarket One Devonshire Gardens, which he opened in 1986, led him to create the lower-priced Malmaison brand, which nevertheless had some of the same flair. "You do not have to spend a fortune. Style does not really cost. A tin of paint costs the same, whatever colour it is," he told me.

"Malmaison and Hotel du Vin created a new sector. We both had the same classical background," he said, referring to Hutson's Chewton Glen days; McCulloch trained at hotels including Gleneagles and Turnberry. "Very disciplined and upmarket. But when we went to do something different, our standards remained the same."

Hotel du Vin and Malmaison together occupy only a narrow segment of the hotel market in Britain – a sector that arguably didn't even exist until the mid-1990s. But their influence has been disproportionate to their size. Patricia Yates, head of publicity for VisitBritain, said: "Along with Jonathan Wix [who opened boutique hotel 42 The Calls in Leeds], Hutson and McCulloch showed that there was a market for decent hotels in city centres.

"The old view was that the only people who went there were businessmen and they would take what they could find. But these hoteliers have revolutionised city centres and made them tourist destinations, because often they discount at weekends, so they attract people into cities at weekends."

Contacts

These hotel groups offer city-centre properties with a stylish, boutique feel:

Abode, www.abodehotels.co.uk

Alias Hotels, www.aliashotels.com

Apex Hotels, www.apexhotels.co.uk

City Inn, www.cityinn.com

The Eton Collection, www.theetoncollection.com

Firmdale Hotels, www.firmdalehotels.com

Hotel du Vin, www.hotelduvin.com

Malmaison, www.malmaison.com

Seaside resorts – the start of a renaissance

Take a long, sandy beach that's just perfect for building sandcastles, for kite-surfing or horse-riding. Add beautiful sand dunes and easy access from London and what do you have? A great day out at Camber Sands in East Sussex.

But add a smart hotel and brasserie, and you have a weekend break. That's the logic behind The Place, a once-bland motel in Camber that was bought up and made over by partners Matthew Wolfman and Mike Ashton.

What the pair did is what a raft of other small, independent hoteliers have done in seaside resorts around the UK. They've spotted a destination with a real draw – in Camber's case, its beautiful beach – but which has lacked a hotel and restaurant of the standard that will induce high-spending couples and families to visit for a weekend. Once these are added, a small resort's fortunes can be given a huge boost, as a new weekend break destination is created.

Two seaside towns are regularly cited as early examples of how a good hotel can turn a small resort into a weekend-break destination: Padstow in Cornwall and Whitstable in Kent. Rick Stein opened his Seafood Restaurant in Padstow in 1975, and has gradually added 32 hotel rooms since then. In Whitstable, the Oyster Fishery Company's popular restaurant has been going for 15 years, while eight converted fishermen's huts and the 29-room Hotel Continental have been added more recently.

The demand for short breaks can be seen all around the coast, as Ruth and David Watson discovered when they took over the Crown and Castle at Orford in Suffolk in 1999, creating 18 stylish rooms and a brasserie. "Orford was already a smartish place but with nowhere to stay," said Ruth. "We had known it for 30 years and it seemed a great location, with river, sea and charming village. We did not need to create the market – just attract the market to it," she said.

In Camber, Wolfman and Ashton put up £1 million of their own money to get The Place going, despite having no background in the hotel business other than as guests. But they have clearly hit a chord. So popular has the 20-room hotel proved that Wolfman has been able to buy another seaside hotel, the Bell at Sandwich in Kent, which he's currently refurbishing, and he has his eye on another property in West Wittering, near Chichester.

They work hard to get involved in the local community, hoping in Camber, for example, to play a key part in the gradual regeneration of this small, rundown resort that grew up after the Second World War as a base for traditional holidays. "But this is not the middle class coming in and doing something that precludes the locals," said Wolfson. "We want them to come here and think, this belongs to me. Most of the diners here are local. People have said it's good value and what the area needed."

Caroline Raphael of the *Good Hotel Guide* agrees that the right hotel, well run, can give a small resort a new lease of life. But for these hotels to work, she believes, they must be aware of the trends that today's customers are looking for. "Informal eating is one trend people like very much, not silver service. And a lot of these places make a point of being child-friendly, especially at the seaside.

"But yes, one property can make a difference. Because if people come to stay at, for example, the Tresanton, they go around the area, shop there... it changes the tone of a place."

The hotelier Olga Polizzi discovered this when she opened Hotel Tresanton in St Mawes, Cornwall, in the late 1990s. "In a village or small part of the world, one property can make a big impact," she said, citing the thousands of pounds the hotel spends with local food suppliers, and the fact that it employs more than 60 staff. She also laments how so many of our seaside resorts are still terribly run down: "We went around the seaside and it's extraordinary – we have ruined some of our best beaches."

Seaside escapes

The Place, Camber Sands, East Sussex, 01797 225057, **www.theplacecambersands.co.uk**

The Victoria, Holkham, Norfolk, 01328 711008, **www.holkham.co.uk/victoria**

The Hoste Arms, Burnham Market, Norfolk, 01328 738777, **www.hostearms.co.uk**

Hotel Continental, Whitstable, Kent, 01227 280280, **www.oysterfishery.co.uk**

Hotel Tresanton, St Mawes, Cornwall, 01326 270055, **www.tresanton.com**

The Crown and Castle, Orford, Suffolk, 01394 450205, **www.crownandcastle.co.uk**

Rick Stein's Seafood Restaurant, Padstow, Cornwall, 01841 532700, **www.rickstein.com**

Hotel Zanzibar, Hastings, East Sussex, 01424 460109, **www.zanzibarhotel.co.uk**

The Bell, Sandwich, Kent, 01304 613388, **www.bellhotelsandwich.co.uk**

Cheap sleeps

When, in 2004, I stayed in the first hotel in the new Dakota chain, I was pleasantly surprised. It seemed to be unpromisingly sited on a business park off the M1 near Nottingham, yet a red Ferrari gleamed in the car park and inside there was a buzz that you rarely find in any hotel on a Saturday night. The restaurant, with its comfortable leather seating and modern gantry lighting, was serving 150 customers, nearly a third of them non-residents who had chosen this as their Saturday night venue, just three weeks after the hotel opened.

The rooms had more than a hint of Malmaison and Hotel du Vin about them too: firm mattress, power shower and slick lighting. Which is no surprise, as Dakota is the latest project from Malmaison founder Ken McCulloch, working with his business partner David Coulthard, the racing driver.

"It's like the field of dreams: if you build it, they will come, and Nottingham is an example of that," McCulloch told me. He has been surprised by how guests use Dakota, as it was expected that business travellers would stay just one night, hence wardrobe space in the bedrooms is limited. "But the average stay is three-and-a-half nights," he said. "People are using it as a base – they know they will eat and sleep well so they can justify the expense. And it is within easy reach of Sheffield, Leeds, Leicester, Birmingham and Nottingham."

The second hotel, Dakota Eurocentral, on the M8 between Edinburgh and Glasgow, is due to open in summer 2006, with the third, Dakota Forthbridge, opening in early 2007. McCulloch told me he is actively working on plans for 10 more and "I do not see any problem doing 30 or 40 in the UK." He also has ambitious plans to create 100 Dakotas in America over the next seven years.

Budget hotel tips

When booking, ask how many people can share a room: sometimes children can sleep in their parents' room for no extra charge. You won't get extras such as room service, although there may be snack dispensers and ice machines in the corridor. Like the budget airlines, the budget hotel groups tend to sell their cheapest rooms first; prices generally rise the later you leave it to book. Often the best rates are online.

Contacts

Dakota, 0870 442 2727, **www.dakotahotels.co.uk**

Days Inn, 0800 028 0400, **www.daysinn.co.uk**

Express by Holiday Inn, 0870 400 8143, **www.hiexpress.co.uk**

Formule 1, **www.hotelformule1.com**

Ibis, **www.ibishotel.com**

Premier Travel Inn, 0870 242 8000, **www.premiertravelinn.com**

Travelodge, 0870 085 0950, **www.travelodge.co.uk**

Pod hotels

In 2006 we have really seen the arrival in the UK of "pod hotels", which offer a way of staying in a city centre location at a very modest price. The downside is that the rooms are tiny, with literally just room for a bed and a shower – and often there's not even a window.

In some of them, however, you get stylish furnishings, plasma-screen TVs and "mood lighting" in return for the lack of space. They have a surprisingly broad appeal – the prospective target market of students, backpackers and budget travellers are rubbing shoulders with families who want two cheap rooms for a night before their flight, and business travellers on a budget.

Contacts

- easyHotel (**www.easyhotel.com**) is based in Earls Court, west London.

- Yotel (**www.yotel.com**), from the same group as the Yo! Sushi restaurant chain, is to open two airport hotels in late 2006 at Heathrow's Terminal 4 (with 40 rooms, known as "cabins") and Gatwick's South Terminal (50 cabins).

- Nitenite (0845 890 9099, **www.nitenite.com**) in Birmingham opened with 104 rooms near the Mailbox in the city centre in March 2006.

- Etap (**www.etaphotel.com**), part of the French Accor hotels group, has one hotel in Birmingham and two in London.

Hostels and backpackers' picks

The Youth Hostels Association (0870 770 8868, **www.yha.org.uk**) has more than 200 hostels across England and Wales offering budget accommodation to couples, singles, families and groups. You no longer have to share dormitories

– many hostels have private rooms – and you do not need to be a member of the YHA to stay in them, although members (£15.95pa) pay a discounted rate and also have access to a network of 4,000 hostels worldwide. It's also possible to hire an entire property for a special event.

Backpackers and budget travellers have other money-saving options where they will be likely to meet fellow travellers. Try these:

- **The Generator** (020 7388 7666, **www.generatorhostels.com**) is an 800-bed hostel in central London, promising a cheap bar and plenty of activities, from £10 a night off season; there's another Generator in Berlin.

- Piccadilly Backpackers (020 7434 9009, **www.piccadillyhotel.net**) in central London offers beds from £12.

- St Christopher's Inns (020 7407 1856, **www.st-christophers.co.uk**) has five UK budget hostels in popular backpacker locations (such as Brighton and Newquay), plus Amsterdam and Bruges; Paris is planned. It offers deals such as £85 per week in a dorm bed.

- The YMCA (**www.ymca.org.uk**) allows budget holidaymakers (both men and women) to book beds in a limited number of its hostels.

Contacts

- **Scottish Youth Hostels Association**, 0870 155 3255, www.syha.org.uk

- **Hostelling International Northern Ireland**, 02890 324733, www.hini.org.uk

- **An Oige, Irish Youth Hostel Association**, 00 353 1 830 4555, www.anoige.ie

Cottage holidays

My brother James was in the kitchen, up to his elbows in flour, making a lemon tart for the evening meal. His wife Jane and I were reading the Saturday papers in the lounge, while baby Emily practised her crawling on the carpet.

Tim had discovered a PlayStation in the TV room (yes, he's 39). Chris, Ken and Stuart were digging bikes out of the garage to head off for a cycle ride while Tim's wife Charlotte was setting out the champagne glasses in the conservatory.

I wasn't sure where Sarah, Sharon and Peter were. Or Rachel and Neil for that matter. With its two large sitting rooms, a couple of kitchens, a pool room, dining room, two staircases and several long corridors, this was an easy house to get lost in.

Thus our happy, lazy Saturday unfolded at the large fishing lodge near Builth Wells in the Brecon Beacons, which we'd booked through cottage company **Rural Retreats** for Tim's 40th birthday. The house, right on the River Wye, had seven *en suite* double bedrooms, which suited us perfectly.

Hiring a large property to celebrate birthdays and anniversaries with friends has never been more popular, as Jane Knight, co-author of *The Big House Party*, and deputy travel editor of *The Times*, explains. "People used to be happy to celebrate birthdays and anniversaries in the local village hall or pub," she said. "Now an increasingly sophisticated travelling public has cottoned on to the fact that you can hire a castle or cottage complex without taking out a second mortgage.

"It means you can get large numbers of people together for a great bash. Cottage rental companies say they can't get enough large properties to meet the demand."

But we're getting much fussier about the sort of properties we'll rent. "People are now expecting to go to a country cottage and have, if not the same quality as at home, then something better," said Bryn Frank, author of *The Good Holiday Cottage Guide*, which he's produced for 25 years, listing hundreds of rental properties around the country. "They want swimming pools, maid service and absolutely spotless interiors, the most expensive beds, and deep pile carpets."

Jackie Dawes of **Helpful Holidays**, a large agency in the West Country, agrees. "People want better quality than at home, with things like *en suite* bathrooms, DVD players and dishwashers now expected as standard." Cottage rental staff also report a growing number of customers who check if supermarkets such as Waitrose or wine merchant Majestic will deliver to the cottage before they will book it.

Of course the downside with self-catering can be doing the chores, which is why there's recently been rapid growth in "serviced self-catering", where cottage complexes attached to hotels allow you to have private accommodation, but with the use of the best bits of a hotel – such as its restaurant and activities such as biking or horse-riding.

Michael Dean of the giant **Holiday Cottages Group**, which includes **English Country Cottages** and **Blakes**, has noticed an increased demand for complexes, which are often converted farm buildings or small groups of individual cottages with central facilities such as an indoor swimming pool. "They are very popular for family reunions," he said. "Rather than booking up one huge property you can book four cottages around a complex, share the facilities, and at night, when you've had your fill of Aunty Doris, you can shut your own front door." Another advantage is that cottages in a complex can be booked separately, meaning each family within the party can make their own booking instead of one person having to coordinate payment for the entire party.

Further information: for details of cottage holiday companies across the UK, *see* the Directory, page 427.

Cottage complexes

There are now many of these popular groups of properties around the country. The following selective list is based on those that have been recommended by *Times* journalists; for further suggestions consult agencies such as Classic Cottages, the Cottage Collection, Premier Cottages, Helpful Holidays, English Country Cottages, Rural Retreats and Toad Hall Cottages (details in the Directory, page 427).

Beacon Hill Farm Cottages, Northumberland, 01670 780900, **www.beaconhill.co.uk**

Celtic Haven, Wales, 01834 870000, **www.celtichaven.com**

Combermere Abbey, Shropshire, 01948 662876, **www.combermereabbey.co.uk**

Eastwell Manor, Kent, 01233 213000, **www.eastwellmanor.co.uk**

Ford Abbey, Herefordshire, 01568 760700, **www.fordabbey.co.uk**

Priory Bay Hotel, Isle of Wight, 01983 613146, **www.priorybay.co.uk**

Tredethick Cottages, Cornwall, 01208 873618, **www.tredethick.co.uk**

Vere Lodge, Norfolk, 01328 838261, **www.verelodge.co.uk**

Wye Lea Country Manor, Herefordshire, 01989 562880, **www.wyelea.co.uk**

Cottage booking tips

When should you book?

Large and popular properties can be booked up a year or more in advance, especially for Christmas and New Year, so if you're planning a big party, give yourself plenty of time. In high summer you may have to rent the property for at least a week, as shorter rentals are usually only available off-season. You may get a last-minute high-season short break if you're prepared to chance it – Hoseasons, for example, releases unsold cottages for sale two weeks in advance for short summer rentals.

What's included?

Rural Retreats will provide a food hamper and wine for you, but most cottage companies don't go that far, or charge extra for stocking the fridge before you arrive. It can be worth bringing your own basics – tea, milk, bread – to avoid having to race to the shops the minute you arrive.

The kitchen should be well equipped. Check that payment for central heating is included, and, if it's a remote area, whether it has mobile phone coverage (most properties will also have a pay phone). If you're travelling with young children, ask if cots, high chairs and stair-gates are provided. Dog owners must also check that their pet is allowed in to the property, and smokers should check if smoking is allowed inside; often it is not.

You are expected to clean up before you check out of your cottage, even though the rental company will send in cleaners to prepare it for the next guests. Leaving it in a mess may mean you forfeit your deposit.

What to do if things go wrong

Contact the owner or the agency when the problem occurs and give them the chance to rectify matters. If you only report a problem after the holiday it is hard for the owner to do anything about it. Take notes, photos or video of the problem and keep a note of who you spoke to about it and when.

If you return home still dissatisfied, write to the owner or agency within 28 days summarising what you feel went wrong and asking for reasonable compensation. Your local Citizens Advice Bureau (details in the phone book, or from **www.adviceguide.org.uk**) may be able to advise. You can ultimately take the owner or agency to the small claims court (details in the phone book or from **www.courtservice.gov.uk**).

Bed and breakfast

B&Bs have improved considerably in recent years, but I was reminded of the vast gulf between good and bad on a recent walking holiday. I hiked the length of Hadrian's Wall from west to east, finding such a paucity of decent B&Bs at the start of the walk that I ended up after day one in a place almost too ghastly to recall, with a hard, single bed, no *en suite* bathroom, and a rather spooky proprietress who served up an almost inedible meal. Unsurprisingly, I was the only guest. (Quite possibly ever.) Fortunately matters improved vastly as I walked east and by the time I reached Hexham I was enjoying smartly decorated, comfortable rooms with TV and bathroom attached, and wonderful home-cooked meals that restored my faith in the British B&B. And all in the very reasonable £30–£45 per night bracket.

These days the best B&Bs will offer homely extras such as proper milk with tea and coffee in your room, home-made biscuits or cake, perhaps even a snifter of complimentary sherry, fluffy bathrobes and decent smellies in the bathroom – habits some of our hotels could usefully imitate.

Regional tourist boards can be a good source of information about local B&Bs. There are also several guides to B&Bs; *see* page 427.

There's also a range of agencies offering B&Bs in **London**, a good alternative to the often-pricey hotels: try the **Bed & Breakfast and Homestay Association** (020 7385 9922, **www.bbha.org.uk**), **At Home in London** (020 8748 1943, **www.athomeinlondon.co.uk**) and the smart **Uptown Reservations** (020 7937 2001, **www.uptownres.co.uk**). Alastair Sawday publishes *London* (£9.99), which lists hand-picked small hotels and B&Bs.

B&Bs with a twist

Several organisations offer B&B in properties that offer a little extra.

- **Distinctly Different** (01225 866842, **www.distinctlydifferent.co.uk**) offers both B&B and self-catering in unusual buildings – a dovecote, a church, a police station.

- **Wolsey Lodges** (01473 822058, **www.wolseylodges.com**) is a collection of 169 upmarket private homes (and a dozen in Europe), such as Victorian vicarages or Georgian manor houses, where you are likely to share meals with the family in a house-party atmosphere.

- **Unique Home Stays** (01637 881942, **www.uniquehomestays.com**) also offers house parties, sometimes for private groups, sometimes with the property owners, at grand houses across the UK and overseas.

Farm stays

If you like the idea of staying in a B&B that's also a working farm, then **Farm Stay UK** (01271 336141, **www.farmstayuk.co.uk**) lists hundreds of farms that offer accommodation across the country, some of them working farms where you can visit the milking parlour and learn more of the farmer's way of life. In the west country, **Farm and Cottage Holidays** (01237 479146, **www.farmcott. co.uk**) has self-catering options that include farms and **Cartwheel** (01392 877842, **www.cartwheel.org.uk**) offers self-catering stays on working farms. For more information contact **National Farm Attractions Network** (01536 513397, **www.farmattractions.net**).

Camping and caravanning

As a teenager, I once took part in a ludicrous charity fund-raising camping expedition on top of Kinder Scout, a wild part of the Peak District National Park. The lunacy of cooking and serving a four-course black-tie dinner to half a dozen invited guests in a howling gale on top of a snowy mountain now seems clear, but at the time it seemed like a marvellous way to pass a freezing night. It was only marginally less disastrous than the time I set my tent on fire in a remote part of the Scottish Highlands whilst trying to cook supper.

Fortunately, camping no longer means you have to rough it. Had I £6,000 to spare, I could have moved in to **Camp Kerala** at the 2005 Glastonbury Festival (01749 860077, **www.campkerala.com**), which offered enormous Indian embroidered tents with private washing facilities, king-size beds and a veranda to sit out with a cocktail. They are nearly booked up for Glastonbury 2007 already, but never fear, **Tangerine Fields** (07821 807000, **www.tangerinefields. co.uk**) offers ready erected tents, kitted out with sleeping bags, airbeds and pillows, at festivals including the Big Chill, Greenbelt and the Hay Literary Festival.

Today there are plenty of jolly alternatives to the wet, uncomfortable camping experiences we may remember (and I certainly do) from our youth. Why go to Mongolia when you can sleep in a yurt in north Devon, with **Devon Yurt Holidays** (01837 810691, **www.devonyurtholidays.co.uk**)? Fancy travelling (and sleeping) in a gypsy caravan? Call **New Forest Gypsy Caravans** (01202 820346, **www.new-forest-gypsy-caravans.co.uk**) and the deed's done. Kids will love sleeping in a proper tipi in west Wales (through **Tipi West**, 07813 672336, **www.tipiwest.co.uk**) or in a wigwam near Berwick-upon-Tweed, Northumberland (through **Wigwam Village**, 01289 307107, www.northumbrianwigwams.com), and big kids will have fun hiring a classic VW Camper Van for a surfing weekend (**Kamper Hire**, 0845 226 7869, **www.kamperhire.co.uk**). Even foodies are catered for these days – **Belle Tents Camping** (01840 261556, **www.belletents.com**) in north Cornwall offers camping with a fully equipped kitchen tent and you can even organise organic vegetable delivery.

For more conventional camping and caravanning trips, the following organisations offer advice and site guides. **The Caravan Club** (0800 521161, **www.caravanclub.co.uk**) offers members (£32pa) access to 200 club sites and a further 2,500 small rural sites across the country. **The Camping and Caravanning Club** (0845 130 7631, **www.campingandcaravanningclub.co.uk**) offers members (£30pa) access to its campsites, plus information and advice. **Camping and Caravanning UK** (http://camping.uk-directory.com) has details of 1,500 sites in the UK, info on camping equipment, and online discussion forums. For caravanners, the **National Caravan Council** (01252 318251, **www.nationalcaravan.co.uk**) lists caravan sites across the UK, and offers advice on how to buy a caravan or motorhome, accessories, insurance and trade fairs. Other useful sites include **www.caravancampingsites.co.uk** and **www.ukcampsite.co.uk**.

Boating holidays

The British Waterways website **www.waterscape.com** is a good starting point for anyone wanting to explore Britain's 3,000 miles of navigable canals and rivers, offering suggestions on where to go, activities on our waterways and lakes, and information such as how to get permits for watersports on inland waterways. The **Waterways Trust** (01452 318220, **www.thewaterwaystrust.co.uk**) is a charity that regenerates canals and riversides and encourages us to spend more time enjoying them. **British Waterways London** (020 7985 7200, **www.britishwaterwayslondon.co.uk**) and **Broads** (01603 610734, **www.broads-authority.gov.uk**) offer water-based suggestions in the capital and the Norfolk Broads, one of the most popular boating areas.

British Waterways collects information on boating holiday operators at **www.waterwaysholidaysuk.com** and **Drifters Waterway Holidays** (0845 762 6252, **www.drifters.co.uk**) can put you in touch with boating companies. Operators include **Crown Blue Line** (0870 428 7119, **www.crownblueline.com**), **Black Prince Narrowboat Holidays** (01527 575115, **www.black-prince.com**), **Blakes Holiday Boating** (0870 220 2498, **www.blakes.co.uk**) and **Anglo Welsh Waterways Holidays** (0117 304 1122, **www.anglowelsh.co.uk**).

Walking in Britain

I was lucky enough to grow up in Bakewell, in the heart of the Peak District National Park, and walking at weekends was a way of life. In our late teens and early 20s, my friends and I would think nothing of roaming 15 to 20 miles over the tough hills of the Dark Peak, so named for the gritstone that gave the landscape a more forbidding appearance than the bucolic limestone-based White Peak to the south. Kinder Scout, Bleaklow and Black Hill were our playground and we grew so familiar with their escarpments and gullies that we'd navigate by streams, trees and the remains of the plane that crashed into the side of Kinder Scout during the war. I still have to remember, when out hiking in pastures new, that "just left of north" is not a technical term and we're all much better off using a map and compass.

Each year such activity would culminate in teams of four of us entering the Four Inns (**www.dynarx.demon.co.uk/fourinns/**), a 45-mile competition hike from Holmbridge, near Huddersfield, to Buxton, which has to be completed within a day. It's tough, as there are six substantial hills to climb along the way, and you must carry kit including a tent, stove, sleeping bag and food. In 1983 I was a member of the first ever all-women team to complete the hike, and we were greeted with increasing astonishment from our male colleagues at each successive checkpoint. By the end of the race we'd won side-bets of free drinks for months to come.

I might not tackle 45 miles at once these days but I still love long hikes, and have recently completed the Great Glen Way in Scotland and the new Hadrian's Wall National Trail, and am slowly working my way, as a weekend walker, along the North Downs Way through Surrey and Kent. There's little to beat the taste of that first decent pint of bitter after eight hours' hiking through some of our loveliest countryside in summer.

And walkers in England, Wales and Scotland have far more countryside open to them today than they had five years ago. In England and Wales, the Countryside and Rights of Way Act 2000 opened up vast areas of open country and registered common land – some 5,000 square miles – in England and Wales to walkers, much of which was previously closed to them. The access rights were introduced in stages in 2004–5 and are now fully in force.

Kate Ashbrook of the Ramblers' Association told me: "It's a break with a long tradition. For the first time, people know that if land has been mapped as access land, and there are no restrictions, they can walk on it freely. It's a lovely feeling, to be in an open space and not to have to worry about where you put your foot."

It's the first time landowners have been forced to allow such access. For details of where you can now walk in England, visit the **Countryside Agency**'s website **www.countrysideaccess.gov.uk**, and in Wales, see **www.ccw.gov.uk/countrysideaccesswales**. The Ministry of Defence has, in the summer of 2006, been encouraging more walkers to use its land, such as training grounds on Salisbury Plain, Dartmoor and Aldershot, that has not previously been open to the public. For details, see **www.access.mod.uk**.

Matters are also much improved in Scotland, where the Land Reform (Scotland) Act 2003, which was implemented in 2005, granted access to most land and water in Scotland. For a copy of the **Scottish Outdoor Access Code**, contact **Scottish Natural Heritage** (01738 458545, **www.outdooraccess-scotland.com**).

Walkers' rights in Ireland, both Northern Ireland and the Republic, are less well protected. There is no legally enshrined right to walk on common land, and the rights of way that exist are not always kept open by landowners. Walkers, concerned that their freedom is being eroded, have formed the pressure group **Keep Ireland Open** (**www.keepirelandopen.org**) and are campaigning for the freedom to roam over rough grazing land, and a network of rights of way across the country.

Walkers are obliged to behave "responsibly" – in practice this means things like shutting farm gates behind you and keeping dogs under control. The **Countryside Code**, promoted by government body the Countryside Agency, is available at **www.countrysideaccess.gov.uk**.

For information about walking and other activities in our 14 **National Parks** (soon to be 15 with the addition of the South Downs), *see* **www.nationalparks.gov.uk**. And for information on national trails in England and Wales, visit **www.nationaltrail.co.uk**. In Scotland, they are known as long-distance paths: see **http://walking.visitscotland.com**.

VisitBritain, the tourist board, has masses of information about walks on its website (**www.visitbritain.com/getactive**) and it also runs the **Walkers Welcome** and **Cyclists Welcome** schemes, highlighting accommodation with features such as a drying room or bike storage.

There are various **walking festivals** around the country each year: look at **www.walkingontheweb.co.uk** and **www.ramblers.org.uk** for suggestions.

Contacts

The British Mountaineering Council, 0870 010 4878, **www.thebmc.co.uk**

The Open Spaces Society, 01491 573535, **www.oss.org.uk**

Ordnance Survey, 0845 605 0505, **www.ordnancesurvey.co.uk**

The Ramblers' Association, 020 7339 8500, **www.ramblers.org.uk**

Walkingworld, **www.walkingworld.com**

Walking companies

There are dozens of holiday companies offering guided walks and services such as luggage transport – which is very useful if you're moving from place to place while walking a long trail. Here are some starting points; others can be found in the pages of magazines such as *Country Walking* (**www.countrywalking.co.uk**) and *Trail* (**www.trailmag.co.uk**).

Contours Walking Holidays, 017684 80451, **www.contours.co.uk**

Countrywide Holidays, 01707 386800,
www.countrywidewalking.com

Footpath Holidays, 01985 840049, **www.footpath–holidays.com**

HF Holidays, 020 8905 9558, **www.hfholidays.co.uk/classicwalking**

Many of the walking companies in the "activities" section of the Directory (chapter 11) also have UK programmes.

Dogs in the countryside

If you want to take your dog for a walk in open country you need to be aware of the rules about controlling dogs. If you're taking advantage of the new "right to roam" legislation over common land and open country, you have to keep your dog on a short lead between 1 March and 31 July, and year-round if you are near farm animals. If you're sticking to public paths there's no need to have your dog on a leash if it is under control. By law farmers can destroy a dog that is worrying their stock so it's in your and your pet's interests to follow the rules.

For a leaflet setting out advice for dog owners contact 0870 120 6466, or visit **www.countrysideaccess.gov.uk** to download it.

Cycling in Britain

Leisure cyclists in Britain have an increasing number of dedicated cycle paths, thanks in large part to the campaigning efforts of **Sustrans** and the **Cyclists' Touring Club** (CTC).

There are now some 10,000 miles of the **National Cycle Network** open across the UK. The network has been created by the sustainable transport charity **Sustrans**, which coordinated its creation by hundreds of local organisations and national bodies. A third of the network is entirely traffic free, using old railway lines or canal towpaths, making it ideal for families or new cyclists. The rest of the network uses quiet, minor roads and traffic-calmed streets.

Within this network are some 30 signposted, long-distance cycle routes, such as the "C2C" (or sea to sea, running from the Cumbrian coast to the North Sea). Dedicated maps for all these routes are available from Sustrans, whose website also details other routes across the country. Sustrans also publishes the handbook *Cycling in the UK*, the official guide to the National Cycle Network (£14.99), with plenty of suggestions for days out.

Visit the **Bike Events** website (**www.bike-events.com**) for details of cycling for fun, kids, sport and charity rides. And **www.bikeweek.org.uk** is the CTC's site with details of the annual June bike week and national events. See also "activity holidays" in the Directory (chapter 11) where many of the cycle companies listed also offer holidays in the UK.

Taking your bike on a train in Britain can be fraught: each of the 25 train operating companies seems to have a different policy on the subject. David Holladay, a consultant campaigning on this issue for the Cyclists' Touring Club, told me: "Part of the problem is that we have lost the culture of taking bikes by train. We also have a culture that cyclists are skinflints and do not pay – but most people taking bikes on trains are leisure cyclists and they are prepared to pay. They want convenience. They do not mind paying if it is not too much, and it is fair."

In general, bikes are discouraged or banned from trains during weekday rush hours (though few leisure cyclists are likely to want to travel then anyway). At other times there may be a charge, or a limit to the number of bikes a train will carry. Call National Rail Enquiries or the relevant train company in advance and, if necessary, book your bike in. Folding bikes go free on trains, if folded up.

For a list of cycle holiday operators, *see* the Directory, page 382.

Contacts

Cyclists' Touring Club, 0870 873 0060, **www.ctc.org.uk;** membership £32pa

London Cycling Campaign, 020 7234 9310, **www.lcc.org.uk**

The London Cycle Network, www.londoncyclenetwork.org.uk

National Rail Enquiries, 0845 748 4950, www.nationalrail.co.uk

Sustrans, 0845 113 0065, www.sustrans.org.uk; membership £15pa

Transport for London has free cycle maps, 020 7222 1234, www.tfl.gov.uk

The rise of "food tourism"

"People want to know where they are when they look at the menu," said Patricia Yates, head of publicity at tourist board VisitBritain. "When people travel, they want to have something that's unique to that area – not just sights and attractions, but also what they eat. There's a new interest in food, and rising standards."

Across the UK, there's now a real buzz about "food tourism". Travel writer Sally Shalam, former travel editor of the London *Evening Standard*, who regularly writes about the British food revolution, identified three reasons why. "We're much more interested in the health and provenance of our food – we listen to what chefs are saying. They have become health gurus," she said. "A second reason is an environmental concern – we're more worried about "food miles", how far food has travelled to get on to our plates.

"And I think we have just become more sophisticated. We eat out more and we're fussier. Once you know that if you go to the Lake District or Lancashire the livestock eats heather, which gives meat a different flavour, that's what you expect to eat there.

"We're mirroring what the French have always done with their *cuisine de terroir*. We've finally stopped being embarrassed about local food, such as Lancashire hot pot, and are making a virtue of it – chefs are cooking these dishes again."

Such is our foodie enthusiasm that these days, we're as likely to hunt out the nearest farmers' market or recommended restaurant on our travels as we are the local castle, museum or stately home. I'm certainly guilty of that, and have recently enjoyed terrific meals on my travels around the UK at places such as the **Felin Fach Griffin** pub with rooms near Brecon (01874 620111, **www.eatdrinksleep.ltd.uk**), **Terroir** at Cley next the Sea in north Norfolk (01263 740336, **www.terroir.org.uk**) and the **Porthminster Café** in St Ives, Cornwall (01736 795352, **www.porthminstercafe.co.uk**).

Chefs in the UK have now racked up 104 Michelin stars across England,

Wales and Scotland, while London was recently given the rare distinction by US-based *Gourmet* magazine of an entire issue devoted to the capital's culinary highlights. Some regional restaurants have become "destinations" in themselves, such as the **Three Chimneys** restaurant with rooms on the Isle of Skye (01470 511258, **www.threechimneys.co.uk**), which has been voted one of the 50 best in the world, or the Michelin-starred **Summer Isles** at Achilitibuie near Ullapool in Scotland (01854 622282, **www.summerisleshotel.co.uk**), which boasts that almost everything it serves – "scallops, lobsters, langoustines, crabs, halibut, turbot, salmon, venison, big brown eggs, wholesome brown bread fresh from the oven" – is locally caught or produced.

But it's not all about Michelin stars and fancy food. Indeed, I have eaten at several Michelin-starred establishments where I found the meals over-fussy and over-priced. But we want to know that when we travel around the UK we can find meals at a high standard that can become an important part of our trip, rather than just refuelling stops.

VisitBritain has produced a dedicated website (**www.visitbritain.com/ taste**) highlighting the diversity of regional food and drink, whether in restaurants, farmers' markets, food festivals or cookery classes. Under the "events" section it lists a staggering number of food festivals held across the land. Here are some more suggestions to get your taste buds going.

British Food Fortnight takes places from 23 September to 8 October, 2006, and encourages shops, restaurants and schools to put local produce to the top of their menus (details: **www.britishfoodfortnight.co.uk**).

The excellent *Trencherman's Guide* highlights 47 restaurants across **southwest England**, many also offering accommodation, and a sprinkling of Michelin stars among them. Ring for copies (0870 442 0880), or visit **www.indulgesouthwest.co.uk** or local tourist information centres. Two Torquay restaurants, The Elephant and Orestone Manor, received Michelin stars in 2006, bringing the region's total to an impressive 18.

The **Cumbria** Tourist Board produces *The Taste District*, an annual guide to its best restaurants and food producers (available to download from **www.golakes.co.uk** or by calling 015394 44444). And **Lincolnshire** County Council has produced **The Tastes of Lincolnshire**, a guide to locally produced food and drink across the region (**www.tastesoflincolnshire.com**).

In **Wales**, many excellent restaurants with rooms are listed in Emyr Griffiths' two guides, *Welsh Rarebits* (01686 668030, **www.rarebits.co.uk**) and *Great Little Places* (01686 668030, **www.little-places.co.uk**). The *Pembrokeshire*

Food Guide (0870 510 3103, **www.visitpembrokeshire.com**) highlights good restaurants, bars and farmers' markets in the region. The book *Dining Out in Wales* reviews 150 establishments and is available for £6.95 from 02920 828986.

VisitBritain also has a dedicated website to regional food producers, festivals and great restaurants (**www.visitbritain.com/taste**). You can also order a brochure from the **Enjoy England** website (**www.enjoyengland. com/taste**).

Also see: **National Association of Farmers' Markets** (**www.farmersmarkets. net**); **Farm Retail Association** (**www.farmshopping.com**), which helps farmers sell produce direct to the public; **English Wine Producers** (**www. englishwineproducers.com**); **Food from Britain**, a marketing company with links to regional food and drink producers (**www.regionalfoodanddrink.com**).

For a list of countrywide restaurant guides *see* the Directory, page 431.

Beaches

My childhood family holidays were spent on the beach at Shoreham-by-Sea, in Sussex, where for two weeks every August we sunbathed outside my grandmother's beach hut to the smell of her frying fish for lunch inside. I learnt to swim in the sea there and, back in the 1970s, long before Blue Flags or Seaside Awards, none of us gave a thought to whether or not the water was clean.

These days there are awards schemes aplenty to help you decide which beach to visit. Some focus on the water quality, others are more concerned with things like whether there are lavatories, pay phones and litter bins. There's also a guidebook published by VisitBritain, *Blue Flag Beaches 2006* (£4.99), which combines the findings of awards schemes with other tourist information.

Would I return to Shoreham-by-Sea now? Reluctantly. It does not hold a beach award, and when I did pop down for a visit two summers ago, I found sparse facilities and rather ancient lavatories. Personally I prefer the wilder, windy strands of Camber Sands or West Wittering in Sussex, and Holkham in Norfolk. And I stumbled across a wonderful, wide, prehistoric-looking beach on the coast near Hastings last summer, from where we could barely see any other signs of human existence. It's hard to find, so the only other visitors were nudists working on all-over tans. Sometimes following your nose, or a friend's recommendation, can be as valuable a guide as any awards scheme.

Award schemes

Blue Flag beaches

This scheme, launched in 1985 in France, is run by the **Foundation for Environmental Education (www.fee-international.org)**. The website **www.blueflag.org** lists the 3,100 beaches and marinas with Blue Flags in the 35 participating countries. In 2005, there were 120 beaches and 9 marinas awarded Blue Flag status in the UK (01942 612618, **www.encams.org**).

Seaside Awards

This scheme is also run by **Encams** (01942 612618, **www.seasideawards.org. uk**). Seaside Awards are only given to beaches in the UK and the criteria are slightly less onerous than those of the Blue Flag beaches. One reason these awards were launched, in 1992, was to stop people driving long distances to the limited number of Blue Flag beaches by highlighting the many others that are worth visiting.

The Seaside Awards are divided into "resort" and "rural" categories, with "rural" beaches not expected to provide as many facilities as those near towns. In 2005, awards were given to 336 beaches in England, Wales, Northern Ireland and the Channel Islands. Beaches that have won Seaside Awards in Scotland (there were 40 in 2005) are listed at **www.keepscotlandbeautiful.org**.

Good Beach Guide

The **Marine Conservation Society** (01989 566017, **www.goodbeachguide. co.uk**) has the most stringent water quality tests: in 2005 it recommended 427 British beaches.

Green Coast Awards

The **Keep Wales Tidy** campaign launched these awards in 1999 to recognise beaches in rural areas of Wales that may not have the attractions to win them a Blue Flag or Seaside Award, but nevertheless have clean water and are in a wonderful, unspoilt environment. In 2005, there were 41 such beaches. Call 01646 681949 or visit **www.keepwalestidy.org** for more information. A similar scheme in the Republic of Ireland, run by **An Taisce, the National Trust for Ireland**, made 11 awards in 2005 (**www.cleancoastireland.org**).

Surfers Against Sewage (0845 458 3001, **www.sas.org.uk**) campaigns to clean up Britain's coastal waters.

CHAPTER SIX
Passports, visas, insurance and money

Introduction

Here comes the science," said actress Jennifer Aniston on a
TV shampoo commercial, as she introduced the unglamorous
technical stuff. There aren't any film stars in this chapter I'm
afraid, but this is where we come to the "technical stuff" – applying
for passports and visas, using money abroad, and taking out travel
insurance. It may be dull, but it's important. Mucking up a passport or
visa application can put a swift stop to your travel plans. Not having
safeguards in place for your travel money can spell disaster if your
wallet is stolen, and failing to buy travel insurance can even cost you
your life.

To cheer you up further, I've found out how expensive it can be to
use your mobile phone abroad, and suggested a few ways to reduce
the costs (page 222). After all that, sorting out your pet passport, so
you can take a dog or cat to the continent, will seem like a doddle by
comparison (page 189).

A good friend of mine always shoves her bills and personal
paperwork behind the sofa, as she hates doing her admin so much.
On the rare occasions she gets around to sorting it out, she invariably
finds several cheques she should have paid in months ago. Sorting out
your travel paperwork isn't that thrilling either – but mentally shoving
it behind the sofa is the worst thing you can do. This chapter will
help you get your documents in order so you can enjoy your holiday
without worrying.

It's worth regularly consulting the useful website of the Foreign
& Commonwealth Office, especially the section called Know Before
You Go (0845 850 2829, www.fco.gov.uk/knowbeforeyougo). As well
as country information it has helpful sections on money, health and
insurance, and regularly updated bulletins on subjects such as bird flu
and security issues.

Passports

A scruffy, visa-filled, dog-eared passport – preferably containing a photograph of you sporting an ill-advised mullet/perm – has long been the traveller's badge of honour. Shown to friends on the plane or in the visa queue at some remote embassy, battered passports are a source of pride among the well-travelled, with the more exotic stamps (Sierra Leone, Iraq, any Antarctic research station) scoring you extra points.

But we would be well advised to take more care of our passports these days. The old joke goes that if you look like your passport photo, you're too ill to travel. These days, if you don't look like your passport photo, you won't get a passport in the first place. Also, if you are using a tatty passport, you may not be allowed on to your plane or, if you are, you may be refused entry at your destination.

Radical change is sweeping through the passport office. On 1 April, 2006, the Identity and Passport Service (IPS) was created, combining the old UK Passport Service and working with the Home Office's Immigration and Nationality Directorate. This new body has been formed to issue both passports and ID cards, under the Identity Cards Act 2006.

The IPS has now started to replace all our passports with "e-passports", also known as biometric passports, as part of a drive to tackle illegal immigration and identity fraud. Biometric passports contain a chip that holds facial recognition data – a computerised version of your photograph. That's why IPS insists we provide extremely clear passport photographs, and rejects any that do not meet its strict new criteria.

In a second move to combat fraudulent passport applications, by late 2006 or early 2007 IPS will start to call first-time adult applicants in for an interview before granting them a passport, a scheme known as "Authentication by Interview". To fund these security measures, passport fees rose by as much as 36 per cent in late 2005, and will rise steeply again in October 2006.

In future, especially if ID cards are introduced, everyone aged 16 or over, whether they are applying for a new or a replacement passport, may be interviewed. The same biometric data used in your passport will form the basis of your national identity card. The British government is also considering using fingerpint and iris scans to give passports further security.

You will not be able to apply for an ID card until 2008 òr 2009, but once they start to be issued most people will receive them when they apply for a passport. However, until 1 January, 2010, you will be entitled to decline the option of being issued with an ID card when you apply for your passport. For more information on ID cards see **www.identitycards.gov.uk**.

Whenever you need to obtain or renew a passport, do so well in advance of your trip – allowing a month or more to apply for it is wise, especially if it's your first passport. When it arrives, check the details are letter-perfect. The slightest discrepancy in the spelling of your name, or any other data, will cause problems when you travel. If anything is wrong, tell IPS immediately.

How do I obtain my first adult passport?

Until 2006 you could apply for a first passport by post, but to counteract fraud, theft and immigration crimes, IPS is tightening the rules. So if you are applying for your first adult passport (this includes children reaching the age of 16 and applying for their first adult passport), you are likely to have to attend a face-to-face interview at a passport office. This system is due to be introduced from October 2006; during 2006 the government has been opening a network of 69 centres across the country where these interviews will take place.

To qualify for a British passport you must be a British citizen, a British subject, or fall into another category such as being a British Overseas Territories citizen. Even IPS's website (**www.ips.gov.uk**) does not list every eligible category, so if you are in doubt, contact IPS on 0870 521 0410. If you are an immigrant living in Britain, remember that permission to live in the country does not mean you can obtain a British passport, unless you apply first for naturalisation. Also, you must be 16 or older, and must be in the UK, when you make a passport application. (Applications for under 16s are made by their parents.)

The application form can be downloaded from the IPS website (**www.ips.gov.uk**) or you can collect the form at branches of the Post Office and Worldchoice travel agents which offer the Check & Send service, or you can call (0901 470 0110, 60p/min) to request an application form.

You will need to supply documents that prove your identity and British nationality. These may include your birth or adoption certificate, your certificate of naturalisation or registration, and sometimes your parents' marriage and birth certificates. You'll need originals – photocopies are not acceptable, although you can submit a new certificate, obtained from the Registrar for the district where you were born. The notes that accompany the application form give full details of the evidence you must provide.

First-time applicants, anyone who is applying for a replacement because their passport has been lost or stolen, or anyone whose appearance has changed dramatically (for example, a child who has grown into an adult), will need to have the application form countersigned. This must not be done by a relative, but by a professional person who knows you, such as a teacher, GP, dentist or vicar.

You must also supply two photographs, which must be identical, have been taken within the past month, show your face clearly and straight-on, and fill 65–75 per cent of the frame. Because IPS is now issuing biometric passports, it has tightened the rules on acceptable photographs. For example, sunglasses, hats, busy backgrounds or a scarf that obscures your features are not permitted. Muslim women who wear a headscarf must tie it back around the face so their features are clear. Laughing, looking to one side or peering coquettishly into the lens at an angle are all forbidden.

One of the photographs must be validated, that is, signed on the back by the person who countersigns your application. They should write "I certify that this is a true likeness of (Mr, Mrs, Miss, Ms or other title followed by your full name)", then sign and date it.

You must include the fee with your application. The current fee for new or replacement, 32-page, adult passports is £51, but this will rise to £66 on 5 October, 2006. If you intend to travel a lot you can request a 48-page passport (currently £62.50 but set to rise to £77).

Once you have sent in your application, you will be contacted to arrange your interview at a passport office (expected from October 2006). After that, if there are no problems with your application, your passport will be sent to you by secure delivery.

This sounds complicated. Can someone help me?

IPS has masses of information on its website (**www.ips.gov.uk**) and it also has a helpline (0870 521 0410). For information on fees, call 0800 056 6654.

There is also a "Check & Send" service offered by main Post Offices or branches of Worldchoice travel agencies (to find their locations, see **www.ips.gov.uk**). For a £7 fee, staff check you have filled in the form correctly and included all the right paperwork. Check & Send applications still take two weeks or more. If these agents make a mistake, you can reclaim the £7 fee from them, but not the passport application fee.

Hugh Stacey, head of travel services at the **Post Office**, said the Check & Send service was good for anyone with "form phobia", adding that the tiniest mistake could mean your application is returned. "If you are one millimetre outside the box when filling in the form, for example, it will be sent back to you," he said. "At the Post Office we are very good at checking these things because we do it all day. People might like to moan about us, but we get it right most of the time – our error rates for this are extremely low."

How do I renew an existing passport that's soon to expire?

Renewing your passport is a similar procedure to obtaining a new one, but you will not at this stage need to attend an interview, although this may change in future. You'll need the application form, two photos and the fee, plus you must send in your old passport. You do not need to produce other documents that prove your identity, and you do not need the form or photograph countersigned, as long as you are still recognisable from the photograph in your current passport, and this passport has not been tampered with.

Your old passport will normally be sent back to you, though damaged passports are destroyed, but it will have been cancelled (the corners are cut off the cover) so any existing visas in it may also be cancelled. However, I found that my US visa in my old passport remains valid – I have to produce the expired passport with the current US visa in it, along with my new passport, when I travel to the USA. But not all countries will accept this arrangement so check with the embassy of the country you plan to visit.

How do I obtain a passport for my child?

If your child was included on an adult passport issued before 5 October, 1998, they can continue to travel on this passport until they reach 16, or the passport expires. However, they must always travel with the adult in whose passport they appear, and it is not possible for a child to travel to the USA on their parent's passport any more. When visiting America, every family member must have a machine-readable passport of their own (for an explanation of "machine-readable", see page 183). If a child is included on his or her parent's passport, he or she will have to obtain a visa for the USA – in which case, it's probably simpler to obtain a separate passport for the child.

Children's passports last for five years, and can be renewed for five years, until the child reaches 16 and can apply for the adult 10-year passport (at which point they will have to attend an interview). Parents must supply suitable documentation, such as the child's birth certificate (full details are on the website **www.ips.gov.uk** and will be sent to you with the application form) and the fee, which is £34, rising to £45 in October 2006.

The trickiest thing can be obtaining two suitable photographs of a baby.

Parents or toys must not be visible, and the child's full face must be shown, which has caused parents endless trouble in photo booths. One tip is to put a white towel over his or her car seat and photograph the baby against that. If it is too fiddly you may have to pay a professional photographer to take suitable photos for you.

The rules about photographs of young children have prompted so many protests from parents who have had trouble getting their babies to "pose" correctly that in early 2006 the rules were relaxed a little. Now photographs of children aged five and under will be accepted "with their mouths open or eyes looking away from the camera... as long as the photo is of a good quality it should meet our simplified procedures for children". School photographs are not permitted.

An increasingly common situation these days is for children to have a different surname from one of their parents, perhaps because the parents are not married, or because the wife has chosen to retain her maiden name. My colleague at *The Times*, literary editor Erica Wagner, had difficulties because of this when visiting America with her son, Theo, who bears her husband's surname. At US immigration she was questioned for some time because she was unable to prove that she was Theo's mother. The advice from the US Embassy, when I put this dilemma to them, was that in this situation the parent should carry the child's "long form" birth certificate (which has both parents' names on it), to prove that mother and child are related.

If your child has been included on your passport and the child is now applying for their own passport – perhaps because they have reached 16, or you are planning to visit the USA – you will need to submit your passport along with the child's application, so the child's details can be removed from your passport. There is no fee for the deletion service.

Does my passport need to be valid for six months beyond the date of my return journey?

The rules vary from country to country. However, within the EU, things are simple: your passport must be valid long enough to cover your entire trip, but there is no need for it to remain valid after that. So even if your passport expires on 15 July and you wish to travel home on 15 July, you will be covered – although it is unwise to leave things quite so late, in case you are delayed and end up returning on 16 July.

Elsewhere some countries insist that your passport remains valid for three or six months beyond the date of your return journey. Travel agents and tour operators often insist on this as a result. Check with the embassy of the relevant country before you travel.

Many *Times* readers have complained that their 10-year passports effectively become nine-and-a-few-months passports because we are being urged to renew them in plenty of time to ensure continuing cover. IPS has now acknowledged this by granting a credit up to the nearest whole month (to a maximum of nine months) in your new passport.

I'm only going to France for the day on Eurostar and I've forgotten my passport. Can I travel?

If you are British, you cannot travel anywhere overseas without a passport, as it is currently the only document that proves both your nationality and your identity. But once the UK's ID cards start to be issued in about 2009, anyone carrying one of those will be able to use it as a travel document within the EU.

Carriers such as Eurostar, the airlines or ferries can be made responsible for the cost of repatriating anyone who is not allowed into the destination country, and they can be fined.

I need a passport in a hurry. What do I do?

You can use the one-week, Fast Track Service. It currently costs £77.50 for an adult passport (£87 for the 48-page passport) and £70 for a child passport. These figures will rise to £91/£97/£80 respectively in October 2006. You must make an appointment to visit one of the seven main passport offices to make the application in person, and you must make a separate appointment for each person, though appointments for different family members will usually be scheduled next to each other if you request this. Call the advice line, 0870 521 0410, to book a slot at the office nearest to you: Belfast, Durham, Glasgow, Liverpool, London, Newport or Peterborough.

Once you're there, you will need the completed and countersigned application form, two photographs and your birth certificate, plus any other documents needed to prove your British nationality and identity. The passport will be returned to you by secure delivery within a week. Note that once the system of interviews starts, this service will no longer be available for first-time adult applicants.

One week?! I'm at the airport now! Is there a faster service?

There is a faster service, but it cannot help in every case. IPS offers a Premium, same-day service, currently costing £96.50 (adult), £83 (child) and due to rise to £108/£93. This service is only available if you wish to renew, extend or amend your existing passport – it is not available if your passport has been mislaid or stolen, or it is your first application. Thus if you reach the airport and find your passport has expired, you can use this service, but if you reach the airport and find that your passport has been lost or stolen, you cannot.

The chances of booking and attending the appointment, collecting the passport (you should expect a four-hour wait after you have handed in the application) and hoofing it back to the airport for a flight later the same day will require superhuman stamina and considerable luck. But this service may well enable you to travel in the next day or two, so here's the drill: call 0870 521 0410 and ask for an appointment for the same-day, Premium service. It is not available on Sundays.

Hurry to the passport office and hand over the application form, two photographs and fee. If your out-of-date passport has children on it, they will need separate, new passports too (and the photos, etc, to apply for them) and the whole rigmarole will take even longer.

You should be able to leave with your replacement passport later that day.

I'm desperate. I cannot get an immediate appointment. Can I just turn up at a passport office and hope for the best?

No. You must have an appointment.

What happens if I lose my passport, or it is stolen, while I'm at home?

If you have lost your passport, or had it stolen, while in the UK, you must first report it as lost/stolen so it can be cancelled and not used by fraudsters. To do this, fill in form LS01, available through the website **www.ips.gov.uk**, from some Post Offices, police stations and Worldchoice travel agents.

Then you must apply for a replacement passport. See above (page 176) for how to do this.

What happens if I lose my passport while on holiday?

You should both report the loss, and apply for a replacement passport – and you will need to do this quickly so you can continue your holiday, and return home easily.

Report the loss at the local police station – the report they give you will help you obtain your replacement passport, and claim on your travel insurance. Occasionally, if you are somewhere remote, this won't be possible.

Next, go to the nearest British Consulate, Embassy or High Commission to obtain a replacement passport. To find out the address of your nearest embassy, visit the Foreign & Commonwealth Office's website (**www.fco.gov. uk**), or call them on +44 870 606 0290. You will be charged £69 for the new passport (or the equivalent in local currency). A child's passport issued abroad costs £45. These fees may rise in autumn 2006.

If your flight leaves soon, you may be given an emergency passport, which is only valid for the flight home and currently costs £43.50. If there is more time, the embassy will issue a proper replacement passport.

I travel a great deal – can I hold two passports?

Normally, no, but frequent business travellers are allowed to hold two passports at the same time, although IPS does not like to publicise this. I have two, because my job as travel editor of *The Times* means I travel frequently, and may need to pop over to Europe on one passport while the other is with an embassy awaiting a visa. To obtain a second passport, you will need a letter from your boss explaining why you need it, as well as the usual application bits and pieces, and you have to send your first passport in at the same time with a covering letter. Call IPS to check before you apply (0870 521 0410). There is no guarantee that it will be granted.

I want a passport in my married name in time for our honeymoon. How do I obtain one?

You must surrender your existing passport in your maiden name, and apply for a new one in your married name, up to three months before your wedding. The new passport only becomes valid on the day of the wedding, which means you will not be able to travel abroad between surrendering the old passport and getting married. As well as the normal passport application you must submit form PD2, available on **www.ips.gov.uk** and from some Post Offices and Worldchoice travel agents, part of which must be filled in by the person conducting your wedding.

Check the visa requirements of your honeymoon destination. If you need a visa, the country concerned may not be willing to put it into the post-dated passport in your married name – so ask their embassy before embarking on this procedure.

If you wait until after the wedding to change your name, you can obtain a new passport in your married name by sending in your marriage certificate with the application.

Can travel insurance help me with passport-related problems?

It depends on what has happened. If you get to the airport, discover your passport has expired and then have to make expensive last minute re-arrangements to your plans, your policy is unlikely to cover you. However, if your passport is lost or stolen while you are on holiday, most travel insurance policies will cover you for the expenses incurred in obtaining a replacement, up to a limit. If you lose your passport or it is stolen while you are at home, your house contents insurance policy may cover you.

What is a machine-readable passport?

Burgundy, machine-readable passports started being issued in 1988 to replace the hard-backed, larger, blue passports that had been the norm since 1972 (now known as "old blues"). Today, almost every British passport is machine-readable. If you want to check that yours is, open your passport to the laminated page that contains your photograph and other personal details. There are two lines of text and chevrons (the <<< marks) along the bottom: this means it is machine-readable.

In 1998 the UK Passport Agency started to make other changes to machine-readable passports to make them more secure. The most obvious of these is that the page of personal information has been moved from the inside back cover to the last page; your signature, digitally scanned in, has been added; and the photograph, instead of being stuck in with glue, is now digitally scanned in too.

What is a biometric passport? Do I need one?

Biometric passports, also known as e-passports, started to be phased in from March 2006. Anyone applying for a new passport, or replacing an existing passport, will now be given a biometric one, so by about 2016 every passport holder in the country should have one. These passports include a biometric chip that uses facial recognition data from your photograph, and biographical data, to confirm your identity. Fingerprint scans are expected to be added from 2008.

The introduction of biometric passports is part of a government crackdown on identity theft and fraud. Until 2006, about 90 per cent of passport applications were made by post or through the Check & Send service, but the big change coming in from 2006 is that, if you are applying for your first adult passport, you will no longer be able to do this by post alone. Instead, as explained above, you will have to attend an interview at a passport office to establish your identity to IPS officials. An IPS spokeswoman said: "As long as it remains possible for passport applications to be processed by post, criminals will attempt to obtain passports in false or stolen identities."

She said that 75 per cent of fraudulent applications that are spotted come from the first-time adult applicant category, which is why this category of applicants is the first to be called for compulsory interviews. In 2004 the Passport Service picked up some 1,500 attempted fraudulent postal passport applications. The spokeswoman added that the new system "should be straightforward for the great majority of cases where the applicants really are who they claim to be".

The new system will mean IPS must undertake an extra 600,000 face-to-face interviews each year, which is why it needs the network of 69 new offices. The aim is that 99 per cent of people will have a passport office within 40 miles of their home. IPS is also looking into adding mobile facilities or peripatetic staff to help applicants who live in remote areas.

The downside for travellers is that applications will take longer and passport costs have risen dramatically to fund the new scheme.

Visas

In my backpacking days, going to the embassy to collect a visa for the next country on my route was a sociable business. You could generally reckon on finding a group of fellow travellers in the queue, and as it was likely they would be crossing the border around the same time as you, chances were you would all meet up again in a café at the next town along.

I still have my "old blue", the hardbacked passport I carried around Asia for many months in the early 1990s, its purple, blue, red and green visa stamps blending into each other following an unfortunate episode in a Vietnamese laundry. But I can still read them and recall the stories behind them: how in 1992, before boarding the Trans-Siberian express in Beijing, I had to obtain visas for Mongolia, Russia and Poland in an embassy merry-go-round that took on the air of a French farce, and how in Vietnam you had to register with the police in every town you visited as a condition of your visa.

Visa rules have changed in many of these countries – Britons no longer need a visa for Poland, for example – but British passport holders do need visas for many countries and usually you must obtain them before you travel. Visa requirements may depend on the category of British nationality you hold; some countries allow British citizens to visit without a visa, but require one for categories such as British subjects, British Overseas Territories citizens, British Overseas citizens or British protected persons.

Some embassies are reasonably efficient at issuing visas on the spot, or allow you to obtain the visa by post. Australia even allows you to complete the entire process online (**www.eta.immi.gov.au**) and charges a modest A$20 (about £8). And I would argue that the Indian High Commission (**www.hcilondon.net**) in London is pretty efficient too, if you are prepared to collect your visa in person. Although at peak times (in winter) you may have to wait a couple of hours, the queue moves fast, the system is well run and there are many counters (and, importantly, lavatories!) inside.

But for other countries it can be a different story. Russia is one the visa experts often cite as troublesome – particularly because most visitors want to travel there in summer, when it is warm. "You usually have to wait many hours," said Shawn Hefner, director of agency The Visa Service. "In summer 2004, we sent staff, on a shift basis, to queue from noon on Sunday overnight to be sure of getting the visas on Monday morning." China is increasingly popular with British visitors, and recently stopped postal applications. Visa applicants must now go to the embassy in person, or use their tour operator or a visa service.

Some countries, such as Egypt and Kenya, will issue visas either on arrival or in advance. If you opt for getting a visa on arrival, you may find yourself queueing at the airport after a long flight. If you are travelling with a group, it helps that everyone does the same thing, so the rest of the party is not kept waiting in the transfer bus while one person holds them up by queueing for their visa.

Many popular tourist destinations, such as Thailand, allow you to stay for a month or so without a visa (British citizens can stay 30 days visa-free, in Thailand's case). Some, such as Turkey, simply see arrival formalities as a revenue-gathering exercise, rather than a check on who is coming into the country – Turkey requires you to cough up £10 in sterling as you arrive.

If you want help obtaining a visa, ask your travel agent or tour operator if they offer this service. Many do, for a fee, especially for more popular tourist destinations. For example, Trailfinders has a service for the 20 or so most popular destinations that require visas, and will obtain a visa for you (for a fee) even if you have not booked your trip with them.

If you have booked through a tour operator it should be able to obtain the relevant visa for you – it may even be included in the cost of the holiday. In 2004 I visited Ukraine with Regent Holidays, which specialises in taking people to communist or former communist countries, and is experienced in obtaining visas for those destinations. It can even, given a fine day and a following wind, get you a visa for North Korea, one of the world's most esoteric destinations.

Even if you hold the correct visa, the authorities do not have to admit you. It is sensible to be prepared to prove that you do not intend to remain in the country after your visa expires. For example, you may need to show your return plane ticket, or proof of sufficient funds to support yourself, to satisfy the authorities.

Contacts

There are many commercial visa services that will sort out the visa for you, for an extra fee. They often offer a one- or two-day service if you are in a hurry.

Gold Arrow, 0870 165 7412, **www.goldarrow.info**

Thames Consular, 020 7494 4957, 020 8995 2492, **www.thamesconsular.com**

Trailfinders, 0845 058 5858, **www.trailfinders.com**

Travcour, 020 7223 5295, **www.travcour.com**

Visa Express, 0906 160 8472, premium rate, **www.visaexpress.co.uk**

The Visa Service, 0870 890 0185, **www.visaservice.co.uk**

Tips for obtaining a visa

• Find out your destination's high tourist season, and assume visa applications will take longer then, especially postal ones, which often have lower priority than personal applications.

• Check how long the visa will be valid for. If you apply too far in advance, it may be out of date before you arrive.

• Find out if visas are date-specific. With a Russian tourist visa, for example, you must enter and leave the country on exactly the dates you specify.

• Do not leave the application too late and try to sort out a visa on arrival. Turning up in a country without the necessary visa will almost certainly get you sent straight home.

• Do not buy a last-minute holiday without thinking about the visa situation. This is particularly important with India: you need a visa for that bargain winter-sun break to Goa.

• Carefully check the visa before leaving the embassy and get any mistakes rectified immediately.

• If you have an Israeli stamp in your passport it may cause trouble when visiting or applying for a visa to some Arab countries. If you go to Israel, ask them to stamp a piece of paper that is kept with your passport, instead of stamping the passport itself.

• If you are visiting an embassy to apply for a visa in person, get there early – some embassies, such as Russia and India, are famous for their long queues.

• Remember you are effectively on foreign soil in an embassy. Getting shirty with staff will not help – they have the right to refuse you a visa.

• You may have to return a few days later to collect the visa. This could mean two expensive trips to London. Consider whether applying by post, or using a visa agency, will be less hassle and cheaper.

• Check the public holidays of the country in question. The embassy is likely to be closed, even if it is not a public holiday in Britain.

• Ensure you have at least two blank pages in your passport – one for the visa, one for entry/exit stamps.

Visiting the USA

There has been a great deal of confusion about the rules for visiting the United States of America since the terrorist attacks of September 11, 2001, caused the US authorities to tighten up their immigration procedures. It is important to understand that most British holidaymakers do not need a visa, but you must have a machine-readable passport (*see* page 183), and you must not have any criminal convictions (including driving offences). If you have a criminal record, you will need to apply for a visa. (For information on applying for a US visa, see below.)

From October 2006, the rules will change. If your British passport is issued after 26 October, 2006, it must be a biometric passport to satisfy the US authorities; if not you will need to obtain a visa. However, as we've already seen, IPS intends to be issuing all new British passport applicants with biometric passports by this date, so this should not pose a problem. For further details, visit the US Department of Homeland Security's website at **www.dhs.gov/dhspublic/interapp/content_multi_image/content_multi_image_0021.xml**.

If you need a visa for the USA (and many travellers, such as certain businesspeople and journalists, do), you must attend a personal interview during which your iris and fingerprints are scanned. First you must book an appointment on 0905 544 4546 (talk fast, it costs £1.30 a minute) and ask to be sent a paying in slip. Take this to a bank to pay the US$100 (approx £60) fee, download an application form from the website **www.usembassy.org.uk** and take that, with your paying-in receipt and a photograph, to your interview. Turn up early and bring a good book.

If you are applying at the US Embassy in London, where I obtained my journalist's visa, there's likely to be a long queue outside, but once through the door, you'll find seats, a coffee bar and lavatories. You will also have to pay a further £10 when you arrive at the embassy to have your passport couriered back to you.

Everyone entering the USA, whether holding a visa or not, will have to go through stringent immigration checks. These now include having your two index fingers scanned, and having a digital photograph taken. These procedures may be repeated when you leave the USA, too, so be prepared for them. Immigration officers are likely to ask you the purpose of your stay, and it's inadvisable to make jokes or give bad-tempered answers, however long you have been queueing. For more details of these procedures, go to **www.dhs.gov/us-visit**.

Since March 2006, the US authorities have required every visitor to supply full details of their first night's accommodation in America, including the post code (which Americans call the zip code), before they can be admitted to the country. It is not enough to put down "Holiday Inn, Orlando" on your form – you will need the exact address. The request forms part of the Advanced Passenger Information (API) system that now applies to all travellers entering the USA. As well as the accommodation information, you must supply personal details such as passport information, full name and nationality.

Many airlines that fly to the USA are now asking passengers to do this in advance, by logging on to the airline's website, to save time at the airport. The API is then sent to the US authorities and checked against various databases.

When you leave America after your trip, you must ensure that immigration staff collect your form I-94 or I-94W that you will have filled in when you entered the country, or you must drop it in the special postboxes at the airport. It should have been stapled into your passport when you arrived. Handing it in on departure ensures your exit from the US is logged, so that if you return, officials do not assume you have illegally overstayed your previous visit.

If for any reason you find you still have the form once you're back home, fill in your departure details and post it, with a covering letter and evidence of your departure (such as your boarding card), to ACS-USCIS, SBU, PO Box 7125, London, Kentucky, KY 40742-7125, USA. Keep a photocopy of your letter and bring it with you next time you visit the USA as proof of what happened. For further information, visit the website **www.usembassy.org. uk/dhs/cbp/i94.html**.

Taking your pet abroad

Since the Pet Travel Scheme (PETS) was introduced in 2000, taking pets in and out of the country has become easier, though there are still important safeguards and restrictions in place. The main impetus behind the scheme was to end the need for every animal to spend six months in quarantine when coming in to the UK, a measure intended to prevent diseases, especially rabies, entering the country. So far 300,000 pets have joined the scheme, according to the Department for Environment, Food and Rural Affairs (Defra), which runs it.

Where can I take my pet under the scheme?

PETS now covers more than 80 countries, including those in the EU, Australia, New Zealand, Japan, various Caribbean islands, Russia, the USA and Canada. For a full list, check the **Defra** website (**www.defra.gov.uk**); click on Pet Travel Scheme on the homepage and go to Factsheet 1. There are no restrictions on pets travelling directly between the UK and the Republic of Ireland.

What preparations must I make before taking my pet abroad?

If you are planning to travel with a dog, cat or ferret – these are treated the same under the scheme – you must first get your pet microchipped, and then, once it is three months old or more, have it vaccinated against rabies. After 30 days it must have a blood test to prove the vaccine has worked. Animals cannot travel until six months from the date of the blood test (so long as it comes back negative, of course).

These procedures must be carried out by a vet who is a local veterinary inspector (most are), and carried out in the correct order. After microchipping, vaccination and blood testing, the LVI can issue your Pet Passport and then you are free to travel with your animal.

At the end of your holiday you must have your pet treated against ticks and tapeworm, visiting a vet to have this treatment carried out no less than 24 hours, and no more than 48 hours, before you travel. Without it your pet will be refused boarding, or will be placed in quarantine.

Transport providers such as Brittany Ferries or groups such as Dogs Away and Passports for Pets have lists of vets in Europe where you can get the tick and tapeworm treatment (contact details below). Colin Silver, founder of Dogs Away, told me he is able to book vets across much of Europe who can carry out this treatment.

Contact the vet in advance to check they will be open when you need to visit, and can carry out this procedure and give you the correct paperwork. If you don't follow the instructions to the letter your pet could be refused carriage or will have to spend six months in quarantine.

Can I travel with other animals?

For rabbits and rodents there is either unrestricted movement, or quarantine – but no pet passport scheme. For details of this, and the rules for transporting other animals and birds, see **www.defra.gov.uk**.

Which routes and transport companies can I use?

The Defra website lists the many cross-channel ferry companies and airlines and the approved routes on which you can transport your pet into and out of the UK – though it is always wise to check with the transport provider when you book. Pets can also travel to France on Eurotunnel, but not on Eurostar (with the exception of guide dogs).

If you are flying in from a country in the scheme, such as Australia, and your flight stops *en route*, you must touch down in another country that is part of the scheme, such as Singapore or the United Arab Emirates, or your pet will have to be quarantined on arrival. Your airline should be able to answer queries on this.

Contacts

Pet Travel Scheme, 0870 241 1710, **www.defra.gov.uk**.

Passports for Pets (020 7589 6404, **http://freespace.virgin.net/ passports.forpets/**) offers advice, such as lists of vets on the continent, as does **Dogs Away** (020 8441 9311, **www.dogsaway.co.uk**), which also offers a vet booking service (£27 in France, £30 elsewhere in Europe).

Also see **Pet Planet (www.petplanet.co.uk)**, or ask your local vet for advice.

The European Health Insurance Card

It sounds like a great deal – a plastic card that entitles you to free hospital treatment overseas. Certainly, everyone should apply for and carry the European Health Insurance Card (EHIC) when they travel within Europe. But it is not valid everywhere, and it is no replacement for travel insurance.

Since January 2006, the EHIC, a plastic card the same size as a credit card, has replaced form E111 as our passport to obtaining reduced-cost, and sometimes free, medical treatment in most European countries. The E111 form, a sheet of A4 paper that you had stamped at the Post Office and had to carry around with you, and which rapidly disintegrated at the bottom of your bag, has now been phased out.

Yet many of us continue to travel without an EHIC, although it could potentially save us thousands of pounds if we fall ill abroad. In 2005, research by the Department of Health, which runs the EHIC scheme, found a shockingly low level of understanding about the system. Its survey found that 35 per cent of UK residents have travelled to Europe without either a valid E111 or travel insurance, potentially leaving them open to huge medical bills. And insurers tell me that the "short-break generation", younger travellers who take advantage of the abundant budget flights to "new" European destinations, often fall into this category, assuming that they'll be covered somehow "because it's just a weekend away, in Europe".

They are wrong. You need both insurance and the EHIC to ensure that you are fully protected for medical emergencies when you travel, as they complement each other.

Carrying an EHIC proves that, if you have a medical emergency on the continent, you are entitled to treatment in that country's state hospitals and surgeries. You'll be treated on the same basis as local people are. For a list of countries where the EHIC is accepted, see page 192. The EHIC also covers routine treatment that you may need if you are pregnant, or have a chronic disease or pre-existing illness (unless you go abroad specifically for treatment, in which case the EHIC does not cover you, and you should take your doctor's advice before travelling).

Where is the EHIC valid?

Austria, Belgium, Cyprus (but not north Cyprus), Czech Republic, Denmark, Estonia, Finland, France, Germany, Greece, Hungary, Iceland, Ireland, Italy, Latvia, Liechtenstein, Lithuania, Luxembourg, Malta, Netherlands, Norway, Poland, Portugal, Slovakia, Slovenia, Spain, Sweden, Switzerland

It's easy to obtain the EHIC. Collect an application form from the Post Office, by phoning 0845 606 2030, or by visiting **www.ehic.org.uk**. When you fill in the form, you will need either your National Health number or your National Insurance number. If you have questions about your application, call the EHIC helpline on 0845 605 0707, or write to EHIC Enquiries, PO Box 1114, Newcastle upon Tyne NE99 2TL. There's also lots of information on the website.

Unlike form E111, which was stamped while you waited at the Post Office and so could be picked up in a hurry, the EHIC is posted to you after a couple of weeks, so you should apply for it well before you are due to travel. Children cannot be included on an adult's card, so parents should apply for a card for each child, too.

If you are taken ill or involved in an accident, you must show the card to access medical treatment from the local equivalent of the NHS. You may be charged for items such as prescriptions, X-rays and dental care. If so, keep your receipts: in some countries you can reclaim part or all of these costs. Consult the booklet *Health Advice for Travellers*, available from Post Offices and sent to you with your card, which tells you how much you can reclaim in each country. In some cases you must apply for a refund while you are still abroad.

Using the EHIC is often speedier than referring everything to your travel insurer back home, especially in places where it is familiar to doctors, such as the popular Spanish resorts. And if the treatment you need is only minor, it may simply be less hassle to use the EHIC than to involve your insurer – plus doing that will save you paying the excess on your insurance policy.

However, there is one cost that the EHIC *never* covers: repatriation to the UK. Being flown home can cost you thousands of pounds, depending on the nature of your illness or injury. The EHIC will also not cover your bills if you are collected in a private ambulance or taken to a private hospital or clinic for treatment. Yet if you have been involved in an accident you are hardly likely to turn the ambulance away because it is a private one, are you?

These are good reasons why you need travel insurance as well as the EHIC.

A good travel insurance policy will cover the private medical care bills, the cost of repatriation, and other incidentals such as the cost of accommodating a relative in a nearby hotel while you are being treated. Skiers should pay particular attention to insurance, because injured skiers may need pricey helicopter rescue or repatriation, and are often first taken to a private clinic, none of which is covered by the EHIC.

If travel insurance is so marvellous, you may be asking, why bother applying for the EHIC in the first place? Well, you need both, because some travel insurers now insist that you carry the EHIC. Sometimes, if you have an EHIC, the travel insurer will waive the excess on your policy when you make a claim, as it can reclaim some of its costs. Plus, the EHIC will cover you for pre-existing medical conditions, whereas travel insurance usually will not cover you for these.

Checklist for action

- Apply for the EHIC.

- Carry it with you at all times.

- Pack the booklet *Health Advice for Travellers.*

- Keep receipts if you have to pay for treatment.

- Ensure you have travel insurance.

- Tell others in your party the details of your travel insurance policy.

- Ask your holiday rep for help dealing with local medical authorities.

Further information

- The booklet *Health Advice for Travellers* is sent to you with your EHIC, and is also available from Post Offices. The information it contains is available on the Department of Health website **www. dh.gov.uk/travellers**. Take the booklet with you when you travel.

- There is also useful information on the EHIC and other preparations for travelling on the government website **www.direct.gov.uk**.

- If you need advice on using the card while you are abroad, you can call +44 20 7210 4850, Monday to Friday, 9am to 5pm UK time.

- If you have questions about obtaining the card, or you lose it and need a replacement, call 0845 605 0707.

Travel insurance

A group of British travellers was on a Land Rover safari in Namibia when the vehicle overturned and caught fire. Everyone was injured and the nearest, very basic medical centre was three hours' drive away.

One traveller, who had 30 per cent burns, was flown out by helicopter under his travel insurance policy, thanks to the quick response of his parents and the insurers. He made a full recovery. Another, who had 40 per cent burns, had allowed his insurance policy to lapse the week before, and despite the best efforts of local doctors and British Embassy officials he died of his injuries. Even worse, his family had to borrow thousands of pounds to cover the cost of repatriating his body.

It's one of many horror stories that British embassies and consulates hear of each year and which could have been avoided had the traveller been covered by insurance. I realise insurance is one of the most boring things we ever buy – especially when compared with the exciting purchase of a dream holiday. It's like writing a will – it feels like tempting fate to think that anything will go wrong. And an astonishing 25 per cent of travellers still leave home without any insurance, according to the British Insurance Brokers' Association. But while you'll survive losing your luggage or facing a delay at the airport without travel insurance, you genuinely may not survive a major medical emergency abroad without insurance. It's a vital purchase.

Where do I start?

As well as the guidance in this chapter, there are several free sources of information. The **Association of British Insurers** has a guide to what insurance should cover you for on its website (**www.abi.org.uk** and click on Information Zone), as does the **British Insurance Brokers' Association** (**www.biba.org.uk**).

Once you have an idea of the level of cover you need, shop around, either by using a traditional broker (you can find one through Biba, for example), or by consulting some of the online comparison sites – **www.insuresupermarket. com** and **www.find.co.uk/insurance** are good starting points, while **www.gapyear.com/travelinsurance** has a more limited selection of providers whose policies are aimed at backpackers making long overseas trips.

Online insurers tend to offer the cheapest policies – but they also tend to offer one-size-fits-all policies, with the insurers trying to minimise the risks they take on, so these companies may not suit you if you have a pre-existing medical condition, or plan to undertake dangerous sports, for example. In these cases, you're better off using a specialist travel insurer or a broker.

Before you buy a policy, read the small print and make sure you understand exactly what you are covered for, and what is not covered – for example, if you have a pre-existing medical condition, or are planning an activity such as scuba diving, you must be sure you are covered as these situations may be excluded from a standard policy.

Be wary if your travel agent offers to sell you insurance when you buy your holiday. Although travel agents sell large numbers of policies, sometimes they are overpriced and you may find a better deal by shopping around. And it's vital to check these off-the-peg policies cover you for everything you may do – such as skiing or bungee jumping. It is not a condition of buying a holiday that you must buy the insurance offered by a travel agency, but travel agents and tour operators are entitled to insist that you have insurance. Buying insurance from your travel agent is far better than not having any at all.

Remember that you generally have to pay an **excess** (such as the first £50–£100) on any claim: insurers say this brings down the cost of your insurance and deters frivolous claims. You may have to pay an excess on every part of the policy that you claim on – so if, for example, you claim for both medical expenses and loss of luggage, you may have to pay the excess on both sections. If the excess is high, you can sometimes offer to pay a higher premium to reduce it, at the time you buy your policy. Using a broker can bring down the amount of excess you must pay (*see* below, page 209). As a general rule, the cheapest insurance policies have the highest excesses.

Finally, ensure you have arranged travel insurance cover for the entire period of your trip abroad before you leave home. Insurers do not generally allow you to extend the cover from abroad, although some gap-year insurers are an exception to this.

In this chapter I cannot tell you which policy to buy or which company to use. Everyone's circumstances are different, so making specific recommendations would not only be difficult, but irresponsible. In this chapter (and in the Directory, chapter 11) I mention a range of insurance companies, but that does not mean their policies are necessarily perfect for you. The market is so large that you may come across an insurer I have not mentioned that offers the right policy for you. Use this information as a guide, then shop around for the best deal.

What your policy should cover

Cancellation or curtailment

It's important to ensure that your holiday is protected if you need to cancel before you travel – for example because you or a close relative falls ill, or you are summoned to do jury service, or you lose your job. The cancellation section of your policy should kick in on the day you buy the holiday.

Typically your policy should cover you for up to £3,000–£5,000 if your trip has to be cancelled before you travel. If your holiday costs more than the amount specified in the policy, ask your insurer if this limit can be raised, or choose another policy with a higher limit.

If your trip has to be curtailed – for example, you have to return home early because of an emergency such as bereavement or a fire or burglary at your home – check your policy will compensate you for the part of the trip that you missed. Again, typical limits are in the £3,000–£5,000 range. Your policy should also cover you for the additional travelling expenses you incur by travelling home early, such as paying for a different flight to the one you had booked (albeit in economy).

Medical expenses

This is the most important part of your policy, as the costs of medical treatment or flying you home on a specially chartered plane can run into many thousands of pounds. If you are uninsured, these costs could potentially bankrupt you or force you to sell your home.

It's wise to look for a policy that offers at least £2 million of medical cover for trips to Europe, and at least £5 million in the USA and the rest of the world. Policies should include the provision of an air ambulance to fly you home, if appropriate. (If you have no cover, this alone can cost in the region of £15,000 from Spain and £35,000 from the USA.) However, just because you are abroad does not mean you will automatically be brought home if you fall ill or have an accident – it will depend on the nature of your illness and where you are when you fall ill. The doctors may decide it is best for you to stay in the overseas hospital until you are well enough to come home on a normal flight.

Some travel insurance policies offer **medical inconvenience benefit**: a sum (typically £20 per day) paid for each day you are in hospital overseas to cover incidental expenses.

If you have a **medical condition**, it is crucial that you tell your insurer about this when buying the policy. It may mean a higher premium is charged, but failing to declare it could invalidate your policy.

While some policies will exclude pre-existing medical conditions, many conditions, such as diabetes and asthma, will be acceptable to mainstream insurers, if you tell them in advance. You should also inform your insurer if you develop a condition after you buy the policy. You are unlikely to cover pre-existing medical needs by buying a cheap off-the-peg policy: this may be a good time to use a broker.

Failing to notify an insurer of a pre-existing condition is crazy, said Hugh Stacey of the **Post Office**. "It's the most stupid thing you will ever do. The first thing that the insurance underwriter does is to look at your medical history from your GP. You should also tell your insurer if your circumstances change after you have bought the policy."

Some insurers and brokers specialise in this area. The broker NW Brown offers a **Freedom Insure** policy aimed at travellers with pre-existing conditions, including HIV and leukaemia. Unless your doctor has forbidden you to travel, Freedom's MD, Terry Green, tells me he reckons he can get travel insurance for most conditions, including terminal illnesses in some circumstances. Broker J&M Insurance offers the **Travelbility** insurance policy, also for those with pre-existing medical conditions, such as wheelchair users, and their carers.

And Chris Jordan of **Orbis Insurance Services**, which specialises in policies for people with "impaired lives", tells me he can find cover for most conditions, unless they are immediately life threatening. "Cancers, for example – people can live for many years with cancer, and we're talking about a short holiday." He can also cover people suffering from depression, who are often rejected by mainstream insurers, and can organise travel insurance for people with pre-existing medical conditions who are going to the USA, where medical bills can be high – though premiums can be high too.

Other insurers worth contacting if you have a pre-existing condition are **Free Spirit** and **MediCover** (contact details are in the Directory, chapter 11).

Another option, if you have a medical condition that is stopping you obtaining insurance through a mainstream insurer or broker, is to contact the national organisation or charity associated with your condition. They should be able to recommend specialist insurers that may be able to offer you cover. Note that all travel insurance policies are aimed firmly at holidaymakers – they will not cover you if you are travelling abroad to seek medical treatment.

As pre-existing medical conditions are more common the older we get, insurance policies aimed at **older travellers** are often helpful here. **Help the Aged, Age Concern** and **Saga** all offer policies with no upper age limit. A spokesman for Age Concern summed up these organisations' approach. He said: "You will be asked about pre-existing medical conditions, and applications will be dealt with on a case-by-case basis. Some people are referred to a medical screening line. Cover will usually be granted, but there may be exclusions, conditions or excesses."

Orbis Insurance Services will insure elderly people aged "up to 99" – it recently insured an 88-year-old to go skiing – and it offers cover for trips of up to a year, though not multi-trip annual policies, to elderly customers, all subject to medical screening. Other insurers that offer cover to older travellers include **American Express, Churchill**, the **Post Office, RIAS** (which covers only the over-50s) and **Marks & Spencer**.

Many mainstream insurers will sell single-trip policies to older travellers, but will not sell them annual travel insurance policies. **Nationwide**, however, launched an annual policy for the 65–80 age group in late 2005, although it is limited to trips within Europe. For more information on annual policies, *see* below (page 204).

If you are travelling in Europe, carry your European Health Insurance Card (EHIC); as explained above (page 193), it works in conjunction with travel insurance.

Loss or theft of possessions and money

Travel insurance policies should cover you for at least £1,500 for loss of baggage and belongings on holidays. Within the luggage cover, policies will specify a limit for valuables – such as £500 total with no item worth more than £300, for example. You're likely to receive a payment that takes into account wear and tear.

Some travel insurance policies offer higher levels of cover for valuables. In 2005 the **Post Office** introduced "extended baggage cover", allowing customers to opt for a single-article limit of £1,000 by paying an extra premium. Hugh Stacey, head of travel services at the Post Office, said the policy was introduced in response to research which showed 25 million of us now regularly travel with high-value toys such as DVD players, laptops and iPods. Another policy that offers more generous cover is **Worldwide Travel Insurance**'s Elite policy, which covers up to £450 of valuables and £2,500 of possessions; the single-item limit is £350.

It's always worth checking to see if you will get better cover for your possessions under the "all risks" section of your **house contents insurance** policy: this may grant you a higher level of cover for each item when taken abroad, and may offer "new for old" cover. If you are covered in this way, you may be able to pay a reduced premium for your travel insurance, because you will not need to buy the luggage cover.

You should also check you are covered for loss of **money** – typically, up to £250 – air tickets, and passport. The level of cover for replacement **air tickets** is usually around £1,500, although if you lose your ticket you should check with the airline immediately in case they can simply reissue your ticket. And look for around £250 of cover in case you lose your **passport** – this helps towards the cost of going to the embassy and sorting out a replacement.

If your luggage is lost by the airline, you should obtain a Property Irregularity Report (PIR) before you leave the baggage hall – see chapter 7 for full details of how to proceed. As well as contacting the airline, do not delay in contacting your insurer about the matter.

With any sort of loss or theft, it's essential to report the incident to the local police, and to obtain a written report from them, within 24 hours. (The exception is if the airline loses your bags, in which case you must obtain a report from them.) This will be used to support your insurance claim and without it insurers are entitled to reject your claim. You need a pretty watertight excuse – for example, you were hospitalised in the incident, or were somewhere very remote when it happened – for your claim to succeed without this report.

And you must take care of your possessions, or your insurance claim for their loss may be invalidated. Don't do things like leaving items on display in your car: cover usually only extends to items that were locked into the boot or glove compartment, out of sight. Use the hotel safe for your valuables, and do not leave them unattended, for example on the beach while you go for a swim. Some policies insist that you keep spare cash either on your person or in the hotel safe, so leaving it hidden in your hotel room will invalidate any claim if it is stolen from the room.

If you're taking specialist equipment on holiday you should seek out a specialist insurer. **Photographers**, for example, will find insurers such as **Photoguard** and **E&L** will offer greater cover for your equipment worldwide than a standard travel policy, albeit at a price.

Golfers should also shop around for cover if they plan to take clubs overseas. Areas to look for include: compensation for the loss or theft of your golf clubs; hire of golf clubs to replace those that are stolen, or delayed in transit; return of green fees if you are injured during the trip or the weather is so poor that you are unable to play pre-booked rounds; public liability insurance in case you injure someone while you play. Insurer **Golfplan** even covers you for up to £300 for the obligatory round of drinks you must stand if you hit a hole in one.

Flight delay and missed departure

If your **flight is delayed**, your insurance policy may pay a sum of money to help you with incidental expenses. This is unrelated to any help you may get from the airline in these circumstances (*see* chapter 3, page 82). Also, there is no excess to pay on this part of your policy – but the amounts paid out are not terribly high.

Typically, this cover kicks in after a delay of eight, 10 or 12 hours, and you receive in the region of £20–£30 for the first period of the delay, and a lesser amount for each subsequent block of eight, 10 or 12 hours, up to a maximum of £100–£150 or so. The cover may be restricted to your main outbound and inbound flights, and may not apply to connecting flights during the holiday. Keep receipts for any essentials you buy at this time.

If you ultimately decide to cancel your trip because the delay is so bad, your insurance policy may pay up again – perhaps a lump sum of a few hundred pounds, or even the entire cost of the holiday to the amount outlined in the "cancellation" section of the policy. This is not a feature of all insurance policies, so check the small print. For this part of the policy to kick in, generally there must have been a delay of at least 12 or 24 hours, and there may be conditions attached – for example the delay must be the result of a strike, breakdown or adverse weather. And in these cases you should also contact your airline or tour operator as well as your insurer. As we've seen in chapter 3, you now have improved rights under EU law when it comes to airline delays and cancellations, and if you have booked a package holiday your tour operator has a responsibility to help you out.

If you catch the flight but your luggage does not, you are usually offered a certain amount by your travel insurer towards the cost of replacing items in your suitcase while you wait for it to arrive. This is usually limited to a couple of hundred pounds and you should keep receipts for everything you buy to back up your claim. If your luggage is ultimately lost for good, any amount you have already received from the insurer for the delay will be deducted from any payment you receive for the lost luggage.

If you **miss your departure** you may also be covered by your insurance, but it will depend on the circumstances, such as whether you had left enough time to reach the airport. The missed departure section of the policy is intended to cover the extra costs (eg hotel, flight) of getting you to your destination after you've missed the original departure.

Accidents

Several parts of the policy will help you if you're involved in, or cause, an accident. The most important section is **personal liability cover**. This protects you against damages claims made against you. It applies if you injure someone, or their property, while on holiday. For example, a British couple on holiday in Spain once unwittingly caused a car crash when they stepped into the road without looking in the right direction. A car travelling towards them swerved to avoid them, and hit another car, injuring its occupants. The couple's travel insurer paid out when they were taken to court. This section of the policy typically pays up to £12 million to cover legal fees and any liability you face if you are sued.

Legal expenses cover, by contrast, will fund a claim that you need to bring against a third party. For example, if you are run over by an uninsured driver on your holiday and you need to take him to court to obtain compensation for your injuries, legal expenses cover will pay for your lawyer. This part of the policy also pays out if you are killed in an accident abroad and your relatives decide to pursue a court case for compensation. Typically up to £25,000 of cover is offered.

Some policies also offer **personal accident cover**: you (or your estate) receive a payment if you are disabled (or killed) while on holiday. Typically you may receive in the region of £25,000–£30,000 depending on what happened. Policies usually only pay out if you have been permanently disabled, for example you lost a limb, or were killed.

Note that if you are **driving overseas** you cannot rely on travel insurance, but must have sufficient cover under your motor insurance policy, if it is your own car. If you have hired a car, you will have to buy insurance to cover you during the time you hire the car. For full details see chapter 8.

Airline failure

Some travel insurance policies protect you if an airline goes out of business, stranding you abroad or, if you're yet to travel, leaving you out of pocket. If you are making your own travel arrangements and do not have financial protection for your holiday (for example like that offered by the Atol scheme – see chapter 3 for details), it may be worth choosing a policy that includes this.

Disasters and terrorism

If you are caught up in a natural disaster such as a hurricane or earthquake, your insurance should cover you for medical costs or loss of possessions if you are injured or lose items because of the event. But it may not cover you for the curtailment of the trip. However, if you have booked a package holiday (*see* chapter 4), your tour operator will be obliged to bring you home and compensate you for the remaining days that you missed, or to switch you to an alternative trip of equal value.

If you plan to visit a country that's affected by war, revolution or terrorism, for example, and the Foreign & Commonwealth Office (FCO) advises against travelling there (check on **www.fco.gov.uk**), your travel insurance is unlikely to cover you for war/revolution/terrorism-related mishaps. In early 2006, the only two countries to which the FCO advised against all travel were Ivory Coast and Somalia, but it also advised against all travel to parts of a further 26, including Afghanistan, Iraq, India, Nigeria and Pakistan. Anyone planning to visit these countries must avoid the blacklisted areas if their travel insurance is to remain valid. If in doubt, speak to your insurer before travelling. (Business travellers who must go to the danger zones, or their employers, should consult an insurance broker for specialist cover.)

These days, however, the FCO is more reluctant to advise against travelling to a specific country than it used to be, so the number of occasions on which insurers are able to use this opt-out is reducing. For example, after the bomb blasts in Sharm El-Sheikh, Egypt, in summer 2005, the FCO advised travellers to be cautious, but did not advise against all travel to Sharm – so subsequent visitors to the area were still covered by their travel insurance.

However, some holidaymakers caught up in the Sharm attacks found that their insurance policies did not cover them for losses sustained because of acts of terrorism. This threw the spotlight on the way some insurers have quietly been changing their policies.

Graeme Trudgill of the British Insurance Brokers Association (Biba) told me: "After September 11, a lot of travel exclusions appeared in policies' small print – you would find that most policies exclude paying out in the event of a terrorist attack. So, for example, if you were caught up in something like the Bali bomb, tough luck.

"But that's when you need your travel insurance the most."

So in 2005 Biba launched a travel insurance policy that includes medical, repatriation and baggage cover in the event of a terrorist attack, through insurers **Arch** (contactable via Biba or through a broker; *see* page 209). "We're still unhappy that a lot of insurers are not covering terrorism – we think they should be doing that," said Trudgill. Other insurers that offer terrorism cover include **Norwich Union** (0800 121007, **www.norwichuniondirect.com**) and **Insure and Go** (0870 901 3674, **www.insureandgo.com**).

Malcolm Tarling of the Association of British Insurers said insurers were now beginning to adjust their policies. "The travel insurance market is adapting to reflect the changing nature of terrorism," he said. "If travellers want cover for the terrorism risk, they should shop around, as an increasing number of insurers now offer medical cover for terrorism-related injuries."

Some insurance policies even pay up if you are involved in a hijack: for example, **Bradford & Bingley** (0800 169 4078, **www.bradford–bingley.co.uk**) pays £50 for each 24 hours of the hijack, up to a maximum of £1,000 (though after 20 days in a hijack situation this may be the last thing on your mind).

The Foreign & Commonwealth Office (FCO) often helps Britons who are caught up in overseas disasters and terrorist attacks. However, concerned that it is seen as providing a catch-all safety net, the FCO is trying hard to get across the message that holidaymakers should always buy insurance, and not simply expect the FCO to help them out. After Hurricane Wilma hit Mexico in 2005, the FCO airlifted some Britons out of the danger zone and it flew them to Dallas. It did not feel its role was to take them home, but simply to get them to safety. In these situations, holidaymakers should be able to call on either their holiday company (if they have bought a package) or their travel insurer to bring them home. Travellers who book their own trips without buying a package, and who do not have travel insurance, will fall through both nets.

Although it is often criticised in these situations, I have some sympathy with the FCO. If it does nothing to help British tourists in a disaster situation, we condemn it as heartless and useless. If it simply takes holidaymakers out of the danger zone, some complain that it will not take them all the way home. But if it did this, the insurance industry would accuse it of encouraging holidaymakers to travel without insurance!

A better outcome might be for insurers to offer policies that we can rely on to help us in times of disaster or terrorist attack, which are not riddled with opt-out clauses and exclusions. For more information on what the FCO can and cannot do for holidaymakers in trouble, *see* chapter 9.

If the FCO declares a region off-limits because of a disease such as bird flu, yet you are still keen to travel there, you should talk to your insurer first. Although the insurer will almost certainly not help if you succumb to bird flu after the FCO has issued such advice, it may still cover you if you have an unrelated mishap – for example, if you break your leg or have your possessions stolen.

Types of policy

Holidays at home

Some policies offer modest cover if you are taking a holiday in the UK, for example if you fall ill and a friend has to stay with you or you need to organise alternative transport home. Cancellation or curtailment cover usually applies too. But it may not cover you for legal expenses or travel delay (except for travel to the Channel Islands). You may have to book at least two nights' accommodation away for the policy to kick in.

Annual policies

An annual travel insurance policy is worth considering if you take more than a couple of trips each year. The most obvious benefit is cost – these policies are generally cheaper than buying several single-trip policies. And you only have to think about buying insurance once a year, instead of every time you take a break. Some annual policies are more generous than individual trip ones, with higher limits on what you can claim. Travellers aged 65-plus may find it harder to buy an annual policy. Try **Help the Aged** (0800 413180, **www.helptheaged.org.uk**), **Age Concern** (0845 601 2234, **www.ageconcern. co.uk**), **Saga** (0800 056 5464, **www.saga.co.uk**) or **Nationwide** (0500 302016, **www.nationwide.co.uk**).

Families

Most insurers offer policies that cover couples, or families, which are much cheaper than everyone in the family buying individual policies. If you travel with children, you can often have them covered on your policy for no extra cost, but as always you must shop around and read the small print. What constitutes a "family" varies from insurer to insurer.

Key questions to ask include: do the adults have to be married? Most policies now allow couples, including gay couples, who have co-habited for six months or more, to be classed as the adults on a family policy. How many children can travel under this policy? Some insurers limit it to two, others are more flexible. Up to what age do the children qualify? The insurer **Simple**

(0870 444 3778, **www.simpletravelinsurance.co.uk**), for example, allows them to count as children up to age 22 if they are in continuous education. Must the children all live at the same address or will the policy allow you to travel with your child's friend, too? Will the policy offer cover if the family members travel separately? Many insurers, including NatWest, will allow this, which is helpful if your child is going on a school trip, for example. But some insurers insist the child must travel with the policyholder.

Companies such as **Leading Edge** (0870 112 8099, **www.leadedge.co.uk**) and **Go Travel Insurance** (0870 421 1521, **www.gotravelinsurance.co.uk**) offer policies aimed at single parents travelling with children. And the **Post Office** (0800 169 9999, **www.postoffice.co.uk/travelinsurance**) and **Flexicover** (0870 990 9292, **www.flexicover.com**), for example, will cover grandparents who want to travel with their grandchildren, though grandparents over 65 may have to pay more.

Second-home owners

If you keep two homes and travel between them, you need to make sure you have proper contents insurance for both properties, and travel insurance for when you are moving between them. Travel insurance alone is not enough to cover the contents of your holiday property. Bear in mind that most home contents insurance policies insist that you do not leave the house unattended for more than 30 or 31 days. If you are likely to be away for longer than this, you must find an insurer that offers cover for extended absence – the easiest way is to consult a broker.

Winter sports

If you are going skiing or snowboarding, insurance is vital. A helicopter lift down the mountain can cost you £4,000 and a broken leg in America could cost £25,000. What's more, the EHIC will not cover search and rescue services, so failing to take out travel insurance is utter madness.

Winter sports cover is not usually included on a standard travel insurance policy – it is usually an optional extra for which you pay a further premium. If you are a regular traveller, it is better value to buy an annual multi-trip insurance policy than two or more single-trip policies, but check how many days' winter sports these policies allow you to undertake in each year. Most limit you to 17 or 21 days per year, though policies from the **Ski Club of Great Britain** (0870 075 9759, **www.skiclub.co.uk**) and Direct Travel (0845 605 2500, **www.direct-travel.co.uk**) do not set limits.

It's crucial that you have good medical cover that includes piste rescue – by helicopter if necessary – and repatriation. Check all the activities you plan to enjoy are covered – including off-piste skiing, tobogganing, snowmobiling, cross-country skiing and skating. Most insurers forbid off-piste skiing unless you are with a qualified guide or instructor, although some – including the Ski Club of Great Britain, Insure and Go and Direct Travel – allow unrestricted off-piste skiing or snowboarding.

Policies should also cover you for the loss or theft of ski equipment, hire of replacement gear, and for the unused part of your ski pack costs (such as tuition, boot hire and lift pass) if you are injured and unable to continue skiing. Check whether you are covered if your skis are pinched from outside a restaurant while you eat lunch – many policies only pay up if they are locked away, although **Snowcard** (01327 262805, **www.snowcard.co.uk**) is an exception. If you are worried, split your skis and store them in different places while you eat lunch – a thief won't bother to hunt for the pair.

Policies may offer cover for piste closure, if there is not sufficient snow, generally covering the cost of travelling to another resort that has snow, or compensating you (typically around £20 per day) if this is not possible. Some will pay out only if the lift system is 100 per cent shut, which is unusual as resort staff usually try to keep at least one lift operational. Direct Travel pays up if 80 per cent of the lift system is closed.

Some policies offer avalanche cover, which is effectively a type of delay cover that comes into effect if an avalanche means your arrival or departure from the resort is delayed, usually by 12 hours or more.

Check that the personal liability part of the policy (*see* page 201) will protect you if you collide with another skier – especially in the USA.

Most insurers offer winter sports cover; good starting points include the Ski Club of Great Britain, whose policies are available to both members and non-members, Direct Travel, Snowcard, World Ski & Travel, Insure and Go, Marks & Spencer, Go Travel Insurance and Dogtag. For contact details, *see* the Directory, on page 394.

Backpackers and gap–year travellers

This group of travellers has markedly different insurance requirements to other groups. Normally these needs include long-term cover for travels lasting up to a year, and risky activities cover; but these travellers are less likely to be bothered about cover for delay (hey, it's all part of life on the road) or loss of possessions (those dirty T-shirts? You're welcome!), so these parts of the policies may be less generous than standard travel insurance policies. Some insurers think particularly imaginatively about what hazards may befall a backpacker – **Boots** (0870 730 3344, **www.boots.com**), for example, offers £1,000 of "incarceration cover" to pay for a parent to visit you if you are jailed overseas!

A standard annual travel policy will not be suitable if you're going backpacking as these policies normally only cover you for trips of up to a month. You need a dedicated "backpacker" or "gap year" policy that will offer cover for six, nine or 12 months of continuous travel. Most such policies lapse if you return to the UK during your trip, although Go Travel Insurance, for example, has a "homesickness" clause, allowing you to return home, then continue your travels without having to take out a new policy.

Tom Griffiths, founder of **www.gapyear.com**, told me he is concerned that a large number of backpackers travel without insurance, and he believes it is only a matter of time before a parent loses their house because their backpacking son or daughter has an expensive overseas medical emergency, and no insurance to pay for it. "Time and again we see backpackers and their parents disregarding the importance of insurance," he said. "Our research has shown that backpackers spend more time buying a penknife for their trip than they spend buying insurance. For less than £1 per day, less than will be spent on beer, they can cover themselves. Our message to parents is: Have you had the insurance discussion with your child yet? And if not, why not?"

Griffiths stresses that outdoor activities are one of the key areas for backpackers to plan for when buying insurance, and urges them to write a list of everything they might get up to – hiring a motorbike, skiing, scuba diving, kitesurfing, etc – before choosing a policy.

One potential problem is scuba diving to below the depth stipulated on your policy (typically, 30 metres). In 2005 a British scuba diver who suffered decompression sickness (known as "the bends") while diving in Egypt faced a £40,000 bill for treatment because his insurer said he had gone below 30m, the depth permissible according to its terms and conditions.

Before buying, consider where your route will take you. If you are not going to the USA and Canada, where medical expenses are potentially high, the cost of your policy may drop. Also check whether you can extend or change your insurance while you are travelling – most firms insist you buy insurance while in the UK, before you set off, and it can be hard to extend it once you start your trip.

Finally, think about what gadgets you'll be taking – iPod, camera, mobile phone – and make sure you are happy with the level of loss/theft cover you have for them. Tell your family back home, and anyone you are travelling with, your insurance policy number and the emergency contact details for your insurer.

Companies that specialise in gap year travel include:

- **American Express**, 0800 028 7573, **www.americanexpress.co.uk**

- **Boots**, 0870 730 3344, **www.boots.com**

- **Columbus Direct**, 0870 033 9988, **www.columbusdirect.com**

- **Dogtag**, 0870 036 4824, **www.dogtag.co.uk**

- **Endsleigh**, 0800 028 3571, **www.endsleigh.co.uk**

- **Go Travel Insurance**, 0870 421 1521, **www.gotravelinsurance.co.uk**

- **Insure and Go**, 0870 901 3674, **www.insureandgo.com**

- **MRL Insurance Direct**, 0870 876 7677, **www.mrlinsurance.co.uk**

- **Round the World Insurance**, 0845 344 4225, **www.roundtheworldinsurance.co.uk**

- **STA Travel**, 0870 160 0599, **www.statravel.co.uk**

Travel insurance offered with a credit card or bank account

I am wary of these policies as I think travellers often assume that, because they have this "perk", they don't need to think about travel insurance any further. Wrong! The travel insurance you're offered with other financial products may suit you – but it may be inadequate.

For a start, it may only be valid if you book the trip using the credit card in question. Barclaycard, for example, offers free travel insurance for a cardholder and up to five companions – but only when you book a holiday through Barclaycard Travel Services, using your Barclaycard.

"You get nothing for free!" said Malcolm Tarling of the Association of British Insurers, when I asked him about "free" travel insurance that comes with financial products. "You should check the policy's limits, as it may not be as comprehensive as insurance from a stand-alone policy – though it may be fine for you."

Note that some credit cards offer you "free travel accident insurance". This is quite a different matter – it is a type of personal insurance that pays up, for example, if you lose a limb in a ski accident. It is not a full travel insurance policy and is no substitute for one. Nationwide, for example, offers this perk with its credit card – it covers you for up to £50,000 for death or serious injury while travelling, if you have bought your travel tickets using the card. But it says on the application form: "This is not a substitute for full travel insurance."

Using an insurance broker

If you have special requirements – such as regular long trips to your second home, or particular medical needs – using a broker may be the best way to find appropriate travel insurance. Unsurprisingly, the **British Insurance Brokers Association** (0870 950 1790, **www.biba.org.uk**) is keen for us to use brokers whatever our circumstances, saying that policies bought through a broker are likely to be more specifically tailored to our needs, offer higher levels of cover, and thus prove better value.

One way they can beat the off-the-peg policies is regarding the excess, according to Biba's Graeme Trudgill. "With travel agents' policies, we often find that you may pay an excess on each part of the policy. But normally with a broker's policy you only pay one excess per person.

"And when you come to claim you find the real benefits, because the cover is that much deeper, and the broker will argue your case with the insurer. They are there to support your claim."

Ian Dickinson of brokers Brunsdon Group said the problems with buying an off-the-peg insurance policy often only become apparent when a claim fails. "Most of the problems are people not being advised at the point of sale what's required of them, and what the implications are if they do not reveal pre-existing medical conditions, for example," he said.

For information on insurance cover when driving abroad, *see* chapter 8.

Exclusions

There are many reasons why insurance companies may refuse to cover you in the first place, or refuse to pay up when something goes wrong. Exclusions can be a good thing in that they keep the cost of the policy down, but you must ensure you do not fall foul of them. Here are some of the most common:

- Pre-existing medical conditions – you must declare them. *See* page 196 for help on finding medical policies for certain conditions.

- Age – some policies have a cut-off age as low as 49. *See* page 198 for suggestions of insurers that help older travellers.

- Destination – if the Foreign & Commonwealth Office advises against travel to a country, you may not be covered.

- Drink and drugs – if you are under the influence of these when an accident happens, your insurer will not pay up.

- Pregnancy – travel insurers usually will not cover you after 28 weeks' pregnancy.

- Hazardous activities – check the small print to find out if you are covered for activities such as rock climbing, skiing, hot-air ballooning or hiring a moped. You may have to pay an extra premium.

- Extended trips to your second home.

- Terrorist acts (though there are exceptions – *see* page 202).

- Business travel (though many insurers will offer specific cover for this).

Insurance tips

- Carry a copy of your policy, the emergency phone number, and your policy number with you; leave a copy at home with a friend or relative.

- Store the emergency phone number in your mobile phone.

- If you are travelling with a friend or relative, tell them your policy details.

- If you incur expenses, and want to claim for them, keep receipts.

- Report any loss or theft to the local police within 24 hours.

- Keep records and take photographs of anything that you intend to claim for.

Contacts

Association of British Insurers, 020 7216 7455, **www.abi.org.uk**

Association of British Travel Agents, 020 7307 1907, **www.abta.com**

British Insurance Brokers Association, 0870 950 1790, **www.biba.org.uk**

Financial Ombudsman Service, 0845 080 1800, **www.financial-ombudsman.org.uk**

Foreign & Commonwealth Office, 0845 850 2829, **www.fco.gov.uk**

Taking money abroad

When I first visited Cambodia, in 1992, I flew in from neighbouring Thailand with US dollars stashed in various different hiding places and pockets. The restaurants barely had cutlery, so I knew I wouldn't find a functioning bank, exchange counter or cash machine. And while for most of my trip I was proved right (the dollar, in former war zones, is always king), there was a moment when I wished I'd had travellers' cheques with me.

I flew north to the Angkor temples, now the country's premier tourist draw. Then, as Khmer Rouge guerrillas were still active, visitors were as rare as hen's teeth, so there was no official admission fee for the temples – but there were plenty of "officials" driving around in shiny new Mercedes cars and extorting "entry fees" from anyone they could catch. They rushed me for US$50. The backpacker I was travelling with had travellers' cheques with him, and handed over one for US$50 – without validating it by countersigning it. Our new friends had never seen a travellers' cheque before, but accepted the unsigned cheque delightedly. Back in Phnom Penh, my companion rang his bank to cancel it and had a new one issued. Well, why not? Effectively he'd been mugged. Meanwhile, I was US$50 down.

Time was when it made sense to carry travellers' cheques, because they offered security and versatility – you could get them replaced if they were stolen, unlike cash, and they were more widely accepted than credit cards. But the growth in the number of shops and other outlets that take plastic, and the wide availability of cash machines worldwide, means the travellers' cheque is dropping out of fashion in many corners of the globe.

They are starting to be replaced by a recent invention, the **pre-paid travel cash card**. These plastic cards are loaded with cash before you travel, and you can use them to withdraw money at cash machines and pay for goods overseas (*see* page 219). These are also a great way to send emergency funds to a backpacking son or daughter. But some readers have reported teething troubles with them, as vendors overseas are still getting used to them, so it's too soon to sound the death knell for the traveller's cheque just yet.

These days, wherever I go, I take a mixture of plastic and cash. I take both a debit and a credit card, a charge card, some local currency and sterling. I always carry an emergency stash of US dollars as dollar bills are accepted as tips in any country, and can be useful if you have just arrived somewhere, have no local currency and wish to thank your driver or bellhop.

I'm cautious about how I carry my money. Holidaymakers are easy prey for pickpockets and fraudsters, and the hassle of losing your wallet when you're on holiday is far greater than if you're at home.

These days you will need to know your four-digit PIN (personal identification number) to use your credit and debit cards in many countries, and always when taking cash from machines. If you do not know your PIN, obtain one from your card provider before you travel.

Money safety tips

- Take several different payment methods with you on holiday.

- Leave one of the cards in the hotel safe unless you need it for a big purchase that day.

- Leave most cash in the safe and take smaller amounts with you each day.

- Keep a separate note of your card numbers and the emergency phone number of the issuing banks; store the phone numbers in your mobile.

- Never write down your PIN.

- Empty your wallet before you travel – you won't need your gym membership card on holiday, but if your wallet is pinched it's one more thing to replace.

- Just because you're relaxed, don't drop your guard. Zip your wallet into a pocket, keep tight hold of your handbag, and don't leave your stuff unattended on a beach.

- Beware the classic trick of street children pretending you have bird droppings on you. In their eagerness to "clean you up", they "clean you out" – by picking your pocket.

- Cash machines and exchange bureaux are likely places for thieves and pickpockets to lurk.

- See **www.cardwatch.org.uk** and **www.chipandpin.co.uk** for more security advice.

Credit cards

Credit cards are a convenient and largely secure way to spend money abroad. The exchange rate used by banks on credit card transactions is usually better than the tourist rate, so it should be cheaper, as well as safer, to pay for goods with a credit card than with cash.

Another bonus is that in March 2006, the Office of Fair Trading won an important victory for consumers at the Court of Appeal. Judges ruled that, under the 1974 Consumer Credit Act, card issuers must offer you a refund if the goods you buy are faulty, or the service you paid for did not materialise, wherever you use the card, for purchases between £100 and £30,000. (Up to then, this protection had only applied to credit card purchases made from a UK-based company.)

This ruling means, for example, if you buy a ticket on an overseas airline and it goes bust, you buy a carpet from a shop in the souk but they never post it to you as they promised, or you have a dispute with an overseas hotel you booked online, you can apply for a refund from the credit card company – though you should try to sort it out with the vendor first. This protection does not extend to purchases made with a debit or charge card, though you should always speak to your bank, as some will help in these cases.

The downside of credit cards is that you're likely to face extra charges, some of them hidden, every time you use the card, whether to make a purchase or to withdraw cash.

Making purchases with a credit card overseas

Whenever you buy something overseas using your credit card, most issuing banks add a foreign currency conversion charge, sometimes known as a "currency fee" or "loading fee", to the cost of your purchase, typically at a rate of 2.75 per cent. So every time you buy something that costs the equivalent of £100, you will be charged £102.75. This fee is usually hidden within the exchange rate your bank uses so it does not show up on your statement as a separate item.

A few card issuers do not levy this charge. **Nationwide Building Society** (0800 302010, **www.nationwide.co.uk**) is the only credit card issuer I can find that charges no currency fee on overseas purchases. **Saga** (for the over 50s; 0845 601 2740, **www.saga.co.uk**) charges nothing on purchases within the EU and 1 per cent on purchases worldwide. **Liverpool Victoria** (0800 134134, **www.liverpoolvictoria.co.uk**) also charges nothing within the EU, but 2.75 per cent worldwide.

To see what credit card companies charge you for shopping overseas, go to **www.moneysupermarket.com**, click on the credit card comparison link, then click on "using your card abroad". The "EU loading" column is the amount added when you make a purchase in the EU, and "worldwide loading" is the amount added when you buy something elsewhere overseas. (This useful website also lists the emergency loss telephone numbers for many credit card companies.)

However, choosing a credit card based on what it charges you for overseas purchases is pointless unless you pay the balance off in full each month. If you don't, the interest charged each month by the bank is likely to wipe out any gains you might make by using a card that charges a low, or no, currency fee.

Withdrawing money using a credit card overseas

Taking cash from an ATM using your credit card is to be avoided – wherever you are. Even if you're in the UK you will be charged a fee for withdrawing money this way.

First, on all overseas cash withdrawals, there's our old friend the currency fee – most credit card companies charge 2.75 per cent. As we've already seen, this fee is hidden within the exchange rate, so doesn't show up on your statement. Once again, Nationwide is the only card issuer I have found that does not charge this fee.

Second, most credit card companies will charge you another fee for using the machine – typically, 2 per cent of the amount withdrawn, often with a minimum amount of £2.50. Nationwide, Saga and Cahoot are slightly more generous, charging 1.50 per cent with a minimum of £1.50 each time, while others, such as Abbey Cashback, Ryanair.com Platinum Plus and MBNA Platinum Plus, charge 2 per cent with a minimum of £3 for each cash withdrawal. (The table on **www.moneysupermarket.com** lists these fees, under "withdrawal charge".)

I have only found two credit cards that do not charge this cash withdrawal fee: the **Abbey Flat Rate** credit card (0845 972 4724, **www.abbey.com**) and **Co-operative Bank Clear** credit card (0845 600 6000, **www.co–operativebank. co.uk**). But both charge the currency fee, at 2.75 per cent. So by using your credit card to withdraw cash from a machine, you will incur, in many cases, typical charges of a 2.75 per cent currency fee, and a 2 per cent cash withdrawal fee – adding £4.75 to the cost of withdrawing £100.

It doesn't stop there. Credit card companies do not offer an interest-free period on cash withdrawals, as they do on purchases (on which you may have an interest-free period of up to 56 days). So you will be charged interest on the withdrawal from the day you make it. I cannot find any credit card company that does not adhere to this practice.

As if all that wasn't enough, most credit card companies then charge you a higher rate of interest on cash withdrawals than on purchases – often much higher, perhaps more than 20 per cent APR. Given that this is charged from the moment you withdraw the money, using your credit card to withdraw cash really is not an attractive option.

My advice is to use credit cards overseas only for making purchases, not for withdrawing cash from a machine, because of these extra charges.

Tips for using your credit card abroad

Before travelling...

- Make arrangements to pay your credit card bill if payment falls due while you are on holiday.

- Tell your credit card company you're going abroad as they are then less likely to query or turn down transactions from that country.

- Make sure you know your PIN but do not write it down.

- Check the distribution of ATMs on the websites **www.visa.co.uk** and **www.mastercard.com**.

- Consider taking out Nationwide's credit card for making overseas purchases.

When abroad...

- Check the amount and currency carefully before signing a bill or entering your PIN.

- You have the right to insist your bill is given in the local currency, not already converted to sterling, which can result in you losing out on the exchange rate.

- Keep all receipts in case of a problem later.

- Don't use your credit card to withdraw money from a machine except in an emergency.

Debit cards

Most bank accounts come with a debit card that you can use to pay for goods or to withdraw cash from an ATM. (In the UK your debit card also acts as a cheque guarantee card.) When you use these cards the cash comes straight out of your bank account.

Debit cards may display the Visa, Visa Delta or Visa Plus logos, or the

Mastercard-backed Cirrus or Maestro logos. You can use your card in the overseas ATM or point of purchase that displays the corresponding symbol. For more information, visit **www.visaeurope.com**, **www.maestrocard.com** and **www.mastercard.com**.

Making purchases with a debit card overseas

Depending on your card issuer, you are likely to face one or two fees whenever you buy something overseas with a debit card.

As with credit card purchases, the currency fee (typically 2.75 per cent) is charged on overseas debit card transactions, and once again this is a hidden charge, wrapped up in the exchange rate and not itemised on your bank statement. Nationwide is the only provider that does not charge this fee.

On top of this, some banks charge a transaction fee as well. Halifax is the most expensive, charging £1.50 on each overseas purchase, while Lloyds TSB charges £1 and NatWest charges 75p. But other institutions, including Smile and Nationwide, do not charge a transaction fee.

Once again, Nationwide Building Society comes out best, charging nothing – neither a currency fee nor a transaction fee – on debit card purchases overseas. To obtain a Nationwide debit card you must open its FlexAccount.

Withdrawing money using a debit card overseas

Broadly speaking, when you use your debit card at an overseas cash machine, the rules are the same as for credit cards. Banks usually charge a currency fee, typically 2.75 per cent, plus a withdrawal fee of up to 2% of the value of the cash you take out.

Lloyds TSB, for example, charges a 2.75 per cent currency fee, plus 1.5 per cent of the amount withdrawn (with a minimum of £2 and a maximum of £4.50). So withdrawing £100 from a machine overseas with your Lloyds TSB debit card would cost you an extra £4.75, made up of the £2.75 currency fee and a £2 withdrawal fee. Smile bank charges 2.75 per cent plus £2 or 2 per cent of the amount withdrawn, whichever is the greater. HSBC charges a 2.75 per cent currency fee plus 1.5 per cent (with a minimum of £1.75) for withdrawals. Nationwide, once again, comes top – charging nothing extra for cash withdrawals with its FlexAccount debit card.

Barclays charges 1.5 per cent (with a minimum of £1.50) per withdrawal, but if you use a cash machine in its Global Alliance network this charge is waived. The Global Alliance members are Bank of America, Deutsche Bank, Scotiabank, Westpac, and BNP Paribas and their machines are found mostly in countries across North America, the Caribbean and Australasia.

Using debit cards to withdraw cash is cheaper than using credit cards because you are not charged interest on the withdrawal, as you are with a credit card. Instead, the money comes straight out of your bank account, so before travelling you should ensure you have sufficient funds in the account.

Tips for using your debit card overseas

- Memorise your PIN but don't write it down.

- Don't be scared of foreign cash machines – they work much like they do at home and will offer you the option of choosing instructions in English.

- Withdraw at least £100 or so each time you use a cash machine because taking smaller amounts out more frequently is more expensive.

- Always request a receipt and keep it in case of problems later.

Charge cards

American Express and Diners Club cards offer useful services to travellers, at a cost. They are charge cards, which means you have no set spending limit, but you must pay the bill off in full every month. You are also charged an annual fee to carry the card.

The benefits for cardholders include a points-based rewards scheme, which can earn you money off goods and travel services, quick card replacement if your card is lost or stolen, and perks such as access to airport lounges through Diners Club and travel inconvenience insurance with American Express.

Diners Club (0870 190 0011, **www.dinersclub.co.uk**) can be used wherever the Diners Club symbol is displayed or, in North America (Canada, Mexico and the USA), where the Mastercard symbol is displayed. You can withdraw cash from a machine that carries the Cirrus logo, but whenever you do so, whether at home or abroad, you are charged £4 or 4 per cent of the amount withdrawn, whichever is greater. When shopping with a Diners Club card overseas you are charged a 2.70 per cent currency fee. Cardholders pay a fee of £50 a year to carry the card.

American Express (0870 600 1030, **www.americanexpress.co.uk**) has four levels of card membership – Green, which costs £37.50 a year, Gold (£95), Platinum (£300) and Centurion, the black card, at £650 a year, for invited cardholders. They offer increasing levels of travel and other benefits, and cards can be used wherever the American Express symbol is displayed (though not in Cuba). Cardholders are charged a 2.73 per cent currency fee on purchases when using the card overseas, and they are charged 1.5 per cent of the amount withdrawn when using the card in cash machines.

Foreign currency

Banks, building societies and bureaux de change sell foreign currency, and it is worth shopping around for special offers such as zero commission. If you want currency delivered to your home, you may have to pay a delivery charge of up to £5, though if you are ordering a lot (say £300 or more) some providers will deliver it free of charge. You can usually order currency online and in some cases you can collect it at the airport before you fly.

Unsurprisingly you generally get a better exchange rate if you buy foreign currency in advance, rather than at the airport. In 2005, research from the Co-op Travel and Travelcare agency chains revealed that exchange counters at UK airports offer a worse deal than high street outlets. You should also check, by shopping around, that a zero-commission deal does not mean you are getting a poor exchange rate to compensate. However, it's still better to buy your currency at a UK airport than to buy it once you arrive overseas, where the rates will often be even worse. And UK airports offer convenience – for example, you can find a bureau de change at 6am at Heathrow which will sell you Thai baht on the spot, which you cannot say of the high street.

The currencies of countries less popular with British visitors can be hard to obtain here before you travel, although some providers can source the currency if you order in advance. The **Post Office** has one of the widest ranges of foreign currencies, offering 72, including the taka (Bangladesh), the lei (Romania) and the pula (Botswana).

Many bureaux de change will try to sell you a "buyback guarantee". This means they offer to buy back any spare currency you have on your return home at the same rate at which they sold it to you. If the rate has moved in your favour that can be a good deal; if it has moved in the bank's favour then you'll lose.

Contacts

American Express, 0870 600 1060, **www.americanexpress.co.uk**

Barclays, 0845 600 8090, **www.barclays.co.uk**

International Currency Exchange, 01455 897801, www.currency-express.com

Marks & Spencer Money, 0870 600 3502, www.marksandspencer.com/travelmoney

Nationwide, 0870 010 0719, www.nationwide.co.uk

The Post Office, 0845 722 3344, www.postoffice.co.uk

Thomas Cook, 0870 010 2913, www.thomascook.com

Travelex, 0870 240 5405, www.travelex.co.uk

TTT Moneycorp, 0800 393967, www.ttt.co.uk

Travellers' cheques

Traditionally these were the safe way to take money abroad – but now there are so many cash machines around the world, and so many of us carry debit or credit cards, that the demand for travellers' cheques has slumped.

They are also a bit of a hassle compared with paying by plastic. You must sign them when you buy them, and then you have to go to a bank, hotel reception or bureau de change overseas to cash them in.

However they are still popular with many travellers. "They are convenient, and I still use them," said Hugh Stacey, head of travel services at the **Post Office**. "You know what you are getting – they are a very simple concept, and a simple budgeting mechanism. You are ring-fencing your money."

They also remain popular in less developed parts of the world, particularly African countries such as Nigeria, and they are safe, because if they are lost or stolen you can cancel them. If you shop around when buying them they are likely to be cheaper than paying with plastic – you may find commission-free deals. And in many establishments in the USA, travellers' cheques denominated in US dollars are accepted as cash, so you do not have to bother changing them.

Keep a note of the serial number of each cheque, in a separate place from the cheques, in case of loss.

Pre-paid travel cash cards

These new plastic cards are starting to replace travellers' cheques. Some of the biggest foreign currency players – American Express, Western Union, The Post Office, Travelex and International Currency Exchange – issue them, and more cards are likely to appear on the market soon.

Pre-paid cash cards allow you to spend funds that you have loaded on to the card before you travel. You buy a card by putting typically between £100 and £3,000 on to it, paying by credit or debit card or cash if you're buying it over the counter. You can ask for the card to be loaded in sterling, US dollars or euros, depending on where you are travelling. You cannot have a mix of currencies on one card.

You can also have cards for other family members, so if, for example, a child is going off on a gap year, parents can load one card back home and their offspring can access those funds using their own card overseas. In an emergency a parent can load fresh funds on to the card in the UK, and within 15 minutes or so their son or daughter overseas will be able to withdraw the money from a cash machine. Which is really quite astonishing. When I first travelled in India and someone posted me a money order, it took me an entire morning of drinking tea with the manager of Grindlay's bank in Shimla before he would hand over my rupees. It was charming, but I was glad I didn't have a train to catch.

However, these cards are not yet as widely recognised as other types of plastic. One *Times* reader has reported finding it nearly impossible to find anywhere that would accept her American Express Traveller's Cheque Card in Morocco, though this will change as they become better known. Take several payment methods when you travel and do not rely on one alone.

As ever, you must look out for the fees and charges. There is a fee to set up the card (Western Union charges £9.95; American Express charges £20) and there are further fees when you use the card – typically, £1.50–£2.50 for each cash machine withdrawal, though there is not usually a fee for buying goods with the card, so long as the items you're buying are priced in the same currency as you have loaded on to your card.

Because there are limited funds on the card, you cannot use it to guarantee things like hire cars or hotel rooms. In some cases your name is not printed on the card, so there may be occasions when you are asked to show other ID. Any leftover funds on your card can be carried over to your next holiday, although you should check the small print as some issuers declare the card invalid after a certain time and you will need to switch your funds to a new card.

Contacts

American Express Traveller's Cheque Card, 0800 085 0023, **www.americanexpress.co.uk/tcc**, also available through Thomas Cook travel agencies

International Currency Exchange's Cash2Go card, 01296 380030, www.cash2go.com

Post Office, 0845 722 3344, **www.postoffice.co.uk**

Travelex, 0870 240 5405, **www.travelex.co.uk**

Western Union Travel Cash Card, 020 8535 7000, **www.wutcc.co.uk**

Cash in an emergency

If you are stuck overseas and need money fast, there are several ways to get your hands on some. Using a **money transfer service** is perhaps the best-known method. A friend or relative back home can use money transfer to get the cash to you within minutes.

The person sending the money takes cash into an agency that offers this service, such as Western Union, the Post Office or Travelex. Some branches may allow you to pay with a credit or debit card (and you can pay this way through Western Union if you do the transaction online), but usually you will need hard cash. The sender pays a fee, and the money is made available to the recipient, wherever they are in the world, often within a few minutes. The recipient goes to their local currency office to collect it, on production of ID.

Fees for this service can be quite hefty – the Post Office's MoneyGram service, for example, charges £18 to send £200 abroad, £46 to send £1,000 and £180 to send their maximum, £5,500. But in an emergency you may feel that the charges are a small price to pay.

Contacts

MoneyGram, 00800 8971 8971, **www.postoffice.co.uk**

Travelex, 0870 240 5405, **www.travelex.co.uk**

Western Union, 0800 833833, **www.westernunion.co.uk**

Holders of American Express or Diners Club **charge cards** should be helped by their card company in an emergency. American Express customers have Global Assist, a 24-hour helpline and card replacement scheme. A Diners Club spokesman said cardholders should phone them and they would be able to arrange help such as transferring funds to your hotel in an emergency.

You can also sign up with a **consumer assistance** company. For example, if you sign up with **CPP** (0870 120 1251, **www.cpp.co.uk**), in an emergency it will cancel all your credit and debit cards with one (free) phone call from you, whether you're at home or overseas, and can lend you up to £1,500 (or £3,000 with its premium policy) to help you continue your holiday. It can also lend you £1,500/£3,000 to cover hotel bills, and £2,500/£5,000 to cover travel tickets – loans are interest-free for 28 days.

It insures you for lost cash and reissuing passports and driving licences. A policy costs £20 per year for the "classic" scheme, or £29 a year for the "plus", which has the higher cash limits. Policies cover up to five people at the same address.

A similar scheme is operated by **Sentinel** (0800 414717, **www.sentinelcardprotection.com**), which also charges £20 per year for cover.

Finally, don't expect the British embassy or consulate to help out if you run out of money. They do not usually lend money to holidaymakers, although they might offer advice or allow you to make a phone call to sort things out. For further details of their services, *see* chapter 9.

Phoning home

Most of us travel with a mobile phone, which makes it much easier to keep in touch with friends and family back home, and to organise elements of the holiday (such as booking a restaurant table) while we're on the move. Unfortunately, phone companies are now notorious for charging us high rates when we use our mobile phones abroad – which is known as "roaming".

Not only is the cost of making calls higher, but you must also pay to receive calls on your mobile, and to listen to voice messages, while you are abroad – services which are often free at home.

The problem is so acute that the European Commission has for several years been investigating the high cost of roaming and urging companies to bring down their roaming charges. And in early 2006 Ofcom, the independent regulator for the UK communications industry, condemned the high charges that mobile phone companies impose on their customers when they go abroad, and suggested ways we can keep our bills down. This report is available on the Ofcom website at **www.ofcom.org.uk/advice/mobile_abroad/**.

In March 2006, the EU Information Commissioner Viviane Reding announced fresh proposals to force down the cost of roaming. Under plans that could be introduced as early as summer 2007, mobile phone companies could be forced to cap some charges, and abolish others, such as the cost of receiving a call while you are overseas.

Before you go away

Check that your phone will work in the country you are visiting. Dual-band handsets – which many of us have – work in many countries. However, the USA, Canada, and some 20 countries in that region, including Mexico and Peru, operate on tri-band phones while Japan and Korea operate on quad-band phones. In these countries you must upgrade to a tri- or quad-band phone, or hire one through a company such as **Cellhire** (0800 610610, **www.cellhire.co.uk**).

Then check that your handset is able to make and receive international calls, because often they are "barred" from making overseas calls. Ask your phone company to remove the international call bar that is sometimes placed on phones when they leave the factory. To do this, you must be in the UK. You may also need to set up your voicemail before you go abroad, if you have not already done so.

Next, check the rates for making calls when you are abroad, listed on your phone company's website, or consult **www.onecompare.com** and click on "international roaming". For detailed information about network coverage around the world, and maps of each provider's coverage, visit **www.gsmworld.com** and click on "GSM roaming". Your phone company's website will give details of the actual charges.

Mobile phone tips

- Find out the code of the country you will be dialling from abroad. If it is the UK, for example, you need to dial the international access code (which is often 00, but if in doubt simply dial the + symbol instead, which you bring up by pressing * twice), then 44, the UK country code, and delete the first 0 of the number you are calling.

- If you are a pay-as-you-go (PAYG) customer, top up your credit before travelling, to save hassle on holiday.

- If you want to avoid paying for voicemail retrieval when on holiday, leave a message on your phone telling callers you will not be picking up voicemail, and that they should text you if it is urgent.

- Alternatively, you may be able to change your phone settings to automatically divert calls to your voicemail when you are abroad.

- Check overseas call tariffs with your service provider before you go.

- Check your mobile phone is covered by your travel insurance policy.

• Ask friends which mobile network they use. If they are on the same network as you, it may be cheaper to call them than if they are on a rival network.

• Sending texts can be expensive, so it might be cheaper to make a quick call than send several texts – but you can receive texts for free.

• Don't forget to pack your phone charger and an electrical adaptor to plug it in.

• **Carphone Warehouse** (0800 925925, **www.carphonewarehouse. com**) offers advice on using phones abroad. It also offers a "memory master" service, which for £1.99 copies all the numbers from your SIM card. If you lose your phone, it then uploads the numbers on to your new SIM card, avoiding phonebook trauma.

• If your phone is lost or stolen, you may need to give your phone company its IMEI number (serial number). This 15-digit number can be found by dialling *#06#. Keep a note of this, and the contact details of your phone company, separately from your phone.

• Programme into your phone the numbers of your holiday company, its rep in resort, and the nearest British Embassy or consulate, in case of emergencies.

• Spinvox (0870 033 7300, **www.spinvox.com**) will convert your voice messages to texts or emails, which saves you expensive voice message retrieval calls when you are abroad; from £5 per month.

• There's worldwide electrical and phone data at **www.kropla.com**.

• eKit (**www.ekit.com**) offers a range of services including reduced cost phonecards, SIM cards and other communications tools.

Sort out your price plan

Phone companies offer different tariffs for overseas use. Many of them split the world into regions and charge you depending on which region you are in. Many of them also offer special deals to help bring your bill down (such as Vodafone's International Call Saver; details below); these are often only available to customers who have a contract with their phone company, not to PAYG customers.

What the phone companies offer travellers

- **easyMobile** (0845 612 4500, **www.easymobile.com**) only offers PAYG phones and requires you to register a credit card to top up your phone before you can use it abroad.

- **O2** (0870 521 4000, **www.o2.co.uk**) offers contract customers its International Traveller Service: for £2.99 a month you can save 40 per cent or more on calls when you are abroad (and you can buy this service for just one month). PAYG customers can buy a "Euro bolt-on" for £1.99 a month which offers up to 50 per cent off calls from Europe.

- **Orange** (07973 100150, **www.orange.co.uk**) offers talk and text "bundles" at special rates for travellers.

- **T-Mobile** (0845 412 5000, **www.t-mobile.co.uk**); in June 2006, it introduced a flat 55p charge to make or receive calls to 29 European countries, Canada and the USA. This service is available to both contract and PAYG customers, with no need to sign up.

- **Vodafone** (0800 068 6695, **www.vodafone.co.uk**) has Vodafone Passport for both contract and PAYG customers, which is a good deal if you are making longer calls. Vodafone's other service for travellers is International Call Saver, which costs £2.50 a month extra (and is only available to contract customers) but cuts your overseas phone bill by up to 61 per cent.

Use a pay-as-you-go SIM card

The SIM card is the electronic chip that connects your phone to a mobile network. As a response to the high cost of using our mobile phones abroad, a whole new industry has grown up around selling SIM cards that will keep our overseas call costs down, by switching us into the local phone network of the country we are visiting. You use your phone as a PAYG customer while using these SIM cards, even if you are on a contract.

Some of these SIM-card companies, such as uk2abroad, allow you to keep your UK mobile phone number while using the SIM card abroad – but with most of them, you will be given a new phone number when you buy the SIM card, which is a bit of a hassle. They all claim to save you 60-80 per cent or more on your phone bill when you travel. However, your friends may have to pay more to call you.

Before you can use one of these SIM card services, ensure your handset is unlocked. (This is not the same as having the international call bar lifted.) Around 30 per cent of handsets are "locked" by the phone company in an attempt to keep you using only their services. To find out if your phone is locked, put the SIM card from a friend's phone that uses a different network into your handset. If it does not work, your phone is locked.

Phone companies are obliged to unlock your phone if you ask them, but they may charge a fee for this – typically around £20, though Three charges a hefty £215 if you are still under contract (£15 if your contract has expired). Unlocking your phone through the service provider takes 30 days. You can do it more quickly by using the SIM card services listed below (**0044** offers a free unlocking service to its customers). If you have a Nokia phone, you can unlock it via **www.unlock123.com** for £4.99. Otherwise you can go to an independent phone service and repair centre (look them up in the phone book) to ask them to unlock the phone.

SIM card services

0044, 0870 950 0044, **www.0044.co.uk**

Gosim, www.gosim.com

Sim4travel, 0870 126 4879, **www.sim4travel.co.uk**

uk2abroad, 0870 922 0825, **www.uk2abroad.com**

Buy a local SIM card

You can buy a local SIM card overseas, and providing your handset is unlocked (see above), you can then use your phone on the local network and start saving money.

Phonecards

Don't forget the good old phone booth. You can buy phonecards at numerous shops abroad, and use pay phones to make calls that will be at far cheaper rates than your hotel or mobile phone provider offers. It also solves the problem of poor mobile coverage in remote areas.

You can buy phonecards at local newsagents and tobacconists' kiosks everywhere, or you can pre-order some via **1st Phone Cards** (0845 123 5858, **www.1st-phonecards.co.uk**) or **Planet Phone Cards** (0870 145 1016, **www.planetphonecards.com**). In the UK, the **Post Office** sells the Post Office Holiday Phonecard, which works in many popular holiday destinations.

CHAPTER SEVEN

Packing: it's in the bag –
but should it be?

Introduction

The art of packing is not simply about taking as little as possible. You can take too little, as I found to my cost during my backpacking days when a group of us were thrown out of a restaurant in Berlin for – allegedly – being too smelly. The three guys I'd been travelling with didn't have so much as a spare T-shirt between them, and after two days on the train from Moscow, I suppose they did pong a bit. I was only guilty through association, obviously.

These days there is increasing pressure to travel as light as possible. In March 2006, two budget airlines, Ryanair and Flybe, started to charge us a few pounds for each piece of luggage we check into the hold (see page 243). Other airlines are likely to follow this money-spinning example. And the airport security alert of August 2006 has forced us all to rethink how we pack for a plane journey.

But if you are heading off with the family for two weeks in a villa in Italy, you don't want to spend the holiday rotating two T-shirts – you want a stylish, if carefully chosen, wardrobe, some books, your camera, beach gear, the kids' favourite toys – your checked luggage is soon up to the 20kg limit that airlines typically impose on anyone travelling in economy.

However the weight question becomes pretty much irrelevant if you're driving to the Continent and can take as much as your car boot can hold. So I think packing smart means working out exactly what you need for each type of trip – and what you do not need.

The more I travel, the less I take – unless I'm off on a trip where lots of gear is essential, as it was when I went to Antarctica, my luggage rarely weighs more than 10–12kg. My dirty secret is list-making. I don't just have a master list, but I have lists for "European city breaks", "villa with friends", "long-haul, always hot", "adventure, cold at night, nothing smart", and I simply try really hard never to do a trip that involves three days on a train followed by dinner with the ambassador.

So in this chapter I'll look at the items you may choose to put on your packing list – and the pitfalls to be wary of, especially when flying – and I'll start with a look at the luggage you'll use to carry it in.

Suitcase or rucksack?

Rucksacks are starting to shed their rough-and-ready backpacker image and smarten up, with some even offering trolley wheels so you can pull them along. But if you won't need to carry your luggage too far, a sturdy suitcase is probably the answer.

Suitcases

If you check your suitcase in with an airline, expect it to be thrown from a height on to hard tarmac, left out in the rain, then chucked on to the airport carousel where it will be further bashed around with everyone else's cases, and jammed against part of the mechanism, which can tear fabric. Hard-shelled cases therefore make most sense: when buying, check the lock mechanisms, zips, wheels and handles are sturdy as these are the bits that break off. Like so many travellers, I am a fan of the wheeled cases that can be pulled along with little effort. You should pull a few around the shop before buying – some have short handles that tall people find uncomfortable; cheaper ones may have wonky wheels, or wheels that are not protected by the shell of the case and so are more likely to snap off. Consider the case's weight, too. Some weigh several kilograms, which will all count towards the total weight of luggage you can take on a plane.

It's not necessary to spend a fortune to get a decent suitcase – the likes of Samsonite, Delsey and Antler make perfectly good, reasonably priced cases, though if your budget stretches, companies such as Tumi, Mandarina Duck and Bill Amberg are good starting places for quality luggage that makes a statement. But designer bags may attract the attention of thieves, as Victoria Beckham found to her cost when three of her expensive Louis Vuitton cases were stolen after she flew from Miami to London on British Airways in April 2000. The problems of lost, delayed or damaged luggage are among the most common subjects in the postbag at *The Times* travel desk, so I'll look at these issues later in this chapter (*see* page 251).

Effective packing involves separating your gear into logical sections. Toiletries should go in a waterproof, sealable bag (*see* "Towels and toiletries", page 235) and medical items should go into clear Ziploc bags or small Tupperware containers. Plastic bags are always useful, for wet swimwear, dirty underwear or muddy boots, so pack a few extras. I've never found a packing technique that stops clothes getting wrinkled, but rolling clothes instead of folding them minimises creasing, as does hanging them up in a steamy bathroom. Some travellers suggest filling extra space in your suitcase with bubble wrap, which stops items moving around and breaking, and gives you space for purchases made abroad. If you are using a pull-along case, pack heavier items nearest the wheels so lighter ones lie on top when you pull it.

Rucksacks

These are not only the obvious choice for gap-year students on round-the-world trips, but are also the best luggage for adventurous travellers on shorter holidays on which you will be hauling your luggage on and off different types of transport, and may have to carry it for some distance.

The key consideration when choosing a rucksack is how it fits you. We're all shaped differently so you should try on your rucksack just as you would an item of clothing or a pair of boots, preferably having filled it to see how it feels when loaded. A cheaper model may fit you better than a more expensive one.

It's essential that the waist strap fits snugly above your hips – if you're buying your first rucksack you may be surprised at how much weight you carry on your hips, rather than on your shoulders, when it is correctly worn. Check the shoulder straps fit properly – their function is to ensure the pack fits snugly against your back, rather than to bear its weight, so they should be padded and should sit on your shoulderbone, not your collarbone. Good packs give you the option of adjusting the distance between hip and shoulder straps, to suit people of different heights, and have a chest clasp for extra stability. All straps should be easily adjustable. When you're carrying a full pack, it should feel like an extension of your body, not an alien weight on your shoulders – if you turn, it should turn with you and not sway loosely, for example – so I think it is vital to buy a rucksack from a shop where you can try it on, rather than buying it by mail order.

Rucksacks are measured by their capacity in litres, and I think 65 litres is big enough for everything except a serious mountaineering expedition. Old-style rucksacks open at the top and have a zipped-off section at the bottom, which is useful for carrying items such as a sleeping bag or hiking boots which you can get at without having to pull everything else out.

Over the past few years, the "sideloader" type of rucksack has become very popular. This is a soft pack that unzips around the sides rather like a suitcase, but has the straps of a rucksack. It also has a canvas cover that can be zipped over the straps, converting the bag to a smarter-looking holdall, which can help if you're trying to wangle an upgrade on a plane or convince a suspicious border guard how respectable you are; it also stops the straps getting caught on the airport carousel. Paul Goodyer, owner of the **Nomad** chain of travel gear shops, says "sideloaders" are by far the most popular type of rucksack he now sells.

The latest refinement is a rucksack-suitcase hybrid: a rucksack that also has wheels and a pull-out handle, produced by the likes of Eagle Creek, Vango and Berghaus. I have not used one, though I have used other Eagle Creek bags and found them to be practically indestructible. The "rucksack on wheels" seems ideal if you're going on a clubbing holiday to Ibiza or Greece, for example – it's not as square as a suitcase, not as scruffy as a rucksack – but before buying one think about the type of holidays you take, and ask yourself if these bags are too expensive or elaborate for your needs.

Rucksacks are never fully waterproof, and even if you don't expect to encounter wet weather, they can emerge wet from the hold of the plane. The best protection is to pack your gear inside several waterproof nylon bags with sealed seams which roll over at the top and clip together; they are widely available from outdoor shops for around £6–£8. Cheaper still is lining your rucksack with a dustbin bag.

Shoulder bags

Every traveller needs a bag for daily use, and for most holidays or business trips you're bound to possess handbags, briefcases and the like that do the job well. But for more adventurous trips you'll need a small, sturdy rucksack to carry your camera, water bottle and guidebook while leaving your hands free.

The new sideloader-style rucksacks often come with an attached "day sack" that can be zipped off and used on its own; in my experience these are too small to be useful. I'd recommend you buy a bag specifically for the purposes you have in mind – a small rucksack is not madly expensive but you will probably have it with you every minute of the day, so it's important to buy one that has the right amount of space and easily accessible compartments for your essentials.

The one I've used for years is made by **Eagle Creek** – it's extremely strong, with plenty of pockets, and straps that allow me to carry it either as a rucksack on my back, or shoulder-bag style across my body. This looks far less silly than wearing it "backwards" across your chest while carrying your big rucksack on your back. I see travellers doing this the world over, and it screams, "I'm carrying all my worldly goods, the valuable ones are in this bag at the front, and I really can't move very fast if you grab it."

Locking your luggage

If your suitcase has a combination lock, you avoid the problem of losing keys. Otherwise ensure your case or rucksack has sturdy double zips whose zippers can be padlocked together (and check the holes in the zipper are big enough to accommodate a good padlock).

It's worth investigating **Catch 22** (01942 511820, **www.catch22products. co.uk**) whose founder, Lincoln Yates, has spent a lot of time developing safety gadgets for travellers. For example, he's come up with Saklocks, locking devices for rucksack buckles (though they cannot stop the pack being slashed open) and also sells the Sakbag, a padlockable nylon rucksack cover that will deter thieves and stop straps catching in the luggage carousel at airports.

It is possible to be too paranoid. Travellers in South America used to put chicken wire inside their pack to prevent it being slashed open. These days you can buy in outdoor gear shops a chain "exomesh" that covers your pack and does the same job. This strikes me as a step too far: it's heavy, you might snag your clothes on it, and sight of such a precaution could make a thief think you have something worth stealing. Instead, carry a bike chain or strong cable with a padlock to hook through your rucksack straps or suitcase handle to secure it to the luggage rack of a train or a car roof rack. It will be useful if you hire a bike while on holiday, too.

Some airports offer a service where your bag is wrapped in a type of industrial clingfilm before you check it in, which makes it harder for thieves to tamper with it, although once this has been done it's difficult to pick the bag up. You're more likely to find this offered in parts of Africa and South America where there is a history of pilfering by baggage handlers.

Don't have your bag wrapped like this if you are flying to the USA, however, where security has been radically revamped since the terror attacks of September 11, 2001. In January 2003 the US Transportation Security Administration (TSA) asked passengers travelling through American airports not to lock their luggage so it could be inspected by security officials. Passengers complained: if they complied, they risked items being stolen, but their insurance claim would be nullified because the bag was unlocked. If they locked the bag, US customs officers might force the lock to search it under these new powers.

A solution has emerged: there are now locks on the market for which American security officials have a master key. They are made by **Travel Sentry** (**www.travelsentry.org**) and **Safe Skies** (**www.safeskieslocks.com**) and are available in Britain through most outdoor gear shops, such as **Nomad Travel Stores** (020 8889 7014, **www.nomadtravel.co.uk**), and the excellent US mail order company **Magellan's**, which has a UK office (0870 600 1601, **www.magellans.co.uk**).

If your suitcase is normally locked by a combination rather than a key, see if you can lock the zippers together with a TSA-approved lock instead, if visiting the USA. If it has catches rather than zips, consider leaving it unlocked but securing it with a luggage strap with TSA-approved locks, available from Catch 22. Further information from the TSA (**www.tsa.gov**).

What to pack

If you take every item I suggest in this chapter, you'll curse me every day of your trip as you lug an enormous bag of junk around the planet. Instead use this master list for suggestions of what you might need, then refine it to suit your preferences and the sort of trip you'll be taking.

Clothes

If you're off to the Med for your summer holiday, or whizzing over to a European city on business, your only clothing considerations are the weight of your luggage, and the temperatures you will encounter. But if you expect very hot, cold or wet weather, or rough travel, it's worth visiting an outdoor gear shop to look at high-tech performance clothing.

This specialist gear used to look pretty nerdy, but manufacturers such as **Columbia** and **The North Face** are now producing outdoor gear that's much better cut and even comes in modish styles such as three-quarter-length trousers. Women should check out **Thaw** which makes stylish and practical clothing designed specifically for them. (Contact details in the Directory, page 397.)

Think about the type of trip you'll be taking before you get carried away buying the most expensive gear. If you're going somewhere hot, simple cotton clothes can be the best – they keep you cool and, if you get wet, they dry quickly. Some clothes now come with a Sun Protection Factor (SPF) – Columbia, for example, has a good lightweight range with this feature. But ordinary T-shirts, so long as they have not been worn thin, offer a certain level of sun protection anyway, especially if they are in dark colours.

Synthetic gear tends to come into its own if you are visiting places with extreme temperatures, either hot or cold. It's crease-resistant, lightweight, tough and less likely to rot in humid conditions, although it can feel clammy in hot weather. It folds up smaller in your pack than conventional clothing, and is designed to be easy to wash and drip dry. Synthetic materials "wick away" sweat from your body, which is great in cold conditions, but less important in hot climates where your body needs some perspiration to cool it down. Essentially, for cold climates you need a base layer that wicks sweat away from your body, a fleece layer to keep you warm, and an outer layer (jacket) that's wind- and rain-proof. Insulated jackets, like sleeping bags, can be filled with down or with synthetic material; the former is lighter but doesn't work properly if it gets wet; the latter is usually cheaper and bulkier but can better withstand wet conditions.

Always check the details when you are buying high-performance gear. Does the hood close snugly around your face, but still allow you to see when you turn your head? Are the zips covered to stop rain leaking in through them? Are there pockets in the places you need them?

Silk underwear and long johns are great in cold weather, and extremely light to carry. Wool is warm but very bulky. Modern fleece is much lighter: for example, check out The North Face's new Apex range of "softshells", fleeces that are wind- and shower-proof. You should also carry a light waterproof jacket.

Jeans are hopeless for serious travelling: they are heavy, they are too hot in warm weather but don't keep you warm in cold weather, and once wet they take ages to dry. But if you're going on a summer beach holiday you'll probably want to take your most stylish pair.

I never travel without a sarong (also known as a pareo). It has myriad uses: skirt, towel, headscarf, picnic table, dressing gown among them. It's fun to buy a new one for every trip, as they are cheap and widely available.

Footwear

As with rucksacks, buying good walking boots is something you should take time over, visiting a specialist store and quizzing staff about the sort of conditions the boot is suited to. Modern boots do not need the endless wearing in that old-fashioned leather ones used to, but it is still wise to walk in them at home before you travel. Buy good socks, too, and thin silk socks as liners if you are going somewhere cold. Wear the socks you will be travelling in when you try on your boots. Feet expand while you walk, so ensure there is some room in the boots when you try them on.

Durable sandals with Velcro straps (made by companies such as **Teva**) are very useful in hot countries – they are surprisingly comfortable for city walking and will dry quickly, although you'll get a stripey tan on your feet. Flip-flops are also worth packing, and are particularly useful in less-than-clean bathrooms or at swimming pools. But while flip-flops have become fashionable summer footwear in Europe, in other countries, particularly in Asia, they are seen as poor people's footwear and their use is confined to the bathroom, so it may be frowned on to wear them in smart situations.

Hat

Vital on most trips, to protect from the sun (particularly important for babies and children) or to keep your head warm in cold weather. It's essential to find one you feel comfortable with – if you feel like a prat in a hat, you won't wear it. Baseball caps might not suit William Hague but they're fairly inoffensive and widely available. Legionnaire-style ones with fabric at the back protect your neck from the sun. Canadian firm **Tilley** makes popular travellers' hats that come with a lifetime guarantee; their style – with an all-round wide brim – is sensible if you're going to be in the sun.

Outdoor-gear shops sell plenty of fleeced-lined varieties for cold conditions – and a balaclava is useful if you're skiing somewhere very cold, for example. Men may wish to invest in a proper Panama or other hat at an outfitter such as **Edward Bates** of Jermyn St in London where it will be steamed to fit you.

Money belt

Having spent two years backpacking around Asia, I have taken some time to cut the umbilical cord with my money belt. In the 1980s, before we had cash machines and internet cafés on every street corner, losing your money caused real problems and most travellers I met wore a money belt under their clothes and slept with it under their pillow at night.

It's still a sensible purchase if you are on the road for any length of time, or going somewhere rather rough and ready. Wear it under your clothes, out of sight, and never open it in public – transfer the day's money into your wallet so no one ever sees the money belt. As it will be against your skin, choose one made of cotton, and keep money, plane tickets, etc, in a plastic bag inside the belt so your sweat does not soak into them.

Towels and toiletries

Independent travellers find it useful to carry a towel, which should be large enough to preserve your modesty should you need to use a dormitory or communal changing room. I do not like the microfibre travel towels which supposedly have excellent water absorbing properties, but which fold up very small when dry: I find they quickly become smelly, and are not, in fact, so absorbent, but many travellers swear by them and they are widely available in outdoor-gear shops. If you are showering before checking out of a hostel or hotel which does not provide towels, dry yourself on the hotel's bedsheet to avoid having to pack a wet towel.

If you stay in the sort of hotels that provide smellies in the bathroom, pinch them — the pots are usually perfect travelling sizes. Fill bottles of shampoo, etc, only three-quarters full if you are flying as they have a tendency to burst open in the air. Wrapping them individually in cling film will stop leaks from spreading. Look for a toiletries bag that has a hook so you can hang it up in the bathroom; bags with transparent zipped pouches, so you can see at a glance where everything is, are useful too.

Medical kit and sunscreen

You should always pack a simple first-aid kit, even if you are only going to be lying on a Spanish beach for a week. I suggest what you might put in it in chapter 10.

Even if you're not heading for the beach, you're likely to be outdoors for far more of the day when you're on holiday than when you're at home, so it's important to pack sunscreen. For more on this, and what to do if you have too much sun, see chapter 10.

Practical accessories

Alarm clock

Essential for catching early morning flights, etc. Most mobile phones also have an alarm clock feature that works even if the phone is switched off.

Binoculars

Only really essential if you're going on safari or a bird-watching trip, when no one will want to lend you their pair for fear of missing a flash of elusive prey. Otherwise, they are a luxury, though it's wonderful to have them with you if you can justify the space and weight in your luggage. They can be useful even in cities, for example for inspecting the beautifully decorated roof of a cathedral.

Books

Novels are my downfall when it comes to travelling light. After once being stranded on an island in the Philippines with only Sidney Sheldon for company, I vowed never again to be short of reading matter, so I often end up carrying two or three novels. John Hatt, author of the classic guide *The Tropical Traveller*, writes: "If, say, I need to visit a government office for a visa extension, I wouldn't consider going without the safety net of 300 unread pages." I couldn't agree more.

If I'm travelling alone I quiz fellow travellers to see if they have something decent to swap. If I'm travelling with friends or family, I encourage each person to take something we all want to read so we can swap among ourselves. If you are looking for novels overseas, head for backpackers' cafés where book swaps can be arranged or second-hand books purchased. Paharganj in Delhi and the Khao San Road in Bangkok are particularly good places to buy books.

Compass

Essential kit if you're on a walking holiday, but also surprisingly useful on other trips, such as if you're somewhere you cannot read the local script. I'd still be in the back streets of Beijing now had I not had a compass to help me navigate in a city where street signs are only in Chinese characters. Learn how to use it before you go. Silva make excellent compasses; available from outdoor shops.

Diary, address book, notebook

It's lovely to look back on a travel diary, so consider keeping one even if you do not do so at home. If you do not want to risk losing your address book, or you only store addresses in your computer, print off a set of address labels before you travel, which you can simply stick on to postcards. A notebook and pens are always useful.

Documents and paperwork

This is a checklist of items you will probably need on most holidays; for detailed information on issues such as visas, insurance, EHIC and carrying money abroad, *see* chapter 6.

- Passport and relevant visas.

- Plenty of spare passport photographs.

- Air/rail/ferry tickets and accommodation vouchers.

- Insurance documents, including a note of the emergency phone number.

- European Health Insurance Card.

- If you are a student, bring ID as it can qualify you for discounts.

- Money: cash, including local currency if available here, debit card for using at cash machines, credit card, travellers' cheques.

- Cards showing membership of frequent traveller schemes, for airlines, Eurostar etc.

- Vaccination certificate, details of any allergies, your blood group, glasses prescription, etc. If you are on medication bring your prescription.

- Driving licence and international driving licence, plus certificate of motor insurance and vehicle registration documents if you are taking your car abroad.

- Receipts for expensive camera or other equipment.

- Photocopies of the above documents, placed in different parts of your luggage (and one set left at home with a friend or relative).

- Business travellers should carry plenty of business cards.

Door guards

If you are staying in a hotel where you feel security is not all it should be, you can buy a Door Guard from **Catch 22** which stops the door being forced open from outside. A low-tech option is to carry a rubber door wedge to shove under your door, or to place a chair under the door handle to prevent it being opened. For more on personal safety, see chapter 9.

Ear plugs

On holiday on the Greek island of Skiathos, our villa was in a quiet village – but it was across the bay from Skiathos Town, and the thumping bass from the disco carried clearly across the water every night until 6am. Ear plugs were vital and I've carried them everywhere since. You might also be a victim of barking dogs, roadworks, noisy neighbours in thin-walled hotels, or planes taking off if you're at an airport hotel.

Electrical adaptor

There are broadly two types, for Europe, and for North America and Australia. However some countries, such as Cyprus, use the same type of square three-pin plug as we use in Britain. Consult a guidebook before you travel to see what type you'll need; the website **www.kropla.com** also has a useful guide.

Expedition gear

A sleeping bag or sheet sleeping bag, mosquito net and sleeping mat can be useful even for relatively short, adventurous holidays. Outdoor shops sell a wide range and can give advice based on the type of trip you are undertaking. Also consult *The Backpacker's Handbook* by Chris Townsend (McGraw-Hill, £11.99).

Sleeping bags can be bulky, so think hard before taking one – a sheet sleeping bag may be sufficient. Down bags fold up smaller, but take ages to dry out if they get wet. If you are camping, a Therm-a-Rest is more comfortable than the old-fashioned foam mat – it is inflatable yet rolls up fairly small. However it may develop a puncture for which you will need a puncture repair kit.

Gaffa tape

A roll of this strong tape has more uses for the traveller than I could possibly list, but here's a start: for temporary bike puncture repair, covering a hole in a mosquito net or a tear in a tent, taping up a broken suitcase, fastening together the legs of two single beds to make a double, taping a stash of spare cash to the top (underside) of a bedside cabinet drawer, forming spare cycle clips, to stop your drink moving around on the tray table on a plane, to repair a watch strap, to create a sticky tape trap on the floor for ants, to hold bandages or splints in place, to fix the broken wing mirror on to your hire car, to repair shoes...

Games

Even if you're travelling light, Travel Scrabble, backgammon or a pack of cards can be lifesavers if you face a long delay. I've found numerous uses for a Frisbee, too – it is light to carry, makes a useful picnic plate and makes a great ice-breaker for playing games with new friends. Once, on a train in Russia, when the carriage attendant refused to unlock the lavatory door, a friend of mine used the Frisbee as an alternative receptacle, throwing the contents out of the window afterwards. We didn't use it as a plate again after that, I should add.

Guidebooks and maps

It's much easier to buy these before you go; good maps can be particularly hard to find in many countries. For a detailed look at what's on the market, *see* chapter 1.

Miscellaneous items

- Sunglasses (and a note of your prescription, if appropriate).

- Gym kit, if your hotel has a gym or you fancy a jog; swimsuit and goggles, snorkel and mask.

- Camera (for tips on travel photography, *see* chapter 9).

- Multivitamins.

- Umbrella.

- Small sewing kit.

- Teaspoon (useful for snacks and eating fruit).

- Box of matches or cigarette lighter.

- Cheap watch.

- Simple gifts for people you meet (postcards from home, good pens, small souvenirs).

- Short-wave radio.

- Small stapler to keep receipts together.

- Inflatable pillow, a lifesaver if you are travelling on hard-seated buses.

Mobile phone

There's the obvious ease of keeping in touch with home, and the pleasure you gain from bypassing the often heinous hotel telephone charges, but mobile phones can also be useful *in situ*. During guided tours of both Mexico City and Sydney, for example, I have stored my guide's mobile number in my phone to make meeting up much easier. (To avoid arguments with your significant other, it's wise to delete the number for Benito/Jim/Luisa once your tour is over.)

The downsides of taking your phone are that overseas calls both to and from your mobile can be expensive; and you will need to carry a phone charger and the appropriate electrical adapter for the country you are visiting. For more information on taking your phone abroad, *see* chapter 6.

Penknife

There's little to beat the classic Swiss Army knife, made by either **Victorinox** or **Wenger**, though some are heavy and have more features than you'll ever need. I think the most useful are knife, corkscrew, bottle and tin openers, small screwdriver for repairing sunglasses, scissors, tweezers and saw. Having scissors in your knife saves taking a separate pair in your medical kit.

Other popular brands of pocket knife are made by **Gerber** and **Leatherman**. These have pliers and would suit anyone undertaking a long drive across Africa or other expedition, but are rather unwieldy for less adventurous trips. But backpackers might find Leatherman's Micra and Juice ranges suit them.

All manufacturers say that their stainless steel knives are not "rustproof", but "corrosion resistant" – you must look after your knife to prevent it rusting, especially if you are using it around salt water. Wash it in soapy water, dry it thoroughly above a stove or using a hairdryer, and oil it with a light machine oil such as WD-40. Finally, remember that you cannot carry a penknife in hand luggage on a plane.

Phrasebook and small dictionary

I think it's always important to learn at least a few words of the language of the country you're visiting – not only is it polite to be able to greet other people in their native tongue, but your holiday will be far more relaxing if you are able to read simple signs for "washroom", "exit", "cash desk" and so on.

String and dental floss

String can be useful for improvising a washing line and is less bulky than portable clothes lines that are sold at airports. Dental floss is useful for more than the obvious; a boyfriend I was travelling with in the Philippines sewed my rucksack up with some when it tore, as it's so strong.

Torch

On a camping trip many years ago a member of our party became ill in the middle of the night, and I was dispatched to a nearby farmhouse to summon help. In the confusion I forgot to grab my torch – and walked straight into an enormous pig slurry. My fellow campers later made me sleep with my legs sticking out of the tent.

A torch is useful on every type of trip, whether you break down in the hire car and need to look under the bonnet, there's a power cut in the hotel, or the walk back to your villa is ill-lit and the pavement uneven. For years, **Maglite** was the unchallenged choice of travellers. It's a well-designed, hard-wearing American torch in various sizes. However Maglites are under threat from the new LED torches which last far longer, and whose bulbs rarely need replacing. **Petzl** produces a range of these with elastic straps so you can wear them on your head. Yes, you look a bit of a twit with a torch on your head, but the girl who runs into the pig pen because she did not have a torch at all looks sillier. Head torches are brilliant for jobs such as fixing the car or putting up a tent in the dark or for reading in bed if there is no bedside lamp.

Water bottle

Time and again I meet holidaymakers who have become ill simply through drinking too little water (sometimes, but not always, combined with drinking too much alcohol). I cannot overstress the importance of drinking plenty of water to maintain good health.

For most holidays, there's no need to buy a special water bottle – a plastic mineral water bottle is fine. Think of the planet and try to refill the same bottle instead of buying different ones every day. Good hotels provide drinking water for free. Although our tendency is to be wary of tap water overseas, in many western countries it is perfectly drinkable. But if in doubt, ask, and if still in doubt, avoid.

If you're going on a more adventurous trip, you should probably invest in a sturdy water bottle, such as those made by **Sigg**. It should be able to tolerate boiling water, as boiling is the simplest method of ensuring water is safe to drink. A lid that's attached to the bottle by a chain is a lid you're less likely to lose. Never fill your water bottle with anything other than water, as you won't get rid of the taste thereafter, so carry a sturdy mug for making up other drinks.

Whistle

Women in particular may like to carry a whistle to attract attention in situations where they feel threatened. It is a light and innocuous object, whereas a rape alarm carried for the same purpose might attract unwanted attention from customs officers. Hikers and skiers may also find a whistle useful, if for example they are injured and fall out of sight of potential rescuers.

For a list of suppliers of all items listed here, see the Directory, page 397.

Transporting your bags

Checked baggage

There is no legislation governing the amount of luggage airlines allow us to check in to the hold, but many carriers follow guidelines compiled by the Geneva-based International Air Transport Association (IATA). These state that you should be able to check in 20kg luggage if you are travelling in economy, 30kg if you're in business class and 40kg if you're in first class. But there are variations – for example, British Airways allows economy passengers to check in 23kg – so it's important to check with your travel agent or airline the limits that apply to your journey.

You should also ask if the more generous "two piece" rule applies. On flights to some destinations, you are allowed to check in two pieces of luggage rather than a certain weight of luggage. This applies to journeys to, from or via the following countries, though you should check before you travel in case it has changed: USA, Canada, Mexico, Central America, the Caribbean, Bermuda and Nigeria.

Under the two-piece rule you are usually allowed to check in two cases of up to 32kg each, making a back-breaking 64kg of luggage, even if you are travelling in economy. However, the rules are starting to change. In November 2005 **American Airlines (www.aa.com)** started charging international passengers US$25 for each bag that weighed between 23kg and 32kg, and in March 2006 **Air New Zealand (www.airnewzealand.com)** reduced the weight of bag that economy passengers can check in from 32kg to 23kg. From October 2006, **British Airways (www.ba.com)** will also reduce the weight limit for each bag to 23kg. **Virgin Atlantic** has a good explanation of the two-piece rule on the baggage section of its website **(www.virgin-atlantic.com)**.

Airlines are within their rights to charge an excess baggage fee if you carry more than they allow. This might be calculated according to the number of extra bags you are taking, or the bags' weight above the limit; a typical guideline is for the airline to charge 1.5 per cent of the full one-way economy fare for each extra kilo of luggage. It is perfectly possible for you to be charged this on one leg of the flight but not on another.

In 2006 the budget airlines **Ryanair (www.ryanair.com)** and **Flybe (www.flybe.com)** started to charge passengers for checking in luggage to the hold. Since February 2006, Flybe has charged passengers £2 for each piece of checked luggage (or £4 if they do not book it in online in advance). Ryanair charges passengers £3.50 for each piece of checked luggage (£7 if not booked online). In return, the airlines claim to be reducing fares for passengers with hand luggage only, and have introduced online check-in, although with Ryanair this is only available to hand-luggage passengers (for more on check-in procedures, *see* chapter 8). Both airlines allow 10kg of hand luggage, and claim that the system is fairer on people who do not carry much luggage, and that it speeds up the system for those who do. I expect other budget carriers will follow their lead.

Most airlines allow two people travelling together to pool their checked luggage, but Ryanair does not and will charge a traveller if their suitcase exceeds the limit for checked luggage (in Ryanair's case, 20kg), even if their partner's bag is well under this weight.

If you are travelling by train, cruise ship, bus or ferry, you rarely need to worry about luggage limits: it's more a question of how much you can comfortably carry. Cruise ships do not bother with weight limits (though if you are flying to join a cruise you will have to consider the airline's limits).

Packing tips

- Never pack anything on impulse at the last minute – make a list and stick to it.

- An immutable law of air travel says that you will buy three magazines, a large bottle of water, a novel, an oversized bar of Toblerone and some tax-free moisturiser in the airport lounge. Try to save room in your carry-on bag for these extras.

- When planning what to take, mug up on the cultural mores of the country you're visiting to avoid no-nos such as wearing camouflage trousers in Barbados (this can get you arrested), or short skirts in a Muslim country, which could cause offence (see chapter 9).

- The old saw about taking half the amount of stuff but twice the amount of money you originally intended is worth repeating, although there's little need to carry large amounts of cash or travellers' cheques these days given the availability of cash machines overseas (see chapter 6).

- If you forget something, don't panic – they sell nappies/toothpaste/ batteries overseas. For less obvious items it can be fun to nose around foreign markets or grocery shops to hunt down the nearest equivalent.

- For an entertaining and useful website about packing light, visit www.onebag.com.

Carry-on luggage

Most airlines allow you to take only a meagre 5kg–7kg of hand luggage into the cabin – although Ryanair and Flybe allow 10kg, and easyJet and British Airways have no weight restriction "within reasonable limits" – you should be able to put the bag into the overhead locker without help. IATA's guidelines, which are followed by many airlines, suggest carry-on bags should be no more than 22in (56cm) long, 18in (45cm) wide and 10in (25cm) deep, making a total dimension of 45in (115cm), which is how this measurement is often expressed by airlines. But in August 2006, the rules changed (see below, page 246).

There are legitimate reasons for the weight limits – no one wants heavy bags to fall from the overhead locker and hit passengers on the head. But when I ask airlines why passengers are then allowed to buy heavy bottles of alcohol and take those on board too, they are reluctant to give me the honest answer – which is that airlines and airports make a profit from such sales, which appears to be enough to override the much-vaunted safety concerns. Personally, I would sooner have a small rucksack fall on my head than a bottle of whisky, but perhaps I am missing the point.

In your hand luggage you should have your passport, tickets and money, travel insurance documents, valuables such as your camera and, if your camera is the old-fashioned sort, camera film, and basic toiletries in case your checked luggage is lost or delayed. But check the new rules, page 246.

You must pack any medicine you are taking in your hand luggage, and bring a copy of the prescription. In spring 2005 a British holidaymaker was imprisoned for eight weeks in Dubai because traces of the drug Codeine were found in her urine. The presence of this substance in your body is illegal in the United Arab Emirates unless you can produce an appropriate prescription, which the woman was unable to do. She was only released once the prescription was obtained from her doctor in England, translated into Arabic and presented to the court.

Rules post-September 11

After the Twin Towers attacks, airlines and airports swiftly introduced new security rules governing what could or could not be taken on board. Newspapers were full of pictures of the sharp items, such as scissors, tweezers and nail files, which had been confiscated from passengers' hand luggage before they boarded a flight.

These rules have now been somewhat relaxed. You can now carry in your cabin luggage tweezers, round-ended butter or plastic knives, plastic scissors and other items previously banned (for a detailed list see the **US Transportation Security Administration** website at **www.tsa.gov** or the IATA website at **www.iata.org/bags**). Sharp items such as scissors and penknives are still banned from being carried in the cabin. If you are diabetic, for example, and need medical syringes with you during the flight, they must be properly packed and documented. If in doubt about what is permitted, consult your airline.

Rules post–August 2006

Following the major security alert at Britain's airports in August 2006, new hand-luggage rules emerged. These remain in place for the foreseeable future and apply to all classes of traveller, but they may change, so check with your airline. You may now take only one item of hand luggage, no bigger than 18in (45cm) by 14in (35cm) by 6in (16cm), and nothing in your pockets. Liquids, including drinks and cosmetics, cannot be taken through security, except essential medicines and baby milk or food. Once airside, you can buy items in duty-free shops and take them on board, but you cannot take liquids on flights to the USA or Canada. Details: **www.dft.gov.uk**.

Sports equipment

Golfers, skiers, cyclists and other wanting to take their equipment on the plane face different rules from airline to airline. Ryanair charges you £17 per flight to carry golf clubs, fishing tackle etc, regardless of weight. Budget airline **bmibaby** (**www.bmibaby.com**) charges a flat £10 to carry golf clubs or other "outsize" bits of sports equipment, as does **easyJet** (**www.easyjet.com**). On British Airways the rules vary depending on destination and what you wish to carry: for golf clubs, typically your checked baggage allowance is increased to 30kg to accommodate the extra weight of the clubs, after which excess charges apply. Ski equipment, however, must come within your existing weight allowance.

Airlines, particularly the budget carriers, often specify that they only accept sports gear on a "limited release" basis, which means they won't pay up if it is lost or damaged – so good travel insurance is vital.

On most airlines, cyclists must remove or fix sideways the pedals, fix the handlebars sideways and pack the bike in box or bag – some airlines, such as American Airlines, offer boxes specially made for this purpose – and the bike usually counts towards your normal weight allowance.

Luggage delivery services

Two companies, **First Luggage** (0845 270 0670, **www.firstluggage.com**) and **Carry My Luggage** (0845 009 0362, **www.carrymyluggage.com**), will transport your bags for you, saving you the hassle of lugging them to and from the airport and checking them in. You book your bags to be collected and a courier picks them up; they are then flown by FedEx to your destination and should be delivered to your hotel or villa before you arrive.

The services operate across Europe and much of the Americas and Asia, but don't yet operate to Africa. First Luggage also goes to Australia and New Zealand.

Bringing it all back home

Going on a "booze cruise" to France now seems like the inalienable right of every British citizen, whether they're stocking up on cheap beer for a student party or fine wine and champagne for a country wedding. But this phenomenon has really boomed since 1 July, 1999, when the European Union (EU) changed from a system of duty-free, under which you could only bring a measly couple of bottles of wine and 200 cigarettes into Britain, to a system of duty paid.

Under the duty-paid rules, you can now bring pretty much anything from another EU country into Britain, although in the case of "excise goods" (basically, tobacco and alcohol), everything you bring must be for your personal use.

On the Customs & Excise website (**www.hmrc.gov.uk** and click on "travel information") there's a table showing at what point Customs officers are likely to become suspicious that what you carry is not just for personal consumption – if, for example, you are bringing in more than 10 litres of spirits, 90 litres of wine, 110 litres of beer or 3,200 cigarettes. If you are visiting some of the newer EU countries, including Hungary, Poland and the Czech Republic, there are still strict limits on how much tobacco you can bring back to Britain.

Who's in the European Union

Austria, Belgium, Cyprus, Czech Republic, Denmark, Estonia, Finland, France, Germany, Greece, Hungary, Ireland, Italy, Latvia, Lithuania, Luxemburg, Malta, the Netherlands, Poland, Portugal, Slovakia, Slovenia, Spain, Sweden, the UK.

Some popular holiday destinations are not in the EU – including Turkey and Croatia. These countries, along with Bulgaria and Romania, are being considered for future membership.

The rules are much stricter if you are coming back to Britain from outside the EU, where the old duty-free system still applies. Rather confusingly, this also includes Gibraltar, the Canary Islands and the Channel Islands, because these three territories are outside the EU's tax framework. From all these destinations you can only bring in the following amounts of "excise goods" without having to pay UK tax or duty:

- 200 cigarettes or 100 cigarillos or 50 cigars or 250g of tobacco.

- 60cc of perfume.

- 2 litres of still table wine.

- 250cc of eau de toilette.

- 1 litre of spirits or strong liqueurs over 22 per cent volume or 2 litres of fortified wine, sparkling wine or other liqueurs such as port or sherry.

- £145 worth of all other goods including gifts and souvenirs.

Yes, that's right: a mere £145 of other goods. Spend more than this and you must pay both duty and VAT on the entire amount you have spent (not just the bit over £145). So if you fancy a shopping spree in America, where for the last couple of years the dollar has been very weak against the pound, you need only pop an iPod and a few CDs into your shopping basket and you will quickly reach that limit. Coleen McLoughlin, the girlfriend of footballer Wayne Rooney, was famously caught out by this rule when she had to pay thousands of pounds in duty and VAT after being stopped by British Customs officers after a shopping trip to America.

Be sure to choose the correct channel when leaving the baggage hall. Take the red channel if you have goods to declare. If you have nothing to declare and have come from the EU you go through the blue channel, and if you have nothing to declare but have come from outside the EU you go through the green channel.

Anyone choosing the red channel meets a Customs officer who will work out what you owe. First you must pay duty on all your purchases. Rates of duty are confusingly varied: there is no duty on books, digital cameras or laptops, but there's 3.5 per cent on CDs, 4.9 per cent on camera film and

12 per cent on most clothes, for example. You then pay VAT at 17.5 per cent on the new total value of your shopping. Customs officers tell me that altogether you will typically face a bill of another 25 per cent or so on top of what you spent overseas.

The **Customs & Excise** department has an advice line: call 0845 010 9000, or if you're calling from outside the UK ring +44 20 8929 0152. C&E also publishes a useful leaflet, imaginatively entitled "Customs Notice 1" and available on its website (**www.hmrc.gov.uk**), or call the advice line to have it posted to you.

The £145 duty-free goods allowance is set to rise to about £340 from 1 January 2007, under a European Union directive announced in Brussels in February 2006. For details, check the Customs & Excise website closer to the time.

Leaving it all behind

There are some things you should not bring home. Where most holidaymakers are concerned, the areas where you might unwittingly fall foul of the rules concern food and plants, items made from endangered animals, and antiques.

Food and plants

If you are coming back to Britain from an EU country you are able to bring in food and plants with few problems. The only real no-nos are unpasteurised milk or its products, and anything that may be diseased. There are special rules if you are coming back from Iceland, Greenland, the Faroe Islands, Switzerland or Liechtenstein: you can bring in food products, but only up to certain limits. Note that wherever you bring food in from, it must only be for your personal consumption.

If you are coming back from any other non-EU country the rules are much stricter. To prevent the spread of disease, many food and plant items are banned from being brought into the UK. You can bring in up to a kilo of some animal products such as honey, fish or eggs, but you can't bring in any meat or dairy products. There are also strict rules about bringing plants or soil back to Britain from outside the EU: items such as potatoes and citrus plants are banned outright; other items are subject to restrictions. You can check what's allowed and what's forbidden by contacting the rather Orwellian-sounding **Plant Health Service Delivery Unit**, part of the Department for Environment, Food and Rural Affairs (Defra), on 01904 455174.

The rules are summarised in two Customs & Excise leaflets, both entitled "If in doubt, leave it out", one referring to plants and animals, the other to meat and animal produce; they are available on the Customs & Excise website (**www.hmrc.gov.uk**) or by calling 0845 010 9000 for copies to be sent to you. But while Customs & Excise are the guys who enforce the rules, it's Defra that sets them in the first place, so if you have specific questions about bringing any food items into Britain, call Defra on 0845 933 5577 (or +44 20 7238 6951 if you're outside the UK) or check its website at **www.defra.gov.uk**.

It is not only essential to watch what you are bringing back into Britain. Some countries, notably Australia and New Zealand, have strict laws about importing items such as food and plant material. Flying in to New Zealand, my hiking boots were taken off to be checked for stray seeds that might be stuck to them. Something as innocuous-seeming as an apple core should be disposed of before clearing Customs in these countries.

Items made from endangered species

I loved travelling in Vietnam, but I hated seeing tacky souvenirs made of beautiful coral for sale by the roadside as I drove up Highway No 1. Likewise I was disappointed to find combs and hairgrips made of pretty turtleshell on sale in markets when I visited Bali. But if you try to explain to a poor stall-holder that the coral looked better when it was in the water you'll be greeted with incomprehension. They make their living by selling this stuff. So the only way for holidaymakers to help stop the trade in endangered species is to refuse to buy any items that look as if they might be made from a protected or endangered species. Ivory carvings, reptile skin handbags and boots, traditional medicines containing tiger bone or rhino horn – avoid them all. If the demand disappears, stallholders will sell other items.

The trade in exotic items like this is regulated internationally by the Convention on International Trade in Endangered Species of Wild Fauna and Flora (CITES), a body run by the United Nations Environment Programme and to which the UK is a party. In this country, Defra is the government department that administers it, and if you are determined to buy something overseas that might be on the CITES list, check with Defra first to see if you can import it – some items are banned, but others can be brought in with the correct CITES permit. Details from Defra's Global Wildlife Division (0117 372 8749). Further information from CITES (**www.cites.org**) and CITES UK (**www.ukcites.gov.uk**).

Finally, remember that it may be legal to buy these items overseas – but it may be illegal to import them into Britain. If in doubt, don't buy.

Ten souvenirs to avoid

- Turtle-shell jewellery from Sri Lanka and the Maldives
- Giant clam shells from the Philippines
- Shahtoosh shawls from India, Nepal or Pakistan
- Snakeskin briefcases from Thailand
- Coral souvenirs from Cuba
- Queen conch shells from the Caribbean
- Traditional medicine made from rhino or tiger from Hong Kong
- Orchids from South Africa or the Caribbean
- Ivory from Africa
- Leopard or tiger skins from the Himalayas

Antiques

Import rules never bothered Lord Elgin when he brought back those marbles from Greece, but these days travellers must think before they buy antique or historically important arts and crafts overseas. It's possible the item you buy will need an export licence, or that it is forbidden to export it, no matter what the shopkeeper tells you.

Reputable salespeople overseas (particularly in official government-run shops) know the export rules and will explain the relevant procedures and paperwork, but if you are in doubt make inquiries elsewhere, such as with the tourist board, before parting with your cash. Ask for a receipt, which will help if customs officers stop you.

What to do if the airline loses your luggage

The scale of the problem

Breakfast in Paris... lunch in New York... and yes, bags in Buenos Aires. There's nothing more gut-churning than waiting at the luggage carousel after a long flight, with the excitement at the start of your holiday gradually being replaced by the realisation that your luggage has not arrived. It has happened to me on several occasions, most memorably when I flew with KLM to Lima in Peru for an adventurous two-week trip. I was pretty fed up to find my bag hadn't made the connection at Schiphol Airport in Amsterdam – how does a girl trek the Inca Trail without her boots?

Fortunately the bag arrived on KLM's next flight, 24 hours later – and this is fairly typical. These days, improvements in baggage tracking mean that in most cases, your luggage has simply been delayed, rather than lost for ever. According to SITA, the IT provider that tracks baggage information for airlines, a whopping 30 million bags are mishandled each year worldwide, but "only" 204,000 turn out to be lost or stolen. But sorting out the mess and reuniting bags with their owners costs the airline industry US$2.5 billion each year, according to SITA.

The Lockerbie disaster of 1988, in which a bomb in a suitcase was loaded on to a plane, but the passenger did not travel with it, was the impetus for huge improvements to safety standards concerning luggage. Since then the UK is one of the few countries to achieve "100 per cent hold baggage screening", meaning that every piece of checked luggage leaving a UK airport is X-rayed. Running in parallel with baggage screening is the process known as "reconciliation", whereby airlines must know to whom every bag belongs, and must ensure that the passenger and the bag travel on the same flight.

Of course sometimes we get to the plane on time, but our luggage does not. However, airlines take the view that if the baggage has been screened and the passenger has already travelled, the bag can safely be put on the next flight.

Budget airlines such as Ryanair tend to have a better record on lost luggage than national carriers such as British Airways, because they tend to use small airports, which reduces the chance of the bag being put on another plane, and do not have connecting flights, which is the point at which most bags get lost. Scheduled carriers by comparison compete for passengers by offering tight connection times, which sound attractive in theory – less waiting around at the airport – but it can mean your bags struggle to make the connection.

What you should do

Before leaving home, label bags both inside and out with your name, address, phone number and destination hotel. Make your bag stand out, for example by wrapping a bright-coloured webbing strap around it, which also prevents suitcases spilling open. However, I do not recommend straps with your name woven on to them – con artists find it easier to engage jetlagged travellers in distracting conversations if they can address you by name. Likewise ensure your address label is not visible to others on the way to the airport, thus advertising a house likely to be empty for the next week or two.

Make sure you have insurance to cover your luggage (for more details on insurance, see chapter 6). Keep a copy of the policy and emergency contact phone number in your hand luggage. If you are travelling with someone else, put a few essentials in each other's cases, so if one bag goes missing no one is left completely empty-handed.

If you have ever travelled in first or business class, keep the luggage label you were given then on your bag – it is likely to be treated better than the luggage of economy passengers (and may be unloaded more quickly, too). If you have never travelled in first or business, try to pinch a label from someone who has. Sometimes spoilsport check-in staff rip them off if you are travelling in economy, but it's worth a try, as is sticking a "fragile" label on the case.

Next, ensure that the check-in assistant tags your bags with the correct three-letter airport code for your destination – this is particularly important at check-in desks where they are boarding several different flights. To find out your airport's code visit **www.world-airport-codes.com**. Keep the sticky barcoded receipt for your bag that the check-in staff give you.

On arrival, if your bag does not appear on the carousel, don't give up hope until you've scoured the baggage hall. Sometimes airport staff pull bags off the carousel and stack them in a corner. And when I flew from London to Havana, my luggage eventually appeared on a neighbouring carousel that claimed to be for a Caracas flight.

If you cannot find your bag you must report this immediately to the airline, or their representative (known as their ground-handler), at their office in the baggage hall. Sometimes a scrum develops at this office if many passengers' luggage has not arrived: this is a bore, because it takes longer to complete the formalities, but it can be a good sign. It suggests the airline simply could not load a whole group of bags at the last minute, and thus they are likely to be sent together on the next flight.

Fill in a Property Irregularity Report (PIR) form and keep a copy. Also ask if the airline can help with cash to cover essentials. As a rule of thumb, many airlines say you can spend up to £25 per day, for up to three days, on essentials such as toiletries and clothes. This is KLM's policy, for example, and a KLM spokeswoman told me that claims beyond that amount need to be realistic: "For example, passengers travelling for a business meeting can claim against the loss of business suits from the moment they discover the loss." It's essential to keep receipts for anything you buy. Also check your travel insurance, as this may offer more generous amounts.

Ask for the phone number of the person at the airport dealing with missing luggage, and call them twice a day to check on progress. They will tell you that such calls distract staff from their job, but I say the squeaky wheel gets the grease.

If you are travelling with a tour operator, tell the rep what has happened and ask them to keep in touch with the airport for you. Good reps will even help by waiting in your villa or chalet if you are out on the day the luggage is due to be delivered — for when delayed luggage does turn up, the airline should deliver it to your holiday accommodation or home.

Baggage tracking services

i-TRAK, 0870 127 0002, **www.i-trak.com**

Globalbagtag, 0870 765 7280, **www.globalbagtag.com**

Yellowtag (**www.yellowtag.com**), which also sells its services through Holiday Care (**www.holiday-care.co.uk**)

Compensation for lost luggage

Usually your bag turns up within days. If it is lost for good (which is deemed to have happened after 21 days), you need to decide how to claim compensation.

The best approach is to let your travel insurer sort it out. Not only will they take on the hassle of trying to reclaim costs from the airline, but the level of compensation provided by your insurance policy is likely to be higher than that offered by the airline. You may, however, write to the airline to claim the cost of the excess that you have to pay on your insurance policy from them. The Air Transport Users' Council has heard reports of many passengers successfully reclaiming their excess (typically £50–£100) from airlines.

If you do not have insurance, ask the airline for compensation. Under the Montreal Convention they are obliged to pay up to about £800, but you may not get that much. If you disagree with the amount the airline pays you, you can take it to the small claims court (details in the phone book or from **www.courtservice.gov.uk**), or contact the **Air Transport Users' Council** (020 7240 6061, **www.auc.org.uk**) for help.

CHAPTER EIGHT
Getting there

Introduction

To travel hopefully is a better thing than to arrive," said Robert Louis Stevenson, but if you are stuck at Heathrow during a strike in August, surrounded by suitcases and screaming children, you may beg to differ. Getting through the airport, especially with heavy luggage and kids in tow, can be so stressful that you may need your holiday simply to recover from it. But with a little preparation, you can smooth out the bumpy bits of the ride. Online check-in, valet parking and pre-bookable airline lounge passes are some of the ways to make life easier at the airport, and if you are driving, taking the ferry, a train or a bus, there's advice in this chapter to make those journeys easier, too. Sanity-saving tricks need not cost you much more than doing things the hard way – but you will need to spend a little time planning and booking some services in advance.

Imagine: the day before your holiday, the courier turns up to collect your suitcases. That evening, you log on to check in online, reserving four seats together for your family and double-checking that your daughter's vegetarian meal has been logged. The next morning, you drive to the airport and drop your car at the valet parking booth by departures, so you need not worry about finding the long-term car park.

With no luggage, you breeze through the terminal and head straight for security – online check-in means you printed your boarding cards at home, so you bypass the check-in queues. You have pre-booked a private lounge so you spend a pleasant hour before boarding the plane. On arrival, you're first in the queue for the hire car as you didn't have to wait by the carousel for your luggage. When you arrive at your villa, your bags are already there.

When you come home, you decide to save money by not using the luggage service, but while you wait to collect your bags you ring the valet parking company to tell them to fetch your car so it is there when you emerge from the airport. It's lovely and clean, as it has been serviced and valeted while you were away.

This need be no fantasy – with a little preparation, you can reach your destination easily, safely and with the minimum of stress. Here's how to do it.

Flying into the future – Terminal 5

There is a big "wow" factor when you step into the departures hall on the top floor of the new Terminal 5 building at Heathrow. Although the building is still a shell, the wave-shaped roof and soaring walls made of glass allow the light to flood in and give it the feel of a modern cathedral.

"There is a wonderful, British, Brunellian feel to the architecture," said Tony Douglas, managing director of the Terminal 5 project, as we toured the site. "And I'm a passionate believer in presenting a gateway to the UK that we can all be proud of. So many people are going to come here and judge this country and its culture, and I can think of no better way to start that process off."

Douglas, 43, is overseeing the largest construction site in Europe, where they are currently spending £4 million a day in preparing the new terminal for its opening date, 30 March, 2008. The job of managing a £4.2 billion project, which covers a site the size of London's Hyde Park, would give most of us nightmares. "One 40ft lorry is going through the door every 31 seconds for four-and-a-half years, bringing in construction material. If you were predisposed to unnecessary worry, this would not be the line of business I'd recommend," he deadpanned.

Our hard-hat tour gave me a fascinating insight into the way we will be travelling once T5 opens. Take that vast, 400m-long departure area, for example. The first thing passengers will come to is a bank of 40 self-service "bag drops", which will replace conventional check-in desks.

Although the exact design and operation of these machines has not been finalised, the idea is that you will be encouraged to use them to check in, if

Make your journey easier

- Luggage delivery services, *see* page 246
- Online check-in, *see* page 268
- Choose your seat, *see* page 270
- Airport parking, *see* page 261
- Valet parking, *see* page 262
- Airport lounges, *see* page 274

you have not already checked in online (see page 268). Then your bag will be weighed, the baggage label and your receipt will be printed out, and you will attach the label to your bag. You will also answer security questions by pressing buttons. The bag will drop out of sight to start its journey to the plane. You will then move straight ahead to the security area.

If your bag is heavier than the permitted limits, or you do not want to use the automated system, there are help desks where you can check in the old-fashioned way. There will be staff around to help, too. "But we want the bag drops to be the first option, so you have to consciously decide you do not want to use them before you effect a conventional check-in," said Douglas.

To prepare us for this new way of checking in, British Airways – which will be the only airline based at T5 – has already introduced online check-in for many of its flights (see page 268). In the run up to March 2008 it will be hammering home the message that online check-in is the simplest way to get through the airport quickly and effortlessly. Douglas hopes 80 per cent of passengers will be using this method by the time T5 opens.

Once you are through the security area, you pop out, surprise surprise, by the shops – the T5 team aims to attract upmarket retailers of the type that already operate in Terminals 3 and 4. There will also be a large lounge for members of British Airways' Executive Club, for frequent flyers, and everyone will enjoy amazing views, through the soaring glass walls, of the planes which will be parked on three sides of the building. Two satellite terminals, connected to the main terminal by an underground train, will provide further stands for aircraft – there will be 60 in all, with 14 designed to cope with the enormous Airbus A380 planes that are due to start flying by the end of 2006. The second satellite terminal will not be finished until 2011.

A lot of thought has gone into how we arrive at T5. A six-platform railway station is being built at basement level, with two platforms for tube trains running on the Piccadilly line extension, two for trains on the Heathrow Express extension, and two more in case further rail links are added. A new slip-road is being built off the M25, near junction 14, and a coach station and 4,200-space short-term car park are under construction at the terminal. After arriving by car or public transport, everyone will then either walk through, or cross on glass bridges, the "interchange plaza".

The plaza is another key part of Douglas's aim of providing a calm, pleasurable experience at the airport. Thirty metres wide, the plaza is an outdoor space that will have fountains and water features, mature plane trees and cafés. Douglas also has a vision of large screens, perhaps showing

Terminal 5 facts

- The terminal has been designed by the architect Lord Rogers, who also designed the Millennium Dome and the Pompidou Centre in Paris.

- The protracted planning disputes over the new terminal included a 46-month public inquiry, the longest ever in the UK; permission was finally granted in November 2001.

- Once T5 opens, Terminal 2 will close for reconstruction, which is due to finish before the 2012 Olympics.

- T5 will be able to handle 30 million passengers a year; British Airways, the only airline that will use it, currently handles about 27 million a year at Heathrow.

- The £4.2bn project is funded by BAA, which owns Heathrow, not by the taxpayer.

- The high-tech baggage system will have 18km of belts.

- After clearing security, it should take you no more than six minutes to reach your plane.

- An underground train will depart every 90 seconds to take passengers to the satellite terminals.

- Most short-haul flights will go from the main terminal, and long-haul ones from the satellite terminals.

- There are five floors at T5, each the size of 10 football pitches.

- The main terminal building is the length of 40 London double-decker buses parked bumper to bumper.

- Earth moved during the building of T5 could fill the new Wembley Stadium one-and-a-half times over.

- The new control tower is 87m high – one-and-a-half times the height of Nelson's Column.

- A 600-bedroom Sofitel hotel will open at the same time as the terminal opens.

- Further information: www.heathrowairport.com or http://tinyurl.co.uk/3b2f

news or football, along the sides of the plaza, giving movement, colour and animation to the space. It will give people who are waiting for an arriving passenger a pleasant environment in which to wait for the flight to land.

Builders have had to divert two rivers and are now landscaping the site with thousands of native riverbank plants, and planting 25,000 trees around the terminal's perimeter. But all the window-dressing in the world won't matter to passengers if they encounter long queues once T5 opens. Tony Douglas's aim is to ensure that check in, baggage movements, security and the smooth operating of the aircraft give us a seamless journey through T5. We'll have to hope he gets it right. Meanwhile, we can play our small part by getting used to using the online check-in technology that is fast becoming the norm.

Before you leave home

House sitters

What price peace of mind? Many holidaymakers like the security of having someone to mind their property while they are on holiday. If you don't know your neighbours, and can't rely on Aunty Doris to pop in regularly, there are professional agencies to help. House sitters can be expected to water plants, do light gardening duties and look after pets. They will be empowered to deal with emergency maintenance issues, complex burglar alarms, and they will be vetted, and insured, by the agency.

Contacts

Absentia, 01279 777412, **www.home-and-pets.co.uk**

Animal Aunts, 01730 821529, **www.animalaunts.co.uk**; claims to cater for any type of animal – from llamas to lizards – and its sitters can milk the goat or feed the chickens.

Home and Pet Care, 016974 78515, **www.homeandpetcare.co.uk**

The Home Service, 0845 130 3100, **www.housesitters.co.uk**

Homesitters, 01296 630730, **www.homesitters.co.uk**

Minders Keepers, 01763 262102, **www.minders-keepers.co.uk**

National Association of Registered Petsitters, 0870 350 0543, recorded info 0870 950 4030, **www.dogsit.com**

Leaving home checklist

- Make sure your pets are looked after.
- Ask a neighbour to take in the post and, if you park on the street, to keep an eye on your car.
- Water plants and ask someone to look after them while you're away.
- Set a timer so that lights come on and off.
- Adjust the thermostat and switch off electrical appliances.
- Lock all windows, doors and the garage.
- Tell your home insurer if you are away for a month or more.
- Cancel milk and paper deliveries.
- Leave photocopies of essential documents, including passport and insurance details, with a friend or relative.
- Book grocery delivery for the day after your return.

Getting to the airport
Airport parking

Having wandered around Gatwick South's long-term car park at 3am looking for my car, only to realise that I'd left it at Gatwick North's long-term car park the week before, I know how stressful parking your car at the airport can be.

Stephen Moss, MD of BCP Airport Parking, one of the biggest parking agencies, said travellers can reduce their stress levels by booking a car park place in advance. "People find going on holiday quite stressful. That's part of the magic of doing things like booking airport parking in advance – it takes the stress out of it.

"People are travelling more, and are more cost-conscious, so they want to sort more out in advance. And things like parking are fairly easy to transact on the web."

Parking prices are usually substantially higher if you simply turn up without a booking – this is one area where you really can save by booking in advance. And although car park operators try to ensure they have enough space for everyone in peak season, if you turn up without a booking you could be turned away.

Nick Caunter, MD of airport parking firm APH, said customers can make further savings by booking an "off-airport" car park, which is further away from the terminal. "On-airport parking is typically 15–20 per cent more expensive than off-airport," he said. "People should shop around for car parking."

Parking off-airport doesn't necessarily add that much extra time to your journey, because some off-airport car parks park your car for you, close to other cars, to maximise space. This means all the passengers are taken to the airport from one bus stop, rather than having to catch a bus that drives around the car park picking up other people, which is what happens at on-airport car parks.

Finally, if you're planning to stay at a hotel near the airport at the start of your holiday (see page 266), ask if it offers parking as part of the deal – many do.

Tips for airport parking

- Book in advance for the best rates.

- Shop around.

- If an agent says the car park is full, it may just mean their allocated spaces are all sold – but another agent may have room.

- Check if there are minimum-stay requirements.

- Ask how long the bus to the airport takes and how frequently it runs.

- Check there is plenty of time between your plane landing and the time your car park ticket expires, in case you are delayed on the flight home.

- Keep the car park ticket with your valuables, in the hotel safe, while you are away.

- Make a note of which car park, and which row, you parked in.

Meet-and-greet and valet services

As well as booking you a car park space, airport service companies such as BCP, APH and Holiday Extras sell "meet and greet", or valet parking services, which are a great help to people like me, who forget where they've parked – and they're real stressbusters if you're travelling with kids, or have lots of luggage, such as skis or golf clubs.

With these services, you drive up to the airport terminal, hand your car to the appointed driver (they will be waiting at their company's booth outside the departures hall), and your car is whisked off to a secure car park. The driver is insured to drive your car, of course. On your return you are met at the arrivals hall by the company's driver with your car. (You can ring them while you wait at the luggage carousel to tell them to fetch the car for you.) You pay extra for this service, but it may be no more than the price of an ordinary car park space if you had turned up without a booking.

Some agencies will organise to have your car valeted for you, or taken to the nearest main dealer for a service, while you are away.

There are also limo services, where a posh car will pick you up from home or work, deliver you to the airport, and take you home on your return. These are likely to be more expensive than your local minicab firm, but may appeal if you are on a honeymoon or anniversary holiday, or a business trip and want to impress a contact. Check whether the service costs a set price (which it does with BCP, for example), or whether you must pay a waiting fee if your plane is delayed.

Finally, consider one-way car hire to the airport instead of taking and parking your own car. It costs between £35 and £60 to hire a car for 24 hours from a company such as Europcar, Avis or Hertz, which often allow you to collect a car near your home and leave it at the airport.

Contacts

Many of these companies are agencies which offer a range of services as well as parking, such as meet-and-greet, chauffeur transfer, airport hotels, airport lounge passes, travel insurance, foreign currency and other extras. As ever, it's worth shopping around because prices change by the day, if not the hour, and different operators have different deals.

- **Airparks** (0870 844 2384, **www.airparks.co.uk**) owns car parks at five airports, Birmingham, Cardiff, East Midlands, Luton and Manchester, and can sell spaces at many more.

- **Airport Parking and Hotels** (0870 733 0515, **www.aph.com**) operates car parks at 16 UK airports.

- **BAA** (0870 000 1000, **www.baa.com**), which owns seven airports (Heathrow, Gatwick, Stansted, Glasgow, Edinburgh, Aberdeen and Southampton), owns on-airport car parks at each. You can book them either direct with BAA or through agents listed here.

- **BCP** (0870 013 4580, **www.bcponline.co.uk**) offers on- and off-airport parking at 22 airports across the country.

- **Chauffeured Parking Services** (0870 411 1118, www.parkwithcps.com).

- **Eparking** (01279 666060, **www.eparking.uk.com**) offers parking at Stansted.

- **Flight Hotel Reservations** (0870 745 6377, **www.fhr-net.co.uk**) offers car park spaces at airports countrywide.

- **Help Me Park** (0870 300 6009, **www.help-me-park.com**) is a Gatwick-based valet parking service.

- **Holiday Extras** (0870 844 4186, **www.holidayextras.co.uk**) offers parking at airports across the country.

- **MBW Valet Park** (020 8759 5252, **www.mbwvaletparking.com**) – this valet parking service at Heathrow allows you to book up to an hour before arrival.

- **NCP Flight Path** (0800 128128, **www.ncp.co.uk**); offers parking at a dozen UK airports.

- **Parking Express** (0871 222 0222, **www.parkingexpress.co.uk**); offers on-airport parking at Heathrow and Gatwick.

- **PAS Gatwick** (0870 242 4670, **www.parkinggatwick.com**) offers valet services at Gatwick.

- **Pink Elephant** (0870 060 7071, **www.pinkelephantparking.com**); offers secure parking at Heathrow, Southampton and Stansted.

- **Purple Parking** (0845 450 0808, **www.purpleparking.com**); offers secure parking at 19 airports.

- **Q-Park** (0870 013 4781, **www.q-park.co.uk**); parking and valet-parking at a range of popular airports plus parking in central London for Eurostar passengers.

Manchester

Airlink Parking, 0161 490 2482, **www.manchesterairlinkparking.co.uk**

Chapel House, 0161 903 9016, no website

Clough Bank Car Storage, 0161 904 0615,
www.cloughbankcarstorage.co.uk

Premier Parking, 0161 489 3723, www.manchesterairport.co.uk

Also try www.parkandsave.co.uk, www.airport-parking-deals.co.uk, www.airport-car-parking.com, www.happyparking.com. The website www.compare-airport-parking.co.uk compares the main airport car park players.

Travelling to the airport by public transport

If you are travelling by public transport, the worst bit is carrying your luggage, so consider using luggage delivery services (*see* page 246).

Countrywide

National Express (0870 575 7747, **www.nationalexpress.com**) has an extensive coach network with links to UK airports. For train travel, contact **National Rail enquiries** (0845 748 4950, **www.nationalrail.co.uk**).

London

Four dedicated services from central London are:

- **Heathrow Express** (0845 600 1515, **www.heathrowexpress.com**) from Paddington Station.

- **Heathrow Connect** (0845 678 6975, **www.heathrowconnect.com**), a new stopping service from Paddington.

- **Gatwick Express** (0845 600 1515, **www.gatwickexpress.com**) from Victoria Station.

- **Stansted Express** (0845 600 7245, **www.stanstedexpress.com**) from Liverpool Street Station. Book tickets through the Ryanair website (**www.ryanair.com**) for a discount.

- The **Thameslink** line (0845 748 4950, **www.thameslink.co.uk**) runs frequent services from King's Cross to Luton Airport – note that they depart from the dedicated Thameslink station, which is 300 metres up the road from the main King's Cross station.

- The **Piccadilly line** on the London Underground (020 7222 1234, **www.tfl.gov.uk**) goes to Heathrow, with one stop for Terminals 1, 2 and 3, and another for Terminal 4, which is currently closed while work on the new Terminal 5 underground station is under way. If you want to reach Terminal 4, hop off at Hatton Cross, from where a bus transfer is provided to Terminal 4 while this work continues.

• The **Docklands Light Railway** has recently been extended to London City Airport (**www.tfl.gov.uk/dlr**).

Airport hotels

Spending the night before you fly at an airport hotel can be another stress-buster, if you live far from the airport or have an early morning flight. Most airport hotels offer free shuttle buses to take guests to the airport, if it is not within walking distance – though some hotels are connected to the airport by a walkway. Many will also allow you to leave your car there during your holiday. Most of the airport parking agencies (listed above) also sell airport hotels, as do many tour operators and hotel booking sites such as **www.laterooms.com**, **www.lastminute.com**, **www.priceline.co.uk** and **www.superbreak.com**. Don't forget to book that early morning alarm call...

Here is a selection of hotels very close to major airports.

Gatwick

Hilton, 0870 242 1351, **www.hilton.co.uk/timetofly**

Holiday Inn, 0870 400 9670, **www.holidayinn.co.uk**

Le Meridien, 0800 028 2840, **www.lemeridien.com**

Heathrow

Crowne Plaza, 0800 405060, **www.crowneplaza.co.uk**

Hilton, 0870 242 1351, **www.hilton.co.uk/timetofly**

Park Inn, 020 8759 6611, **www.parkinn.co.uk**

Premier Travel Inn, 0870 242 8000, **www.premiertravelinn.com**

Sheraton Skyline, 020 8759 2535, **www.sheraton.com/skyline**

Stansted

Express by Holiday Inn, 0800 405060, **www.hiexpress.co.uk**

Hilton, 0870 242 1351, **www.hilton.co.uk/timetofly**

Radisson SAS, 01279 661012, **www.radissonsas.com**

Manchester

    Bewleys Hotel, 0161 498 0333, **www.bewleyshotels.com**

    Hilton, 0870 242 1351, **www.hilton.co.uk/timetofly**

    Radisson SAS, 0161 490 5000, **www.radissonsas.com**

Birmingham

    Novotel, 020 8283 4530, **www.accorhotels.com**

Glasgow

    Holiday Inn, 0141 887 1266, **www.holidayinn.co.uk**

Belfast International

    Park Plaza, 02894 422033, **www.parkplazabelfast.co.uk**

At the airport

Arrival

At all Heathrow and Gatwick terminals you can book the **Skycaps porter service** (020 8745 6011, **www.maclellan–skycaps.com**). A porter will meet you as you arrive at the airport and take your bags to check in for you; you can also book a porter to meet you on your return. If you have up to five pieces of luggage the service costs £8, and rises if you have more bags (but it's free for the over 65s or those with special needs).

Airport escalators, trolleys and baggage carousels look like the best playground in the world to a curious toddler, so pin a label to them with your mobile phone number in case they disappear while you are distracted. **IdentiKids** (0845 125 9539, **www.identifyme.co.uk**) sells wristbands to help you keep track of your kids.

Checking in – how to beat the queues

At Heathrow's Terminal 4 recently I saw a lengthy queue of people waiting to check in for British Airways flights – but next to them were four unused self-service check-in kiosks. Given that 76 per cent of all BA flights are made by passengers holding an electronic ticket, or "e-ticket", a large proportion of those passengers could have used these machines to check in, thus avoiding a long wait.

Self-service kiosks are not the only time-saving way to check in. Online check-in is rapidly catching on, with British Airways leading the way and other airlines, including easyJet and Ryanair, introducing it in 2006. Others are set to follow.

Online check-in

You can hardly have missed **British Airways'** recent advertising campaign – glossy magazine ads and posters ask "have you clicked yet?". The adverts are alerting you to the new system that allows you to check in and, in many cases, print your boarding pass from your home or office computer.

To do this, you log on to **www.ba.com**, go to the "manage my booking" area of the site, and input your e-ticket details. You can check in online and reserve your seat on 95 per cent of BA's routes, and on most of its European and American routes you can also go as far as printing out your boarding pass from your home computer, in the form of a bar code. For routes where you can check in online but not yet print your boarding pass, and for the handful of routes where you can do neither, you must check in, or obtain your boarding pass, by going to a conventional check-in desk, a self-service kiosk at the airport or the fast bag drop (see below) – BA's website, or its staff at the airport, will give you instructions. Up to summer 2006, families and groups were not able to use online check-in, but by the time you read this, they should be able to.

There's more. Since April 2006, on all its flights within the UK, BA has banned passengers from using conventional check-in. All domestic passengers must either check in online, or use the self-service kiosks in the departure area. This shows how BA sees the future – online check-in is here to stay.

Other airlines are following suit. **Bmi** launched an online check-in service, which allows you to print your boarding card at home, on most of its short-haul routes in February 2006. Although you cannot yet print your **Virgin Atlantic** boarding pass at home, you can check in for Virgin flights via its website. You then collect your boarding pass at Virgin's fast bag drop. By late 2006 Virgin hopes that its passengers will be able to print out their boarding passes at home.

In March 2006, **easyJet** launched online check-in for passengers who only have hand luggage, and by the end of summer 2006 this service should be available on most of its flights. Travellers with luggage to check in to the hold must use the check-in desks or self-service kiosks (see below).

Ryanair also launched online check-in for passengers who only have hand luggage, on all its flights, in March 2006. And the budget airline **Flybe**

introduced online check-in for passengers with both hand luggage and checked luggage, in April 2006. Passengers log on between 24 and two hours before their flight, print their boarding pass, and at the airport go straight to security (if they have luggage for the hold, they leave it at the fast bag drop).

Other airlines, such as **KLM**, are introducing online check-in – consult your airline's website before you travel to see if you can use it.

Self-service kiosks

Airlines including BA, Virgin, KLM, easyJet and bmi have introduced self-service check-in booths in airport departure halls. You need either an e-ticket, or a cardboard printed ticket (but not the old-fashioned carbon copy variety), or a form of ID such as a credit card or passport, to feed into the machine to start the process (no payment is taken if you use a credit card). Your boarding pass is printed, then you take your bag to the fast bag drop, avoiding check-in queues.

"Twilight" check-in

Some airlines let you check in for the flight the day before it leaves, reducing queueing time and stress in the morning. It works well if you live near the airport, or are staying in a nearby hotel the night before your holiday, and can be very helpful for families as they will not have to queue up to check in with fractious children and all their luggage.

During 2005 and 2006, Gatwick's South Terminal trialled a "Day Before" programme. Passengers flying with Thomson, Excel, MyTravel and Thomas Cook Airlines could check in at a dedicated desk from 4pm to 10pm the night before they flew, for any flight departing up to 9am the following day, then go straight to security the next morning. This scheme is likely to continue in some form, so check with your airline or Gatwick Airport for updates (contact details below).

Elsewhere, Thomas Cook Airlines offers this service at Manchester, and First Choice Airways offers it from Gatwick North Terminal, Manchester and Birmingham (but for £5 per person). British Airways offers day-before check in at Gatwick North Terminal between 4pm and 10pm, for flights departing before 3.15pm the following day. Virgin Atlantic offers twilight check in for all its flights from Gatwick, and bmi offers it for its long-haul flights from Manchester and Heathrow.

At Gatwick during 2006, easyJet has been trialling "all-night" check-in. You can check in from 8pm the night before for any flight leaving before 8.30am the following morning. The check-in desks are open all night.

Special check-in services

Thomsonfly offers priority check in at Gatwick, Manchester and Birmingham for £35 per person. You have a dedicated check-in desk, guaranteed seats with other members of your party, and lounge access.

In Barbados, Antigua, St Lucia, Grenada and Tobago, Virgin Atlantic allows you to check in from your hotel for the return journey, then spend the day by the pool before going to the airport. In Barbados, British Airways' Club World passengers have a drive-through check-in, while those in First are driven straight to an exclusive lounge to be checked in.

Virgin offers its Upper Class passengers kerbside check-in from the limousine which picks them up from home – all part of the ticket's perks.

Contacts

bmi, www.flybmi.com/onlinecheckin

British Airways, www.ba.com

easyJet, www.easyjet.com

Excel, www.xl.com

First Choice Airways, www.firstchoice.co.uk

Flybe, www.flybe.com

Gatwick Airport, www.gatwickairport.com/daybefore

KLM, www.klm.com

MyTravel, www.mytravel.com

Ryanair, www.ryanair.com

Thomas Cook Airlines, www.flythomascook.com

Thomsonfly, www.thomsonfly.com

Virgin Atlantic, www.virgin-atlantic.com

Choosing your seat

Some scheduled airlines will allow you to choose your seat online, even if you do not check in online. Ask your travel agent or check the airline's website for details of this service. It's helpful if you want to be sure you have an aisle or window seat, or are seated away from the lavatories, for example. The website **www.seatguru.com** is a useful tool – it shows the interior layout of a large number of types of aircraft.

However, airlines will typically only release half the seats for pre-booking, with the remaining seats only made available 24 hours before departure. You are not usually able to book emergency exit seats online – the ones with extra leg room, by the emergency doors. Airlines have to be sure that you are fully able bodied if you are going to sit in these seats, and so they are allocated at the check-in desks on a first-come, first-served basis. Likewise seats by the bulkheads, which is often where skycots for babies are placed, will generally be reserved for check-in staff to allocate.

Many charter airlines also allow you to pre-book your seats, to ensure your party can sit together, which is best done at the time you book your package holiday or charter flight. As we've seen in chapter 4 (page 113), there is usually a charge for this service on charter flights.

Many budget airlines, such as Ryanair and easyJet, do not allow anyone to book a seat. Their "free seating" arrangement means you sit wherever you like: those who board first (generally, those who have checked in earliest) get the most choice. But some budget airlines, including Flybe, Sterling Airlines, Air Berlin and Monarch Scheduled, now allow you to pre-book seats, for a fee.

An alternative approach is offered by a New York-based website, **Airtroductions (www.airtroductions.com)**, set up by traveller Peter Shankman after he found that a flight from Houston to New York passed in a flash when he was fortuitously seated next to Miss Texas 2002. Travellers register their personal details, travel plans and, if they wish, a photograph, and can arrange to sit next to other people who are booked on the same flight as them. It's been used for making business contacts and, inevitably, for dating. The majority of flights on the site are US-based.

Can I have an upgrade, please?

All sorts of rubbish is written about getting upgrades. Saying that you are tall/ill/very important usually cuts no ice. Being aggressive to check-in staff is disastrous: woe betide the idiot who shouts to the check-in assistant, "Do you know who I am?!" (The apocryphal tale goes that a quick-witted check-in assistant once responded loudly, "Can anyone help? This man has forgotten who he is!")

The reality is that it is extremely unlikely that you will be upgraded if you travel on the airline only once a year and have booked a cheap ticket in economy. If you have paid full price in economy, are a regular traveller with the airline and are a member of its frequent flyer scheme, your chances are a little better. There's no harm in asking about the possibility of an upgrade, but you will need to be polite, charming and well dressed to stand any chance of success.

THE TIMES HOLIDAY HANDBOOK

Occasionally the plane is overbooked in economy but has space in business class. If the staff are so minded, they may decide to upgrade full-fare economy passengers. If you are travelling with children, or have ordered a special meal, this will count against you – children won't be upgraded, and the special meal request is tied to your (economy) seat and, for reasons I've never quite fathomed, cannot be moved.

Airlines bestow their favours as they see fit – there's no rule book you can throw at them when it comes to upgrades. I've even known planes to take off with empty seats in business class, yet leaving some economy passengers behind. It may come down to the mood of the senior check-in staff or cabin crew on the day – which is why your best bet is to turn on the charm, but not the smarm.

Ultimately, the only way to guarantee a seat in business class is to buy a business-class ticket. See chapter 3 for the best ways to get a good deal.

Security at the airport

Since the September 11, 2001, attacks prompted airports to increase security, more detailed passenger checks have been introduced, and inevitably the process is taking longer. You can easily spend half an hour queuing to go through security at busy times.

These days you are likely to see armed police officers at the airport, and hear regular announcements warning you not to leave your luggage unattended. "We take a layered approach to security – some layers are visible, some are not," said Ian Hutcheson, director of security at BAA, which owns seven UK airports including Heathrow and Gatwick. "Clearly, to keep the terrorists or criminals guessing, we do not wish to reveal some of the behind-the-scenes layers, but it is fair to say that all checked luggage leaving UK airports is screened before being placed on board aircraft. There is also extensive CCTV at UK airports, some of which is visible, some of which is not."

As a passenger, you must go through the security area once you have checked in. Follow the sign for "departures" which will take you into the security area. You'll have to show your boarding card, and sometimes your passport, at this point. You may see a separate lane called "fast track" or "fast lane". This is for holders of business-class tickets, or people travelling in the premium cabins of charter airlines such as Excel and Monarch, and it should be faster than the normal queue.

Once you step beyond the screens into the security zone, you must take off your jacket or coat and put it into a large plastic tray, along with your hand luggage, and put the tray on the rubber belt so it can be passed through the X-ray machine. Laptops and mobile phones are safe in the machinery, whether turned on or off, and cameras should be too, though if you are concerned about your camera film you can ask to have it hand-searched (the request is not always granted).

Since the security alert of August 2006, you have not been allowed to carry anything in your pockets, and more travellers are now being hand-searched too.

You then step through a metal detector, which sometimes bleeps at things like belt buckles, so don't be alarmed. If it does you'll then be body-searched by someone of the same sex who may pass a scanner across your body or feel around your body to make sure you are not carrying a banned item. Anyone with a heart pacemaker or in a wheelchair should also have a hand search.

Items you must not carry in your hand luggage (but may pack in your checked luggage) include scissors, knives, cutlery (except spoons), hypodermic needles (unless you have a medical note explaining why you need to carry them), corkscrews and toy guns. Items you cannot take on a plane at all include gas canisters, car batteries, fireworks, weedkiller or other poisons and non-safety matches. Your travel agent or airline can supply a full list of banned items.

On no account think it worth trying a "bomb" joke out on staff (and impress this message on your children). Even the slightest mention of the word, or any indication that you are carrying a firearm, for example, will prompt a full-scale alert. You will quite probably be arrested and if found guilty, imprisoned.

At some airports you are asked to take your shoes off to have them inspected as you go through security. You may also find that your bags are pulled over to one side for a further inspection once they have come out of the X-ray machine. These are routine procedures. Once all the inspections have finished you are free to move through to the departure lounge.

Passing the time

Even if your flight is not delayed, you will probably have time to kill at the airport, once you've gone through security. There will inevitably be plenty of shops – often rather expensive luxury goods ones, offering "tax-free" prices, and bookshops that often sell books from overseas publishers that are not yet available elsewhere in the UK. A few airports have cosmetics outlets where women can have their make-up done (such as my favourites, MAC, at Heathrow's Terminal 3, 020 8745 7165), which is a fun way to pass the time, especially since restrictions on carrying cosmetics through security were introduced in August 2006.

If you are travelling through one of the seven BAA Airports (Heathrow, Gatwick, Stansted, Edinburgh, Glasgow, Southampton and Aberdeen) you can use its **Shopping Information line** (0870 850 2825) to find out about shops at the airport, and whether particular goods are in stock. You can order items to collect at the airport, and if you are travelling within the EU, you can delay collecting them until your return journey, so you do not need to lug them around on holiday. BAA also has a frequent shopper scheme, **BAA WorldPoints** (0500 844844); when you shop at a BAA airport you earn points that you can turn into discount vouchers.

Keeping the children happy

First things first: dress your kids in brightly coloured clothes to make it easier to spot them if they dash off in the lounge. Bring healthy snacks with you so you do not need to rely on expensive, sugary or fatty meals from the airport cafés, and pack a few favourite toys and games. Wet wipes are ever useful.

Many children will simply enjoy watching the planes come and go through the windows, and airports often have dedicated viewing areas. Gatwick Airport recommends the Aqua Bar at the North Terminal, while Heathrow recommends the views from Café Nero at Terminal 1. Many airports also have specific play areas for children – there are unsupervised play areas at both Gatwick terminals, at Heathrow's Terminal 1 by Café Nero, at Manchester Airport's Terminal 1 and near Hamley's toy store (oh-oh!) in the Stansted departure lounge.

You can also take children into some airport lounges (see below).

Airport lounges

Escaping the mayhem of the departure lounge for the peace and quiet of a private airport lounge can be a real sanity-saver, especially if your flight is delayed. Some travellers will have automatic access to a lounge – for example, if you have reached a certain tier of an airline's frequent flyer scheme, if you have a business or first-class ticket, and if you hold certain types of American Express or Diner's Club cards. But anyone can buy lounge access on a one-off basis, and it's a growth area of business for the "extras" companies that have already sold us our airport parking and hotel stay.

Stephen Moss, MD of BCP, said: "A lot of airports are getting increasingly frenetic, so it's quite nice to get away from the madding crowds." Typically BCP charges £17–£18 per person for a visit to a lounge at a UK airport, and hopes soon to add overseas airport lounges, because "delays are inevitably on your way back rather than your way out," said Moss, rather patriotically.

Once in the lounge, you'll usually find free refreshments, newspapers, TV, wi-fi access and sometimes free-to-use computers. There may be a smoking room and sometimes showers. If your flight is delayed you can usually stay beyond the allotted three hours that a typical booking offers, though if you are held up on your way to the airport and don't have time to use the lounge, you forfeit your money. When you book, check what time the lounge closes – at smaller airports they may not stay open into the evening.

Many lounges do not accept children under 12, so always check when booking. At Gatwick, families can use the **Aviance lounge** in the North Terminal or the **Servisair lounge** in the South Terminal (book on 0870 850 2825, **www.gatwickairport.com**) for £17.95 (no child discount), while at Heathrow, the **KLM Holideck lounge** at Terminal 4, open to passengers of any airline, offers a family area, free refreshments and an aircraft viewing area (**www. holideck.co.uk**). Children aged 2–15 pay £9; adults aged 16-plus pay £18.

A free alternative to the lounge is to hunt out the airport's chapel, though you will have to settle for spiritual riches rather than free drinks and newspapers.

Contacts

APH, 0870 733 0515, **www.aph.com**

BCP, 0870 013 4542, **www.bcponline.co.uk**

Holiday Extras, 0870 844 4186, **www.holidayextras.co.uk**

These are three of the airport service companies that offer lounge access. Many tour operators and travel agents can book this for you, too, or you can book direct by calling the airport.

Lounge pass schemes

• **Priority Pass** (020 8680 1338, **www.prioritypass.com**) gives members access to 450 lounges worldwide. You pay an annual membership (from £69pa) and then £15 per visit, and can take in a guest for £15.

- **Lounge Pass** (020 8253 5146, **www.loungepass.com**), Priority Pass's sister programme, is aimed more at leisure travellers, with 128 lounges on offer at varying rates, but no annual fee.

- **Regency Premier Lounges** (01205 761176) offers lounges worldwide, from £17 in the UK and £18 overseas, with no annual fee.

- **Executive Lounges** (**www.executivelounges.com**) offers access to 50 lounges worldwide either on a one-off basis from £13.50, or using annual membership at £250pa.

On the plane

The rapid growth of the budget carriers has turned us into a nation that treats airline travel like bus travel. It's also meant that many people who until recently had never been on a plane now take flights regularly. Sitting in a sausage-shaped tin can for hours is hardly the most natural of experiences, but if you know what you can expect, it will seem less alien. In this section I'll look at what happens on a typical flight. For more information about the experience of flying, consult **www.airlinequality.com**, or the books *Flying* by Serge Barret and Thierry Lamiraud (Beacon, £5.99) and *The Flying Book* by David Blatner (Penguin, £7.99).

Boarding the plane

Families and people with poor mobility are often invited to board first, especially on the budget airlines which do not allocate individual seats.

If you're travelling in economy, it's worth trying to be one of the first to board because you will have more chance of putting your bag in the overhead locker nearest to you. The Law of Sod dictates that if you board last, the only space left to squeeze your bag into will be 10 rows behind your seat, so when you land, you will have to wait until everyone else has got off before you can retrieve it.

If you are sitting in emergency exits rows or at the front of the cabin, you must put everything into the overhead lockers – elsewhere, you're allowed to put bags under the seat in front of you.

Business or first class passengers need not worry about these trivialities: they are normally allowed to board at any point, have plenty of room to stow their bags, and are offered a hot towel/glass of champagne/selection of newspapers once they deign to sit down.

Safety announcements are always made before take off, and wise travellers will pay attention. The exits on different types of planes are in different places, and life jackets can be too. The chances of you needing to act on the information in the safety briefing may be slim – but that does not mean it is not worth hearing.

Flying with children

When booking flights, make sure you ask for a skycot or bassinet for your baby – children under two generally fly for free, or for a token sum, but they are not given their own seat. If you do not request a bulkhead seat, where a skycot can be placed in front of you, the baby will have to sit on your lap throughout the journey. However, on short flights, for example on budget airlines, bulkhead seats and skycots are not usually available.

If you are flying long-haul with a child under two, consider buying them a seat, even though it is not essential. "Can you imagine flying 24 hours to Australia with a toddler on your knee? Imagine what it is like trying to eat an airline meal with that going on!" said journalist Jeannette Hyde, a regular contributor to *The Times* who has two young children. "Anyone I have ever met who has done that says they will never do it again."

If you have booked a skycot, call the airline again a few days before your flight to check the request is in the system. At check in, ask again. You can usually take your baby's carry cot or car seat on to the plane, but if you have a pushchair you must relinquish it when you reach the aircraft, whereupon it will be put into the hold. When you land, you won't get it back until you reach the luggage carousel. At some airports, such as Palma in Majorca, this may involve a long walk carrying the baby and all your clobber before you are reunited with the pushchair.

Once on board, you may find that feeding the baby as you take off helps to calm them, because changing pressure in the cabin can otherwise be uncomfortable. Give older children a sweet during take off and landing for the same reason. Most airlines, but not all, give parents an extra lap belt to restrain their baby for take off and landing, during which time skycots are packed away. Changing a baby's nappy in a plane's lavatory is a test of agility at the best of times, so keep essentials in one small bag that you can take in with you rather than lugging a large changing bag in. Pack a spare shirt or jumper, in case the baby is sick on you.

If your children are prone to motion sickness, discuss this beforehand with your doctor and consider packing something like Kwells. It's good to have a bag of tricks with you to keep kids occupied. Small toys, drawing games or books can be produced at regular intervals to counteract boredom. Make sure your children (and you) drink plenty of water or juice to counteract the dehydrating effects of the cabin.

Food and drink on board

Airlines are not obliged to offer passengers free food and drink – budget airlines tend only to offer snacks, which they will charge you for – but scheduled carriers generally offer one or two free meals and drinks, depending on the length of the flight. On some airlines, and usually in the premium cabins, you will be offered a menu and may eat off a china service.

It's long been axiomatic that vegetarian meals on airlines are better than the usual beef or chicken option – and are often served first – and many scheduled airlines offer a wide range of special meals, including vegetarian, Kosher, lactose-intolerant and low-sodium options. Check on your airline's website, or ask your travel agent, when booking to request these special meals, and ask again at check in. At *The Times* we regularly receive complaints about these meals being unavailable, despite being ordered in advance. Unfortunately there's not much you can do about this in mid-air, so pack some snacks in case the meal you ordered is unavailable.

It's also worth considering the nationality of the airline you are flying with. Some of the best aeroplane food I have tasted was the vegetarian option on an Air India flight to Delhi. Curry, dahl and rice lend themselves rather well to being wrapped in foil containers.

The grimly compulsive website **www.airlinemeals.net** carries pictures of airline meals sent in by contributors, and lots of info on how airline meals are put together.

Entertainment and etiquette

On-board entertainment varies from the usual films and music to fashion shows, courtesy of Air Jamaica, whose cabin crew parade down the aisle showing off clothes from Jamaican stores, while some airlines offer seat-back gambling.

On a short-haul flight you'll probably only have the in-flight magazine to flip through, but flying long haul, you may have several channels of films and TV shows, pre-recorded radio channels and programmes aimed at kids. In economy cabins these are sometimes shown on big screens at the front of each cabin, or on overhead TVs, but increasingly airlines have individual seat-back TVs. There's also usually a TV channel showing a map of the plane's route, how far you have flown, the height, air temperature, speed and other data.

In business and first-class cabins you're often given a personal DVD player and offered a choice of dozens of films that you can watch, and pause, whenever you want to during the flight, rather than being tied to set screening times. Whatever cabin you're in, the films are always bang up to date, with the latest releases shown alongside a selection of classics. On Virgin Atlantic flights, crew hand out ice creams as the movie starts – honestly, there are worse ways to spend a few hours than snuggling up in a dark cabin and gazing at George Clooney.

After take-off on a long-haul flight, you will be given a toiletries bag which usually contains socks (it's a good idea to take your shoes off while on board), an eyemask and ear plugs if it's an overnight flight, and perhaps a disposable toothbrush and paste, some moisturiser or lip balm. Passengers in the premium cabins get fancier bags with more toiletries, often brands of Molton Brown quality and above. You should be given a blanket and pillow on a long flight.

During the flight there will sometimes be announcements from the flightdeck – such as when there is a great view to one side of the plane, or to give arrival information. Sometimes the seatbelt signs will be illuminated, meaning it's compulsory to return to your seat and fasten your seatbelt. This is really annoying if you've just got to the front of the queue for the lavatory, but it's done for a reason, usually because the plane has hit turbulence. When you are in your seat it's sensible to keep your seat belt done up all the time. If you plan to go to sleep, fasten the seat belt over your blanket, so staff can see it and do not need to wake you up if the seatbelt sign comes on.

Meal service and the films are all ways of helping you pass the time without bothering the cabin crew by moving around the plane too much. Staff will also try to sell you tax-free goods, such as perfume and jewellery, after they've served the meal. You can ask cabin crew if you need items such as headache tablets, more water, or tissues.

It's considerate, when eating airline meals, to raise your seat to the upright position so the person behind you is not pinioned to the back of their seat when their tray table is down.

I do not know of any international airline that now allows you to smoke on board, though there may be domestic services in some countries where smoking is still permitted. If you try to sneak a crafty cigarette in the loo it will set the alarms off, and staff are able to open the door from the outside to catch you. You can even be arrested for this when the plane lands. Most airports still have smoking areas, which are often heavily air-conditioned and rather cold.

Health on the plane

Dehydration is one of the most common problems among passengers, especially on long flights; if permitted, carry your own bottle of water, and ask for more when the cabin crew serve drinks. Dry cabin air can also make wearers of contact lenses uncomfortable, so it's worth swapping to glasses for the flight. When the plane lands you may find your ears "pop" – if you have a cold this can be quite painful – but it can be relieved by pinching your nose, closing your mouth and blowing out or swallowing. Babies may like to feed, or children to suck on a sweet, at this time.

Scuba divers should time their last dive a day or so before their flight home to avoid decompression sickness on the plane.

Airlines always provide airsickness bags in case of emergency. If you find these to be things of beauty and interest, you may wish to visit the collectors' site (I'm not joking) **www.bagophily.com**.

For more information on how to stay healthy on holiday, *see* chapter 10, and the Bibliography, page 431.

Deep vein thrombosis (DVT)

This is often, misleadingly, referred to as "economy-class syndrome". Such a term suggests that those most at risk are passengers flying in the cheap seats, but any traveller can suffer from DVT, whichever part of the aircraft they are in, or if they are travelling by car, bus or train. The problem is exacerbated by immobility, so however you travel, it's important to take regular breaks to stretch and walk around.

A DVT is a blood clot that forms in a vein, usually in the calf, and it can, in rare cases, move up through the body and lodge in the lungs to cause pulmonary embolism, which can be fatal. Certain people are at higher risk of developing DVT than others: those over 40, women on the pill or HRT, smokers, overweight people, those with varicose veins, and pregnant women. Passengers on long flights are obviously at greater risk, but however short your flight, try to move around the cabin every hour, if possible. Consult your doctor before flying if you are concerned.

Other ways to reduce the likelihood of a DVT include drinking plenty of water and limiting your alcohol intake, doing stretching exercises both in your seat (these are often described in the in-flight magazine) and standing up in the aisle, and keeping your feet as high as possible, but not crossing your legs. Choosing an aisle or bulkhead seat makes it easier to get up and move around. Wearing elastic compression stockings is also recommended by many doctors. It's a good idea to take some vigorous exercise, such as swimming or walking, before and after a long flight.

Some doctors recommend you take half an aspirin per day for the three days before a flight, which will slightly thin the blood, thus reducing the risk of clots. As ever, consult your doctor before you do this as some people have an adverse reaction to aspirin.

For further information and advice contact the **Aviation Health Institute** (01865 715999, **www.aviation-health.org**).

Jet lag

If you are flying anywhere that is more than about four hours behind or ahead of UK time, you're likely to experience a certain degree of jet lag. Many travellers say that it is less pronounced when flying east to west, but I have found it can strike after any long journey, sometimes even kicking in a few days after you arrive. It's said that it takes you a day to adjust for every hour of time zone you cross – certainly visitors to Australia can expect to feel jet-lagged during their first week in the country.

There are a few tips for reducing jet lag, though ultimately you should expect to have to deal with it and try not to be in a stressful situation straight after a flight (which is why it might be wise to collect your hire car a day later). On the flight, immediately set your watch to the time at your destination, and act accordingly. If you are to land at breakfast time, try to sleep for as long as possible before you land. If you are to land in the evening, try to stay awake for the flight. Once you arrive, try to stay awake until a normal bed time, then arise at a normal breakfast time.

Limiting your intake of alcohol and food on the plane may help stave off the worst effects of jet lag, and drinking lots of water will help you feel better, too.

Popping a pill

Some travellers swear by melatonin to combat jet lag – it is available over the counter in the USA – while some nervous flyers, and others who simply want to pass the journey painlessly, advocate taking a sleeping pill to knock them out for a long flight.

I would seek a doctor's advice before popping any pills. Staying immobile for hours on a plane, as you will after taking a sleeping pill, can increase the risk of DVT, and when you awake you can feel extremely groggy and dehydrated – which is not the best state to be in when you have to negotiate customs and immigration in a strange country.

Health tips

- Drink lots of water while on a plane.

- Keep your alcohol, tea and coffee intake to a minimum.

- Move around the plane every hour.

- Read the in-flight guide – most suggest stretching exercises you can do in your seat.

- Eat lightly.

- Wear loose clothing, and take your shoes off during the flight.

Fear of flying

Airports can be overwhelming, stressful places, unlike anywhere else we go in our daily lives, and if it's this stressful and confusing on the ground, it's hardly surprising that some people find the experience of flying quite terrifying.

If you are a nervous flyer, consider these tips to reduce your stress:

- Arrive at the airport early, as rushing to the gate will raise your stress levels.

- Tell cabin crew of your anxieties.

- Learn breathing exercises, and try to focus on the relaxing holiday you will have when you arrive.

- Bring a good book or some music to help distract and calm you.

- Avoid alcohol and sedatives if possible.

If you simply cannot get on a plane, several airlines offer courses that help you master this fear. Experienced pilots explain how the plane works, and the meaning of the various engine noises and beeps and aircraft movements that you may experience – often this information is highly reassuring to worried flyers. Staff also discuss subjects such as turbulence and security issues, and answer questions. In the afternoon participants go on a 45-minute flight accompanied by staff who explain what's happening at every stage.

- **Aviatours** (01252 793250, **www.aviatours.co.uk**) runs one-day courses at Heathrow, Gatwick, Manchester, Edinburgh, Bristol, Birmingham and Southampton, using British Airways pilots, for £235.

- **Flying Without Fear** courses (01423 714900, **www.flyingwithoutfear.info**) are run by Virgin Atlantic at Gatwick, Heathrow, Luton, Birmingham, Manchester and Newcastle, for £199 per day.

- *Ask the Pilot – Everything you Need to Know about Air Travel* by Patrick Smith (US$14 from **www.penguin.com**) is both funny and fascinating, and explains a lot of what happens on a plane – the author is a former pilot. Also see **www.askthepilot.com**.

Travelling by train

Reaching the continent: Eurostar

I recall feeling very worried about the idea of taking a train under the Channel in the run up to Eurostar's launch in November 1994. Wouldn't it feel claustrophobic? What would happen if we broke down in the tunnel? Could the tunnel leak?! But since Eurostar (0870 518 6186, **www.eurostar.com**) started operations I have, like many of us, become a convert.

Eurostar's convenience – a 30-minute check-in, and city-centre to city-centre routes – has won many of us away from planes on routes between London and Paris or Brussels. Indeed, because of Eurostar's impact on the environment, by causing the more polluting airlines to reduce their frequency on these routes, it won an award in the 2004 Responsible Tourism Awards, sponsored by *The Times*.

In late 2007, the Eurostar terminal will move from Waterloo to St Pancras, in north London, when the final stage of the high-speed link from London to the Kent coast will be finished, reducing journey times as trains will be able to travel at 186mph all the way. Travelling from London to Paris will then take 2hr 15min (down from the current 2hr 35min), the Brussels route will come down from 2hr 15min to 1hr 53min, and Lille will come down from 1hr 40min to an almost commutable 1hr 20min.

Eurostar can also take you to Calais, Disneyland Paris, Avignon during the summer, and French ski resorts Moutiers and Bourg St Maurice in the winter (on either a daytime or night-time service). When the high-speed link opens, two new stations will be added in the UK, at Stratford in east London and Ebbsfleet in Kent (to be known as Dartford International).

There are three classes on Eurostar – Standard, Leisure Select (you get roomier seats and a meal with champagne) and Business Premier (benefits include late check-in and use of the smart lounges). To obtain the cheapest Standard fares you must book as soon as fares are released, which is four months (120 days) before you travel. Mark this in your diary, or use an agent such as European Rail (see below) to do the work for you. Eurostar has adopted the pricing structure used by many airlines whereby ticket prices rise as demand increases.

A perk of buying a ticket to Brussels is that it allows you free onward travel on the Belgian rail network within 24 hours of your arrival; the same applies before your return to London.

Trains within Europe

Arriving by Eurostar at Paris, Lille and Brussels, it's easy to connect with other services across Europe. See **www.hacon.de/hafas_e/www.shtml** for links to the timetables of various European rail companies and bus services, including the rail networks of France, Belgium, Italy, Denmark, the Netherlands and Switzerland. Thomas Cook publishes an invaluable timetable (details below).

Recently, continental train companies have started working together to compete with the airlines, such as the French-Spanish company **Elipsos**, which offers high-speed night trains linking Spain with France, Switzerland and Italy. **Artesia Trains** are fast trains between various Italian cities and Paris and Lyons, while the major cities of Germany and France are linked by **DB NachtZug** (night trains).

A great place to start, if you want to book tickets yourself, is the website **www.seat61.com** (see box, page 289). Although he's not a sales agent, Mark Smith, who set up this site, offers knowledgeable step-by-step instructions on how to book trains direct.

But you may find it easier to use a rail agent with specialist knowledge, who will be able to advise on things such as the types of seats and sleepers available, and whether it is worth upgrading to first class. An agent will usually charge a fee, typically £6 or more, to book trains for you and if you are buying tickets priced in euros you need to watch the exchange rate used if you are paying in sterling.

The agent **RailEurope**, as it is part of the French railway company SNCF, is particularly knowledgeable about train travel in France and can book tickets to every station in that country.

A constant complaint is that you cannot book rail tickets very far in advance. While Eurostar allows a four-month booking window, French Railways offers three months and many European rail networks allow you to book only two months before you travel. This can be nail-biting, especially in high season when you may feel it is essential to book your hotel rooms much further ahead than this. Some rail agents' websites allow you to register so that when the tickets you want go on sale you are alerted by email and can buy straight away.

Train timetables tend to change before Christmas, and again in late spring, so be sure to use an up-to-date timetable when planning a trip (such as the Thomas Cook publications, below).

Inter-Rail Passes

Twenty years ago I headed off on the boat train to Paris with my university friend Bettany Hughes. We spent a few weeks taking the train through France and Italy, getting into various scrapes along the way (running out of money, finding our hotel was a brothel, hitching a lift in a funeral hearse) but loving our time exploring the classical sights of Florence and Siena, clutching a dog-eared copy of Vasari's *The Lives of the Artists*. In 2006 we both travel in a little more comfort – Bettany recently retraced our trip to prepare the Radio 4 series *Amongst the Medici* – but we still have fond memories of our budget journey.

We weren't alone. Many of our friends spent weeks each summer criss-crossing Europe on its trains – in the 1980s it was much more common to travel around Europe than to head off on a backpacking trip to Asia, as so many do now. But while Inter-Railing has for years been synonymous with student travel, Inter-Rail Passes have, since 1998, been available to anybody, of any age, although the under-26s pay less.

Today the Inter-Rail Pass allows you to travel in 29 European countries plus Morocco, in second class, in trains on the national networks. The continent is divided into eight zones and you can choose a pass that allows you to travel in one, two or all eight zones, for 16 days, 22 days or a month. The scheme's website **www.interrailnet.com**, or a rail agent (listed below), will explain how it works.

Single-country rail passes

The **EuroDomino pass**, a scheme run by most European countries, suits travellers who are sticking to one country. These passes give unlimited travel in that country for between three and eight days – these need not be consecutive days but can be spread over a month. With a EuroDomino Pass you can usually travel on the high-speed trains without paying a supplement, unlike with an Inter-Rail Pass, but you will still need to pay seat reservation, sleeper or couchette charges.

EuroDomino passes are available to all ages, though the under-26s pay a lower price. They run in parallel with rail pass schemes offered by individual countries: for example you can buy rail passes for countries including Germany, Switzerland and Holland or regions such as Scandinavia (the **ScanRail Pass** covers Denmark, Finland, Norway and Sweden) and the Benelux Countries (Belgium, Holland and Luxembourg) from agents such as **Rail Pass Direct** (0870 084 1413, **www.railpassdirect.co.uk**) or **Rail Choice** (0870 165 7300, **www.railchoice.co.uk**).

In France the EuroDomino pass has been replaced by the new **France Railpass**, offering three to nine days' travel during one month, on any train on the SNCF network including the TGV (available from agents including RailEurope). In Italy the EuroDomino pass has been replaced by the **Trenitalia Pass**, valid for three to 10 days' travel within a two-month period.

The way single-country railpasses are issued in Europe is likely to change in 2007; check with a rail agent. Agents can also sell passes to long-haul destinations such as the USA, Canada, Australia, New Zealand and Japan.

Taking the car on the train

Eurotunnel

Eurotunnel (0870 535 3535, **www.eurotunnel.com**) allows you to put your car on a train to go under the Channel from Folkestone in Kent to Calais in France. There are up to four departures an hour, all day, every day. As with Eurostar, ticket prices rise according to demand, rewarding early bookers. Standard fares start at £49 one-way – in this class you must take the departure you have booked. The Flexiplus fares are a set price of £199 each way, and these allow you to hop on the next available train, and give you a few other benefits such as dedicated check-in and a lounge.

Motorail

Putting your car on the train to save making long drives across countries such as France and Spain seems to be enjoying something of a revival. The most popular services for British travellers leave Calais and head south across France, operating only in summer, but there are also Motorail services across much of the continent, such as from Germany into Austria and Italy, and across Spain. One reason for French Motorail's increasing popularity may be that from summer 2006 it is allowing 4x4 vehicles to be transported for the first time, and has improved the sleeping compartments.

Also in 2006, specialist Motorail agency **Railsavers** (0870 750 7070, **www.railsavers.com**) got together with a Dutch train operator to offer de luxe Motorail services from Denderleeuw, near Zeebrugge, into Italy and the south of France, with restaurant cars (which French Motorail does not provide) and comfortable sleeper compartments.

French Motorail is bookable through **RailEurope** (0870 241 5415, **www.raileurope.co.uk**), and all Motorail services are available through Railsavers.

Further information

The *European Rail Timetable* and the *Overseas Timetable* for the rest of the world (both £11.50 from Thomas Cook Publishing) are essential planning tools. The former is updated monthly, the latter bimonthly. Seasonal versions of both, with more tourist information, are published at £13.99. Thomas Cook also publishes a Rail Map of Europe (£7.95) and the guidebook *Independent Travellers Europe by Rail* (£12.99). See **www.thomascookpublishing.com**. *Europe by Train* by Katie Wood (Robson Books, £12.99) is also useful.

Contacts
France

- SNCF (**www.voyages-sncf.com**): the French railway company offers fares to major cities in France and beyond. It has also recently launched a low-cost TGV service from Paris to the south of France. Book on **www.idtgv.com** (in French only), tickets from £13.

- TGV (**www.tgv.co.uk**) is the high-speed French train service.

- Thalys (**www.thalys.com**) also offers high-speed services, for example linking Paris to Amsterdam and Cologne.

Germany

- **German Railways** (0870 243 5363, **www.bahn.co.uk**) offers ticket booking across Europe using this site.

- **www.nachtzug.de** is the site for Germany's cross-European night trains.

Spain

- **www.elipsos.com** has details of international overnight services to Spain.

- **www.renfe.es** is the Spanish train service.

Italy

- **Trenitalia** (**www.trenitalia.com**) or **www.italiarail.co.uk**.

- **Trenok** (**www.trenok.com**) offers low-cost services (in Italian only).

UK

- **National Rail** (0845 748 4950, **www.nationalrail.co.uk**) can give you advice and book tickets for you in the UK.

Rail agents

These agents sell point-to-point tickets and rail passes to destinations worldwide, and some also sell Motorail tickets and rail-based package holidays:

European Rail, 020 7387 0444, **www.europeanrail.com**

Freedom Rail, 0870 757 9898, **www.freedomrail.com**

Rail Pass Direct, 0870 084 1413, **www.railpassdirect.co.uk**

Railbookers, 0870 458 9080, **www.railbookers.com**

RailChoice, 0870 165 7300, **www.railchoice.co.uk**

RailEurope, 0870 584 8848, **www.raileurope.co.uk**

Simply Rail, 0870 084 1414, **www.simplyrail.com**

The TrainLine, 0870 084 1417, **www.internationaltrainline.com**

Trainseurope, 0871 700 7722, **www.trainseurope.co.uk**

Motorail

French Motorail, 0870 241 5415, **www.raileurope.co.uk**

Railsavers, 0870 750 7070, **www.railsavers.com**

The Man in Seat 61

Mark Smith is a man with a mission. Passionate about trains, and having spent years working in the rail industry, he decided there was a need for clearer information about how to get the best deals. "Getting to Europe by train is very easy," he said, "but finding out about it is like trying to find an NHS dentist."

So he set up his website, **www.seat61.com**, to offer travellers information about travel by train and ship, both for people who dislike the impact aviation has on the environment, and for rail, ferry and bus travellers who simply prefer these forms of transport to the airlines.

Running the site, named for Mark's favourite seat on Eurostar (seat 61 in first-class compartments 7, 8 or 11 is an individual seat that lines up with the window), is only a hobby, and he updates the site during his hour-long commute to work, but in 2005 it received 1.8 million visits. It tells people what trains are like, with plenty of detail about the services you can expect, as well as how to buy tickets. There are also pages of detail about everything from booking trains in India to taking the bus in Laos.

The site covers trains worldwide, and, perhaps surprisingly, the most popular page is on Malaysia. Smith reckons it's because he gives travellers details of how to do the classic Singapore to Bangkok journey on a local train for £35 in first class, compared with the £1,000 or so that Orient-Express charges on the Eastern & Oriental Express. "It's the same scenery," he pointed out.

He's keen to encourage more business travellers to use trains, especially in Europe. "On the continent I bet a lot of people use a plane because it's all their business travel agent can book," he said. "But Paris to Geneva, for example, is three hours 20 minutes by train, round lovely Alpine valleys." Once you've checked in at the airport for that flight, there's probably not much of a time difference.

Holidays by rail

One of the most memorable trips I have ever taken was the week-long journey on the Trans-Siberian train, from Beijing to Moscow. Fearing boredom might set in during seven days on a train, I packed plenty of reading material, but by the time I arrived in Moscow I had read just 20 pages.

I was lucky with my travelling companions, and this is the key to an enjoyable long-distance train trip. I was travelling alone but the travel agent put all 20 foreigners who were booked on that train into one carriage. Although this created a slight ghetto – and we were one night targeted by thieves – this was more than compensated for by the great company my travelling companions turned out to be. Our mixed group of Europeans, Americans and Australians organised games of cards and backgammon, with the winner getting a bottle of Russian champagne (the loser got two); we shared food bought at stations along the route, we fell in and out of love, argued, told stories, sang songs, teased the grumpy *provodnitsa* (cabin attendant), and gradually got whiffier and whiffier (this was definitely "goat-class" travel, with no showers, only a hand basin and lavatory).

There was another reason the journey was more comfortable for foreigners sharing the same compartment: many Russians, Chinese and Mongolians use the train to transport bales of cheap silk and other clothes bought in the markets of Beijing to points along the railroad. Their compartments are stuffed with boxes and bags of contraband, making living conditions extremely cramped. At stations along our route they would sell cheap jeans and trainers to local people out of the train windows. Of course we mixed with local passengers in the restaurant car (where, after perusing the 20-page, three-language menu for half an hour, the waiter took great pleasure in telling you that the only things on offer were fried eggs and more Russian champagne), and we enjoyed racing along the platform to barter with the tradespeople who came to meet the train. They'd sell us home-made bread, strawberries, cooked chicken, boiled potatoes in wraps of newspaper, and pots of cream cheese, essential supplements to our limited diet.

I have made many memorable journeys on trains elsewhere, especially in India, where I never cease to be amazed by the efficiency with which your name and seat number will be pasted up on the door to your compartment, weeks after you bought your ticket. Mortifyingly, they also insist on listing your age, which is taken as a red light for locals to ask why you are not married at such an advanced age (anything over 21), whether your honoured parents are still alive, how much can someone of your age expect to be earning, etc etc.

Time-keeping, however, is not such a strong feature of the Indian train system. Journalist Stephen McClarence, a regular contributor to the travel pages of *The Times*, who spends each winter in India, recalls once seeing his train arrive early at the platform. He was so astonished by this that he turned to an Indian friend to comment on it. The friend shook his head, sadly. "Oh no, that is not today's train, half an hour early. It is yesterday's train, 23 and a half hours late."

Most of my memorable, long train journeys – such as the spectacular, high-altitude ride from Lake Titicaca to Cusco in Peru, or the gruelling 33 hours across central China – have been on normal passengers trains, which offer a wonderful slice of life – hawkers selling bags of peanuts, colourfully dressed women dandling their babies, cheeky shoe-shine boys touting for business. But I've occasionally stepped on to the five-star "experience" trains such as the Orient-Express, which offer an entirely different, though equally memorable, journey. It's hard to resist the urge to dress up and imagine yourself back in the 1930s – though without the Agatha Christie-style murders, thank you. Here I've listed some of the world's great train journeys, and tour operators that can book them for you.

Classic trains

Blue Train, South Africa, **www.bluetrain.co.za**

The Ghan, Australia, **www.railaustralia.com.au**

Glacier Express, Switzerland, **www.glacierexpress.ch**

Palace on Wheels, India, **www.palaceonwheels.net**

Rocky Mountaineer, Canada, **www.rockymountaineer.com**

Royal Scotsman, UK, **www.royalscotsman.com**

The **Trans-Siberian** and **Trans-Mongolian Express** trains can be booked through operators including **Regent Holidays** (0870 499 0911, **www.regent-holidays.co.uk**) and **On the Go Tours** (020 7371 1113, **www.onthegotours.com**).

Travellers aged 18–35 can join budget trips through China, Mongolia and Russia, including long-distance train trips, with **Vodkatrain** (020 8877 7650, www.vodkatrain.com). The Venice Simplon-Orient-Express, the Northern Belle and British Pullman journeys in the UK, the Eastern & Oriental Express in Asia and the Hiram Bingham in Peru are all bookable through **Orient-Express** (0845 077 2222, **www.orient-express.com**).

Guidebook publisher **Trailblazer** (**www.trailblazer-guides.com**) has guides to rail journeys in Japan, Canada, Australia and Russia.

Rail holiday operators

- **Cresta** (0870 238 7711, **www.crestaholidays.co.uk**) has a dedicated Eurostar brochure for train-based holidays to Europe.

- **Enthusiast Holidays** (020 8699 3654, **www.enthusiasthols.com**) offers steam train tours around the world.

- **eRail** (020 7387 0444, **www.erail.co.uk**), sister company of ticketing agency European Rail, offers tailor-made train-based holidays in Europe.

- **Ffestiniog Travel** (01766 512400, **www.festtravel.co.uk**) offers group and tailor-made train holidays worldwide.

- **French Travel Service** (0870 241 4243, **www.f-t-s.co.uk**) offers rail-based holidays across France.

- **Great Rail Journeys** (01904 521900, **www.greatrail.com**) is an experienced specialist operator, offering rail holidays worldwide on the great scenic routes and luxury trains.

- **Railtrail** (01538 382323, **www.railtrail.co.uk**) offers escorted group rail-based journeys around Europe and the UK, some featuring historic or steam railways.

Anyone heading for **India**, where train travel is one of the best ways to get around, should consult the site of **SD Enterprises**, set up by the legendary Dr Dandapani, in Wembley, north London (020 8903 3411, **www.indiarail.co.uk**). It's the official UK ticket agency for Indian Railways and I have found it to be extremely efficient.

Coach travel

Within Europe, the major provider of coach services is **Eurolines** (0870 580 8080, **www.eurolines.co.uk**), which links 32 independent coach companies across 25 countries under the Eurolines brand. From the UK, prices include the ferry crossing to the continent and journeys such as London to Prague or Barcelona take the best part of 24 hours. If you have time but limited funds, you can even travel to Moscow, which takes three and a half days, from £159.

The most popular routes are to Paris, Amsterdam, Dublin and Bruges; fares to Paris, for example, start at £32 return if bought 30 days in advance. The trip takes seven and a half hours, city centre to city centre, which is not much longer than a flight would take once you factor in travel to the airport and checking-in times. Prices rise as the departure date nears.

In winter there is a popular ski service costing from £79 return to a dozen French resorts, including the transport of skis. The Eurolines Pass allows 15 or 30 days' travel in Europe between 41 cities; a 15-day pass costs £115 for under-26s or £135 for over-26s; a 30-day pass costs £159/£205. Coaches typically have videos playing on board, reclining seats and a lavatory. Eurolines Plus coaches, on routes from London to Paris, Amsterdam and Dublin, have more legroom.

Coach-based holidays

Tours of Canada combining coach travel with the Rocky Mountaineer train, and tours of China adding in a boat trip on the Yangtze, are among the most popular coach holidays sold by specialist agent **Coachtrips.com**, according to its owner, Tony Radstone. And anyone who still thinks coach holidays are the preserve of the infirm elderly will find that myth scotched by operator **WA Shearings**, whose most popular tour outside the UK is an exhausting 15-night trip around Russia. "People want to see Russia, as there's so much history, but they are nervous about making the arrangements and getting the visa," said Karen Gee of WA Shearings. "So it's great that we can organise that for them. There's something nice about delegating all the responsibility."

Indeed, coach tours are ideal for countries "where you cannot read the road signs," said Radstone.

Coaches are now more comfortable, with WA Shearings offering their Grand Tourer on some European trips, which has 36 seats, giving the same sort of legroom as some business-class seats on planes. Some coaches have TV screens, and all have lavatories, though drivers stop regularly for breaks. When booking, you may want to ask if you have the same seat throughout the trip (as with WA Shearings, for example), or if you are rotated through the coach (as with Cosmos Tourama, for example) so everyone gets the best seats at some point.

Check the itinerary to find out how much time you spend on the road, compared with how much time you have at each destination. Some trips involve a change of hotel most nights, which can be tiring. Also find out where your pick-up point is on the list – some trips start by collecting people from different pick-up points, which can be a bore if you are one of the first to be picked up.

Coach holiday operators

Archers Direct, 0845 600 1910, **www.archersdirect.co.uk**

Consort Travel, 0845 345 0300, **www.consorttravel.com**

Cosmos Tourama, 0800 083 9837, **www.cosmostourama.co.uk**

David Urquhart Travel, 0845 700 0400, **www.davidurquharttravel.co.uk**

Insight Vacations, 01475 741203, **www.insightvacations.com**

Leger Holidays, 0800 018 9898, **www.legerbreaks.com**

Page & Moy, 0870 833 4012, **www.pageandmoy.com**

Saga, 0800 096 0089, **www.saga.co.uk**

Thomas Cook Tours, 0870 443 4436, **www.thomascooktours.com**

Titan HiTours, 01293 455345, **www.titanhitours.co.uk**

WA Shearings, 01942 824824, **www.washearings.com**

Travel agent **Coachtrips.com** (020 8450 5354, **www.coachtrips.com**) sells holidays from many of these companies.

Travelling by ferry

Until recently, you practically needed a degree in advanced mathematics to work out the price of a ferry ticket across the Channel. As David Stafford of Hoverspeed admitted: "We used to have terrible timetables that no one could understand, with different prices and colour zones. It was a nightmare for those that worked in the ferry industry, never mind the poor public."

But now, ferries are largely following the simpler pricing model of the budget airlines, whereby the cheapest tickets are available first, and prices rise with demand – so the closer to departure you buy, the more expensive the ticket. This is partly because the likes of Ryanair and easyJet, flying into popular

Spanish and French towns such as Biarritz, Nantes and Bilbao, or across to the Republic of Ireland, are now offering serious competition to the ferries.

Daragh O'Reilly, passenger manager for Irish Ferries, said: "Passenger perception is that the best fares have been on the airlines, so we have been forced into making our fares much more attractive and easier to understand. We used to quote them on a return basis for a car plus five passengers, now that's outmoded. Fares are cheaper than ever."

Marianne Ilum of Speedferries, which introduced fast Dover–Boulogne crossings in 2004, claims credit for the change. "We did to the ferry industry what Ryanair and easyJet did to the low-cost airline industry," she said. "We have low-cost fares, fully flexible tickets and the price is dependent not on the duration of your stay but on the capacity available. It's benefited the consumers because the average price of a cross-channel fare has come down by 50 per cent since we started." It's also now possible to buy one-way tickets, which was previously not an option.

Enjoying the on-board shopping, and bringing back tax-paid goods that you have bought on the continent, is one of the main reasons travellers take their car on the ferry. For details of the limits on the amount of goods you can legally bring back to the UK, see chapter 7 (*see* page 247).

Booking

You can book ferry tickets through your travel agent, direct with the ferry companies listed in the Directory, *see* page 423, or through these specialist agencies that offer tickets from a variety of ferry lines: **www.ferrysavers. com** (0870 990 8492), **www.directferries.com** (0871 222 3312), **www.eurodrive. co.uk** (0870 442 2440), **www.ferrybooker.com** (0870 442 2418) and **www. cheap4ferries.co.uk** (0870 111 0634). The **Passenger Shipping Association** has got leading ferry companies together to form the site **www.sailanddrive. com**, which promotes the benefits of taking ferries, and has information about on-board services.

Rail and sail

These services offer a combined rail and ferry ticket: the **Dutchflyer** service connects London with Amsterdam and other Dutch destinations (0870 545 5455, **www.dutchflyer.co.uk**); **SailRail** links the UK and Ireland (0845 075 5755, **www.sailrail.co.uk**).

Driving abroad

I love driving and I'm always happy to hire a car when I travel. As well as driving all over Europe and the USA I've hired cars in far-flung places such as Bali, Mexico and Zimbabwe and, while there may still be the odd Twingo on Majorca without a wing mirror, I've generally managed to avoid getting into any scrapes.

But while the freedom of having your own wheels is great fun, organising a rental car and sorting out the insurance can be a nightmare. This industry has raised jargon to an artform – CDW, non-waivable excess, and third-party liability are just some of the confusing terms you may encounter – and we're all wearily familiar with arriving at the pick-up point only to be told to "initial here, here and here" before we can collect the car. What are we signing up for? Is it a rip-off – or vital insurance?

Even driving your own car on the continent isn't entirely straightforward. Breakdown insurance and a certain amount of paperwork need to be considered before you head off.

Taking your own car overseas

Insurance

If you are driving your own car overseas, your UK motor insurance policy will provide the basic legal minimum cover that's required by law in the EU and some other countries. But this generally means just third-party cover, so that if you have an accident and injure someone, they can make a claim on your insurance.

That's a far cry from the comprehensive, or the third party, fire and theft policy you will have in the UK. So the first thing to do is to call your insurance company. Some will automatically extend your cover for driving in Europe up to the same level that you have in the UK, for no extra charge. Other insurers may charge you for this. And all insurers are likely to limit the number of days per year that you can drive overseas on your insurance policy, typically to a month or six weeks per year. If you go abroad and do not notify them, you may only be covered for the basic third-party minimum cover, so every time you're driving overseas, it's vital to let them know.

Your motor insurance does not include **breakdown cover**, but it can be worth buying this, either from your motor insurer or a motoring organisation such as the RAC or the AA. If you're a member of such an organisation, you already have breakdown cover in the UK, but this does not extend overseas, so you need to buy an extra policy.

Typically, breakdown insurance should give you 24-hour access to an English-speaking operator, who will arrange for someone to repair the car at the side of the road, or if that's not possible, to tow it to a garage. It should cover a certain amount of labour (perhaps £150 or so) but it does not cover parts. It should also get you and your vehicle back home if it cannot be repaired abroad, or if the driver is incapacitated, and it should offer help with other travel arrangements, such as a hotel stay, that you must make as a result of the breakdown. Some policies will offer a replacement car so you can continue your holiday.

You generally pay for breakdown insurance by the day, so you can tailor it to the exact length of your trip. Some insurers offer annual breakdown insurance policies which are worth considering if you regularly take your car to the continent. Have your car serviced before you take it abroad, or at least check essentials such as water, oil and tyre pressures before each trip.

Companies offering breakdown cover include:

The AA, 0800 444500, **www.theaa.com**

Direct Line, 0845 246 8704, **www.directline.com**

Europ Assistance, 0870 737 5720, **www.europ-assistance.co.uk**

Green Flag Motoring Assistance, 0800 400638, **www.greenflag.co.uk**

The RAC, 0800 550055, **www.rac.co.uk**

Paperwork

It's essential to take your driving licence (both the photocard and the counterpart), your motor insurance certificate, and your proof of vehicle ownership – either the registration document, or a letter from the owner authorising you to drive the car. It is wise to carry your passport with you in the car, too (but do not leave it there).

Green cards are not compulsory but they can be useful, particularly in the 10 new EU member states. A green card is a document, available free from your insurer, that proves you have minimum motor insurance and is widely recognised on the continent. Ask your insurer for a standard accident form too – if you are in an accident it's useful for recording what happened, which will help with any insurance claim.

The International Driving Permit (IDP) is no longer needed in the EU, although it is in certain other countries – the AA's website has a list of countries where you should carry it (see **www.theaa.com** and enter IDP into the search field). If you are still driving on an old-fashioned paper licence in the UK, which does not have photo ID, it may be worth carrying an IDP even in Europe.

IDPs are available from the **DVLA** (0870 240 0009, **www.dvla.gov.uk**), from some Post Offices and from organisations such as the AA and the RAC. They are valid for a year, and cost £5.50. You should carry it with your UK driving licence – it is not a substitute.

What to take with you

There are various bits of kit you need if you're driving overseas. Most basic is the GB sticker on the back of your car. If you are in the EU, you do not need this if your car has a "Euro-plate" numberplate that displays a circle of 12 stars above the GB symbol on a blue background.

Some countries, such as France, insist you fit headlamp adjusters to avoid dazzling oncoming drivers, and carry warning triangles in case of breakdown. Spare headlight bulbs, fire extinguisher and first aid kit are compulsory in some countries, and you must carry a reflective vest in Austria, Spain, Portugal and Italy, to be worn while standing next to the car in the event of a breakdown. Check with motoring groups such as the AA or RAC, or the relevant tourist office, to ensure you have everything you need.

Getting around

The modern way to navigate is to use a Global Positioning System – *see* **www.globalpositioningsystems.co.uk** for a selection. Ensure the mapping software is as up to date as possible. The old-fashioned way is to use a road atlas – and it's always worth packing one even if you have GPS. The AA (**www.theaa.com**) sell masses. A middle way is to use internet-based route services to help plot your journey: try **www.viamichelin.co.uk**, **www.mappy. com** or **www.theaa.com**. In France during high summer, you can encounter huge tailbacks: consult **www.bison–fute.equipement.gouv.fr** for the dates of expected jams and other roadworks information (in French). The site **www.autoroutes.fr/index.php** also has traffic, route and toll information for France, some of it in English.

You often have to pay a toll to use motorways, especially in France and Italy, so be prepared with plenty of euro coins in change. In Switzerland and Austria, to use the motorways you need a vignette, which you can buy from the **Swiss Centre** in London (020 7734 1921), for driving in Switzerland, and at frontiers, post offices and petrol stations when you're there.

Rules of the road can vary across the continent – it's not simply a case of remembering to drive on the right. Traffic priorities can be different and countries have different laws – for example in several European countries, including throughout Scandinavia, Austria, Croatia, the Czech Republic, Hungary and Slovenia, you are expected to use dipped headlights during the day (this also applies in Italy outside towns). Speed limits can vary and drink-drive laws are often stricter than in the UK, and the minimum age for drivers may be 18, rather than 17 as in the UK. For useful country guides, see the AA or RAC websites.

Recently police forces in Europe have got better at notifying other countries if a foreign driver is caught breaking the law. So if you rack up a speeding fine overseas, you can expect the DVLA here to be notified and for it to appear as points on your licence.

Driving overseas – tips

- Talk to your insurer before travelling.

- Consider buying breakdown cover.

- Read up on the rules of the road for the country you're visiting.

- Carry driving licence, insurance and car ownership papers.

- Bring a spare set of car keys.

Hiring a car to drive overseas

Driving down the Florida Turnpike in a red convertible, Santana playing on the radio, was terrific fun – in fact I almost forgot what a hassle I'd had picking up the rental car in the first place. But with a little preparation you can take much of the stress out of hiring a car.

Booking the car

Whenever possible, organise your hire car at home before you set off on holiday, rather than once you get overseas – it's likely to be much cheaper, and you'll be able to compare prices from different companies and brokers (prices can vary widely, even for the same make of car in the same country).

If you are flying long-haul, consider whether you will want to pick up the car the moment you get off the plane. I once collected a car at Las

Vegas airport after an 11-hour charter flight and was so jet-lagged, and so overawed by the city's extraordinary hotels (I could see the enormous black pyramid of the Luxor from the plane) that it was very hard to concentrate on the road – or should I say, the Strip. It can be wise to take the transfer bus straight to your hotel for the first night and collect the car on day two – plus there's more chance you will avoid the long wait that usually occurs when everyone from your flight picks up their car at once. Some car hire firms will even bring the car to your hotel – I used this service in Antigua, for example – which makes life very easy.

You should also consider whether you'll want air conditioning, or need a child seat, or snow chains in winter, a luggage rack, or a saloon with a covered boot so your possessions can be kept out of sight. Most of these "extras" incur extra charges. If you want an automatic car, get the hire firm to confirm this in writing – in the USA most rental cars are automatic, but in Europe you may find them harder to come by.

It can be better to take your own child's car seat with you than rely on the rental office having one, even if you have pre-booked it – in high summer they sometimes simply run out. You can usually transport your car seat for free on the plane, but you must pay to hire one from a car rental firm.

You must also check how old the driver(s) must be. The minimum age of driver permitted by many firms is 21, although in Antigua we found it was 25 and as Roy, the photographer I was working with, was only 24, he got to be the designated drinker. Sometimes you are not allowed to hire a car if you are aged over 65, although older drivers with a clean record should be able to shop around for a deal. And if you want to share the driving, you usually have to pay a charge for every extra person whose name goes on the form.

You will need to declare any penalty points on your licence, too. "Usually, if you have three to six points on your licence for speeding, or a drink-drive conviction more than 10 years ago, you will be accepted," said a spokeswoman for broker Carrentals.co.uk. "But if you have more points, or the conviction was more recent, you may have problems." She added that, in the broker's experience, Ireland takes the toughest line of any European country on these matters.

Check exactly when and where you have to return the car – it may be possible to arrange one-way drives, leaving the car at another depot, but you should organise this in advance, and there may be an extra charge.

Car rental insurance

Yes, I'm afraid this is where our eyes start to glaze over, but it's important to understand what insurance you need, and what you can safely decline.

Collision damage waiver (CDW) is the first box to tick. This limits the amount you must pay if your car is damaged – if you don't have it and you write the car off, for example, you could end up paying for the entire cost of the car. It usually comes as standard in rental agreements anyway, and you'd be wise to accept it. In America it is sometimes known as loss damage waiver (LDW).

You may also encounter **theft waiver** too – accepting this, which I'd recommend, means that if the car is stolen you will not have to pay the rental firm for it.

However with both these types of waiver, you still have to pay an **excess**, just as you do with a travel insurance policy. But while on most travel insurance policies the excess is typically £50 or £100, which most of us can swallow, the excess if the car is damaged or stolen can run into hundreds of pounds – and in some cases, well over £1,000. In 2005, figures from **Insurance4carhire. com** revealed a theft excess of £1,077 on a small car hired in Pisa, Italy, from Europcar, and a damage excess of £515 on a small car hired there from Hertz. In other words, *even though you have insurance*, you would still be stung for these amounts if the car was stolen or damaged.

To avoid paying these big excesses, you are usually offered the chance to buy insurance to reduce them to a lower figure, or to zero. These policies are sometimes known as "super CDW" or "damage excess waiver" and, although you can buy them when you book the car, you may also be asked to buy them when you collect the car.

These **excess insurance** policies can themselves be fairly expensive, adding perhaps £5 to £10 per day to the rental cost. In the Italian examples quoted above, the excess insurance was £9.06 per day with Europcar and £12.35 per day with Hertz. Insurance4carhire.com has an interest in publicising these high charges, because it sells annual excess insurance policies from £51.45 for a year in Europe to £124.95 for a year worldwide. The company reimburses policyholders for the entire cost of any excess they have to pay.

If you have bought excess insurance before you travel, either from your rental company or through Insurance4carhire.com, you can safely decline it at the car collection desk. It is not compulsory, but if you have an accident and do not have it you could face paying a hefty excess charge.

Fuel charges are another bugbear. Make sure you know what's required – whether you must bring the tank back full or empty – and factor in time to find a petrol station near the drop-off point when you return the car. Keep your petrol receipts, timed and dated, to prove when and where you filled up the car in case of a dispute later.

Mileage charges are increasingly a thing of the past, but do check you have unlimited mileage when you book, and if not, consider whether the free mileage allowance is sufficient.

Glass and tyres is a classic car rental cop-out. Usually, your hire car insurance does not cover you for damage to tyres, wheels, windows or windscreen, wing mirrors, the car's interior or its underside. When I asked one car firm why this was so, they told me it was because "when these items are damaged, it is usually down to driver negligence", which I find hard to accept in all cases. Some firms will cover these items, but if not, Insurance4carhire.com will cover you for damage to windows, tyres and the car's underside, up to £2,000.

There are other types of insurance you may be offered by your rental firm, such as **personal accident** or **possessions cover**. These should be covered by your travel insurance policy, in which case you can decline them. If you have no travel insurance, you're potty – go back to chapter 6 to find out why.

Collecting and returning the car

If you're collecting your car at the airport when you fly in, send the driver in your party to the car hire desk while the rest of you wait for the luggage to appear on the carousel – it often takes ages to sort out car rental paperwork, so you want to be at the front of the queue. You must present the credit card with which you made the booking, as well as driving licences for everyone who's to drive the car.

But one reason why you may choose to collect the car the day after you arrive is so you can inspect it in daylight, without a tired family or bored friends urging you to get a move on. If you plan to do this, always tell the rental company beforehand, and check their office opening times. Offices at some of the smaller airports popular with budget airlines may only open when flights are due to arrive.

It's important to check the car very carefully for dents and other damage before you drive away in it – otherwise you may be charged for causing them. Check the bodywork, that the tyres are not bald and that the spare is in good condition. Rental staff should give you a diagram of the car indicating any pre-existing damage you find. If you are sent off to an outlying car park to pick up your car and you find it is damaged, you'll have to go back to the office to report the damage or risk being charged for it.

Also check how much petrol the car has in the tank, and note down the mileage before you drive off. Be sure that rental staff have given you their emergency contact details and instructions about what to do if you have an accident. Finally, make sure you know what type of fuel the car uses. If you put diesel into a petrol engine, or vice versa, you're in real trouble – and it's unlikely your insurance will cover you.

Sometimes you have to return the car when the depot is closed and so no staff are there to check it over. But they hold your credit card details, so can charge you subsequently if they detect any damage. So why not take photographs of the car to show that the bodywork is as it was when you hired it? If staff are there, insist that they inspect the car with you. If they are too busy, write on the agreement that they declined to inspect it, and keep a copy. If you have damaged the car, try to get a quote from an independent garage for repair work, so if the car rental firm sends you a much higher bill you have some comeback. (Do not ask the garage to do the work, however.)

You may have to return the car when the office is very busy – so build in extra time for this, if you have a flight to catch. Ask for a copy of any notes that the car rental staff make when you return the car, and cross a line through any blanks on the form. If you had to give an open credit card voucher when you collected the car, ask for it back and tear it up.

Further information

- **Insurance4carhire.com** (020 7012 6300, **www.insurance4carhire. com**) sells excess insurance and has a useful "FAQs" section on its website covering many aspects of car rental.

- **The British Vehicle Rental and Leasing Association** has a guide to renting a car on its website (**www.bvrla.co.uk**).

- **Citizens Advice Bureaux** offer free advice if you have a dispute, and there's also useful information on the website **www.euroconsumer.org.uk** (click on holidays).

- In the USA you can deliver a car across the country: contact **Autodriveaway** (**www.autodriveaway.com**).

Car hire firms

Alamo, 0870 400 4562, **www.alamo.co.uk**

Avis, 0870 010 0287, **www.avis.co.uk**

Budget, 0870 156 5656, **www.budget.co.uk**

Europcar, 0870 607 5000, **www.europcar.co.uk**

Hertz, 0870 848 4848, **www.hertz.co.uk**

National, 0870 400 4560, **www.nationalcar.co.uk**

Sixt, 0870 156 7567, **www.e-sixt.co.uk**

Brokers

Car Hire Warehouse, 01233 500464, **www.carhirewarehouse.com**

Carrentals.co.uk, 0845 225 0845, **www.carrentals.co.uk**

easyCar, 0906 333 3333, 60p/min, **www.easycar.com**

Holiday Autos, 0870 400 0000, **www.holidayautos.co.uk**

OnAirport, 0870 902 8021, **www.onairportcarhire.com**

Suncars, 0870 500 5566, **www.suncars.com**

Motorhomes

• **Motorhome Bookers** (020 7193 2873, **www.motorhomebookers.com**) specialises in motorhome and campervan travel.

• Many companies offering holidays in North America and Australasia, which are popular destinations for hiring motorhomes, can organise hire of these vehicles, which are often known as RVs (recreational vehicles). *See* the Directory (chapter 11).

CHAPTER NINE
Staying there

Introduction

Towels on the sunbeds at dawn. I expect many of us remember the lager advert that so memorably summed up the tensions between the British and some of our northern European neighbours when we go on holiday. We Brits like a lie-in and we don't like to come down to the pool mid-morning to find all the best sunloungers have been bagged by other guests arising at 6am to "claim" them with their towels.

Small niggles like this can really mar your holiday in a way that's easily blown out of all proportion. But I'm afraid claiming your sunbed is not the only potential holiday hurdle. From unclean swimming pools to locked fire doors, from dangerous taxi drivers to con-artists and muggers, numerous hazards await the unwary traveller.

Most of us enjoy uneventful, relaxing, safe holidays. But when something goes wrong in a foreign land it can seem like a bigger problem than it might at home, because you may not speak the language or know who to contact for help. So in this chapter I'll look at some of the most common holiday hazards and the best ways to deal with them.

Hotel and villa hazards

Whether you are spending one night in a hotel, or two weeks at a villa, it makes sense to spend a few minutes thinking about your safety. Some of the concerns in this section are more relevant to hotel guests, but many apply if you're staying in a villa, too.

Balconies

These pose one of the greatest potential hazards, especially if you have children: you must watch them like a hawk, and never leave furniture up against the balcony in case an inquisitive toddler clambers up on it. Request a ground-floor room when you book if this is a worry.

Peter Cornall of the Royal Society for the Prevention of Accidents (RoSPA) said: "Balconies should be at least 1.1m high, so the top is above your centre of gravity, and they should have vertical rails, not horizontal, which encourages kids to climb up them.

"The rails should form a solid barrier, so a child cannot squeeze through them, and should be set at the edge of the balcony, not leaving a gap that you might be tempted to climb on to." He didn't add "if you're drunk", but I will: every summer there are accidents in hotels caused by drunken guests trying to climb from one balcony to another. What's worse, if you are injured in this way while under the influence of drugs or alcohol, your travel insurance is unlikely to cover your medical bills.

Security

Solo women travellers should be especially cautious in hotels – and should be wary of male staff as well as guests. Use spy glasses or door chains if they are provided, and do not open the door to anyone you are not expecting – especially at night. Call reception first to check them out, and report any unsettling incidents to the management.

It's not a bad idea to shove a door wedge under your hotel door for extra security. Alternatively **Catch 22** sells a nifty door guard that works on many doors, for £7.99 (01942 511820, **www.catch22products.co.uk**). Personally I avoid ground floor rooms when possible, as I like fresh air at night and don't feel safe with an open window in a ground floor room.

If the receptionist asks your room number you can write it down for them if you do not want people nearby to overhear what you are saying. Some business hotels (such as the London Hilton on Park Lane) have "women-only" floors where male guests and staff are not permitted.

If you are worried about theft from your room, keep valuables in the room safe, or the hotel reception's safe (at least if items are stolen from a safe behind reception you should be able to claim for them on your insurance). I'm reluctant to advise you to leave lights on while you are out of the room to deter thieves, as burning extra electricity isn't great for the planet, but you could leave the radio on if you wanted to give the impression to an opportunist thief that the room is occupied.

Fire safety

Many years ago I interviewed a survivor of the fire at the Heliopolis Sheraton Hotel in Cairo in 1990, in which 17 people died and 70 were injured. Her stark terror at what had happened – she was convinced she was going to die, and had a very narrow escape – stayed with me, and ever since we spoke, I have been careful to check my hotel room and surroundings with fire safety in mind.

When you arrive, check the fire escape information in your room (it is usually on the back of the door). Then conduct a little test, following the directions to the fire escape, and counting how many bedroom doors you pass to reach the emergency stairs from your room. Hotels with long corridors and rows of identical doors can be confusing places at the best of times, so trying to find your way out when smoke fills the corridor is a scary prospect. Check the fire doors are not blocked or locked (if they are, tell the management and get them opened), and walk your way out of the fire escape to ensure it leads outside, not to a dark basement or other potential trap.

The Childers backpacker fire in Australia is a dreadful example of how a lack of essential fire safety measures can lead to tragedy. In June 2000 a disgruntled former resident of the Palace Backpackers Hostel in Childers, Queensland, set fire to the timber building, and the ensuing blaze killed 15 backpackers, including seven Britons (the arsonist was caught and jailed for 20 years). Later reports revealed that the hostel ignored many fire safety measures: the alarm was disabled, there were no extinguishers or sprinklers, furniture blocked fire exits and the premises were over-occupied. But do not make the mistake of thinking that it is only cheaper hotels that are at most risk: fires can and do occur at expensive hotels. For example, in May 2004, three people died in a fire at the five-star Parco dei Principi Hotel in Rome.

Experienced travellers often ask for rooms on the first to the fifth floor of large hotels. Avoiding the ground floor helps from a security point of view, but fire ladders rarely reach much higher than the fifth floor (and can only be used to access rooms where there is enough space to park the fire tender below the window).

If you hear a fire alarm, do not assume it's a test – get out immediately. Hotel fires can spread with astonishing speed. In 1986 a fire at the Dupont Plaza Hotel in Puerto Rico killed 98 people within 13 minutes.

Fire safety tips

- When you go to sleep, put your room key somewhere you can easily find it, such as on the bedside table or by the door.

- Keep a small torch by your bed. Baroness Thatcher has carried a torch in her handbag since she was caught up in the Brighton hotel bomb attack of 1984.

- If it seems safe to leave your hotel room, follow the fire escape signs, do not use lifts, and take your room key with you (in case you need to retreat to the room).

- If the corridor is full of smoke, crawl, as smoke and heat rise.

- Cover your face with a wet flannel: you could even wet your clothes before you leave the room, and remove any made with synthetic fibres.

- If you are stuck in the room, fill the bath and place damp towels at the bottom of the door to keep smoke out.

- Attract attention from your balcony or window, but be wary when opening a window in case it draws smoke or flames into the room.

- I have heard of people who threw bags of clothes or mattresses out of the window to provide a soft landing when they jumped out.

Swimming pools

Ah, the bliss of a good swimming pool. As a keen swimmer I always try to stay in hotels with a great pool for doing laps first thing in the morning. La Mamounia in Marrakesh, with its gigantic pool surrounded by palms and orange trees, is hard to beat, as is the wonderful 32m pool at the Hotel

Cipriani in Venice. Legend has it that the designers gave the pool's length in feet, but the builders accidentally built it in metres, unintentionally doing keen swimmers a big favour.

But while a well-maintained pool can add immeasurably to the pleasure of a holiday, so the reverse is true. Every summer we hear a litany of dreadful stories of illness and injury caused by poor pool maintenance, irresponsible or stupid behaviour by swimmers, or simply awful bad luck.

Villas with pools

The bad news, for parents wanting a relaxing break, is that if your villa has a swimming pool you cannot drop your guard for a second if you have young children. Every summer we hear dreadful stories of young children drowning in the pool of a holiday villa. "Families using private villas with swimming pools must realise that they will have to be lifeguards for their children 24 hours a day," said Peter Cornall of RoSPA. "It might be safer to book a property without a pool if you have young children."

In France, all villa owners have had to take child-safety measures around their pools, such as adding a pool cover, a fence, or a sensor that sounds an alarm if a child falls in. But these are no substitute for eternal vigilance.

Hotel pools

Arriving at a holiday hotel is terribly exciting for kids, while parents may simply want to get up to the bedroom, unpack and have a nice cup of tea. But the worst thing they can do is to tell the kids it's OK to go off to explore the hotel. That's when accidents can occur. It's much better for one parent to go and explore with the children.

Take a stroll by the pool. Are there depth markings around the edge? A hotelier once told me that they spoiled the look of his trendy hotel, so he didn't bother to paint them on. You need to work out where the deep parts are. "Freeform", or irregularly shaped pools, common in resort hotels, may vary in depth from area to area, seemingly at random, and sometimes the floor of the pool may shelve steeply.

Other hazards may lie under water. I once stayed at a hotel on the Kenyan coast which had a wide, raised, concrete ledge around the bottom of the pool in the deep end. Anyone diving in might not have seen it and could have hit their head on it.

Lifeguards are sometimes, but by no means always, on duty at large resort hotels. There may be pool attendants who give out towels (and if you're lucky, monitor use of the sunbeds) but they are not there to act as lifeguards, so it's essential to watch your children. If you have had a large lunch and a few glasses of wine, make sure someone else is able to watch them in case you doze off on the sunlounger.

The most common dangers, however, tend to be unseen. Stomach upsets caused by bugs and germs in swimming pools are one of the most unpleasant problems encountered by holidaymakers.

A shocking report by *Holiday Which?* in 2004 revealed that only two of 80 hotel pools they tested in Corfu and Majorca were fully up to safe standards. The rest had various problems including contamination with faecal bacteria (bugs found in animal or human faeces), too much chlorine or not enough disinfectant. "Our results reveal stomach-churning evidence of gross bacterial contamination," said the report. "Coupled with most hotels' apparent incompetence at maintaining effective levels of water and disinfectant, it seems that hotel swimming pools can be serious health hazards."

Two major outbreaks of cryptosporidiosis at hotels in Majorca in the past few years have turned the spotlight on the problem. Cryptosporidiosis, which can be fatal in babies or those with a weak immune system, is a serious gastric complaint caused by the parasite cryptosporidium, and causes acute diarrhoea. It can occur when a pool's water becomes contaminated, perhaps by a baby with an ill-fitting swim nappy or by an adult swimmer who did not wash before entering the pool.

Mark Harrington of **CheckSafetyFirst**, which runs inspection schemes for hotel swimming pools and kitchens, said: "If the pool is murky, it may be over-chlorinated and you have to ask why that is – perhaps there are a lot of children in the pool wearing swim nappies and one has had a tummy upset. That means there's a risk of cryptosporidium in the pool, which causes diarrhoea."

In 2000 holiday company JMC had to compensate more than 1,000 guests who fell ill at the Aguamar Hotel in Majorca with cryptosporidiosis. In 2003, another outbreak at the Alcudia Pins Hotel, also in Majorca, affected more than 1,000 holidaymakers travelling with the tour operator MyTravel.

Finally, note that in France it is the law that men must wear tight-fitting Speedo-style briefs, rather than baggy trunks, in public pools, and all swimmers must wear bathing caps. The rules may not be enforced in all outdoor or hotel pools but it is wise to be prepared. From a hygiene point of view, it's best if everyone wears a bathing cap, whether or not it's the rule. Bathing caps are also compulsory at public pools in some central and eastern European countries.

Swimming pool safety tips

- If you want to swim with your baby, ensure they wear a well-fitting swim nappy.

- Keep babies in the smaller baby pool, if there is one, which is easier to drain and clean than the adult pool if there's a problem.

- Make sure you and your children shower thoroughly before swimming.

- Don't swim if you have had a stomach upset in the last few weeks.

- If the pool smells of chlorine, it may mean the chlorine is overworked and no longer active, so don't swim.

- If the water is murky, it can be dangerous to swim as you cannot see the bottom, and it may mean that the water is not properly chlorinated.

- Tell the rep or hotel staff if you notice any problems, and fill in a complaint form.

Swimming in open water

Statistically, rip tides and currents are a far more serious threat to the swimmer than a more headline-grabbing shark attack. I once reported on the story of a British tourist who drowned in Goa, India, while paddling in water that came up only to his knees. The current was so powerful that he was suddenly dragged out to sea and drowned. So look around for warning flags or notices, and if no one else is swimming where you want to swim, ask why.

Avoid drinking alcohol or eating heavily two hours before you swim, and be wary if the water is cold. "Even in summer, temperate seas are rarely warmer than 15°C, and at these temperatures swimmers easily get into trouble and drown," warned Dr Jane Wilson-Howarth, author of travel health guide *Bugs, Bites & Bowels*.

Make sure you wear waterproof sunscreen, though even this can wash off, so you should reapply the lotion as soon as you get out of the water.

It's particularly important to consider sun protection when you are snorkelling, as you may be floating for some time, so absorbed in the wonderful underwater life that you forget that your back and the backs of your legs may be frying. Try not to touch anything underwater – touching coral harms it, and it can scratch or sting you, and jellyfish are to be actively avoided. I was once snorkelling in the beautiful lagoon at Aitutaki in the Cook Islands when I was stung by a jellyfish. We had a nervous boat ride back to our resort while waiting to see if I developed an allergic reaction, for we were a long journey from any real medical help.

Never go scuba diving unless you are with an accredited dive operator who works to a recognised programme, such as the **Professional Association of Diving Instructors (www.padi.com)** or the **British Sub-Aqua Club (www.bsac.com)**, and offers appropriate training for your skill level.

Hotel meals

I'm afraid more dangers lurk within the innocuous-seeming hotel buffet and in other meals you may eat on your travels. This is an important subject and I've looked at it in depth in chapter 10 (*see page 358*).

Electrics and gas safety

Safety with electrics

Electrical appliances in the room may not be made to the same safety standards as in the UK. When plugging in anything you have brought with you, check it's compatible with the local supply.

Safety with gas

Carbon monoxide is a silent killer, which has caused the deaths of several holidaymakers. It's a particular concern for anyone in self-catering accommodation – a cottage, villa, apartment or even a caravan – where you have a gas water heater, but it can be produced by any sort of fuel where there is inadequate ventilation.

"Anything that burns can give rise to carbon monoxide when the appliance does not have proper ventilation and oxygen," said barrister Stephanie Trotter, who runs the **Carbon Monoxide and Gas Safety Society (www.co-gassafety. co.uk)**, a charity that campaigns for tighter legislation in this area. "It can affect people having a barbeque in an enclosed space, or working on their car in a garage, cooking or taking a shower. Always make sure there is a flue, and if you have a fire indoors, check the smoke is coming out of the chimney."

Ms Trotter advises holidaymakers to carry and use a small carbon monoxide detector (one that sets off an alarm, rather than the sort that simply changes colour), which are available from as little as £20, and to keep windows open and rooms well ventilated. "Whenever you use gas, open the window, and never sleep with the gas on in any way," she said. The charity's website has further advice and information.

Contacts

- **CheckSafetyFirst (www.checksafetyfirst.com)** runs hygiene training programmes for resort hotels to help them improve standards in food preparation and swimming pool maintenance. It lists hotels that have reached high standards.

- **Holiday Which? (www.which.co.uk)** fights for consumer rights and publishes magazines and books to help people make an informed choice.

- **RoSPA (www.rospa.co.uk)** is actively involved in the promotion of safety and the prevention of accidents.

When your holiday goes wrong

Houston – we have a problem

You might not be lost in space, but when you have a problem on holiday you may well want to call Ground Control. The swimming pool's a building site, your room has a view of the car park, the disco keeps you awake all night, the shower leaks, the hotel's restaurant is closed for redecoration, the shuttle bus to the resort is out of action... you have saved hard for this holiday only to find it isn't what you expected. So what do you do?

If you have booked a package holiday, you are entitled, under the Package Travel Regulations that I discussed in chapter 4, to the holiday that you have paid for, so if there are any problems the holiday company knows it must act to put them right.

Take things up with your rep immediately. It's essential that you give the holiday company the opportunity to put things right there and then – over the last few years, tour operators have given their reps far greater powers to sort things out on the ground, so hopefully the rep will be able to fix the problem straight away. And if you do not take matters up with the rep at the time, you may find any subsequent claim you make against the holiday company is rejected.

If you do not have a rep (as we've seen in chapter 4, some holiday companies do not always offer a rep service), there will be someone who works for the holiday company in your resort, so speak to them and also take matters up with the hotel management. (If you simply cannot track anyone down, you may have to call the head office of the company in the UK.) Fill in a complaint form and ask the company rep and hotelier to sign it.

Let's take a common example: the four-star hotel you booked was full when you arrived, and you have been switched to a three-star hotel down the road. You've complained to the rep, but it's high season and they say there's nothing more they can do.

The holiday company is obliged to do everything it reasonably can to give you the holiday you have booked, so if, for example, you find there's a four-star hotel up the road with rooms available, but it's not in your company's brochure so the rep doesn't know about it, you can suggest to the rep that they move you there. They will need a good excuse not to accept this sort of deal.

If you stay put, make notes about what you have missed out on – for example, the four-star hotel might have been offering a wider choice of restaurants, a bigger bedroom, air conditioning, or entertainment which you are not getting at the three-star hotel. Continue to register your complaint with both the rep and the hotel manager. Sometimes you can be moved after a couple of days – I'm a great believer in the squeaky wheel getting the grease. If you make a polite but persistent fuss you may find the rep fixes the problem just to get you out of their hair.

You may be offered, say, £100 in compensation on the spot. Should you take it? If you feel that £100 is adequate compensation for the switch from four-star to three-star accommodation, then accept it, consider the matter closed and get on with your holiday. If you think the £100 goes some way towards compensating you, but you think you are owed more, then only accept it if you can do so without signing away your rights to complain in future.

A final option – but a very high-risk strategy – is to move to another hotel, paying for it out of your own pocket, in the hope that you can claim the money back from your tour operator later. If you do this, make sure you keep your rep informed, and move to a hotel that has the same star rating as the one you originally booked. If you upgrade yourselves to the best hotel in town when you had originally booked a standard four-star property, the holiday company will certainly not cough up. Keep receipts, and be aware that there is no guarantee that you will get your money back. However, you may feel it is better to be out of pocket and have an enjoyable holiday, than to stay put and stay miserable.

Another common problem is that building work is going on at your hotel. You complain to the rep and ask to be moved, but they cannot help, and you cannot afford to move elsewhere. It's important to gather evidence: take notes, photos and video footage (this can capture the noise of the building work) and ask other guests to write a note in support of your complaint. Indeed, if you have any problem with a hotel or villa, keeping records of the problem is very important if you intend to pursue the holiday company for compensation.

In really disastrous cases, you can ask that the holiday company flies you home early, if possible, and you can try to claim compensation for the part of the holiday you lost, and for the discomfort of the bit you experienced. But this really is the nuclear option and most holiday companies will try very hard to fix the problem before it gets to this stage.

Since the 1990s there have been a series of large group compensation claims, where hundreds of disgruntled holidaymakers who stayed at the same hotel have banded together to demand compensation for problems such as illness caused by poor swimming pool or kitchen hygiene. Sometimes English solicitors go to the hotels as soon as problems are reported and collect witness statements. But barrister Alan Saggerson, who specialises in travel and tourism law and often acts for tour operators in such cases, said large group actions are becoming less common, as holiday companies insist that the hotels they work with improve hygiene standards. "I believe group claims are being eased out of the system because of the hard work that tour operators have done over the last 10 years to sharpen up the act of the hotels," he said.

The pressure group **Holiday Travelwatch** (0121 747 8100, **www.holidaytravelwatch.co.uk**) has long campaigned on behalf of holidaymakers whose package holidays have gone wrong, sometimes organising group actions and legal representation. It has information and resources on its website for anyone considering bringing a claim for compensation.

Claiming compensation

If you booked a package holiday

Once you are back home, if you think you are entitled to compensation for the problem you encountered, you must first decide who to bring your claim against. In most cases, it will be the tour operator, which is legally obliged to provide you with the holiday that you booked. But in some cases you may need to claim against the travel agency, if you think it has been negligent

– for example, because it did not pass on to you some information from the tour operator about a change of flight time or hotel.

Next you must decide what it is you are claiming for. If you simply did not enjoy the holiday because you booked the wrong place for your tastes, or it rained all week, that's not the tour operator's fault and you cannot expect compensation. But let's say you had a legitimate problem, you tried unsuccessfully to tackle it with the rep in resort, and you have notes and photos from the trip to back up your claim. Your first task is to write to the tour operator setting out why you are unhappy and what sort of recompense you are seeking. Do so soon after returning home. A subsequent compensation claim may be damaged if you took months to send in your original complaint, as that suggests you weren't particularly upset by the problem. If you are complaining to an Abta member, you must file your complaint within nine months of returning home, but waiting that long is inadvisable.

You must make "reasonable" demands, although there is no clear definition of what "reasonable" is. Let's say, for example, that you had the first two days of your holiday in a sub-standard hotel, and spent considerable time sorting out a move to a better hotel with the rep, but after you moved, the holiday went well. A claim for the cost of those two lost days will probably be considered reasonable.

To work out what you might claim, subtract the cost of the flight from the overall package holiday price – it's usually thought to constitute around 60 per cent of the total – and then divide the remaining 40 per cent by the number of days of your holiday. This gives you a rough daily amount that you paid for your accommodation, so in this example you would multiply that figure by two for the two lost days.

Another item you can claim for is out-of-pocket expenses that you would not have expected to pay if the holiday had gone according to plan. For example, if you booked an all-inclusive holiday and one of the hotel's restaurants was closed so you had to eat lunch outside the hotel, you could claim for the extra meals. Or if you were supposed to stay at a hotel that had a free shuttle bus to the resort, but you were moved to another hotel that had no shuttle bus, you could claim for the extra taxi fares you incurred.

A third part of your claim might be for disappointment or distress. This is also hard to quantify but if you were very upset by the problems you encountered then it is reasonable to ask for compensation for this too. But remember that it is extremely rare to get the cost of your entire holiday back unless something has gone dramatically wrong.

Write a polite letter to the company setting out your grievances and what you want by way of recompense. If you are unhappy with the company's response, you can take proceedings against it.

The two ways to do this are through a trade body's arbitration or dispute resolution scheme, or by using the small claims court. If one route fails, you cannot then try the other because the decisions in both cases are binding. So you need to work out which system will suit you best.

Dispute resolution schemes

If the company with which you have a dispute is a member of the **Association of British Travel Agents** (Abta, 020 7637 2444, **www.abta.com**), you can take your case to Abta's arbitration scheme. Complaints are adjudicated independently, by the Chartered Institute of Arbitrators. If your holiday company is a member of the **Association of Independent Tour Operators** (Aito, 020 8744 9280, **www.aito.co.uk**), you can use its Dispute Settlement Service.

The Abta scheme is the best known. Before you can proceed with it, you must have written *twice* to the company with your complaint, as outlined above, and still be unhappy with its response. Under Abta's code of conduct, the company must give you a "substantive" response (that is, one that addresses your concerns, rather than just an acknowledgement) within 28 days, each time you write to them.

You then send your case off to Abta, including any photos or video footage. The case is passed to the arbitrators and will be decided on the merits of the evidence you submit, and the written response from the company – there is no court hearing and you do not give evidence in person.

The fee for putting in this claim is £72.85 for claims up to £3,000, £98.70 for claims up to £5,000, £129.25 for claims up to £10,000 and £164.50 for claims up to £25,000. You can claim up to £5,000 per person, and £25,000 per group booking, but you can only claim up to £1,500 for illness or personal injury. If you win the case, you will probably get your fee back as well as any compensation that the arbitrators decide you should receive. If you lose, you will probably have to pay that same fee again to the holiday company.

"Arbitration is the last resort," said Sean Tipton of Abta. "We get between 15,500 and 17,000 complaints each year, but only about 10 per cent go to arbitration, because mostly we manage to sort it out with the company before it gets to that stage." He said that once you had sent in your complaint to Abta, the arbitrators should give you their verdict within two months. "Eighty per cent of cases go in the customer's favour, though there are no guarantees," he said.

If your complaint suggests that the Abta member has breached Abta's code of conduct, Abta may make a separate inquiry into the company's behaviour.

The Association of Independent Tour Operators' scheme works in a similar way, and is also paper-based rather than involving a court appearance. Holidaymakers pay a £94 non-refundable fee and can claim for up to £2,500 per person, or £10,000 per booking. The independent adjudicators' decision is final. You must submit your claim within nine months of returning home from holiday.

Small claims court

An alternative way to pursue compensation is to take your complaint to the small claims court, a division of the county court. You can do this whether the company concerned is an Abta member or not, and you can put in a claim for up to £5,000, but only up to £1,000 for illness or personal injury. No one is awarded costs, so the idea is that you will not need a lawyer. (Some claimants employ lawyers to help them, but must pay their fees out of any compensation they win.)

You normally have to appear in person in court, which may mean taking a day off work. If you win, you can normally claim travel costs and loss of earnings for the day. If you think you can get your grievances across more effectively to the judge in person than in writing, this may be the best route for you.

Bruce Treloar, trading standards lead officer for the holiday and travel industry, said holidaymakers must be wary when deciding to go to court. If you plan to present video or photographic evidence, the tour operator is entitled to see it before the hearing, and if your video includes some happy holiday scenes it will detract from your claim.

Claiming up to £1,000 costs £80, and claiming up to £5,000 costs £120. Some industry observers, such as *Holiday Which?*, feel that the small claims court finds in favour of holidaymakers, and awards higher levels of compensation, more often than the Abta scheme does.

For courts in England and Wales, contact **www.courtservice.gov.uk** or look up your nearest county court in the telephone directory. For courts in Scotland, see **www.scotcourts.gov.uk**. There is useful advice on using the small claims court at **www.compactlaw.co.uk**.

Personal injury claims

If you became very ill or suffered an injury while on a package holiday, the amount of compensation you can claim through Abta's scheme or the county court is limited. So for larger negligence claims you must consult a solicitor about the advisability of bringing a court case. It is always essential to have travel insurance, which will cover the cost of hospital treatment and, if necessary, repatriation if you fall ill or are injured while on holiday.

If you did not book a package holiday

If you put the holiday together yourself, perhaps by buying a flight online, then renting a villa from a different company, and finally making a booking with a car hire firm, you are not protected by the Package Travel Regulations if something goes wrong, because you have not technically bought a package. This means there is no single body to sort out any problems.

The first thing to do is to register your complaint on the spot, even if you do not have a tour operator's rep to deal with. The provider of your holiday cannot put things right if it does not know what the problem is, so seek out a representative of the airline or car hire company, the hotel manager or the villa owner, and put your complaint to them, in writing if necessary. If the matter cannot be resolved on the spot, request a written acknowledgement of your complaint. This will help if you need to write to head office later to press for compensation. Take photographs or video footage too, if appropriate.

The help you can then expect depends on what part of your trip went wrong.

Problems with flights

If your flight is delayed or cancelled, you have some rights. Broadly speaking, if you are delayed for two hours or more, you'll get refreshments and perhaps accommodation, and if the flight is cancelled or overbooked you should get compensation too, and a replacement flight.

But the airline's obligation is simply to get you from A to B – not to make sure the rest of your holiday goes well too. So if, for example, you arrive a day late because of a delayed flight and the hotel has sold your room to someone else because you didn't show up on time, the airline is not obliged to help you resolve that problem – you'll have to fight it out with the hotel. By comparison, if you had booked a package holiday and the flight was delayed for a day, it would have been the holiday company's duty to sort out your accommodation and ensure that when you finally arrived, everything was ready for you.

See chapter 3 (page 79) for full details of what rights you have if something goes wrong with your flight.

Problems with accommodation

With hotel or villa bookings, you must work out who your contract is with before you can start to fight for redress if things go wrong. If you booked direct with an overseas hotel or villa owner, or via a booking agency that is merely acting as the agent for the property, your contract is with the hotel or villa abroad. (Read the terms and conditions of your booking if you are not clear who your contract is with.) In these cases it's essential to sort out any problems as amicably and quickly as possible, because if the problem escalates and you want to take the accommodation provider to court, you will have to do so in their country, not in the UK. This will almost certainly not be worth the time and money.

However if your contract is with a UK-based hotel booking website you can deal with them if anything goes wrong, which is much easier. Some accommodation providers such as **Apartments Abroad** (**www.apartmentsabroad.com**) offer this level of customer service. The company explains on its website: "Unlike some companies, Apartments Abroad takes responsibility for the products and services it provides, which in plain English means if you have a problem it is the company's responsibility to resolve the issue with you in the UK and not leave you pursuing the matter overseas."

Problems with car hire

If you book a hire car when you are overseas and there are problems, you will have to take on a foreign firm in a foreign court. So it is safer (and usually cheaper) to book car hire before you go on holiday, with a UK-based broker or hire firm. For detailed information on hiring and driving cars overseas, see chapter 8 (*see* page 299).

It's always advisable to book your travel using a credit card. If you spend more than £100 and there's a problem with the goods or services you have paid for, and you cannot get satisfaction from the company concerned, you can apply for a refund from your credit card company under the 1974 Consumer Credit Act.

Understanding the culture

Any country you visit will have unfamiliar cultural habits that it will benefit you to try to understand. The farther you travel, the greater these differences can be. Good guidebooks will explain country-specific customs, but observing a few general rules will make your trip much easier and more enjoyable.

Language

Learning a few words of the local language can make life immeasurably easier for you. Local people invariably respond well to a greeting in their native tongue, and speaking a little of the language will mark you out as a more experienced tourist than others around you, and may mean you are treated better and with more respect by local people.

What to wear

It's not just about modesty (though this is important) – it's about understanding what is considered acceptable, and unacceptable, in your chosen destination. After all, in Papua New Guinea or parts of Africa it can be the norm for women to display their breasts – though it would be unacceptable for tourists to follow suit – while in India, the sari reveals a woman's stomach. Men can cause offence in some countries by wearing vest tops or shorts, especially in temples, and it can be insulting to wear flip-flops in public, as these may be used by local people only when visiting the bathroom.

Long, flowing, loose cotton clothing is a safe bet in hot countries for both men and women. As a general rule, aim to keep elbows and knees covered. Before exposing shoulders, legs, stomach or too much cleavage, take advice. Confine swimwear to the beach or pool.

Religious observance

Dozy tourists can unwittingly cause huge offence by not being aware of religious customs. There was a shocking example of this in Sri Lanka, where in 1993 a German woman sat on one of the Buddha statues at the Dambullah Caves to have her photograph taken. So great was the offence this gave that she was deported, the caves were closed to tourists for six months while they were purified and when I visited in 2003, the authorities had only just allowed tourists to take photographs once more.

You will have to remove your shoes in many temples. Be careful not to point the soles of your feet at a person or Buddha statue, and be wary of patting children on the head, as this can cause offence in some cultures. Walk around *stupas* (Buddhist monuments) in a clockwise direction. Be prepared to cover your legs and shoulders and have change ready to donate to churches, temples or other religious establishments. If in doubt about how to behave, watch what local people are doing.

Losing face

In many parts of the world, insulting someone, creating a scene or otherwise making someone "lose face" is the worst thing you can do. The moment you understand this, life magically becomes much easier.

By the time I reached Nepal, after six months in India, I had learnt the importance of not allowing anyone to lose face. So when I was hauled off a bus at the border and told by the guards that there was a "problem" with my visa, I looked grave, and told the head border guard that I was delighted he had noticed this dreadful administrative error, and that I was sure someone as senior as him would be able to sort it out. He disappeared to his hut, chest puffed out, and pretended to make a phone call to Delhi. Some time later he emerged, dignity intact, to announce in front of his subordinates that he had sorted out the problem and I was now free to continue my journey.

Even something as simple as asking directions can potentially cause a loss of face. If, for example, you want to know whether a bus is going to a particular town, do not say, "does this bus go to X?" The answer you receive will invariably be "yes". This can mean either "yes", "I don't know but I don't want to lose face by admitting my ignorance", or "no, but I don't want to be the person to give you the bad news". The best thing to do is to ask, "where does this bus go?"

Waiting

The concept of waiting hours for a train or bus is alien to most of us in the fast-paced west, but in much of the developing world it can seem perfectly normal to spend eight or 10 hours at a train station waiting for a connection, or several hours simply waiting for a bus to fill up with passengers before the driver will depart.

For travellers, the waiting game can come as a surprise at first, but there's nothing wrong with learning a little patience and expecting things to take longer than they might at home. Carrying a good book is always wise.

Tipping

Judging from our postbag at *The Times*, this subject worries many holidaymakers. Perhaps it is because in the UK tipping has fairly strict parameters and we do not go through our daily lives constantly palming a few coins to people here and there. Yet in many countries you are expected to tip far more often simply to get basic things done. It is hard to generalise – for example, in China, Japan or Australia, tipping is practically unheard of – but a few suggestions might help:

- If you are staying somewhere for a few days and want to encourage good service, a judicious tip to the doorman or bellhop at the start of your stay is a wise investment – though handing them something when you depart is a nice gesture, too.

• If you wish to tip the chambermaid who has cleaned your room, leave the money under your pillow.

• If you are going on a cruise, where you are normally expected to tip, find out when booking what the protocol is – the website **www.cruisetip.tpkeller.com** suggests appropriate amounts.

• In restaurants in America, it is customary to tip double the amount of tax charged on your meal – which usually works out at about 15 per cent.

• Keep a stash of US$1 bills to hand if you want to tip but do not have local currency – a dollar bill is acceptable pretty much anywhere.

• If you are not sure whether or not a tip is appropriate – and sometimes it can offend – think about the status of the person who has rendered the service. Say, for example, the proprietor of your villa collects you from the airport – they would be insulted by the offer of a tip, whereas if they had sent a driver from the local cab firm to collect you, he would probably be pleased to receive one.

• In many resorts, particularly in developing countries, staff are poorly paid and rely on tips to sustain a basic standard of living. It's good to tip in these situations – and it's also good to pass on your concerns about low staff wages to the hotelier and tour operator.

• Sometimes boys will gather round your parked hire car and offer to "guard" it for you in return for a tip – the implication being that if you do not pay them, they will damage the vehicle. Frankly, I pay up every time – just think of it as an extra insurance policy.

Washing

Even in the dirtiest slums, people wash daily and wear clean clothes. They are shocked to see westerners travelling around with dirty or torn clothes, however fashionable this may be back home. If you want to gain the respect of local people, keep on top of your washing. In Africa and parts of the Muslim world, women should not give their underwear to be washed by hotel launderers, who are often men, as this can cause offence.

Lavatories

We all have a travel horror story on this subject, I'm sure. The best advice I can offer is this: if you see a decent loo, use it, as you never know when the next one's coming along.

In many countries, including Greece, the plumbing cannot cope with lavatory paper or sanitary products, so a basket is provided for the disposal of these items. Use it, however unfamiliar you find the system. You will also often find, particularly in Asia, that a tap or pot of water is provided instead of lavatory paper. The norm is to use your left hand to clean yourself – so you must never put food into your mouth, or offer someone a gift, with your left hand, as this causes great offence.

Staying safe

One of the creepiest stories I ever heard was a hoary old travellers' tale told over *caipirinhas* in a bar one night in Gran Roque, in the beautiful island archipelago of Los Roques off the coast of Venezuela. A group of us had spent a few days sailing among these tiny islands, dropping anchor occasionally to go ashore and buy exotic fish for supper, or to snorkel in the aquamarine sea. That night, our captain told us of a similar group of young sailors who had all jumped off their yacht to swim in the calm sea, miles from land. No one thought to check how many people were left on board, until eventually they realised that everyone had jumped in – but nobody had remembered to lower the ladder.

No one could clamber up the steep, slippery sides of the yacht. They were too far from land to swim to safety. Their bodies were eventually found floating around the boat, the desperate scratch marks of their fingernails on its hull the only clue as to what had happened...

It was a warm night, but we shivered anyway. And I've never jumped off a yacht since without checking I could get back on board. I hope it's an apocryphal tale, but whenever a group of travellers get together you can bet that most of them have tall stories of misadventure, disaster or skullduggery to relate.

The reality is, whether you are popping over to Paris for the weekend or embarking on a round-the-world gap year adventure, you can fall victim to con artists and thieves, encounter terrorist attacks or otherwise fall into dangerous situations. Yet if you stay at home, exactly the same can happen. I've travelled all over Asia on my own for the best part of two years, but the scariest thing that's happened to me was being mugged 500 yards from my front door in London. And you need only to think of the recent terror attacks on New York, Madrid and London to realise that danger can lurk anywhere these days.

I don't think everyone you meet on holiday is out to get you – on the contrary, I think most people you meet are helpful and honest – but to stay safe you need to be aware of what's going on around you, wherever you are, whatever time of day or night.

Scams, dodges, rip-offs and tricks

I have my own roll-call of minor misfortunes from more than 20 years of circling the planet. One story that usually resonates around the travellers' bar is how I nearly fell victim to one of the oldest cons in the book. I was in my mid-20s and backpacking around Asia, and in Bangkok I bumped into Vicky, a girl I vaguely knew from London. One day we decided to visit Jim Thompson's House, a centre of Thai silk, arts and crafts, and were walking down the road towards it when a well-dressed Thai gentleman approached us and started chatting in perfect English.

Jim Thompson's House was closed, he said, for a bank holiday (it wasn't, of course, as we later discovered), but if we cared to accompany him to his good friend's jewellery shop he could help us to buy gems at rock-bottom prices that we could then sell on in Europe or Australia – for a fortune! What luck!

At this point I was saved by the fact that I did not have a credit card with me, so I was of no interest to our new friend and his pals at the jewellery store. It was a respectable-looking joint where we were plied with Cokes and shown tray after tray of gems. Vicky was keen to buy. They told us that if you bought jewellery in Thailand, you could sell it overseas for a huge profit – they showed us letters and photos from travellers who had done this to back up their claims. As Vicky planned to go to Australia anyway it all sounded too perfect. She even rang home to get her credit limit extended. She asked my opinion and I said I thought she was mad – what did she know about jewellery prices in Australia? – but, astonishingly, she said she didn't think my attitude was very supportive and ignored my advice.

We parted company at this point and so I never found out if she so much as made her money back, but I doubt it. I started to spot letters stuck on travellers' noticeboards from others who had fallen victim to the scam, telling their tales of woe. On reaching Australia they had been told the gems weren't even worth what they had paid for them in Thailand.

The Thai jewellery scam is now well known. The current Lonely Planet guide to Bangkok even warns visitors to Jim Thompson's House: "Beware of well-dressed touts in the *soi* [street] who will tell you Thompson's house is closed – it's just a ruse to take you on a buying spree." But as sure as night follows day there will be another con to replace it, and there will be just as many fresh-faced travellers losing their money somehow. "To date, no British traveller has made any money out of buying gems, carpets or anything else and selling it on," warns the Foreign & Commonwealth Office bluntly, in a new booklet, *Travel Safe*, published by Lonely Planet. "If something sounds too good to be true, it is."

Travel cons go in cycles, judging by the readers' letters we receive at *The Times*. For a while the Barcelona Bird-Muck Scam was a particular favourite. Tourists in prime spots such as Las Ramblas would be approached by a few youths who would gesticulate wildly and start dabbing at the tourists' clothes and shoes, claiming they had bird muck on them. After a whirlwind of dabbing and fussing, the gang would shoot off, having picked the tourists' pockets or stolen their handbags.

Prague's cabbies have had their moment too, being regularly accused of overcharging wildly, sometimes with menaces. Then there was handbag-snatching by boys on Vespas on the streets of Rome, chloroform attacks on passengers sleeping on overnight trains in Europe, and a series of carjackings in France and Spain. In these, drivers were encouraged to pull over to inspect a "blown tyre" and while distracted at the rear of their car, their bag would be stolen from the front seat by an accomplice.

What can you do to protect yourself? Short of developing the cynicism of a murder detective and the suspicious nature of a tax inspector, packing a healthy dose of common sense is a good starting point. Just because you are on holiday and feeling relaxed, don't drop your guard entirely.

It hardly needs saying, but you immediately put yourself in far greater danger if you do anything that's illegal, such as changing money on the black market or buying or consuming drugs. I have changed money on the black market in places such as Burma (Myanmar), where the official exchange rate is 100 times worse than that on the street, and in China and Vietnam in the early 1990s, when going to a bank took all day. I always tried to use a moneychanger who had been recommended by a fellow traveller.

If you must change money this way, go into a café to do the transaction discreetly, rather than doing it on the street. Insist that only one person comes with you. Count the money you're given and then pocket it – do not let the moneychanger take it back on the basis that they have miscounted (they never do). That's when they may try to switch your bills for worthless ones using sleight of hand. Another trick to watch out for is the "fake policeman" number: just as they are about to hand over the cash to you, an accomplice runs up, claims police are on the way, and both men scarper, leaving you with nothing. Or a fake policeman approaches and tries to arrest you before taking the cash back off you... oh, you get the picture. You're taking a risk, and if it goes wrong, no one in officialdom will be remotely sympathetic.

Tips for avoiding travel scams

- Keep valuables out of sight – leave flashy jewellery at home, and use the hotel safe for the bulk of your cash.

- Be wary when carrying and using cameras, mobile phones or iPods.

- Keep essentials in a rucksack or handbag that has straps across your body, so it cannot easily be snatched from your arm.

- Develop a constant awareness of where your bag is – hook the strap through your foot, for example, when you're eating a meal in a restaurant.

- If you are driving and someone indicates that you should pull over, try to drive to the next town and find a police station. Otherwise, stop in a busy area and keep the doors locked and your mobile phone at the ready until you know what is happening.

- Be especially wary at railway and bus stations. Thieves love to strike just as a train moves off, as I know to my cost, having once had a camera bag stolen from a train in India as we left the station.

- Read current guidebooks to find out the latest scams.

- Take the same care of your personal safety as you would at home.

- If you are mugged, give them your wallet and don't put up a fight.

I look at the problems associated with drugs below (page 339).

Caught out?

If you are the victim of crime, you need to sort things out quickly. If you are not injured, go to the local police to report the incident – and not just because you need a police report before you can claim on your travel insurance.

There's a chance they will catch the perpetrator, and logging crimes against tourists helps police to realise when a real problem is developing and crack down on it. If your passport has been stolen you will also need to visit the nearest British Consulate to obtain a replacement.

If you've had a medical emergency, contact your insurers as soon as practicable. If your wallet has been stolen, you may need to call a card protection service or your bank to get your credit cards cancelled. If you need emergency money sending to you, there are various ways to have it transmitted (see page 221).

Contacts and resources

In recent years, several travel safety courses have sprung up to cater for the increasing desire by backpackers (or, just as likely, their parents) to find out about staying safe on the road.

- **PlanetWise** (0870 200 0220, **www.planetwise.net**) offers one and three-day courses (£145/£395) for gap year travellers, and courses for business travellers.

- **Objective Travel Safety** (01788 899029, **www.objectivetravelsafety. com**) offers one-day courses (£150). Topics covered include preparation, what to take, getting around, medical issues and staying safe.

- **The Suzy Lamplugh Trust** (020 7091 0014, **www.suzylamplugh.org**) is a personal safety charity set up by Paul and Diana Lamplugh, the parents of 25-year-old estate agent Suzy Lamplugh, who disappeared and is presumed to have been murdered as she showed a client around a house in London in 1986. The charity raises awareness of personal safety issues and offers training and advice to anyone, including travellers. It produces the useful *Your Passport to Safer Travel*, aimed at independent and gap year travellers (£7.99, available from the trust).

- **The Foreign & Commonwealth Office** (FCO) provides masses of information on safe travel through its Know Before You Go programme (0845 850 2829, **www.fco.gov.uk/knowbeforeyougo**), which it launched in 2001 to help travellers to be more prepared for their trips. It has a special website for young travellers (**www.gogapyear.com**). For more on what the Foreign Office can and cannot do for travellers, see below (page 334).

- *Travel Safe - Know Before You Go*, published by Lonely Planet in association with the FCO, is available free to travellers at **www.gogapyear.com**, **www.lonelyplanet.com**, by downloading it from the FCO website (**www.fco.gov.uk**) or by emailing **fcoleaflets@ accelerated-mail.co.uk** to request a copy.

- **Red 24** (020 8080 0220, **www.red24.info**) sells travel security services.

Terrorism and natural calamities

In recent years we have witnessed, and an unfortunate few have experienced, a dreadful series of terrorist attacks and natural disasters. The events of 11 September, 2001, may be the most memorable terrorist atrocity, but the recent roll call includes bomb blasts in Bali, Sharm el-Sheikh, Istanbul, Madrid and London. In autumn 2005, Hurricane Katrina caused death and destruction in New Orleans while Hurricane Wilma shredded the Yucatan coast of Mexico. And the tsunami of 26 December, 2004, brought us all to a horrified standstill as we watched people being washed away on beaches familiar to many of us from our holidays in Thailand, Sri Lanka, south India and the Maldives.

As if that wasn't bad enough, there have been outbreaks of SARS and, more recently, bird flu, although I believe their risk to travellers is often exaggerated. (If you want to worry about your health, at least worry about something you're likely to get – see chapter 10 for advice on avoiding stomach upsets, heatstroke or malaria.)

Until the turn of the 21st century, few holidaymakers considered that they might be caught up in such horrors when they headed off to relax on a beach or explore a city. In the 1990s I regularly reported on smaller-scale bomb attacks on beaches in Spain and Turkey, usually attributed to the Basque separatist group ETA or the Kurdistan Workers' Party PKK respectively, and, while clearly appalling for those affected, these incidents were viewed by most British visitors as no more alarming than the constant, low-level threat of an IRA attack that they were accustomed to at home.

But in the early 21st century the bar has been dramatically raised – and our holiday industry has taken a while to work out how to deal with these unfamiliar and uncomfortable situations. For some years, there was a knee-jerk response. After an incident, the Foreign & Commonwealth Office (FCO) would rule that it was too dangerous for us to travel to destination X any longer, and once they put a destination off-limits, travel insurers would refuse to cover us if we went there. So tour operators, in turn, would rule that it was too risky to take us there.

But these days, the sad and seemingly endless catalogue of atrocities has prompted a new outlook. Among travellers there's now a rather stoic view – particularly since the attacks on London of July 2005 – that horrible things can happen anywhere, so why stop travelling? In March 2006 a Mintel report found that 67 per cent of British adults said they will not let terrorism prevent them from visiting places that have been attacked.

"British holidaymakers are becoming more resilient to catastrophes and, while taking on board FCO advice, some may switch destinations but very few will cancel altogether," said Richard Cope, senior travel analyst at Mintel. "As terrorism attacks have now also happened here in the UK, the threat is no longer externalised or alien and… it is apparent that many holidaymakers refuse to be put off travelling."

Others travellers have told me that the tsunami was the incident that made them realise how important it is for holidaymakers to continue to travel, because so many of them had been to the affected destinations, and knew local hoteliers or shopkeepers who had been caught by the waves, and so wanted to go back and support them and their families.

Within the travel industry, there's now greater sophistication in the analysis of where problems really lie and how we should respond to incidents. It's now far less likely that the FCO will declare an entire country off-limits following an incident. As this book went to press in mid 2006, the only two countries to which the FCO advises against *all* travel are Ivory Coast and Somalia – even Iraq and Afghanistan are not in this category, though you are nevertheless strongly advised to give them a miss (see **www.fco.gov.uk/travel**).

"We wanted to get a balance so we were not doing the terrorists' work for them," said Paul Sizeland, director of consular services at the FCO*, when I went to see him in his Whitehall office. "So we would not advise against travel unless there was a specific and immediate threat to British citizens. The idea of trying to get travellers to make an informed choice is at the heart of this."

He said one of the first real tests of this new policy was the terrorist attack on the resort of Sharm el-Sheikh, Egypt, in July 2005, after which the FCO did not advise against travelling to the area. "It put us on the cusp," he admitted. "We did not stop travel [to Sharm], but we told people what was going on. It's quite a fine judgement."

The FCO's new approach has been welcomed by many holidaymakers and tour operators, who had become frustrated by the old, inflexible approach which blacklisted some destinations long after operators on the ground felt they were safe. But the FCO's new reluctance to blacklist destinations puts a greater onus on the traveller to read up on where they're going.

* Note: British diplomatic missions overseas take the form of British High Commissions or Deputy High Commissions in Commonwealth countries, and British Embassies in other countries. Sometimes British staff will work in separate buildings known as Consulates General, or Consulates, which may be in regional centres. In countries where there is no British presence, there may be an Honorary Consul who can offer limited help. I have used the term "consul" to refer to the appropriate member of the British diplomatic staff in the country you are visiting, and "consulate" to describe the British diplomatic mission's base there. If there is no British mission in a country, you should contact the mission of another EU member.

How should travellers prepare?

It's not just where you go that matters – it's how you travel, according to Bruce Newsome, a former lecturer on terrorism and security at the University of Reading. He argues that taking mainstream package holidays in developing countries in Africa and South East Asia is a bad idea, as they often oblige you to travel on western-style tour buses emblazoned with the holiday company's name, and to stay in big resort hotels that are a world away from the lives of the poorer local people outside their gates.

He sees tour buses, hotels and even cruise ships as ideal terrorist targets, because they offer a concentrated group of westerners in one place, often with poor security. It's a chilling analysis, but given the attack on an Israeli-owned hotel in Mombasa, Kenya, in November 2002, which killed 15 people and was followed by an unsuccessful attempt to shoot down an Israeli charter plane, it's not without some logic.

His solution? Fix your own itinerary, avoid big chain hotels, use local transport, dress appropriately, travel in pairs or small groups. In other words, behave like a backpacker, avoiding obvious over-consumption. It's an interesting point, and although we're not all about to give up our package holidays, we are all starting to think about dealing with disaster if it arises.

Travel insurance should be your starting point. It's never been more important to have good insurance, with medical cover that includes repatriation if necessary. Then check the FCO's latest advice (0845 850 2829, **www.fco.gov.uk/travel**). Gap-year travellers can consult its sister site at **www.gogapyear.com**.

By the time you read this, the FCO may have launched its **Online Traveller Registration** scheme, planned for late 2006. It will be accessed via its website and will help officials to work out who is likely to be in the area at the time of a terrorist attack or natural disaster. Backpackers and expatriates will be particularly encouraged to sign up, although any holidaymaker can register. You complete your itinerary, personal information and next-of-kin details, and update this information if your plans change as your trip progresses.

If a terrorist incident or natural disaster occurs, your family can ask the FCO to search the database – which will not be made public – to see if you might have been in the area at the time. Meanwhile travellers in the vicinity of an incident will be encouraged to log back in to their online profile and leave a message to say they are safe, which can be passed on.

Last but not least, don't forget about the benefits of booking a package holiday rather than an independent trip where you have no consumer protection (for an explanation of the difference, see chapter 4). If you are caught up in a terror attack or natural disaster, your tour operator is obliged to help you.

"A lot of people say, I do not need a rep," said Sue Biggs, MD of **Kuoni**, the UK's leading long-haul tour operator. "But when things go wrong, nothing beats the reassurance of having someone who knows what to do, and who can charter aircraft at an hour's notice to get you out of trouble."

She speaks from experience. Within 24 hours of the Asian tsunami, Kuoni had chartered a plane to fly to Sri Lanka to bring back anyone who wanted to return. "The British are wonderfully resilient and most wanted to stay!" said Biggs. "Though we filled the plane with other tour operators' clients. We have now funded three field hospitals in Sri Lanka – tour operators do have a social responsibility to these destinations."

Safe travel checklist

- Take out good travel insurance.

- Consult the FCO website (**www.fco.gov.uk/travel**).

- Register with the FCO, once Online Traveller Registration starts.

- Keep a note of the phone number of the nearest British Consulate (details on the FCO website).

- Register yourself with the local British Consulate, if advised to do so by the FCO website.

- Dress modestly and do not draw attention to yourself when travelling.

- Avoid political demonstrations or rallies.

- Tune in to World Service radio or international TV channels to keep updated.

- Be very careful if taking photographs.

- Leave passport and insurance details with your family.

- Fill in the next-of-kin section in your passport.

- If an incident occurs in the country you're visiting, contact family to let them know you are OK, even if the incident was far away.

- Read up on local laws, particularly concerning alcohol and drugs.

- Refer to the advice "Understanding the culture" and "Staying safe" earlier in this chapter.

Can the Foreign Office help?

The Foreign & Commonwealth Office (FCO) came in for considerable criticism in late 2005 in a report by the National Audit Office into how the FCO had responded to the Boxing Day tsunami. The problems it noted included: inability of call centre staff to cope with the number of calls; no method of sifting out non-emergency calls; no rapid deployment team sent from London to Thailand until January 8, nearly two weeks after the tsunami; and other problems including poor communication with local officials, lack of resources, and inadequate coordination with other government departments.

The then Foreign Secretary Jack Straw apologised for these shortcomings and there's a new determination at the FCO to be more prepared for future disasters. Rapid deployment teams, volunteers drawn from FCO staff, are kept on standby, with their passports in the office; many of them have training in such areas as communications technology or bereavement counselling.

But a further problem, identified by the House of Commons Select Committee on Foreign Affairs in early 2006, is that the public doesn't understand what the FCO can, and cannot, do to help them in an emergency. "In recent years excessive and unrealistic expectations have arisen of what the FCO is able to do for people who get into difficulties abroad, including in circumstances such as natural disasters," said the committee's report. "We recommend that Ministers take a firm line in explaining to the public... that there are practical limits to the consular support that British citizens who choose to travel abroad are entitled to receive, not least because of the FCO's duty to make efficient and effective use of public funds."

The aftermath of Hurricane Wilma, which struck the Yucatan peninsula of Mexico in October 2005, is a good example of the confusion in some travellers' minds. The FCO airlifted 117 Britons, mostly independent travellers, from Cancun in Mexico to Dallas in the USA, which was chosen as a place of safety where there is also a British consulate. From there the travellers had to make their own way home. (Holidaymakers on package tours to Mexico, by contrast, were helped by their tour operators either to return home, or to continue their holidays elsewhere.)

Some of the Dallas evacuees were cross that they were not flown all the way home. But the FCO felt it had discharged its duties to its citizens by taking them to safety. It is adamant that it will not act as some sort of insurer to help travellers who do not have their own insurance policy or tour operator to fall back on.

In March 2006 the FCO published a booklet about its services for travellers, *Support for British Nationals Abroad: a Guide*. The FCO has staff in nearly 200 countries, who receive 3.5 million inquiries from travellers each year, including 860,000 personal visits to a consulate – given this demand, the guide is clearly overdue. It's available, free, from libraries, Citizens Advice Bureaux and at the website **www.fco.gov.uk/travel**.

The guide makes it clear that the British consul is not going to lend you a few hundred quid if you've been mugged, get you out of jail if you have been arrested, or pay to send you home if you've lost your air ticket. Help is much more limited. Here's a summary.

What will consular staff do for you?

- Issue a replacement passport (for a fee).

- Explain how to transfer funds, if you need money.

- Cash a sterling cheque up to £100, secured against a banker's card, into local currency (for a fee).

- Provide help if you have been assaulted or are in hospital (for example, by accompanying rape victims to the local police).

- Contact you within 24 hours of being told that you have been arrested or hospitalised, and visit you as soon as possible.

• Give details of local lawyers, interpreters, doctors and funeral directors.

• Offer basic information about the local legal system, such as whether a legal aid scheme is available.

• Give you information about local prison conditions, including visiting arrangements, mail and censorship.

• Approach the local authorities if it appears your case is not being dealt with according to internationally accepted standards, or is unreasonably delayed compared with local cases.

• Offer help in cases of child abduction, kidnapping or forced marriage.

• Contact your friends and family.

• Ask UK police to contact next of kin if someone dies abroad.

• Offer advice on registering the death in the country where the person died.

• Work closely with families of anyone who has been kidnapped and, if they are released, provide local accommodation, medical help and travel to the UK.

• Give information about the customs and laws of the country if your child has been abducted, put you in touch with local support groups or alert Interpol.

What will consular staff *not* do for you?

• Get you out of jail.

• Interfere in criminal proceedings, or investigate your case.

• Help you if your visa for that country is invalid.

• Give you legal advice.

• Search for missing people.

• Get you better treatment in prison or hospital than local people receive.

• Pay your bills or lend you money.

- Make travel arrangements for you.

- Pay a ransom to release a kidnapped person.

- "Rescue" a child from abduction.

In major catastrophes, some of these rules may be relaxed, and the FCO may make contingency funds available to help stranded or injured travellers. It may also set up a telephone helpline and send extra staff to the region, and arrange for evacuation of the injured and to fly home the remains or bodies of the dead. But you cannot normally rely on help of this sort.

Contacts

- **FCO's Child Abduction Section** (020 7008 0878 or 020 7008 1500).

- **Forced Marriage Unit** (020 7008 0151 or 020 7008 1500, **fmu@fco. gov.uk**). If you are abroad and worried about this, try to visit the nearest British Consulate.

- **Kidnap Victim Support (www.kidnap–support.com)** is a support group for relatives of British hostages.

- **Prisoners Abroad** (020 7561 6820, **www.prisonersabroad.org.uk**) is a welfare charity that can help by providing advice, support, and in some cases money for food and living costs in foreign jails.

- **Support After Murder and Manslaughter** (020 7735 3838, **www.samm.org.uk**) can help if a relative dies overseas in suspicious circumstances.

Women travellers

An awful lot of nonsense is written about women travellers, as though we are delicate creatures who can't get our luggage off the carousel without having a nervous breakdown and heading for the nearest spa to recover. In fact some of the scariest people I've met on the road have been solo women travellers, and few of them considered their sex to be anything other than a fact of life – if not an advantage.

Certainly there are huge bonuses to travelling solo as a woman. You're not (usually) a threatening prospect, so you're easily invited to share families' meals on long trips, as I have been often on those endless Indian train journeys, or to visit their homes in a way that few male travellers would be. You're often accorded a respect or status that is lacking in the west – whether you're helped to the front of a bus queue, or given the top berth on an overnight train as it's a little more private. And people generally look out for you.

Of course, almost everyone you meet in most of Asia, the Middle East or Africa will think you are completely potty. If you travel around alone in a society where women are normally married by their mid 20s, and in which it would be inconceivable for them to go travelling for months on their own, you're bound to be seen as exotic, unusual and possibly quite mad. You'll get endless questions about your personal life, salary, weight, romantic prospects, children – and raised eyebrows if you don't have a husband in tow. However, sometimes a solo western woman is treated as an honorary man – invited to eat with men or drink alcohol with them, while local women are excluded. This is usually well intentioned and a result of your hosts not quite knowing which box to put you in, although I would be very wary about joining in too enthusiastically with a male drinking scene.

Guidebooks often suggest solo women travellers wear a wedding ring to deter unwanted advances. In my experience, wearing a wedding ring has never deterred, and in fact has often encouraged, unwanted advances – plus it's another item of jewellery to worry about losing. It's a trick that might work for some people, but I can't be bothered with it. I think it's much better to carry some snapshots of your family and friends and use these as ice-breakers.

Travelling solo is very freeing, whatever your sex. You're the master of your own destiny, can go where and how you like, and change your itinerary whenever it suits you. There's a huge sense of achievement to be gained from negotiating your way around a foreign country on your own, and ironically you'll find it's easy to meet people – there's always room for one more around a dinner table, in the bar, or sharing a dorm or a taxi to the next town.

Safety tips

- Move around purposefully and try not to consult maps in public.

- Dress appropriately and modestly to avoid causing offence or sending out the wrong signals.

- Don't feel you have to respond to shouted questions or approaches from passing men. A polite dismissal may be taken as an invitation to pursue you.

- Turning away while covering your head with a shawl or scarf is widely seen across Asia as a polite way to tell a man to get lost.

- Don't hitchhike on your own.

- Book seats in women's carriages in trains, where offered (such as in India), though be prepared for crying babies.

- Wear shoes you can run in.

- Sit near other women or families in restaurants or on public transport – and avoid the back of the bus.

- Plan journeys to arrive in a new town in daylight hours.

- Learn a little of the local language to make getting around easier.

The website **www.journeywoman.com** has interesting, occasionally eccentric advice and reports from women on the road, and *Women Travel: First Hand Accounts from More Than 60 Countries* by Miranda Davies and Natania Jansz (Rough Guides, £12.99) is a useful read.

The trouble with drugs

Do you remember the case of Sandra Gregory, the British woman caught trying to smuggle heroin out of Thailand in 1993? She was given a 25-year sentence, and only released early (in 2000) because she was pardoned by the King of Thailand.

But perhaps you remember the 2004 film *Bridget Jones: the Edge of Reason*? In this, Bridget Jones is briefly imprisoned in Thailand after drugs are found in her luggage but soon the hero, lawyer Mark Darcy, rushes to her rescue and she is quickly freed. Surely that's what really happens when holidaymakers are caught in the system? Especially if they are British?

"I wish we all had a Mark Darcy in these cases – but the film's misleading, and I hope people see it for the fiction it is," said Pauline Crowe, chief executive of the welfare charity Prisoners Abroad. Through her work supporting Britons in foreign jails, she has seen all too often how British citizens – whether guilty or not – can spend years in prison awaiting trial or serving their sentences.

It's easy to distance yourself from someone like Gregory, who knowingly set out to smuggle drugs – she wasn't just having a crafty puff on a joint on the beach. But in some countries even the most casual connection with drugs, or an association with someone else involved with drugs, can be enough to have you arrested, tried, and if found guilty fined or imprisoned – sometimes for many years.

The Foreign & Commonwealth Office (FCO) points out that in Greece and Cyprus, for example, possession can lead to a hefty fine or even life imprisonment, and Thailand, Malaysia, Singapore and Indonesia are among countries that impose the death penalty for some drugs offences.

"Any traveller should think really seriously about behaving any differently abroad to the way they behave at home," said Crowe. "If something is not acceptable at home, it's almost certainly not going to be acceptable abroad." She cites the example of Amsterdam, where it can be OK to smoke a joint in a café, but to walk down the street smoking one is brazenly breaking the law.

Stephen Jakobi of Fair Trials Abroad, which helps British citizens it believes have been unfairly imprisoned overseas, reinforces the point. He has no time for anyone who knowingly breaks the law, but said: "What worries me is the way people can get into trouble by being unwittingly used, or breaking rules that their common sense would tell them are not rules, but unfortunately they are." He cites the case of Marianne Telfer, a care manager from Essex whose boyfriend died in the Dominican Republic while they were on holiday there in 2004 because condoms of cocaine he had swallowed, intending to smuggle them, burst open. Ms Telfer, then 28, knew nothing about the drugs, but she was blamed and imprisoned for four months before pressure from Fair Trials Abroad and others helped to get her released.

Jakobi urged anyone who has suspicions that a fellow traveller is involved with drugs to report their concerns to the British Consul, rather than to local police, in case they come up against a corrupt policeman and unwittingly get drawn into trouble.

He has particular concerns about the Indian judicial system. "Let's not mince words," he said, "it's a corrupt cesspit. The law is in incredible disarray. There are states where cannabis is part of the culture and is legal, and in other places the minimum is six months in prison for possessing less than 25g of cannabis." He advises anyone who is asked by police for a bribe in return for dropping the charges to pay up. "If it's only £100, it's a good investment. But the best advice is not to take drugs."

If you are arrested, you can expect to be treated in the same way as citizens of the country you are in – being British will not mean you get any special treatment. You have a right to insist that the British Consul be informed. You can expect consular staff to visit you in prison and they can pass messages to your relatives and friends, and help you to find a lawyer or interpreter.

But the British Consul cannot get you out of prison, interfere in court cases, give you legal advice, investigate the crime or get you better treatment than is given to locals. They will not give you money for prison food, though they can pass on money from your family or from Prisoners Abroad. In some countries, you are expected to pay for your food in prison, which is why a network of support from family, friends and Prisoners Abroad can literally be a lifesaver for some prisoners.

In other words, you're pretty much on your own, in the hands of the judicial system of whichever country you are in. So resist gulping down that ecstasy tablet at a Thai beach rave, or lighting up a spliff in an Indian beach bar – or you could suddenly find that you have plenty of time on your hands to regret it.

Drug dangers

- Never buy, carry or consume illegal drugs, no matter who offers them to you – you may be under surveillance by local police.

- Never agree to carry a package on to a plane for someone, no matter how well you know them.

- What are considered soft drugs in the UK may be seen as hard drugs according to the laws of the country you are visiting.

- If you are caught with drugs abroad, you will end up with a criminal record in the UK.

- Avoid driving across borders with people you do not know.

- Be cautious about accepting gifts from someone overseas.

- If you leave your luggage unattended, such as at your hotel before you go to the airport, inspect it before you check in to ensure it has not been tampered with.

- If you take prescription medication, carry the prescription or a note from your doctor with you.

- If you have an accident while under the influence of drugs (or alcohol), your travel insurance will be invalidated.

- If you think you have been drugged – for example you think your drink has been spiked – ask a friend to look after you and call for medical attention.

Contacts

- **Fair Trials Abroad**, 01223 319009, **www.fairtrialsabroad.org**

- **Foreign & Commonwealth Office** (0845 850 2829,
www.fco.gov.uk/knowbeforeyougo) has information on drugs issues,
on its website and in the leaflet *Drugs: Information for Travellers*

- **Prisoners Abroad**, 020 7561 6820, **www.prisonersabroad.org.uk**

Combating child sex tourism

When Gary Glitter was given a three-year jail sentence in March 2006
for molesting two young girls in Vietnam, it threw the spotlight on to a
particularly nasty corner of the holiday business: child sex tourism.

Although many observers felt the disgraced singer's jail sentence was
too lenient, the case at least highlighted a problem that few in the tourist
industry want to talk about. Christine Beddoe, director of **ECPAT** (End
Child Prostitution, Child Pornography and the Trafficking of Children for
Sexual Purposes), said holidaymakers can help stamp out the abuse of
children by sex tourists. "It's about looking at what's appropriate, and what's
inappropriate behaviour," she said. "If you are in a tourist environment and
you see someone alone with a local child, it may be a pattern of inappropriate
behaviour. It's always worth asking, and reporting suspicions of abuse either
locally or back home.

"We have to encourage people to speak out," added Beddoe. "It's only
when the public speak out and do not tolerate it that it will change. Challenge
it when you see it."

Some holiday companies are now taking this problem very seriously,
introducing training for their staff to help them, and their customers, be
aware of the problem. Tour operator First Choice has been working with
ECPAT, in a project funded by tourism charity the Travel Foundation, to train
reps in 10 mainstream holiday destinations where child sex tourism has
been identified as a problem. The project was launched in 2006 in Cuba, The
Gambia, Mexico, Kenya, Thailand, Tunisia, Morocco, Sri Lanka, the Dominican
Republic and Goa.

"It's a difficult situation because there's not usually a witness to the crime,"
said Jane Ashton, head of corporate social responsibility at First Choice. "It's
based on a suspicion, and we have to be careful that our reps do not become
vigilantes or accuse innocent people." The reps are being trained to look for

warning signs and to respond to concerns from holidaymakers. They report these to their manager and they are passed to local police.

"It might be hard to tie things down, but the police are interested in any information that gives them a sense of where these issues are becoming more prevalent," said Ashton. Tour operators TUI, which owns Thomson Holidays, and The Gambia Experience have also been focusing on the issue.

At ECPAT, Beddoe welcomed First Choice's efforts but said there's a need for more action by tour operators. She added that as travel patterns change – for example, as eastern Europe opens up with more cheap flights – so the abuse can migrate from country to country, meaning no destination can be considered free of the problem.

Under the Sexual Offences Act 2003, British tourists who commit sex crimes against children overseas can be prosecuted in the UK. Some offences carry penalties up to life imprisonment, and those convicted will be placed on the sex offenders register. In January 2006, a 56-year-old man from Milton Keynes was jailed in the UK for 17 sex offences committed in Ghana, including raping and taking indecent photographs of children. As if to demonstrate how tourists can help, he was arrrested in 2005 when a French holidaymaker voiced concerns after seeing him handing out toys to local children.

The Foreign & Commonwealth Office is urging all tourists to be alert to the problem. If you see anything suspicious, or are approached by anyone asking if you want a sexual relationship with a child, report it to your holiday rep, hotel manager, the local consul or the local police.

You can also call **Crimestoppers** to report it. If you are overseas, call +44 800 555111 from a landline (you are charged for this); if you're in the UK it's a free call (0800 555111), and you can remain anonymous.

Contacts

> **ECPAT**, 020 7233 9887, **www.ecpat.org.uk**
>
> **www.thecode.org**
>
> **www.child-safe.org.uk**
>
> **www.fco.gov.uk/knowbeforeyougo**

Communications on the road

In my backpacking days I loved going to the Poste Restante, the section of a main Post Office that held letters and parcels, to pick up my mail. Visiting the

Poste Restante in Bangkok was a particularly sociable experience as it was such a well-used address, so you'd always meet fellow travellers there. But I found the system worked well in Hong Kong, Manila, Beijing and Delhi, too, though I suspect I may still have letters waiting for me in a dusty back corner of the Ulaan Baator Poste Restante.

Part of the system's charm (some might choose a different word) was the element of pot luck that accompanied each visit to the post office. There was no guarantee that my letters, even if they had arrived, would be filed under "U" so I would ask the post master to search under "C" and "M" for "Ms", too. Sometimes I received a dozen, sometimes none at all, and inevitably some would never reach me. The system also worked as an unofficial message board, as travellers could leave notes there for each other.

These days the Poste Restante has largely been replaced in travellers' affections by the ubiquitous internet café. "The vast majority of travellers probably don't even understand how Poste Restante works now," said Tom Hall, a spokesman for guidebook publishers Lonely Planet. "I did a round-the-world trip six years ago and even then it felt like it was dying out. I wonder what's happened to those old boys in the post offices in places like Quito and Santiago?"

Internet cafés might not be as romantic as those cobwebby rooms full of crumpled, light-blue airmail letters, but they offer the sort of convenience (sending email, checking your bank balance, uploading photographs) that we could only dream of 20 years ago.

But I have mixed feelings about internet cafés. Sure, I use them, and they can be extremely useful, but it's worth questioning whether you need to keep emailing home to find out the progress of Aunty Doris's cat's hernia operation when you're backpacking around Thailand. How can you fully absorb the wonderful experiences open to you on holiday if you're spending hours hunched over a computer? Isn't that what you went travelling to leave behind?

But the march of modern technology presses ever onwards, and these days using humble email to keep in touch with home is old hat. The modern traveller signs up to a service such as My Trip Journal or Rough Guides' intouch to create their own webspace, and then uploads their diary and photographs so those at home can immediately read about their trip. Or they start a blog, or they carry a light laptop to watch DVDs, or they buy overseas SIM cards for their mobile (as discussed in chapter 6) so they can call and text their friends on the road at modest prices. On a recent family holiday in

France I had to keep the men in the party informed of the England cricket team's progress, because I could access breaking news via the internet on my mobile phone even as we sipped our morning coffee in a remote village in the depths of the French countryside.

But while there are lots of benefits to being able to stay in touch, sometimes it's important to switch off. You are on holiday, after all. More and more travellers tell me that peace and quiet, a lack of internet access, and being out of mobile phone range are what makes a holiday special. May I suggest Bhutan? Your mobile won't work and they only got telly in 1999 (and it's not very gripping).

Another sign of the growing backlash is that one tour operator, the Adventure Company, is offering "mobile-free" holidays in places such as Peru and Costa Rica on which they confiscate the phones of every participant. The company's spokesman, Mick Thompson, told me the trips were introduced following complaints from customers: "People get to the top of Kilimanjaro at dawn, only to hear other people's phones ringing. Or they get a call from a mate back home, but it's the middle of the night where you are, and it wakes up everybody in the camp or dormitory."

Communication tips

- Be considerate when using your mobile phone in public.

- Use email to stay in touch but don't spend all your holiday in an internet café.

- Post a list of emergency phone numbers on an email to yourself, or use an online vault to store data, such as the eKit communications package (**www.ekit.com**).

- Don't expect friends back home to be that interested in lengthy bulletins – while they'll enjoy hearing from you, only your mum will really care that you got ripped off for a Coke at the bus station in Kathmandu.

- When you're away, keep communication with the office to a minimum – by having a refreshing holiday you'll be better equipped to tackle problems once you get back.

- For advice on keeping mobile phone bills down, *see* chapter 6.

Further information

There are now numerous websites that allow you to create an online travel diary, upload pictures and video, plot your route on maps and contact your friends when you've added new material. They usually charge a few pounds per month and it's worth checking that you can download the journal to your PC or burn it to a CD when you've finished the trip. Suggestions include **My Trip Journal** (**www.mytripjournal.com**), **Rough Guides "intouch"** software (**www.roughguidesintouch.com**) and **Where Are You Now** (**www.wayn.com**).

Travel forums are useful for picking other travellers' brains or posting your advice as you go. Lonely Planet's **Thorn Tree** travellers' forum (**http://thorntree.lonelyplanet.com/**) has 300,000 registered users and receives 4,000 new posts each day. **Travellers' Point** (**www.travellerspoint.com**) provides an online forum for travellers to keep in touch and exchange tips and advice. **Igougo** (**www.igougo.com**) claims, with 350,000 registered members, to be one of the largest online travel communities.

To find hotspots where you can use a laptop with wi-fi technology, visit **www.hotspot-locations.com**; hotels, libraries, airports and coffee shops are popular locations. For a list of internet cafés worldwide, visit **www.cybercafes.com**.

Photography

If you find yourself passing your snaps or digital camera round in the pub and notice your friends flipping through the pictures quickly, past the cut-off heads and out-of-focus faces, you'll probably wish you had done a better job.

But with a little thought and preparation, most holiday snappers can come home with a really good set of pictures that their friends will genuinely enjoy viewing.

I have worked with two professional photographers, Doug McKinlay and Steve Benbow (**www.wordsandpix.co.uk**), in more than 20 countries. Most of my best photos are the same as theirs, except you'll find Doug's or Steve's shoulder in the foreground – I just take the picture they're taking.

We've had a few lively times. Steve and I were nearly deported from Zimbabwe when officials clocked his camera gear, then he had me paddling a canoe far too close to a hippo on the Zambezi for my liking while he lined up his shots. In The Gambia we had to fight off a mugger who wanted to pinch his socks, and in Vietnam we had a near-death experience in the ill-named De-Militarised Zone when I tripped over an unexploded bomb as we went in search of a "better vantage point". Doug meanwhile spends a lot of time taking pictures that seem to get up the nose of the local police, so I like to brush up on the Spanish for "no officer, I don't know this man" when we head to South America together.

But somehow or other I've picked up plenty of tips from watching them work (and not just how to stay out of jail, either). Here are their top 10 suggestions for improving your holiday snaps:

- Read the manual – to get the best out of your equipment, whatever it is, you need to know exactly what it can and cannot do.

- Be prepared to get up early to get the best light, which is at sunrise and sunset.

- Think of the "rule of thirds" – the most pleasing images are those that have the horizon, for example, one third of the way from the top or bottom of the frame.

- Get as close as possible to the subject (unless they are members of the armed forces/police/local border guards).

- Focus on the eyes when you are taking pictures of people, animals or even statues.

- Panoramic landscape shots don't always work – try to look for a point of interest and focus on that to draw the viewer in.

- Experiment with different viewpoints – crouch down, climb to the first floor, turn the camera at an angle.

- Watch what's going on around you, and be prepared to sit and wait for the right shot to come along.

- Make friends with people you wish to photograph and take time to chat – the pictures will be more relaxed. Ask beforehand, especially when photographing women or children.

- Take more pictures than you think you need – you'll never be able to capture that exact scene again.

Ethical concerns

Photographing your wife or husband on the beach isn't going to raise too many ethical questions, but there are times when taking a photograph may be inadvisable. "Inside a church or monastery, photography is usually forbidden," said McKinlay, "and you shouldn't intrude on grief, for example by photographing a funeral. Anywhere near a police station, border or military installation is obviously out, too." You should also be wary of photographing beach scenes if there are small children or topless sunbathers in view.

Another thorny question, particularly in developing countries, is whether you should pay people for taking their picture. "If it's someone who's making a living from it, such as the dancers in the Djemm el Fna square in Marrakesh, that's fine because it's their job, but if you give money for every picture you start to create a begging culture," said McKinlay. It's better to talk and joke with the people you're photographing, show them the picture you've just taken, if you have a digital camera, and never promise to send a copy of the picture to them unless you can keep the promise.

Equipment

Traditionally a good film camera gave better results than a digital camera, but the gap's now disappeared. Digital has the advantages that you can see straight away if the picture's worked, you can email pictures home to friends, and you don't have the hassle of carrying camera film around. But make sure you have enough memory, or the ability to download the pictures, and that you'll be able to charge the battery easily.

Always keep your camera gear with you on the plane – never check it in – and if you are carrying film through an airport where you don't trust the X-ray machines, try asking politely for your film to be hand-searched (keep film in a see-through bag that you can pull out of your hand luggage for this purpose).

It can also be worth carrying photocopies of the receipts for your camera, especially if you have expensive equipment, in case customs officials ask you to prove you brought it with you from home.

Finally, ask whether you really need to carry a camera at all. In Calcutta I once met a woman who was travelling the world for eight months without a camera. She said that without having to worry about camera angles and F-stops, she had more time to engage with people and really learn about the country. At the time I couldn't imagine not carrying a camera, but a few weeks after this encounter mine was stolen on an overnight train journey, and I spent the rest of my Indian trip without one. It was strangely liberating.

CHAPTER TEN
Travellers' health

Introduction

Tickets, passport, toothbrush...? or loperamide, malaria prophylaxis, antiseptic cream...? When it comes to making a quick mental checklist before you rush out of the door on your holidays, health concerns are rarely to the fore. Many of us think we've done all we need to if we've bought travel insurance, packed the aspirin and thrown in some Alka-Seltzers in case we overdo it on the sangria.

But good travel planning includes thinking about your health before you find yourself making a desperate dash around Boots at Heathrow (or, what's worse, a desperate dash for the bathroom after overdoing it at the hotel buffet).

The good news is that there is no reason why any of us should fall seriously ill on holiday if we spend a little time preparing, and learning how to avoid the most common dangers. Upset stomachs are not normal, sunburn is preventable, and small bites and scratches shouldn't cause trouble if you treat them promptly. More serious diseases are far rarer, but these too can usually be dealt with successfully if you are prepared and alert.

But there's a growing problem. Because so many of us are booking holidays at the last minute, we often do not leave ourselves time to visit our GP or a travel health clinic for advice before a trip. Dr Richard Dawood, author of *Travellers' Health, How to Stay Healthy Abroad*, told me: "Over the last few years everyone has become their own travel agent. People travel right at the last minute, and so they either do not know about the health risks, or they think they have left it too late to bother about them."

If you buy a late package deal to The Gambia, for example, where taking malaria tablets is essential, you may not have time to get hold of the correct drugs and start taking them the recommended one week before departure. It's no idle threat – British travellers have contracted malaria in that country, and several have died.

Travel health and medicine is a huge subject and in this chapter I can only scratch the surface of it. And while I've spoken to experts in travel health about getting the basics right, the information here is limited and general – so consult your GP before travelling, and a doctor in your resort if you are worried about your health when you're on holiday.

Preparation

Ensure you buy **travel insurance** that includes good medical cover, and repatriation if necessary. If you are travelling within the 28 countries covered by the European Health Insurance Card (EHIC), make sure you pack it. Full details, chapter 6.

You should pack a simple **first-aid kit**, even if you intend to do nothing more than drift between the hotel bar and the beach for a week. You might pick up a cold on the plane, sprain your ankle on some steps, or get dehydrated in the heat, and having your own first-aid supplies to hand means you can start to treat yourself with familiar remedies that your body is used to.

Pack treatments you normally take for colds, pain relief, indigestion, high temperatures in children or motion sickness. You will probably need sunscreen, lip salve and after-sun cream. Treatments for minor wounds, such as plasters, dressings and antiseptic, are also important (an antiseptic spray, such as Savlon dry spray, is often more effective than a cream in hot countries). I always pack Anthisan cream, which soothes insect bites.

Oral rehydration salts (such as Dioralyte), which contain essential sugar and mineral salts and are mixed with water, are useful in any hot environment – and very effective for hangovers! Insect repellent is useful on many trips, and if you are going to a malarial area it's vital.

First-aid kit essentials

- Sunscreen and lip salve.
- Insect repellent.
- Painkillers.
- Indigestion tablets.
- Motion-sickness tablets.
- Oral rehydration salts.
- Plasters, dressings, bandages.
- Antiseptic.
- Bite and sting cream.
- Malaria tablets, if required.
- Support bandages.

- Blister treatment.

- Condoms and other contraception.

- Any prescription drugs you are taking.

Paperwork

- Your own contact details.

- The number of an emergency contact.

- Your blood group.

- A list of any immunisations you have had.

- A note of any health problems, allergies or conditions you suffer from.

- GP's contact details.

- Insurance policy and emergency helpline details.

- The prescription for any medicine you are taking.

- A note of your glasses prescription, if you need one.

If you are travelling with children, going to the tropics, or are on an adventurous holiday or expedition, you will probably need to add to this basic first-aid kit such items as sterile syringes and needles, or any medicines that you regularly give your children. Ready-made first-aid kits are widely available, and there's nothing wrong with buying one so long as you take the time to understand what you can use its various components for. But it's better – and essential if you are going anywhere for which vaccinations or malaria tablets are required – to visit a doctor.

Not every GP is a travel specialist, so it may be worth seeking out a travel clinic (see page 369). Simply having the recommended vaccinations is not, on its own, sufficient trip preparation – ideally your consultation should include a chat about the type of trip you're going on, your health and any particular concerns the trip might pose (particularly important if you are, say, diabetic, a smoker or overweight).

You are likely to be charged for most vaccinations whether you have them at your local surgery or at a travel clinic (though you may be able to get vaccinations for typhoid, tetanus and diphtheria on prescription) and as charges can vary from clinic to clinic, and even from GP to GP, you might want to shop around.

But travel health planning is about more than just jabs. "Accidents take many travellers' lives, others succumb to malaria and many suffer from travellers' diarrhoea or dysentery, and yet there are no vaccines against these health risks," said Dr Jane Wilson-Howarth, author of the travel health guide *Bugs, Bites & Bowels*. "So it is necessary to think 'prevention', not just 'what jabs do I need?'"

Start your trip planning a couple of months before you leave, if possible, in case several vaccinations are required. And keep records of what you have had; although you do not usually need to produce these at borders, they will help you keep your protection up to date. Sometimes you will have to show a yellow fever certificate when entering a country, if you are travelling from an endemic area.

Visit the dentist, and have your eyes checked before embarking on a long trip. Although there's recently been a rise in "tooth tourism" to countries such as Poland and Hungary, where dentists are well trained but cheaper than in the UK, it is usually an expensive hassle to get your teeth fixed while you're overseas. Carrying a copy of your glasses prescription makes it easier to get a spare pair made up on the road. Even if you wear contact lenses all the time, bring a spare pair of glasses as dry or dusty conditions at your destination may irritate your eyes.

It's important to think about your sexual health before travelling. Too much sun, sea and sangria can lead to sex, so both men and women are wise to carry condoms in case. Unwanted pregnancy is not the only concern – unprotected sex can expose you to hepatitis B, HIV and other sexually transmitted infections (about 100 British travellers each year pick up HIV overseas, according to Dr Wilson-Howarth).

Tampons can be hard to find in some countries so women may wish to carry extra supplies (consult a guidebook to find out the situation in your intended destination). If you are on the pill, a bout of traveller's diarrhoea may reduce its effectiveness; condoms may be a useful alternative. Check you have sufficient contraceptive supplies to cover your holiday. Flying through several time zones may make it harder to work out what time of day to take the contraceptive pill; try using two watches, one set on UK time, until you have established a new routine (try not to change the time you take the pill by more than an hour a day).

Getting there

Flying, particularly long distances, can be a tiring, dehydrating and for some people, a frightening experience. In chapter 8 (*see* page 280) I look at how to stay healthy in the air.

While much has been written about the risks of deep vein thrombosis when flying, sitting in one position for any length of time can be dangerous, no matter how you are travelling. So move around the train carriage, get out to stretch your legs whenever the coach stops, and build in regular breaks if you are driving. Do some stretching exercises, and drink plenty of water. Taking exercise before and after any long journey will also make you feel better.

When you're there

Culture shock

I was once staying at Ringo's, a popular budget guesthouse in the centre of Delhi, when out on the street I saw a young backpacker from New Zealand, who I'd earlier met in the hostel, trying to hail a taxi. Several drivers were cajoling her into taking their auto-rickshaw and a lively argument was in progress over the fare. Suddenly the woman, clearly enraged at what she thought was a rip-off price, spat at one of the drivers.

I hardly need tell you the horror with which this offensive act was greeted, both by the drivers (who saw the noisy negotiations as an entirely normal method of doing business) and by other tourists who witnessed the scene. I didn't really know the woman but she had not stood out in the hostel as being rude or aggressive. But at that moment, an anodyne encounter by the standards of Delhi street life had flipped her over the edge into shockingly rude behaviour.

Culture shock can take many forms. I suspect that backpackers, who tend to have far more, often exhausting, dealings with local officials, ticket-sellers, hoteliers and the like, may be more prey to it than the upmarket package tourist who is collected in an air-conditioned car from the airport and cossetted in a five-star hotel. But culture shock can affect anyone and you should mentally prepare for challenges to your values, belief systems and sense of fair play.

Arriving in an unfamiliar place, you are likely to be jet-lagged and tired. You may have had an exhausting encounter with a taxi driver, it may be extremely hot, and you may be worried about finding a hotel or what you can safely eat.

As your trip unfolds, you may be surprised to find that you have somehow turned into the tourist attraction. If you are white, in much of Africa and Asia you will stand out from the local population and thus you may well attract beggars, street children or, in more remote places where few tourists visit, a veritable crowd of onlookers – "staring squads", as some call them, as it is culturally acceptable in many countries to stare at people in a way that makes westerners feel most uneasy (it doesn't work in reverse, either, so don't stare back).

Often you may be followed, not aggressively, but because people are simply curious to see how you behave. I once travelled around the Mekong Delta in Vietnam with a blond, 6ft 4in American model with a penchant for wearing a one-piece Lycra bodysuit in public (it's a long story) and, while I admit he was going to stand out anywhere, I have to say that by the end of day two I felt like the Pied Piper of Hamlyn, so many people were following us around. Ed barely had any hairs left on his arms – the local kids, fascinated by his blond body hair, had been pulling them out.

And in many places, particularly across Asia, the concept of personal space that we carry with us in the west does not exist, so you may find a press of bodies in a restaurant, waiting room, queue, etc, that is much greater than we would normally encounter, and which may make you feel claustrophobic or uncomfortable.

Meanwhile you may be feeling homesick, missing your friends or family, unhappy that you cannot understand the language or read the street signs, fatigued by the change of climate and diet, and so increasingly prone to mood swings, mild depression, anxiety or irrational anger.

It's important to recognise that culture shock is a common, understandable, usually short-term phenomenon, and that a good way to deal with it is to be especially nice to yourself during your first few days in a strange country. Pre-order a taxi from the airport to your hotel, or arrange for a friend to meet you, to ease your arrival. Re-read a favourite book or listen to your favourite music to help you relax. Arrange to phone home or encourage friends to email you to counteract any feelings of loneliness or displacement. Visit a beautiful temple or other attraction to remind yourself why you have come here.

But don't try to pack too much activity into the first few days. I am often asked for advice on visiting India by friends who have two weeks to spare. I remind them that it is the size of Europe, much harder to get around, and can be culturally overwhelming. I suggest they limit themselves to three or four major sights or towns in one region, building in rest days along the way.

No one has yet come back and told me that they had too much time on their hands and could have packed in a few more cities.

Colds and flu

It's the dead of winter, you've escaped the January gloom, and now you're lying on a beach in Barbados. So it's extremely irritating to have caught a cold.

But colds and flu – not bilharzia, diphtheria or yellow fever – are the illnesses that we are most likely to pick up on our travels. "We do not really bother about them, because we can get them anywhere, but people do get more colds and flu when they travel," said Dr Richard Dawood. "We don't know why – perhaps it's because you come into contact with more people than at home."

I find I often pick up a cold on a long plane journey. It seems crazy to have a cold in a hot country, but it's very common. I suggest you pack an extra sweater or shawl for the plane, bring your usual cold remedy with you, drink lots of water, eat healthily and take a multi-vitamin every day. Always wash your hands after shaking hands with others, and before eating. Consider having a winter flu jab.

In the sun

Fashions change, but coming home with a suntan is still one way to provoke envy among your friends, especially during the British winter. But if you are white-skinned, and especially if you are fair- or red-haired, you must take particular care to avoid getting burned, as sunburn is not only very painful at the time, but can lead to premature skin ageing and skin cancer in later life. People with darker skins should not ignore sun protection either: although your skin may be better able to deal with sun exposure, you may still be susceptible to skin ageing and cancers.

These days the dangers of too much exposure to the sun are much more widely known, partly because we travel far more to sunny countries such as Australia, which has a catchy slogan: "Slip, slap, slop – slip on a shirt, slap on a hat, slop on some suncream". But the sun-protection advice is still worth repeating.

Wearing good sunscreen, with a sun protection factor (SPF) of 15 or higher, is essential almost everywhere. Skiers and anyone on the water can be burned by the sun's reflection, even in cold weather, and the sun can also burn you on overcast days. Sunscreen should protect you from both UVA rays and the more harmful UVB rays. The protection against UVA rays is indicated by a star system on the container: five is the highest, meaning it gives you most protection. The SPF (a number up to 60) indicates the level of protection against UVB rays.

Sunscreens with a factor lower than 15 are widely available, but many experts advise against using them. When I asked Boots' sunscreen expert, Mike Brown, why Boots sold them, he said that some holidaymakers are so keen to get a tan that they think factor 15 is too high, and if lower-factor sunscreens were not on sale, they would use no sunscreen at all. "But over two weeks you will still tan, using factor 15," he said. "If you build up a tan over several days, it tends to last longer, so using factor 15 is better for you in the long term."

Experts agree that regular re-application of sunscreen – every hour or two, and especially after swimming – is important. "Most people do not put on enough in the first place, so re-applications are a top-up," said Brown. "You should put it on quite thickly – a blob the size of a £2 coin should be enough for one arm and hand."

Children should always be coated in factor 25 or higher. Anyone enjoying watersports should consider swimming or snorkelling in a dark-coloured T-shirt to reduce the chance of burning while in the water (as well as applying sunscreen). Wear a wide-brimmed hat and good quality sunglasses if you're walking or spending much time in direct sunlight.

The old saw about "mad dogs and Englishmen" going out in the midday sun is still all too true. Britons and others who live in temperate climes still seem so utterly thrilled to be somewhere warm that we will sunbathe during the midday heat, when the sun will do the most damage. You should avoid sunbathing between 10am and 3pm, and you should always start sunbathing in short bursts – just 10 minutes on the first day.

Too much sun?

Sunburn is unpleasant and can easily ruin your holiday. Your skin will feel hot and sore, will turn red, and may swell and peel. Try not to pick at the blisters, take anti-inflammatories to reduce the pain and drink plenty of water to counteract the drying-out effect of the burn. Taking cool baths or showers will offer temporary respite – and, of course, you should stay out of the sun. Apply aftersun lotions such as calamine or aloe vera to the sore skin. If in doubt about the severity of your sunburn, see a doctor immediately.

Sunburn is not the only problem caused by over-exposure to the sun: heat exhaustion and heat stroke are potentially very serious (and even fatal) if not treated quickly. If you suspect someone has had too much sun – perhaps they are sweating profusely, dizzy, vomiting, feeling confused, and/or have a high temperature – call for medical attention. While waiting for a doctor, keep the patient out of the sun, cool them with a wet cloth and encourage them to drink water.

One of my travelling companions succumbed to heat exhaustion in the middle of an overland expedition through the Karakum Desert in Turkmenistan, several days' drive from the nearest doctor. Fortunately we had studied what to do, so we spotted the signs and were able to treat him, monitor him and ensure he recovered. He was unwilling to drink much water, perhaps unwilling to accept how serious his heat exhaustion was, so we took turns to sit with him and bossily made him drink at regular intervals until he had recovered.

Stomach upsets

Delhi Belly, the Egyptian Two-Step, Montezuma's Revenge – we have jokey names for bouts of travellers' diarrhoea. "Travellers' diarrhoea is regarded as being almost inevitable," said Dr Richard Dawood. "Perhaps 40 per cent of travellers get it, and it's dismissed as trivial – but it can have a big impact on your holiday."

But it need not. When I was 18, I spent nine months backpacking around India and Nepal without falling ill. It wasn't just down to the strong constitution of youth, although the fact that I was healthy to start with helped. But a friend who knew India counselled me wisely before I went: be careful about the water you drink, peel fruit, avoid salads, ice, ice cream, meat... so alarmed was I by this advice that I followed a vegetarian diet (which is the norm in India, so that was easy), rarely drank alcohol, made sure street food came sizzling from the pan and learnt enough Hindi to ask for water to be boiled so that I knew it was safe to drink (in those days, bottled water was hard to find).

This routine was not without a certain amount of sacrifice and tedium. I ate more boiled eggs and bananas than I really wanted to and no doubt missed out on some of the more exotic culinary experiences the sub-continent has to offer. And eventually I did fall ill – after eating the in-flight meal on the Pan Am flight home. The minute I left India, I dropped my guard, with unpleasant consequences.

Dr Dawood says travellers may have to make some compromises regarding what they eat if they want to avoid falling ill. He calls it "eating defensively". "It's counter-intuitive. You have paid a lot of money for your holiday, you arrive at the hotel and there's a big buffet. You want to try new foods and get your money's worth." But restraint is necessary, particularly with salads, and with hot dishes that have been left on the buffet too long.

In Egypt, Nile cruises have posed particular problems. The food on most ships is served buffet-style, and prepared in tiny galleys by staff who may not maintain the highest standards of food hygiene. On the two Nile cruises I've undertaken, a significant number of passengers fell ill.

But standards in the cruise ships' kitchens have improved since the late 1990s. Mark Harrington of **CheckSafetyFirst**, a company that helps hoteliers improve food hygiene, said: "In Egypt, we turned the Nile cruise holidays around from being floating hospitals to having very little backlash because of food poisoning." The company introduced basic measures such as better washing facilities in the food-preparation area. Similar problems in some of the all-inclusive resorts in the Dominican Republic in the late 1990s have also been largely resolved since the introduction of the "Cristal" food hygiene programme in hotel kitchens.

Wherever you find that food is served buffet-style, be careful what you eat. Avoid hot food that has been left standing for a long time – choose dishes that have just come from the kitchen, and spoon out a portion of food that is sitting directly over the burner. Avoid salads and raw, unpeeled fruit or vegetables that may have been washed in dirty water, or anything that has been left uncovered so flies can land on it. Ice and ice cream are also potentially dangerous, as is shellfish, and meat should be cooked through, not eaten rare. Raw or lightly cooked eggs (or mayonnaise, for example) and unpasteurised milk should also be avoided.

So what can you eat? The advice in the well-known mantra sums it up: "Wash it, peel it, boil it or forget it." Meals cooked to order are a wise choice – especially simple dishes such as omelettes and pasta. Your children will be thrilled to hear that chips are pretty safe, too, as long as they have been freshly served. Bread and "dry" foods such as biscuits are much safer than "moist" foods such as sauces and salads. Fruit that you can peel yourself is safe (but check the skin has not been punctured). Boiled eggs are good, but be wary of leftover rice served up the next day, for example in a salad. Do not use dirty crockery or cutlery, and be sure your drinking water is clean.

If you want a taste of the exotic, try street food, which perhaps surprisingly can be safe – so long as it is served piping hot from the wok or pan. Noodle soups are generally safe, too. In India, Morocco and Thailand, I've eaten fabulous meals at street stalls without problems, but I avoid pre-cooked items that have been left on display.

How to treat travellers' diarrhoea

"Travel broadens the mind and loosens the bowels," said Dr Sherwood Gorbach, Professor of Public Health and Medicine at Tufts University School of Medicine, Boston. And a bout of gippy tummy can make you reluctant to go more than a few paces from your bathroom.

Don't panic. You might feel dreadful, but most cases of travellers' diarrhoea will resolve themselves within 48 hours without the need for a doctor's visit. The most important thing is to replace the fluids you are losing by drinking lots of water – at least two glasses every time you open your bowels, and more if you can – then gradually reintroduce a bland diet (such as salty biscuits, dry bread, bananas and boiled potatoes). Avoid greasy foods, dairy products and alcohol (you won't fancy them anyway). Rehydration is extremely important if children or babies have diarrhoea, and it is usually wise to seek medical attention for them, too.

Even better than drinking pure water, making up a sugar-and-salt solution to drink is an excellent way to replace the vital minerals you lose with diarrhoea. You can mix your own, using one level teaspoon of salt and eight level teaspoons of sugar to one litre of water, or a pinch of salt and two heaped teaspoons of sugar in a glass of water. If it tastes saltier than tears, throw it away and make it again with less salt. You can also buy plastic measuring spoons for mixing this rehydration drink from travel clinics or from **Teaching-aids At Low Cost** (01727 853869, **www.talcuk.org**). And of course you can buy sachets of ready-made rehydration salts in the shops, such as Dioralyte, but it is important to mix them into the correct quantity of water.

Other drinks can help with fluid replacement: herbal teas, weak black tea or coffee (without milk), fizzy drinks, clear soups, and drinks made from Marmite, Bovril or stock cubes. Adding sugar to salty drinks helps the body absorb the fluids and salt.

Beyond rehydration, common treatments for diarrhoea involve drugs that "block you up", such as loperamide (the active ingredient in Imodium, for example); these can be helpful if you have to make a long journey, but they may also prolong the illness. The other common treatment is antibiotics. Before taking either of these treatments I suggest you consult a doctor. There are occasions when these remedies are not advised.

There are other circumstances where seeking medical help is advisable: if diarrhoea lasts more than three or four days; if you notice that what you pass is mixed with blood; if the stomach pains become constant; if you are running a high temperature; or if any of the symptoms seem particularly severe.

Accidents

The excitement and feeling of freedom we gain from a holiday can make us drop our guard. Dr Richard Fairhurst, writing in *Travellers' Health, How to Stay Healthy Abroad*, says: "Because... of the absence of the usual constraints of home, family and work, most people behave differently abroad, sometimes in quite a reckless, uncharacteristic manner – exposing themselves to risks they would never dream of taking at home."

Oops. I'm as guilty as the next person. I recall a long journey on the roof of a train in Ecuador, and another on top of a crowded bus in the Philippines (indeed the boyfriend I was travelling with jumped off to buy some drinks, and sprained his ankle)... riding a motorbike, helmetless, around Phnom Penh... seeing my life flash before me as my rickshaw driver in Delhi stalled in the path of an oncoming bus...

But accidents do not simply befall those who seek out adventure: the BBC's World Affairs correspondent, John Simpson, relates with some embarrassment how in 1999, when he was covering the bombing of Belgrade, he injured himself, and was hospitalised, not because he was caught in the crossfire but because he slipped on the side of his hotel pool.

Road accidents are among the most common mishaps that befall Britons overseas. They might be caused by something as simple as failing to remember which side of the road you should drive on, or by something more exotic, such as colliding with a moose in Scandinavia or a kangaroo in Australia (both are regular occurrences). One of the most common accidents happens when people hire mopeds in countries such as Greece or Thailand and then tear around without a helmet. According to the **Association for Safe International Road Travel (www.asirt.org)**, a US-based organisation, popular holiday destinations with poor road safety records include Kenya, Greece, Turkey, South Africa and Portugal. It has safe-driving advice on its website.

In essence, you should follow the same road safety rules as you would at home. Never hire a moped without checking that you are covered to do so under your travel insurance policy. Always wear a helmet, even if it is not a legal requirement. Learn the rules of the road, do not drink and drive, and do not get into a car with a drunk driver. Be particularly careful when driving at night, and try to avoid this if possible. When you hire a car, if you are travelling with children insist that proper child seats are fitted. If they are not available you will simply have to drive to the nearest supermarket or car supplies shop to buy one.

On buses, sit near the front to avoid motion sickness and undesirable travelling companions on the back seat, but not right at the front, as you could be thrown through the windscreen in an emergency. Always use a seat belt, where provided. Avoid over-crowded ferries, and make sure you know where your life jacket and the muster station is.

The best way to prepare for accidents, beyond carrying a small first-aid kit, is to take a first-aid course run by an organisation such as the **British Red Cross** (0870 170 9222, **www.redcross.org.uk/firstaid**) or **St John Ambulance** (0870 010 4950, **www.sja.org.uk**). The British Red Cross publishes a useful guide, *Five Minute First Aid for Travel* (Hodder Arnold, £6.99).

Accidents: what to do

- First, consider your own safety – do not touch live wiring, for example.

- Be wary of moving the victim if there is a chance of neck or spinal injury.

- Get someone else to help you.

- Ring for help.

- Remember "ABC":

    A – check the airway is clear.

    B – check the person can breathe.

    C – circulation – check the heart is beating.

- Travel with and know how to use a first-aid kit.

- For detailed advice on dealing with common injuries, consult travel health manuals or attend a first-aid course.

- Find out the emergency telephone number of the country you are in (for example, 999 in the UK, 112 in the EU, 911 in the USA and Canada).

Malaria

In November 2000 a 52-year-old woman about to go to The Gambia for a two-week holiday went to a pharmacy and asked for malaria pills. She was sold chloroquine and proguanil tablets, which are the only anti-malarial pills available over the counter in the UK. Unfortunately, they are not the correct type to take in The Gambia, where mosquitoes are resistant to them. She developed falciparum malaria, the most serious form of the disease, and at one point was not expected to survive. Later complications meant she had to have all her toes and most of her fingers amputated. She unsuccessfully sued the chemist – because she had lost her receipt, she could not prove that she had been missold the drugs.

Dr Richard Dawood of the Fleet Street Travel Clinic, who told me this story, thinks it is wrong that chloroquine and proguanil can be sold over the counter. "If I could change one thing about malaria, it would be that," he said. "You get people going at the last minute to places where chloroquine and proguanil are not appropriate, but because they have not left time to consult a doctor, that's what they take." And as we take ever more last-minute holidays, this is a problem that is only likely to get worse.

Malaria is a serious and sometimes fatal disease that is prevalent throughout the tropics, especially in Africa, and which kills some two million people worldwide each year, mostly African children under the age of five. You get it by being bitten by a female Anopheles mosquito, and symptoms (such as fevers, chills or aches) start to appear after at least a week, though the illness may be delayed for months. The most serious type, falciparum malaria, can kill within 24 hours of symptoms appearing.

Around 2,000 British travellers contract malaria each year, and 10 to 20 of them die. The winter of 2005–06 saw a particularly high number of cases in people returning from The Gambia: the Malaria Reference Laboratory in London reported 27 cases in travellers coming back from the West African state between October 2005 and early January 2006, three of whom died. Nineteen of them had taken no, or inadequate, malaria prevention measures.

Of course it's possible to contract malaria in other popular holiday destinations, including many African countries, and large parts of Asia, including India, Sri Lanka, parts of Thailand and Indochina, and South and Central America including Brazil and even remote parts of Mexico. Consult a doctor to find out if the journey you're planning takes in a malarial area.

Anti-malarial drugs

Travellers going to a malarial area should visit their GP or travel health clinic to find out what type of tablets are recommended for that area. Malaria is constantly mutating, so you should always discuss with a doctor which drugs are most appropriate. All drugs potentially have side-effects. Pregnant women, babies and children are often advised against travelling to malarial areas, as they are particularly susceptible to the disease.

There has been huge publicity about the side-effects of Larium, which was introduced in the early 1990s. Many travellers who took it reported side-effects such as mood changes, strange dreams and nausea. Today, doctors know more about the drug, its side-effects and when prescribing it may be inappropriate, so being offered Larium should now give far less cause for concern if you have had a thorough discussion with your doctor.

Ensure you follow the drug regime to the letter. This usually involves starting the course of tablets a week or more before travelling, taking them throughout your trip, and continuing with the course for four weeks on your return. Often you are expected to swallow them after eating a meal. Do follow this advice if it's given: I once took a malaria tablet on an empty stomach and felt sick for hours afterwards. If you have diarrhoea, the protection the drugs offer may be reduced, which makes bite-prevention efforts even more important.

Bite prevention

Taking anti-malarials will not necessarily stop you getting malaria, so it is essential to take every precaution to avoid being bitten by mosquitoes in the first place.

They are active from dusk until dawn, so at these times you should ensure you are wearing long-sleeved shirts, long trousers, and have covered any exposed skin with a good repellent, reapplying it frequently. Close mosquito screens and retreat to an air-conditioned room to further reduce the chance of being bitten. Spraying insecticide, switching on the fan or burning mosquito coils in your bedroom can also help. At night be sure your mosquito net is tucked in all around the bed, and that it does not have holes in it.

I suggest you use a repellent that is at least 50 per cent DEET (diethyl toluamide) – although children should not be exposed to this level, and some travellers (such as those with eczema) will not be able to use it. Dr Jane Wilson-Howarth, author of *Bugs, Bites and Bowels*, said: "DEET's big disadvantage is that it dissolves plastic and ruins many synthetic materials...

not surprisingly this makes travellers wonder what such a compound might do to their skin and insides. Yet this is a safe compound." And it works.

If you are in a non-malarial area, and simply want protection from irritating bites, you can experiment with DEET-free products such as citronella-based repellents and natural oils.

Do I have malaria?

The symptoms will not appear until a week after you were bitten, so if you have a fever that starts in a malarial area less than a week after you arrive there, it cannot be malaria. Symptoms include fevers, sweating, chills and aches, and if any of these develop, go quickly to a doctor or hospital and mention the possibility of malaria. Other signs, such as diarrhoea, stomach pain or a cough, may indicate that you have malaria, too. If you are not sure, see a doctor as soon as possible. Most travellers become ill within the first month of leaving a malarial area.

But the illness can appear some months after your return, so consult your doctor if you have an acute feverish illness within three months of coming home. It is important to finish the course of anti-malarial tablets on your return from holiday.

Other serious illnesses

There is a seemingly endless list of ghastly poxes you can pick up while travelling – Hepatitis A and B, Japanese encephalitis, rabies, diphtheria, typhoid, AIDS, bilharzia, dengue fever... You can be vaccinated against some, but not all of them, so you should visit a doctor or clinic to discuss which of these may be prevalent in your destination and whether vaccinations are needed. For detailed information about the prevention, symptoms and treatment of these illnesses, consult the medical handbooks and other sources listed at the end of this chapter and in the Bibliography (see page 431).

Altitude sickness

In the town of Puno, on the shores of Lake Titicaca in Peru, I found an unusual item available on room service in my hotel: an oxygen mask and tank. But I was quick to order one, for the high altitude had made me short of breath. That day I had flown from Lima, which is on the coast, to Puno, which is at 3,830m above sea level (asl), and I was feeling short of breath, a little headachey and thirsty – all classic signs of a mild form of altitude sickness.

I soon felt better, but altitude sickness, properly known as Acute Mountain Sickness (AMS), is a serious and potentially fatal condition and its symptoms should never be ignored.

Many people are affected by altitude sickness when they travel to places that are roughly 3,500 metres asl or higher. With the growth of adventurous holidays, increasing numbers of people are finding themselves at these heights, whether they are trekking in Nepal or Peru (backpackers' favourite hangout, Cusco, is at 3,225m asl), climbing Mount Kilimanjaro in Tanzania (5,895m asl), or skiing in some of the higher resorts of North America, such as Breckenridge (where you can ski at nearly 4,000m asl). Altitude sickness is caused by a lack of oxygen – not because there is less oxygen in the air, but because lower pressure means it is harder for that oxygen to get into your lungs. Typical symptoms include dizziness, headaches, lethargy, nausea, depression and loss of appetite.

Usually these symptoms dissipate as you become acclimatised and you can then continue to move higher. But anyone on a trekking expedition should not try to ascend more than 300m per day, and should go back down to sleep at a lower level – "climb high, sleep low" is the mantra. Keep hydrated by drinking at least three litres of water a day and keep an eye on your companions, rather like the buddy system in diving. If someone starts to develop serious symptoms, they may become argumentative or wish to be left alone. Never let them have their way. The way to tackle altitude sickness is always to descend, even if you have paid a lot of money for your trekking holiday. Pushing on regardless of the symptoms can lead to death. Don't hire a horse to transport someone higher, either, thinking they are simply tired – get them back down the mountain.

Travelling while pregnant

If you feel up to it, there's no reason to avoid travelling while pregnant, though the middle three months – typically from the 12th to the 26th week – are considered the safest time to travel, when the risk of miscarriage has largely passed but the risk of early delivery is still low. Think twice about travelling to any country or region without good medical services, and carry a copy of your medical notes with you.

It's important to consult your doctor before going overseas, to have as many of your antenatal checks as possible, and to ensure you have good insurance and have declared your pregnancy to the insurance company. Some travel vaccinations, and some types of anti-malarials, are not recommended for pregnant women, which may dictate your choice of destination. Malaria can be much more serious in pregnant women than in other people. You are also advised to use a more dilute form of DEET if you need to use insecticide.

If you plan to fly you must tell the airline you are pregnant. Most airlines allow you to fly up to 36 weeks, but they may ask for a note from your doctor specifying your due date, and your travel insurance may only cover you for flying up to 28 weeks.

Pay attention to what you eat and drink, and follow the normal health rules you would at home. You should avoid activities such as trekking at high altitudes or scuba diving, and be careful when having spa treatments: take advice from the therapist first. Saunas and hot tubs should be avoided, especially during the first three months of pregnancy.

Your child's health abroad

Children are resilient travellers. Naturally curious, they will enjoy the sights and sounds of an unfamiliar country, and the younger ones will quickly be "adopted" by the locals. In countries such as Greece, Italy and Spain a gaggle of mamas will be cooing over your pram from the moment you arrive. No, the kids will be fine – it can be the parents who struggle, especially if they have not travelled much before having a family.

Preparation

First, the paperwork: apply for your child's passport, check that your travel insurance policy covers all the family and, if you are travelling within Europe, apply for European Health Insurance Cards for everyone, as each member of the family needs his or her own (further details, see chapter 6).

If you're taking the kids somewhere exotic, a pre-trip doctor's visit is important. Doctors can talk you through some of the obvious risks – dehydration, diarrhoea, sunburn – and check your child has had all their normal childhood vaccinations as they fall due and, if necessary, has any others they will need for the planned trip (such as tetanus and polio).

For short trips a simple first-aid kit could include, in addition to the adult kit suggested above:

- Rehydration salts (such as Dioralyte).

- Sunscreen and calamine lotion in case of sunburn.

- Paracetamol tablets or Calpol for fever.

- Antiseptic, such as TCP or Dettol.

- Baby wipes.

- A thermometer.

- Nappy rash cream.

- Plastic freezer bags for emergency sick bags or to wrap dirty clothes while on a plane.

Holiday health risks for children

Upset stomachs, leading to diarrhoea, are potentially far more dangerous in a baby or child than in an adult. Unfortunately diarrhoea is also very common in children when travelling, so be prepared – rehydration is the most important thing, so bring oral rehydration salts and if the outbreak seems serious, consult a doctor immediately. Insist your children wash their hands thoroughly after going to the lavatory and before eating.

Travelling with a baby while it is still being **breastfed** can make life easier. Not only does it cut down on the clobber (bottles, sterilising equipment) that you need to pack, but it's safer too. Once anything other than breast milk is taken, the baby becomes much more susceptible to illnesses such as diarrhoea. It's important for the mother to keep her fluid levels high, especially if she has a stomach upset. Babies (like all of us) need more fluids in hot countries so be prepared to give them bottled water which has been boiled – bottled water is not sterile.

If you are visiting **a malarial area** with your child, it's important to consult your doctor to find out the best anti-malarial drugs for that area, and the correct (reduced) dosage for your child. Get your child into the habit of taking the tablets or medicine at the same time each day, for example when brushing teeth after breakfast, and practise the bite-prevention techniques I've discussed above.

Getting children to take malaria tablets can be a trial, as the tablets taste disgusting. Dr Richard Dawood recommends crushing them up and mixing them into peanut butter or a chocolate spread such as Nutella, as these are fat-based products in which the tablets do not dissolve and release their nasty taste. If, however, you crush them into something like jam, the water in the jam starts to dissolve the tablets, spreading the taste.

Buy an **insect repellent** that contains DEET in a dilute solution (such as 10 per cent) for children, and apply it in a well-ventilated area; don't put it on your child's hands in case they put them in their mouth or eyes. You are advised not to put products containing DEET on young babies.

Sun protection is vital for babies and children – make sure they wear hats, plenty of sunscreen and consider buying clothes made with a built-in sun protection factor (such as those from **Young Explorers**, 01789 414791, **www.youngexplorers.co.uk**).

Accidents are a particular worry if you have active kids. We've already considered the dangers a swimming pool presents (chapter 9), but just running around in unfamiliar territory with bare feet can be dangerous, if they step on glass or tread on a snake, for example. Make sure your first-aid kit has plenty of plasters and antiseptic and that you clean and cover wounds properly to prevent infection spreading.

Travelling with children is a joy, and can open doors to a culture that might otherwise remain shut – local people will often come over to admire your children or coo over your baby, and introductions are made. I have seen grumpy French restaurateurs turn to mush, and suddenly realise that they aren't quite ready to stop serving lunch after all, the minute my baby niece Ruby gave them her toothless grin. If you keep your children well hydrated, protected from the sun and from insect bites, and have had them properly vaccinated, they should enjoy happy, healthy holidays.

Travel health contacts

Travel health clinics

- **E–med** (020 7806 4028, **www.e–med.co.uk**) offers online consultations with a British GP no matter where you are, offers advice on its website, and also has a travel clinic in London. Registration costs £20pa.

- **Fleet Street Travel Clinic** (020 7353 5678, **www.travellers–health.info**) offers travel and vaccination advice on its website and runs a travel clinic. Its medical director, Dr Richard Dawood, has written the invaluable *Travellers' Health* (*see* Bibliography, page 431).

- **Hospital for Tropical Diseases**, London (**www.thehtd.org**) offers a travel clinic (appointments on 020 7388 9600) and recorded, country-specific advice on 020 7950 7799. It also offers emergency treatment for anyone who suspects they have picked up a tropical disease.

- **Liverpool School of Tropical Medicine** (www.liv.ac.uk/lstm) offers appointments at its travel clinic (book on 0151 708 9393) and a premium-rate helpline with country-specific and general travel health advice (0906 701 0095, 50p per minute).

- **Malaria Reference Laboratory**, London (**www.malaria–reference. co.uk**) gives advice on malaria, both on its website and from 0906 550 8908 (£1 per minute).

- **Medical Advisory Services for Travellers** (www.masta.org), at the London School of Hygiene and Tropical Medicine, provides printed travel health briefs tailored to your journey (0906 822 4100, also available online), and a network of travel clinics across the UK.

- **Nomad Travellers' Store and Medical Centre** (**www.nomadtravel. co.uk**) has up-to-date travel health information on its website, a premium-rate line (0906 863 3414, 60p a minute) where you can speak to a travel health expert, and five stores that sell clothing, equipment and medical supplies and have travel health clinics attached.

- **Trailfinders** (020 7938 3999, **www.trailfinders.com**), the travel agency, operates a travel clinic at its branch at 194 Kensington High Street, London.

Travel health advice websites

- **Bradt Guides** (www.bradtguides.com) has a travel health forum on its website, where you can email questions to Dr Jane Wilson-Howarth, author of *Bugs, Bites & Bowels*.

- **Cancer Research UK** (**www.cancerresearchuk.org**) runs SunSmart, a skin cancer prevention campaign, and has information on staying safe in the sun on its website.

- **Center for Disease Control**, Atlanta, Georgia, USA (**www.cdc.gov/ travel**), is a superb site with extensive travel health information.

- **Fit for Travel** is a great website provided by the NHS in Scotland (**www.fitfortravel.scot.nhs.uk**) which has general travel health information, country-specific advice and updates on outbreaks of disease around the world.

- **Foreign & Commonwealth Office** (**www.fco.gov.uk/travel**) has information on travel health risks, including disease outbreaks.

• **International Society for Travel Medicine (www.istm.org)**, a professional body, allows non-members to search for clinics worldwide that specialise in travel health, and has some free information on its website.

• **Malaria Hot Spots (www.malariahotspots.co.uk)** is a detailed malaria awareness and information site sponsored by the drug company GlaxoSmithKline.

• **National Travel Health Network and Centre (www.nathnac.org)** is funded by the Department of Health to promote clinical standards in travel medicine. The website has up-to-the-minute information about diseases and how to stay healthy on your travels.

• **Net Doctor (www.netdoctor.co.uk/travel/)** has an extensive, clearly written section on travel health, with masses of useful advice.

• **Travel Health Online (www.tripprep.com)** has excellent listings of health requirements by country, masses of information for travellers and lists good clinics and hospitals. You must register to use it, but access is free.

• **World Health Organization (www.who.int)** has an online, downloadable version of its detailed International Travel and Health book.

Medical services

• **Blood Care Foundation** (01403 262652, **www.bloodcare.org.uk**) couriers screened blood to you anywhere in the world if you need a transfusion and are worried about the safety of the local supply. Membership, £50pa.

• **International Association for Medical Assistance to Travellers** (001 716 754 4883, **www.iamat.org**) is a non-profit organisation that offers lists of English-speaking doctors and inspected clinics and hospitals in 125 countries. It has free, downloadable charts on subjects such as malaria prevention on its website.

• **Medex** (01273 223002, **www.medexassist.com**); UK branch of the US-based medical insurance provider, which offers services from putting you in touch with doctors worldwide to organising medical evacuations.

Equipment

- **Lifesystems** (0118 981 1433, **www.lifesystems.co.uk**) sells travel health equipment (such as water purifiers, mosquito nets or flight socks) online and through stores.

- **Teaching-aids At Low Cost** (01727 853869, **www.talcuk.org**) sells plastic spoons for mixing rehydration fluids.

- **TravelPharm** (01395 233771, **www.travelpharm.com**) is an online pharmacy for travellers selling everything from malaria tablets to flight socks. You have to provide a doctor's prescription for some items. There is lots of information on malaria on the site.

- For many more stockists of items such as first-aid kits, mosquito repellent and nets or sunscreen, see the Directory (page 397).

CHAPTER ELEVEN
THE DIRECTORY

INTRODUCTION

There are hundreds of holiday companies in the UK, but until now it has been difficult to find out about many of them. If you go to a high-street travel agent, you will be offered holidays from a limited selection of companies, often those owned by the same company as the travel agent, or those that pay commission to agents for selling their holidays. Smaller, specialist travel agents offer a wider choice, but there are still hundreds more companies out there selling excellent holidays over the internet or by direct mail. Unless you know where to look for them, they can be hard to find.

This is where this directory comes in. Over more than a decade of writing about the travel industry I have come across hundreds of travel specialists, but have never found a useful directory that lists them all. So I've tried to compile one here.

There are some useful short cuts to finding your ideal holiday. The Association of Independent Tour Operators (020 8744 9280, www.aito.co.uk) groups together more than 150 specialist tour operators which offer an enormous range of breaks, from mainstream sun and sand holidays to specialist activities. They will send you a brochure listing all their members, who must be independently owned, have a financial bond that protects customers' money, and have signed up to guidelines on responsible tourism. You can also access these holidays through the 130 Aito specialist travel agencies (www.aitoagents.com).

There are some regional trade bodies, for destinations including France and Africa, which I'll list in the appropriate sections and which give details of specialist operators. It's also worth consulting tourist boards for suggestions of holiday companies that feature their country: *see* chapter 1.

In addition to the many travel and holiday specialists listed here, I have also included all the contact details that I have mentioned in the rest of the book, for easy reference under relevant headings. I hope you will find these lists a useful shortcut.

How to use this directory

Smaller specialist companies, such as those that offer only Spanish holidays or cookery tours, find an obvious home in the relevant section of this directory. But many larger companies, which offer holidays on different continents, or a mix of activities, have been harder to categorise. Yet if I were to list every company under every possible sub-section of this directory that they could legitimately appear in, this book would be the size of a phone directory.

So I have listed each company in the section that seems to me to reflect most fairly the strength of their programme. This means you may wish to consult several parts of this chapter for the widest range of suggestions. For example, if you want to rent a villa in Greece, consult the Greece listings (see page 413) and the villa specialists (see page 379). It is also worth checking out Summer Sun (see page 406), which lists companies offering holidays across several countries in the Mediterranean, and for good value bucket-and-spade breaks, check out the deals from the Mainstream Tour Operators (see page 405).

Likewise for holidays in Africa, Asia or South America, start with those specialist sections, but don't forget to look at "Mainstream Tour Operators" and "Worldwide".

Where I have felt it helpful I have included a brief description of a tour operator's programme.

ACCOMMODATION

HOTEL BOOKING WEBSITES

www. asiahotels.com
www. easyjethotels.co.uk
www. hotelclub.co.uk
www. hotelconnect.co.uk
www. hotels.com
www.lastminute.com
www.laterooms.com
www.needahotel.com
www.octopustravel.com
www.priceline.co.uk
www.ratestogo.com
www.ryanairhotels.com
www.viamichelin.com

Hotel price comparison websites

www.cheapaccommodation.com
www.hotelscomparison.com
www.kelkoo.co.uk
www.nextag.com
www.traveljungle.co.uk
www.tripadvisor.com

Online hotel guides

Alastair Sawday's Special Places to Stay,
www. alastairsawday.co.uk
Hip Hotels,
www.hiphotels.com
i-escape,
www.i-escape.com
Michelin,
www.michelin.com
Mr and Mrs Smith,
www.mrandmrssmith.com
Travel Intelligence,
www.travelintelligence.net

Hotel reviews

www.hotelchatter.com
www.priceline.co.uk
www.tripadvisor.co.uk

Free accommodation

www.couchsurfing.com
www.globalfreeloaders.com
www.sleepinginairports.net

HOUSE SWAP AGENCIES

If you fancy a holiday living like the locals,
swapping homes with an owner overseas is a
good way to do it. Often you can use their car,
too, and it can be ideal for families. But check
the insurance situation and get everything in
writing before you swap. To use these sites, you
must generally register and pay a modest fee.

Holswap, 07771 866584,
www.holswap.com
Home Exchange Network, 0141 571 8068,
www.home-exchange-network.com
Homebase Holidays, 020 8886 8752,
www.homebase-hols.com
HomeLink International, 01962 886882,
www.homelink.org.uk
Intervac Home Exchange, 01249 461101,
www.intervac.co.uk
Matching Houses
(www.matchinghouses.com), for those with
special needs
Vacation Homes Unlimited, 001 661 298 0376,
www.exchangehomes.com

HOTEL CHAINS

It's always worth going direct to a hotel's website
to see if it's offering special deals, and to get a
sense of what the hotel is like. These are the big
global brands; for suggestions of UK-based hotel
groups, see chapter 5 and the UK directory on
page 425.

Accor (www.accorhotels.com): this French-
owned chain includes the swanky Sofitel hotels,
business travellers' favourites Novotel and
Mercure, and the more basic Etap, Formule 1
and Ibis brands, plus Motel 6 in the USA.
Best Western (www.bestwestern.com) has more
than 4,000 independently owned and operated
hotels in 80 countries.
Choice Hotels (www.choicehotels.com) has
more than 5,000 budget and mid-price motels
and hotels worldwide under brands including
Comfort Inn, Clarion and Rodeway Inn.
Fairmont Hotels and Resorts
(www.fairmont.com), based in Canada, operates
luxury hotels across North America, plus hotels
in Mexico, Monaco and Dubai; it also owns the
Savoy in London.
Four Seasons (www.fourseasons.com) operates
66 luxurious hotels in 29 countries, with 20
more under development; it mixes formal city
hotels with ultra-luxurious beach resorts.
Hilton (www.hilton.com) owns, manages and
franchises 500 properties around the world; its
brands include Conrad Hotels and
Hampton Inns.
Hyatt (www.hyatt.com) operates more than 200
hotels worldwide under the brands Hyatt, Hyatt
Regency, Park Hyatt and Grand Hyatt.
InterContinental (www.ichotelsgroupcom)
owns more than 3,500 hotels in 100 countries,
including upmarket InterContinental hotels plus
the more affordable Crowne Plaza and Holiday
Inn brands.

Le Meridien (www.lemeridien.com) is a London-based group that has more than 130 upmarket hotels in 53 countries.

Marriott Hotels (www.marriott.com) is a US group that operates and franchises more than 2,600 hotels in 65 countries. Its brands include the luxury group Ritz-Carlton (www.ritz-carlton.com), which has 35 hotels in the USA and another 22 worldwide.

Pan Pacific Hotels and Resorts (www.panpacific.com) has 24 hotels in countries around the Pacific, across Asia (especially Japan) and on the west coast of the USA.

Radisson Hotels and Resorts (www.radisson.com) operates 435 hotels across 61 countries and its brands include Radisson SAS, Regent International and Park Plaza.

Raffles International Hotels and Resorts (www.raffles.com) has more than 40 hotels worldwide – including the famous Raffles Hotel in Singapore – under the brands Raffles and Swissôtel.

Shangri-La (www.shangri-la.com), the Hong Kong-based luxury group, has 47 deluxe properties across Asia and the Middle East under the Shangri-La and Traders brands; it is rapidly expanding, particularly in China.

Starwood Hotels (www.starwoodhotels.com) owns or operates around 750 hotels in 80 countries; its brands include St Regis, Westin, Sheraton, W hotels and it plans to launch the budget brand Aloft.

Boutique chains and designer hotels

Amanresorts (www.amanresorts.com) is a collection of 18 beautiful, individually designed hotels, the majority in Asia, built in sympathy with the local environment.

Banyan Tree (www.banyantree.com): just half a dozen Asian properties, but soon to open another 15 worldwide. Boasts excellent spas and has a strong environmental record.

Mandarin Oriental (www.mandarinoriental.com) is a Hong Kong-based group with 22 luxurious hotels and resorts across 17 countries, many with high-class spas.

One&Only Resorts (www.oneandonlyresorts.com) is owned by the flamboyant Sol Kerzner, who formerly ran Sun City in South Africa. It offers a group of ultra-luxurious resorts in Mauritius, the Maldives, Mexico and the Bahamas.

Orient-Express (www.orient-express.com), a collection of 30 luxurious hotels, including some of the world's most famous, such as the Cipriani in Venice, the Copacabana Palace in Rio, and the Mount Nelson in Cape Town.

Rocco Forte Hotels (www.roccofortehotels.com) offers14 stylish, mostly city-centre hotels across Europe, including classics such as Brown's in London and Château de Bagnols in France.

The Stein Group (www.thesteingroup.com) is a fast-growing group of stylish, upmarket hotels across Europe which includes Son Net on Majorca and the Cadogan in London.

Six Senses Resorts and Spas (www.sixsenses.com) is a Bangkok-based group that manages a dozen elegant resorts in Asia under the Soneva and Evason brands (including the sublime Soneva Fushi in the Maldives), and operates spas in a dozen more hotels worldwide.

UK hotel booking agencies

Superbreak (01904 644455, www.superbreak.com) consistently offers good room rates, and also offers packages such as theatre or concert tickets plus a nearby hotel.

We Do Weekends (0870 240 1111, www.wedoweekends.co.uk) offers breaks at upmarket hotels in the UK with entertainment from bands or comedians.

HOTEL MARKETING GROUPS

Most of these websites offer you the chance to sign up for email newsletters which can bring discounts unavailable elsewhere.

Chic Retreats (www.chicretreats.com) is a collection of around 150 small (no more than 30 rooms), stylish properties worldwide. Membership costs £15, and entitles you to discounts at Chic Retreats' hotels.

Conde Nast Johansens (www.johansens.com) publishes for consumer guides to hotels in the UK and Ireland, Europe and the Mediterranean, and the Americas; details are also available online.

Design Hotels (www.designhotels.com) markets 140 hotels across 40 countries, many of them cutting-edge, modern or minimalist in style.

Great Hotels of the World (www.ghotw.com), is an alliance of luxury hotels worldwide, split into the categories spa, golf, romantic and business. Its sister alliance, Special Hotels of the World (www.shotw.com), has 45 properties worldwide which offer something unique, such as a converted ancient building.

Historic Hotels of Europe (www.historichotelsofeurope.com) is a marketing group with links to 16 European hotel consortia, offering typical heritage properties of their country, such as pousadas in Portugal, or historic palaces in Italy or Germany.

Leading Hotels of the World (www.lhw.com) represents more than 420 of the world's leading hotels, resorts and spas.

Relais & Chateaux (www.relaischateaux.com) is an association of 440 luxury hotels and restaurants with details in guidebook form and online. It's particularly strong on France.

Small Luxury Hotels of the World (www.slh.com) groups more than 350 independently owned, upmarket hotels in some 60 countries, including spas, country houses, golf resorts and game and wilderness lodges. It also offers the brand Great Small Hotels (www.greatsmallhotels.com) which picks small, characterful properties worldwide.

Unusual Hotels of the World (www.uhotw.com). If you fancy staying in treehouses, prisons, igloos or even in an underwater hotel, this is for you.

VILLA COMPANIES

You will find more companies that offer villa rental in the destination categories later in this directory. Many of the companies listed here sell bonded package holidays, but some can only rent the property to you rather than offer a package.

A&K Villas, 0845 070 0618,
www.abercrombiekent.co.uk
Bonnes Vacances , 0870 760 7071,
www.bvdirect.co.uk
Caribtours, 020 7751 0660,
www.caribtours.co.uk
Carrier, 01625 547020,
www.carrier.co.uk
Chez Nous, 0870 336 7679,
www.cheznous.com
Cottages to Castles, 01622 775217,
www.cottagestocastles.com
CV Travel, 020 7384 5850,
www.cvtravel.co.uk
Dominique's Villas, 020 7738 8772,
www.dominiquesvillas.co.uk
Elegant Resorts, 01244 897000,
www.elegantresorts.co.uk
Elite Vacations, 01707 371000,
www.elitevacations.com
Elysian Holidays, 01580 766599,
www.elysianholidays.co.uk
Individual Travellers Company, 0870 078 0189,
www.indiv-travellers.com
Igluvillas, 020 8544 6401,
www.igluvillas.com
Ilios Travel, 01444 880350,
www.iliostravel.com
Interhome, 020 8891 1294,
www.interhome.co.uk

ITC Classics, 01244 355527,
www.itcclassics.co.uk
James Villa Holidays, 0870 055 6688,
www.jamesvillas.co.uk
Meon Villas, 0870 850 8551,
www.meonvillas.co.uk
Mirador Villa Holidays, 01233 611200,
www.miradorvillaholidays.com
Owners in France, 0870 901 3400,
www.ownersinfrance.co.uk
The Owners' Syndicate, 020 7801 9804,
www.ownerssyndicate.com
Palmer & Parker, 01494 815411,
www.palmerparker.com
Private World, 020 7723 5599,
www.privateworldvillas.com
Scott Dunn, 020 8682 5040,
www.scottdunn.com
Simply Travel, 0870 166 4979,
www.simplytravel.com
Sovereign Villas, 0870 900 3290,
www.sovereignvillas.co.uk
Style Holidays, 0870 444 4404,
www.styleholidays.co.uk
Sun Select Villas, 01299 271616,
www.sunselectvillas.com
Sunvil Holidays, 020 8568 4499,
www.sunvil.co.uk
Think Sicily, 020 7377 8518,
www.thinksicily.com
Toad Hall Caribbean, 01548 852407,
www.toadhallcaribbean.com
VFB, 01242 240340,
www.vfbholidays.co.uk
The Villa Agency, 01273 747811,
www.thevillaagency.co.uk
Villa Centre, 01223 513593,
www.villacentre.com
The Villa Collection, 01753 853737,
www.thevilla-collection.co.uk
Villa Retreats, 0870 013 3979,
www.villaretreats.com
Villa Select, 01789 764909,
www.villaselect.com
Villa World, 01223 506554,
www.villaworld.co.uk
Villas of Morocco, 020 7823 2255,
www.villasofmorocco.com
Villazzo, 020 8123 3375,
www.villazzo.com
Vintage Travel, 0845 344 0460,
www.vintagetravel.co.uk
Wimco, 0870 850 1144,
www.wimco.co.uk

ACTIVITIES

CULTURAL HOLIDAYS

ACE Study Tours (01223 835055,
www.study-tours.org), cultural trips and
study tours with specialist lecturers, on
subjects including music, art, history, literature,
archaeology and architecture.

Ancient World Tours (020 7917 9494,
www.ancient.co.uk), part of tour giant Kuoni,
offers culture and history tours, specialising in
Egypt, plus Libya and other destinations.

Andante Travels (01722 713800,
www.andantetravels.co.uk), cultural tours of
the ancient world, mostly Europe and the Near
East; emphasis on archaeology and history.

Andrew Brock Travel (01572 821330,
www.coromandelabt.com), mix of near and
far east cultural breaks, plus other programmes.

Collette Worldwide Holidays (0800 804 8700,
www.collettevacations.co.uk), coach tours
and cultural trips, some in conjunction with the
Smithsonian.

Fine Art Travel (020 7437 8553,
www.finearttravel.co.uk), small programme of
organised cultural tours, mostly to Italy.

Heritage Group Travel (01225 466620,
www.grouptravel.co.uk), cultural tours
worldwide for groups (not individuals).

Inscape Fine Art Study Tours (01993 891726,
www.inscapetours.co.uk), art and architecture
holidays and study tours of high quality for
serious art lovers.

Kirker (0870 112 3333,
www.kirkerholidays.com), the city break
specialist, has a dedicated cultural programme
offering trips to music festivals and its own
specially designed concerts, throughout Europe.

Martin Randall Travel (020 8742 3355,
www.martinrandall.com), cultural tours
including art, architecture, history, archaeology,
gastronomy and music throughout Europe and
the Middle East.

Peter Sommer Travels (01600 861929,
www.petersommer.com), archaeological tours
of Turkey.

Prospect (01227 773545,
www.prospecttours.com), cultural tours
for art and music lovers.

Specialtours (020 7730 2297,
www.specialtours.co.uk), group art and
culture tours, mostly in Europe but also to
countries such as Japan, Ethiopia and Armenia.

Temple World (020 8940 4114,
www.templeworld.com), tours with an
educational twist.

Travel for the Arts (020 8799 8350,
www.travelforthearts.com), classical music,
opera and dance holidays, for individuals or in
small groups, taking in the major opera houses,
dance companies and festivals worldwide.

Travel Editions (020 7251 0045,
www.traveleditions.co.uk), group escorted
tours to destinations across Europe, mostly
with cultural, artistic and historic themes.

The Traveller (020 7436 9343,
www.thetraveller2004.com), large programme
of cultural tours with guest lecturers to
mainstream destinations, especially the Middle
East, and unusual ones such as Gabon, North
Korea and Serbia; it also offers cultural tours
for families.

Food, wine and cookery

Arblaster & Clarke Wine Tours, 01730 893344,
www.winetours.co.uk

Flavours Cookery Holidays, 0131 625 7002,
www.flavoursholidays.com

Gourmet on Tour, 020 7871 0848,
www.gourmetontour.com

Grape Escapes, 0870 766 7617,
www.grapeescapes.net

Great Gastronomy & Spa Holidays, 01733 315522,
www.greatgastronomy.co.uk

On the Menu Holidays, 020 7371 1113,
www.holidayonthemenu.com

Orpheus & Bacchus, 01483 511655,
www.orpheusandbacchus.com

Taste Italia, 01268 711445,
www.taste-italia.com

Tasting Places, 020 8964 5333,
www.tastingplaces.com

Wessex Continental, 01752 846880,
www.wessexcontinental.co.uk

Winetrails, 01306 712111,
www.winetrails.co.uk

Gardens

Boxwood Tours, 01341 241717,
www.boxwoodtours.co.uk

Brightwater Holidays, 01334 657155,
www.brightwaterholidays.com

Military history and battlefield tours

Bartletts Battlefield Journeys, 01507 523128,
www.battlefields.co.uk

Holts Battlefield Tours, 01293 455300,
www.holts.co.uk

Leger Holidays, 0845 458 5600,
www.leger.co.uk

Mike Hodgson Battlefield Tours, 01526 342249,
www.lancfile.demon.co.uk/mhtours

Remembrance Travel, 01622 716729,
www.remembrancetravel.com

Miscellaneous

Dance Holidays, 0870 286 6000,
www.danceholidays.com
Painting holidays: order a directory, 01830 540215,
www.paintingholidaydirectory.com
Space holidays: Wildwings, 0117 965 8333,
www.wildwings.co.uk, offers zero-gravity
trips and the chance to sign up for space
exploration.

Tickets and event information

Keith Prowse (0870 906 3860,
www.keithprowse.com) offers tickets for
cultural events, rock and pop shows, opera,
theatre and musical concerts, theme parks and
other attractions worldwide.
Liaisons Abroad, (0870 421 4020,
www.liaisonsabroad.com), for tickets to
cultural events such as opera, festival and
museums in Europe.
Theme Park Tickets Direct, 0870 040 0210,
www.themeparkticketsdirect.com
365tickets.com (www.365tickets.com), sells
attraction tickets, mostly in the UK and Florida.

MULTI ACTIVITIES AND SOFT ADVENTURE

Activities Abroad, 0870 444 5320,
www.activitiesabroad.com
The Adventure Company, 01420 541007,
www.adventurecompany.co.uk
Exodus, 0870 240 5550,
www.exodus.co.uk
Explore, 0870 333 4001,
www.explore.co.uk
Gecko's Adventures, 01635 872300,
www.geckosadventures.co.uk
Guerba, 01373 826611,
www.guerba.co.uk
Headwater, 01606 720199,
www.headwater.com
High and Wild, 01749 671777,
www.highandwild.co.uk
Imaginative Traveller, 0800 316 2717,
www.imaginative-traveller.com
Inntravel, 01653 617906,
www.inntravel.co.uk
Intrepid Travel, 0800 917 6456,
www.intrepidtravel.com
KE Adventure Travel, 01768 773966,
www.keadventure.com
Lakes and Mountains Holidays, 01243 792442,
www.lakes-mountains.co.uk
Peregrine Adventures, 01635 872300,
www.peregrineadventures.co.uk
Pioneer Expeditions, 0845 004 7801,
www.pioneerexpeditions.com

Polar Travel Company, 01364 631470,
www.polartravel.co.uk
Wild Frontiers, 020 7736 3968,
www.wildfrontiers.co.uk
Wilderness Adventure, 0845 458 4440,
www.wildernessadventure.co.uk
World Expeditions, 020 8870 2600,
www.worldexpeditions.com

Overland tours by truck

Overlanding is a fantastic way to travel,
especially if you're on a limited budget, have
plenty of time, and enjoy meeting fellow
travellers. The group, typically 20 to 24
strong, travels through a continent in a large
converted truck, usually with two drivers/tour
leaders, stopping at night to camp or stay
in cheap hostels, and enjoying activities,
game viewing and sightseeing along the way.
You're expected to share the chores, such as
shopping for food in the market, cooking,
cleaning the bus and pitching your tents. It's
a good value way to see a lot in one trip, will
help you make friends, and should give you
the confidence to return on your own later.

This type of travel started in Africa, but
there are also popular routes through Europe,
Asia and South America. Some trips can
last as much as nine months but others are
as short as two or three weeks and some
companies, such as Dragoman and Guerba,
have special programmes for families.

* Suggested reading: *Africa Overland*, Bradt, £5.99

Absolute Africa, 020 8742 0226,
www.absoluteafrica.com
Acacia Africa, 020 7706 4700,
www.acacia-africa.com
Africa in Focus, 01803 770956,
www.africa-in-focus.com
Bukima, 0870 757 2230,
www.bukima.com
Dragoman Overland, 01728 861133,
www.dragoman.com
Economic Expeditions, 020 8969 1948,
www.economicexpeditions.com
Exodus, 0870 240 5550,
www.exodus.co.uk
Guerba, 01373 826611,
www.guerba.co.uk
Kumuka, 020 7937 8855,
www.kumuka.com
Oasis Overland, 01963 363400,
www.oasisoverland.co.uk
On the Go Tours, 020 7371 1113,
www.onthegotours.com
Overland Club, 0870 460 7085,
www.overlandclub.com

NATURIST HOLIDAYS

Peng Travel (0845 345 8345,
www.pengtravel.co.uk) organises holidays to
naturist resorts worldwide, especially France,
Spain and the Caribbean, and also offers room-
only bookings through the website
www.barebeds.com.

British Naturism, **www.british-naturism.org.uk**,
produces a quarterly magazine.

RELIGIOUS AND SPIRITUAL HOLIDAYS

Highway Journeys
(**www.highwaytrust.org**) offers Holy
Land tours.

Israel Travel Service (0870 794 3333,
www.itstravel.co.uk), specialises in trips to the
Holy Land.

MasterSun and MasterSki Christian Holidays,
020 8942 9442, **www.mastersun.co.uk**.

Pax Travel (020 7485 3003,
www.paxtravel.co.uk), religious and cultural
holidays, pilgrimages, Vatican trips.

St Peter's Pilgrims (020 8244 8844,
www.stpeter.co.uk), runs pilgrimages, for
example to Fatima in Portugal or
Lourdes in France.

Tangney Tours (01732 886666,
www.tangney-tours.co.uk), pilgrimages to
Lourdes and other shrines; also offers trips to
Oberammergau, and, trading as Spes Travel, to
Rome and Turin.

Xclusively Kosher (020 8953 2866,
www.xkuk.com), Jewish holidays.

SPORTS HOLIDAYS
Cycling and walking specialists

When booking a trip, check whether your
luggage is transported from hotel to hotel for
you, and what equipment you need to provide
yourself, plus the insurance situation in case you
have an accident.

Also see "Walking and trekking specialists", page
384

ATG Oxford, 01865 315678,
ww.atg-oxford.co.uk

Belle France, 0870 405 4056,
www.bellefrance.co.uk

Bents Tours, 01568 780800,
www.bentstours.com

HF Holidays, 020 8905 9558,
www.hfholidays.co.uk

LB Freedom Tours, 01442 263377,
www.lbfreedomtours.com

Peak Retreats, 0870 770 0408,
www.peakretreats.co.uk

Sherpa Expeditions, 020 8577 2717,
www.sherpaexpeditions.co.uk

Walking Women, 0845 644 5335,
www.walkingwomen.com

Cycling specialists

Alp Active, 0845 120 9872,
www.alpactive.com

Boots & Bikes, 020 8462 6522,
www.bootsandbikes.co.uk

The Chain Gang, 01392 662262,
www.thechaingang.co.uk

CTC Holidays & Tours, 0870 235 1356,
www.cyclingholidays.org

Cycle Rides, 01225 428452,
www.cyclerides.co.uk

Cycling for Softies, 0161 248 8282,
www.cycling-for-softies.co.uk

Freewheel Holidays, 01636 815636,
www.freewheelholidays.com

Mountain Beach Activity Holidays,
0115 921 5065, **www.mountain-beach.co.uk**

Mountain Bike Holidays, 020 8123 5654,
www.mountainbikeholidays.co.uk

Red Spokes, 020 7502 7252,
www.redspokes.co.uk

Rough Tracks, 07000 560749,
www.roughtracks.com

Saddle Skedaddle, 0191 265 1110,
www.skedaddle.co.uk

2 Wheel Treks, 01483 271212,
www.2wheeltreks.co.uk

UK cycle holiday operators

Bicycle Beano Holidays, 01982 560471,
www.bicycle-beano.co.uk

Byways Breaks, 0151 722 8050,
www.byways-breaks.co.uk

Capital Sports, 01296 631671,
www.capital-sport.co.uk

Company of Cyclists, 01904 778080,
www.companyofcyclists.com

Country Lanes, 0845 370 0622,
www.countrylanes.co.uk

Galloway Cycling Holidays, 01556 502979,
www.gallowaycycling.co.uk

Holiday Lakeland Cycling, 016973 71871,
www.holiday-lakeland.co.uk

Let's Go Devon, 01837 880075,
www.letsgodevon.com

Suffolk Cycle Breaks, 01449 721555,
www.cyclebreaks.com

Wheely Wonderful Cycling (01568 770755,
www.wheelywonderfulcycling.co.uk

UK cycling contacts

Bike Events, 0870 755 8519,
www.bike-events.com

Bike Week, 0845 612 0661,
  www.bikeweek.org.uk
Cyclists' Touring Club, 0870 873 0060,
  www.ctc.org.uk ; membership £12pa
National Rail Enquiries, 0845 748 4950,
  www.nationalrail.co.uk
Sustrans, 0845 113 0065,
  www.sustrans.org.uk, membership £15pa
London Cycling Campaign, 020 7234 9310,
  www.lcc.org.uk
The London Cycle Network,
  www.londoncyclenetwork.org.uk
Transport for London has free cycle maps,
  020 7222 5600, **www.tfl.gov.uk**

Golf

A Golfing Experience, 01923 265858,
  www.agolfingexperience.com
Golf Amigos, 0845 230 3100,
  www.golfamigos.co.uk
Golf Groups Direct,
  www.golfgroups.co.uk
Golf Par Excellence, 01737 211818,
  www.golfparexcellence.com
Longshot Golf, 0808 156 5927,
  www.longshotgolf.co.uk
Momentum Golf Italia, 020 7371 9111,
  www.golfitalia.co.uk

Horse riding

Many Africa specialists and other activity
companies will offer riding trips; also see listings
for North America for ranch holiday companies.

Equine Adventures, 0845 130 6981,
  www.equineadventures.co.uk
Equitour, 0800 043 7942,
  www.equitour.co.uk
FreeRein, 01497 821356,
  www.free-rein.co.uk
Horse Hire Holidays, 01697 371217,
  www.horsehire.co.uk
In the Saddle, 01299 272997,
  www.inthesaddle.com
Inntravel, 01653 617949,
  www.inntravel.co.uk
Ride World Wide, 01837 82544,
  www.rideworldwide.com
Unicorn Trails, 01767 600606,
  www.unicorntrails.com
Wild and Exotic, 01439 748401,
  www.wildandexotic.co.uk

Scuba diving

Aquatours, 020 8398 0505,
  www.aquatours.com
Barefoot Traveller, 020 8741 4319,
  www.barefoot-traveller.com
Dive Worldwide, 0845 130 6980,

www.diveworldwide.com
Regaldive, 0870 220 1777,
  www.regaldive.co.uk

Sporting events

Selling tickets for major events such as the
Olympics, or international cricket, rugby and
football matches, has become big business. Often
to get into these events you will have to buy your
tickets through official outlets such as companies
listed in this section: given this quasi monopoly,
package prices can be extremely expensive for big
events.

For the most popular events, these companies
will often compile a waiting list of interested
customers, giving them first chance to book
when tickets are released, so it can be worth
registering your interest in advance. By "advance",
I mean a year or more – dedicated fans do not
wait until the last minute. If you're after tickets
for the most popular events, such as major
football tournaments, it may also help if you are a
member of the sport's official supporters' club.

These sports holiday companies cater largely
for spectators – for holidays where you can
participate in sport, see other listings in this
Activities section.

Airtrack, 01895 810810,
  www.airtrack.co.uk
ATP International, 0870 990 6787,
  www.atpsportsevents.com
Classic Travelling, 0870 350 0122,
  www.classictravelling.com
Fan Fare Events, 0161 437 0002,
  www.fanfare-events.com
Grand Touring Club, 0870 609 1176,
  www.grandtouringclub.co.uk
Grandstand Sports Tours, 0870 428 4409,
  www.grandstandsportstours.co.uk
Gullivers Sports Travel, 01684 293175,
  www.gulliversports.co.uk
Horse Racing Abroad, 01444 441661,
  www.horseracingabroad.com
Kuoni Sport Abroad, 01306 871038,
  www.sportabroad.co.uk
Mike Burton Sports Travel, 01452 892057,
  www.mikeburton.com
Motor Racing International, 01304 612424,
  www.motorracinginternational.uk.com
Page & Moy, 0870 010 6226,
  www.1st4f1.com
Sports Tours, 01708 336991,
  www.sportstours.co.uk
Sportsworld, 01235 555844,
  www.sportsworld-group.com
Thomas Cook, 020 7853 6485,
  www.thomascooksport.com

Tennis

Jonathan Markson Tennis, 020 7603 2422,
www.marksontennis.com

Walking and trekking specialists

Also look at companies such as Exodus, Explore, Inntravel and others on page 381, which all have extensive walking programmes. And see "Cycling and walking specialists", page 382.

Alpine Exploratory, 01942 826270,
www.alpineexploratory.com
Classic Journeys, 01773 873497,
www.classicjourneys.co.uk
Contours Walking Holidays, 017684 80451,
www.contours.co.uk
Countrywide Holidays, 01707 386800,
www.countrywidewalking.com
Footpath Holidays, 01985 840049,
www.footpath-holidays.com
HF Holidays, 020 8905 9558,
www.hfholidays.co.uk/classicwalking
High Places, 0114 275 7500,
www.highplaces.co.uk
Himalayan Kingdoms, 0845 330 8579,
www.himalayankingdoms.com
Kudu Travel, 01722 716167,
www.kudutravel.com
Langdale Walking and Adventure Holidays,
01539 735108, **www.langdaleholidays.co.uk**
On Foot Holidays, 01722 322652,
www.onfootholidays.co.uk
Ramblers' Holidays, 01707 331133,
www.ramblersholidays.co.uk
The Wayfarers, 01242 620871,
www.thewayfarers.com
Upland Escapes, 01367 851117,
www.uplandescapes.com
Walking Plus, 020 8835 8303,
www.walkingplus.co.uk
Walking Safari Company, 01572 821330,
www.walkeurope.com
Walks Worldwide, 01524 242000,
www.walksworldwide.com
Waymark Holidays, 0870 950 9800,
www.waymarkholidays.com
World Walks, 01242 254353,
www.worldwalks.com

UK walking contacts

The British Mountaineering Council,
0870 010 4878, **www.thebmc.co.uk**
Country Walking Magazine,
www.countrywalking.co.uk
Countryside Access Wales,
www.ccw.gov.uk/countrysideaccesswales.
Countryside Agency,
www.countrysideaccess.gov.uk

Countryside Code,
www.countrysideaccess.gov.uk
Four Inns hike,
www.dynarx.demon.co.uk/fourinns
Keep Ireland Open,
www.keepirelandopen.org
Ministry of Defence walking access,
www.access.mod.uk
National parks,
www.nationalparks.gov.uk
National Trails,
www.nationaltrail.co.uk
The Open Spaces Society, 01491 573535,
www.oss.org.uk
Ordnance Survey, 0845 605 0505,
www.ordnancesurvey.co.uk
The Ramblers' Association, 020 7339 8500,
www.ramblers.org.uk
Scottish Natural Heritage, 01738 458545,
www.outdooraccess-scotland.com .
Trail,
www.trailmag.co.uk
UK walking festivals,
www.walkingontheweb.co.uk
Walking in Scotland,
http://walking.visitscotland.com.
Walkingworld,
www.walkingworld.com

Watersports

Activity Yachting Holidays, 01243 641304,
www.activityyachting.com
Adrift, 01488 71152,
www.adrift.co.uk
Classic Sailing, 01872 580022,
www.classic-sailing.co.uk
Club Med, 0845 367 6767,
www.clubmed.co.uk
Mark Warner, 0870 770 4222,
www.markwarner.co.uk
Minorca Sailing Holidays, 020 8948 2106,
www.minorcasailing.co.uk
The Moorings, 01227 776677,
www.moorings.com
Nautilus Yachting, 01732 867445,
www.nautilus-yachting.com
Neilson Active Holidays, 0870 909 9099,
www.neilson.co.uk
Peligoni Club, 01243 511499,
www.peligoni.com
Sailing Holidays, 020 8459 8787,
www.sailingholidays.com
Sea-Trek, 01386 848814,
www.sea-trek.co.uk
Seafarer Cruises, 0870 442 2447,
www.seafarercruises.com
Setsail, 01787 310445,
www.setsail.co.uk

Sportif, 01273 844919,
www.sportif-uk.com
Sunsail, 02392 222223,
www.sunsail.com
Sunvil Sailing, 020 8758 4780,
www.sunvil.co.uk
Swimtrek, 020 8696 6220,
www.swimtrek.com
Tall Ships Adventures, 02392 832055,
www.tallships.org
Templecraft, 01732 867445,
www.templecraft.com
Top Yacht, 01243 520950,
www.top-yacht.com
Wildwind Holidays, 01920 484516,
www.wildwind.co.uk

UK watersports

The following bodies can give you all the
information you need to take up or develop a
passion for watersports around the UK.

British Canoe Union, 0115 982 1100,
www.bcu.org.uk
British Kite Surfing Association, 01509 856500,
www.kitesurfing.org
British Sub-Aqua Club (0151 350 6200,
www.bsac.com), which along with the
Professional Association of Diving Instructors
(0117 300 7234, **www.padi.com**) trains and
certifies scuba divers.
British Surfing Association, 01637 876474,
www.britsurf.co.uk
British Water-Ski Federation, 01932 570885,
www.britishwaterski.org.uk
Environment Agency – Fishing (0870 850 6506,
www.environment-agency.gov.uk/fish),
explains the regulations governing angling and
how to get a licence.
National Federation of Anglers, 0115 981 3535,
www.nfadirect.com
National Federation of Sea Anglers,
01364 644643, **www.nfsa.org.uk**
National Water Sports Centre, 0115 982 1212,
www.nationalwatersportsevents.co.uk
Royal Life Saving Society, 01789 773994,
www.lifesavers.org.uk
Royal National Lifeboat Institution
(0845 122 6999, **www.rnli.org.uk**), which as
well as operating lifeboats around our shores
runs a lifeguard programme in the West
Country (**www.beachlifeguards.org.uk**).
Royal Yachting Association, 0845 345 0400,
www.rya.co.uk
UK Sailing Academy (01983 294941,
www.uksa.org), residential watersports courses
at Cowes on the Isle of Wight.

Winter sports and skiing

Several of the operators listed under "activity"
or "mainstream tour operators" also offer winter
sports programmes.

Alpine Action (01273 597940,
www.alpineaction.co.uk) offers high quality
catered chalets in La Tania and Méribel, France.
Alpine Tours (01628 826699,
www.alpinetours.co.uk) organises large group
and school ski trips to Austria, Italy, Switzerland
and Spain.
Alpine Tracks (0800 028 2546,
www.alpinetracks.com) offers ski and summer
activity breaks in the Alps.
Club Med (0845 367 6767, **www.clubmed.co.uk**)
offers "village"-based holidays in winter sports
destinations across the Alps.
Crystal Ski (0870 160 6040,
www.crystalski.co.uk) offers a wide range of
trips across the Alps and North America.
CV Ski (0870 062 3425, **www.cvski.co.uk**), part of
villa company CV Travel; upmarket, tailormade
holidays in North America and the Alps.
Descent International (020 7384 3854,
www.descent.co.uk) offers extremely upmarket
chalets across the Alps.
Equity Ski (01273 666500, **www.equityski.co.uk**)
offers 27 resorts in France, Italy, Switzerland
and Austria.
Erna Low (0870 750 6820, **www.ernalow.co.uk**)
offers ski and spa holidays in North America
and the Alps.
Esprit Holidays (01252 618300,
www.esprit-holidays.co.uk) specialises in
family skiing in Europe, plus visits to Santa in
Lapland and a programme of summer holidays.
Family Ski Company (01684 540333,
www.familyski.co.uk) provides catered chalets
with childcare for all ages in three French
resorts.
Finlays (01573 22661, **www.finlayski.com**) offers
high quality chalet holidays in three French
resorts: Val d'Isère, Courchevel and La Plagne.
First Choice Ski (0870 754 3477,
www.firstchoice.co.uk), a wide range of
holidays from the mass market giant.
Flexiski (0870 900 3278, **www.flexiski.com**)
provides tailor-made holidays and weekend
breaks in 13 European resorts.
Frontier Ski (020 8776 8709,
www.frontier-ski.co.uk) specialises in holidays
to Canada.
Inghams (020 8780 4433, **www.inghams.co.uk**)
has a large ski programme across Europe and
North America.

Inntravel (01653 617788, **www.inntravel.co.uk**) specialises in gentle downhill and cross-country skiing in villages in Europe and New England.

Lagrange (020 7371 6111, **www.lagrange-holidays.co.uk**) offers self-catering in France, Switzerland and Austria.

Le Ski (0870 754 4444, **www.leski.com**) specialises in high quality chalets in three French resorts: Courchevel, La Tania and Val d'Isère.

Made to Measure (01243 533333, **www.mtmhols.co.uk**) offers tailor-made ski holidays, including short breaks – plus art history tours, beach holidays worldwide and summer activity breaks in the Alps.

Mark Warner (0870 770 4227, **www.markwarner.co.uk**) offers ski holidays at its dedicated chalethotels in ten resorts across the Alps, with extensive childcare.

Momentum Ski (020 7371 9111, **www.momentum.uk.com**) offers flexible, upmarket ski breaks to the Alps, plus North America and Chile.

Neilson (0870 333 3356, **www.neilson.co.uk**), the active holiday specialist, has ski and snowboard trips to the Alps and North America.

Oxford Ski Company (0870 787 1785, **www.oxfordski.com**) specialises in luxury chalets in France and Switzerland.

Peak Retreats (0870 770 0408, **www.peakretreats.co.uk**) offers skiing in the French Alps in winter, and activities such as mountain biking in summer.

Powder Byrne (020 8246 5300, **www.powderbyrne.co.uk**) offers upmarket, hotel-based, high-service ski holidays, with families well catered for.

Powder White (020 8355 8836, **www.powderwhite.co.uk**) offers upmarket catered chalets in Méribel, Courchevel, Val d'Isère and Verbier.

Premiere Neige (0870 383 1000, **www.premiere-neige.com**) offers luxury hollidays in Sainte Foy, France.

Purple Ski (01494 488633, **www.purpleski.com**) provides chalet holidays in Méribel.

Scott Dunn (020 8682 5050, **www.scottdunn.co.uk**) offers luxury ski holidays in the Alps, with some chalets offering extras such as indoor pools.

Ski Beat (01243 780405, **www.skibeat.co.uk**) offers catered chalets in the French resorts of La Plagne, Les Arcs, La Tania, Méribel and Val d'Isère.

Ski Esprit (01252 618300, **www.esprit-holidays.co.uk**) specialises in family ski holidays across the Alps, plus trips to see Santa in Lapland.

Ski Famille (0845 644 3764, **www.skifamille.co.uk**) specialises in family ski holidays, offering catered chalets with childcare in Les Gets and Morzine, France.

Ski Freedom (01442 263377, **www.skifreedom.com**) offers luxury chalets in the Swiss Alps, especially Verbier.

Ski Freshtracks (020 8410 2022, **www.skifreshtracks.co.uk**), the holiday arm of the Ski Club of Great Britain (**www.skiclub.co.uk**), is offering holidays that link with the club's Respect the Mountain environmental campaign (**www.respectthemountain.com**).

Ski Independence (0845 310 3030, **www.ski-i.com**) has a big programme to North America, plus France and Switzerland.

Ski Norway (020 7917 6044, **www.ski-norway.co.uk**), for Norway and Scandinavia.

Ski Olympic (01302 328820, **www.skiolympic.com**) offers catered chalets in eight French resorts, including Val d Isère and Courchevel, plus overnight luxury coach transfers from Manchester and Leeds to the French resorts.

Ski Peak (01428 608070, **www.skipeak.com**) specialises in holidays to Vaujany in the French Alpe d'Huez ski area. In summer the company offers walking, biking and rafting in the area.

Ski Safari (01273 224060, **www.skisafari.com**) offers tailor-made skiing and snowboarding holidays across the USA and Canada, plus three resorts in Chile for summer skiing.

Ski Solutions (020 7471 7700, **www.skisolutions.com**) is a specialist ski travel agency, offering both the Alps and North America.

Ski the American Dream (0870 350 7547, **www.ski-dream.co.uk**), for North American resorts.

Ski Weekend (0870 060 0615, **www.skiweekend.com**) specialises in short ski breaks and long weekends to Switzerland, France and Italy; will cater for single skiers who want to meet like-minded travellers.

Skiworld (0870 241 6723, **www.skiworld.ltd.uk**) claims to be Britain's largest independent ski company, offering higher resorts, and thus a longer season in France, Austria, Switzerland, Canada and the USA; it specialises in group trips.

Snowbizz (01778 341455, **www.snowbizz.co.uk**), is based in Puy St Vincent, France, offering childcare and its own ski school for families.

Snowcoach (01727 866177, **www.snowcoach.co.uk**) offers holidays to Austria and France.

Snowline (0870 112 3118, **www.snowlinevip.com**), based in 28 catered chalets across four French resorts, has good childcare and the

"Scaredy Cat" programme for nervous learners at Val d'Isère. Its sister company, VIP Chalets (0870 112 3119, **www.vip-chalets.com**), offers more than 60 upmarket properties, many popular with celebrities, across the French Alps.

Stanford Skiing (01223 477644, **www.stanfordskiing.co.uk**) specialises in Mégeve, France.

Thomson Ski (0870 888 0254 **www.thomson-ski.co.uk**) offers an extensive programme.

Total Ski (0870 163 3633, **www.skitotal.com**) offers chalet holidays across the Alps.

Virgin Holidays (0870 220 2788, **www.virgin.com/holidays**) offers ski holidays across North America.

Waymark (01753 516477, **www.waymarkholidays.com**) offers cross-country skiing in the Alps and Scandinavia.

White Roc Ski & Snowboard Weekends (020 7792 1188, **www.whiteroc.co.uk**) offers ski and snowboard weekends, plus longer winter sports holidays in 21 resorts across Europe.

Whitepod (00 41 79 744 6219, **www.whitepod.com**) is a luxury winter eco-camp consisting of five distinctive canvas pods in the Vaudoises Alps in Switzerland. This eco-friendly concept won Whitepod the award for Innovation in the 2005 First Choice Responsible Tourism Awards.

YSE (0845 122 1414, **www.yseski.co.uk**) specialises in chalet holidays in Val d'Isère.

Ski websites

I've asked Mark Frary, ski correspondent of *The Times*, to recommend the websites he finds most useful.

www.beansonline.co.uk – website of ski retailer Beans of Bicester. It doesn't have the bells and whistles of Snow+Rock's site but sells a good range and is enthusiastic and informative in the descriptions of items.

www.ifyouski.com – an online ski travel agency but with good editorial features, frequently updated winter sports news and resort information.

www.igluski.com – best site for searching for package ski holidays.

www.pistehors.com – the most comprehensive online resource for off-piste skiing.

www.skiclub.co.uk – the Ski Club of Great Britain's site is good for snow reports. As well as official snow depths, there are reports from in-resort Ski Club reps that tend to be more realistic. One great new feature is a green database, which is the most detailed resource on what resorts and ski companies are doing environmentally.

www.snow-forecast.com – superb graphical displays of forecast snowfall around the world.

www.snowheads.com – forum for real enthusiasts on everything from the value of helmets to the best places to go in resort.

'Green' skiing

These associations are all concerned with minimising the impact of skiing on the environment and provide lists of companies and resorts that have an ethical policy.

Association of Independent Tour Operators' ski directory, 020 8744 9280, **www.aitoskiholidays.co.uk**

Green Resort Guide from the Ski Club of Great Britain, **www.skiclub.co.uk/skiclub/resorts/greenresorts**

National Ski Areas Association, **www.nsaa.org/nsaa/environment/sustainable_slopes/**

Spa holidays

Erna Low (0870 750 6820, **www.ernalow.co.uk**) a long-established spa holiday operator, offers ski and spa holidays and has a growing business selling property overseas.

Essential Escapes (020 7284 3344, **www.essentialescapes.com**) specialises in spa holidays at five-star hotels worldwide.

inspa (0845 458 0723, **www.inspa-retreats.com**) offers small group yoga, exercise, detox and massage holidays in Morocco, India, Thailand, France and Spain.

La Joie de Vivre (01483 272379, **www.lajoiedevivre.co.uk**) specialises in luxury spa holidays and honeymoons.

Thermalia Travel (020 8385 7070, **www.thermalia.co.uk**) offers spa holidays, primarily in Europe.

Wellbeing Escapes (0845 602 6202, **www.wellbeingescapes.co.uk**) is a provider of a wide range of healthy breaks, including spa, yoga, thalassotherapy, detox, weight loss, holistic and outdoor holidays.

* For more information, consult *The Good Spa Guide*, **www.goodspaguide.co.uk**, Content Consultants, £12.95, which explains spa etiquette and reviews spas in the UK, and *Great Spa Escapes*, Dakini Books, £22.50, by Jo Foley, which reviews spas worldwide. The monthly magazine *Conde Nast Traveller* offers a spa review in its March issue each year. Also see **www.spafinder.com** to hunt for spas worldwide.

Yoga, fitness, retreat holidays

Beyond (020 7226 4044, **www.beyondretreats. co.uk**) offers yoga plus skiing, golf and walking in the UK, Italy and Nepal.

The Big Stretch (0845 430 8621, www.thebigstretch.com) offers life coaching courses in the Picos mountains of Spain plus walking and kayaking.

Body and Soul Adventures (020 3002 0936, www.bodysouladventures.com) offers a yoga and activities retreat, including rainforest hikes and kayaking, at Ilha Grande in Brazil.

Boutique Sri Lanka, 0870 833 3838, www.boutiquesrilanka.com

Health and Yoga Holidays (020 8699 1900, www.yogaturkey.co.uk) offers yoga breaks in Turkey.

The Hill That Breathes (0870 609 2690, www.thehillthatbreathes.com) offers holistic holidays in Italy.

Lotus Journeys (020 8965 5727, www.lotusjourneys.com) offers yoga and holistic holidays.

Neal's Yard Agency (0870 444 2702, www.nealsyardagency.com) specialises in healthy, holistic and yoga holidays worldwide.

Sarah Pilates (020 7722 4373, www.sarahpilates.com) – Pilates instructor Sarah Rosenfield offers small group pilates holidays throughout the year.

Skyros (020 7267 4424, www.skyros.com) offers yoga and other activity holidays in Greece and Thailand.

Wellbeing Escapes (0845 602 6202, www.wellbeingescapes.co.uk) offers holistic holidays.

Wild Fitness (0845 056 8343, www.wildfitness.com) is an adventure camp-cum-fitness centre in Kenya.

Wildwind Holidays (01920 484515, www.healthy-option.co.uk) offers yoga in Greece.

Yoga Travel (07875 102407, www.yogatravel.co.uk) offers yoga in Egypt.

Yoga Turkey (020 8699 1900, www.yogaturkey.co.uk) offers yoga in Turkey.

Yoga Practice (020 7928 7527, www.yogapractice.net) offers Ashtanga yoga in Greece.

Further information

The Retreat Association, 020 7357 7736, www.retreats.org.uk

The Good Retreat Guide by Stafford Whiteaker, Rider, £12.99, details retreats, spas and wellness centres across the UK www.thegoodretreatguide.com www.retreat-co.co.uk.

Wildlife and birdwatching

Birdfinders, 01258 839066, www.birdfinders.co.uk

Bird Holidays, 0113 391 0510, www.birdholidays.co.uk

Birdquest, 01254 826317, www.birdquest.co.uk

Birdseekers, 01752 342001, www.birdseekers.co.uk

Discovery Initiatives, 01285 643333, www.discoveryinitiatives.co.uk

Earthwatch, 01865 318838, www.earthwatch.org

Explore, 0870 333 4001, www.explore.co.uk

Limosa Holidays, 01263 578143, www.limosaholidays.co.uk

Naturetrek, 01962 733051, www.naturetrek.co.uk

Ornitholidays, 01794 519445 www.ornitholidays.co.uk

Reef and Rainforest Tours, 01803 866965, www.reefandrainforest.co.uk

Sarus Bird Tours, 0161 761 7279, www.sarusbirdtours.co.uk

Sunbird Holidays, 01767 262522, www.sunbirdtours.co.uk

The Travelling Naturalist, 01305 267994, www.naturalist.co.uk

Toucan Tours, 01772 787862, www.toucantours.co.uk

Wildlife & Wilderness, 0845 004 4599, www.wildlifewilderness.com

Wildlife Worldwide, 0845 130 6982, www.wildlifeworldwide.com

Wildwings, 0117 965 8333, www.wildwings.co.uk

Windows on the Wild, 020 8742 1556, www.windowsonthewild.com

World Primate Safaris, 020 8740 3350, www.worldprimatesafaris.com

CRUISING

Ocean Cruising

Life the ocean wave is great fun, but the huge variety of ships and trips on offer can be confusing. Start by consulting a good guide – such as the *Complete Guide to Cruising and Cruise Ships* by Douglas Ward, Berlitz, £18.99, which reviews 260 cruise ships in depth and gives masses of information about life on board.

Also consult The Passenger Shipping Association (020 7436 2449, www.discover-cruises.co.uk), an industry body representing dozens of cruise lines, for advice on choosing a cruise. Eight upmarket cruise lines have got together to market themselves as the Exclusive Collection (020 7436 2449, www.exclusive-collection.co.uk) and six smaller specialists are grouped in the Niche Cruise Alliance (020 7620 1960, www.nichecruisealliance.com). The sites

www.cruisecritic.com and
www.cruisereviews.com offer advice and reviews
from regular cruisers.

To book, you can contact the cruise lines direct,
or try specialist travel agents who often have
exclusive deals and discounts, plus they can
compare different cruise lines to suggest the best
one for you. The Leading Cruise Agents Alliance
(www.thelca.com) can put you in touch with
more than 40 specialists across the country. Also
try The Cruise Store (0870 191 3705,
www.thecruisestore.co.uk), part of the
MyTravel group, Thomas Cook travel agents
(0870 111 1111, www.cruisesdirect2u.com) and
independent agent 1st4cruising (0870 010 6241,
www.1st4cruising.com). If you are concerned
about how much and when you should tip people,
the site www.cruisetip.tpkeller.com suggests
appropriate amounts.

Cruise lines and agents

African Safari Club (0845 345 0014,
www.africansafariclub.com) operates cruises
out of Mombasa, Kenya, to the islands of the
Indian Ocean.

Carnival Cruise Lines (020 7940 4466,
www.carnivalcruise.co.uk) has 22 large ships
and offers cruises worldwide, many out of
Florida and the US and some out of Rome.

Celebrity Cruises (0800 018 2525,
www.celebritycruises.co.uk), has nine ships,
sailing predominantly around the Americas but
also worldwide.

Chandlers Travel (01708 224000,
www.chandlerstravel.co.uk), specialist cruise
agent.

Costa Cruises (020 7940 4499,
www.costacruises.co.uk) is an Italian line, and
has a dozen ships operating worldwide.

The Cruise People (020 7723 2450,
www.cruisepeople.co.uk) is a travel agency
specialising in luxury ships as well as freight
and cargo boats.

Crystal Cruises (020 7287 9040,
www.crystalcruises.com) offers cruises
worldwide on two spacious ships, with fine
dining courtesy of celebrity chefs' restaurants.

Cunard Line (0845 071 0300, www.cunard.co.uk)
offers worldwide cruises on the QE2, which will
be 40 in 2007, and the QM2, which also offers
transatlantic crossings. The new Queen Victoria
will enter service in late 2007.

Disney Cruise Line (www.disneycruise.com) has
two ships for families in the Caribbean.

easyCruise (0906 292 9000, 25p/min,
www.easycruise.com), sister company to
budget airline easyJet, has a no-frills, and rather
orange ship cruising the Med in summer,
Caribbean in winter, plus another offering river

cruises in Holland and Belgium.

Fred Olsen Cruise Lines (01473 742424,
www.fredolsencruises.co.uk) offers four
smaller ships with a traditional, British feel,
out of Dover and Southampton on cruises
worldwide.

Hebridean International Cruises (01756 704704,
www.hebridean.co.uk) has two small ships, 49
and 96 passengers, with a strong UK country
house hotel feel, cruising in Scotland, plus the
Indian Ocean, Mediterranean and Scandinavia.

Holland America Line (020 7940 4477,
www.hollandamerica.com) operates 13 ships
worldwide; there's an emphasis on luxurious
surroundings and fine food.

Hurtigruten (020 8846 2666,
www.hurtigruten.co.uk) offers holidays on the
Hurtigruten ships, carrying passengers on daily
services up the coast of Norway, plus longer
voyages to the Arctic and Antarctic.

Island Cruises (0870 750 0414,
www.islandcruises.com), a joint venture
between tour operator First Choice and cruise
line Royal Caribbean International, offers two
ships with mostly Mediterranean itineraries and
plenty for families.

Louis Cruise Lines (020 7383 2882,
www.louiscruises.co.uk), a Cypriot cruise
line, offers cruises around the Mediterranean
including some out of the UK, from Tilbury.

MSC Cruises (020 7092 2880,
www.msccruises.co.uk) is an Italian cruise
line that operates eight ships, mostly in the
Mediterranean.

Mundy Cruising (020 7734 4404,
www.mundycruising.co.uk), specialist cruise
agency.

Noble Caledonia (020 7752 0000,
www.noblecaledonia.co.uk) offers a wide
programme of ocean and river cruises
worldwide, plus land-based holidays, often with
a cultural or wildlife theme.

Norwegian Cruise Line (0845 658 8010,
www.uk.ncl.com) has 12 ships sailing
worldwide; famed for the "freestyle" concept of
relaxed, less formal cruising.

Ocean Village (0845 358 5000,
www.oceanvillageholidays.co.uk) is aimed at
thirty- to fifty-somethings who prefer a casual
atmosphere and exciting shore excursions, such
as horse-riding and mountain-biking. Currently
just one ship, with another soon to join,
operating in the Med in summer and Caribbean
in winter.

Orient Lines (0845 658 8050,
www.orientlines.co.uk) operates the Marco Polo
on adventurous itineraries which can include
Antarctica, the Chilean fjords and the Baltic.

P&O Cruises (0845 355 5333, www.pocruises.co.uk) the UK's leading cruise line, has five ships and operates worldwide, with cruises starting in Southampton, and is trying to attract more families, though two ships, *Arcadia* and *Artemis*, are for adults only.

Princess Cruises (0845 355 5800, www.princesscruises.co.uk) operates large ships on worldwide cruises; it features relaxed dining, study courses in subject such as cookery or computing, and a huge outdoor movie screen.

Quark Expeditions (01494 464080, www.quarkexpeditions.com) takes Russian ice-breakers into the Arctic and Antarctic, with just a few dozen passengers.

Regent Seven Seas Cruises (02380 682280, www.rssc.co.uk) claims to offer "six-star" luxury – all its cabins are suites with balconies, and there are no more than 700 guests on luxurious cruises worldwide.

Royal Caribbean International (0800 018 2020, www.royalcaribbean.co.uk) has 20 ships, including *Freedom of the Seas*, the world's biggest, which even offers on-board surfing! The giant US line is based in Florida, with cruises worldwide.

Saga Cruises (0800 505030, www.saga.co.uk) caters for the 50-plus market; very British, predominantly ex-Southampton worldwide cruises; also river cruises, and the new *Spirit of Adventure* for over 21s.

SeaDream Yacht Club (0800 783 1373, www.seadreamyachtclub.com) operates two large, luxurious yachts for couples wanting casual, no black tie, upmarket cruising in the Med and Caribbean.

Silversea Cruises (0870 333 7050, www.silversea.com) offers upmarket, expensive cruises, champagne on tap, and no signing for drinks on four small ships worldwide.

Star Clippers (01473 292029, www.starclippers.co.uk) offers three tall clipper ships, the largest fully rigged sailing ships afloat, with itineraries in the Mediterranean, Far East and Caribbean.

Star Cruises (020 7591 8225, www.starcruises.com) has ten ships based around Asia; most cruises are in that region, out of Singapore, but it also operates in the Med.

Swan Hellenic (0845 355 5111, www.swanhellenic.com) is an upmarket outfit famed for cultural tours, but is ceasing operations in April 2007.

Thomson Cruises (0870 550 2555, www.thomsoncruises.co.uk), part of the giant TUI holiday group, has five ships offering cruises around the Med and northern Europe.

Voyages of Discovery (01444 462150, www.voyagesofdiscovery.com) offers cultural and historical cruises around the eastern Med, Red and Black Seas, plus long haul destinations including the Pacific, Antarctica and the Caribbean, with expert guest lecturers.

Windstar Cruises (020 7940 4488, www.windstarcruises.com), smaller, sail-assisted ships aimed at a more adventurous clientele.

The Yachts of Seabourn (0845 070 0500, www.seabourn.com) has three luxury, upmarket cruise ships sailing worldwide.

Cargo ships

It's possible to travel as passengers on some of the freight ships that carry cargo worldwide: you may find yourself at sea for up to a month. There are very few other passengers or organised activities, but food and accommodation is of a high standard – just the trip to write your novel!

Andrew Weir Shipping (020 7575 6480, www.aws.co.uk) offers cruises on working freight ships, including cruises on the Royal Mail Ship St Helena (www.rms-st-helena.com) to the Atlantic islands of St Helena and Ascension.

The Cruise People (020 7723 2450, www.cruisepeople.co.uk) also books conventional cruises.

Strand Voyages (020 7766 8220, www.strandtravel.co.uk) is a traditional cruise agent that also specialises in booking passengers on to cargo ships.

River cruises

Assam Bengal Navigation (020 8995 3642, www.assambengalnavigation.com) offers cruises on the Brahmaputra river in eastern India.

Cosmos Tourama (0800 083 9837, www.cosmostourama.co.uk) has a large river cruise programme plus a worldwide programme of escorted coach tours.

European Waterways (01784 482439, www.gobarging.com) offers luxury barge cruises with fine food and cultural visits.

Orient-Express Cruises (020 7805 5100, www.orient-express.com) runs cruises on the Irrawaddy river in Burma and on the inland waters of France.

Page & Moy (0870 010 6230, www.page-moy.com) offers both river and ocean cruising; its sister company Just You (0800 915 8000, www.justyou.co.uk) claims to be the first company to charter an entire ship for single travellers.

Peter Deilmann (020 7436 2931, www.peterdeilmannrivercruises.co.uk) operates ten river cruisers on Europe's great rivers, such as the Danube, Moselle, Rhone and Rhine.

Travel Renaissance Holidays (0870 850 1690, **www.travelrenaissance.com**), cruises across Europe, especially down the Rhine and the Danube, plus some long-haul such as the Yangtze in China and the backwaters of southern India.

Viking (020 7752 0000, **www.vikingrivercruises. com**) operates 24 vessels on the rivers of Europe and Russia.

Boating holidays

Anglo Welsh Waterways Holidays (0117 304 1122, **www.anglowelsh.co.uk**) offers comfortable narrow boat short breaks and holidays for up to twelve people per boat.

Black Prince Narrowboat Holidays (01527 575115, **www.black-prince.com**) offers comfortable canal holidays in the UK.

Blakes Holiday Boating (0870 220 2498, **www.blakes.co.uk**) has a wide selection of boating holidays in Britain and abroad.

Crown Blue Line (0870 428 7119, **www.crownblueline.com**) offers river and canal boat trips on inland waterways across Europe.

RESPONSIBLE TOURISM

GENERAL INFORMATION

The Association of Independent Tour Operators (Aito), 020 8744 9280, **www.aito.co.uk**

The Foreign & Commonwealth Office, **www.fco.gov.uk/knowbeforeyougo**

Green Globe, **www.greenglobe.org**

Green Tourism Business Scheme, 01738 632162, **www.green-business.co.uk**

Greenstop, **www.greenstop.net**

The International Ecotourism Society, 001 202 347 9203, **www.ecotourism.org**

The International Tourism Partnership, 020 7467 3620, **www.internationaltourismpartnership.org**

RESPONSIBLE TOURISM SPECIALISTS

Discovery Initiatives, 01285 643333, **www.discoveryinitiatives.co.uk**

Ecoclub, **www.ecoclub.com**

EcoEscapes, 020 7384 1682, **www.ecoescapes.co.uk**

Ecotravel, **www.ecotravel.com**

Ethical Escape, 01244 570336, **www.ethicalescape.co.uk**

Exodus, 0870 240 5550, **www.exodus.co.uk**

Explore, 0870 333 4001, **www.explore.co.uk**

Green Hotels Association, **www.greenhotels.com**

Guerba, 01373 826611, **www.guerba.co.uk**

The Independent Traveller, 01628 522772, **www.independenttraveller.com**

Natural Discovery, 0845 458 2799, **www.naturaldiscovery.co.uk**

Responsibletravel.com, 0870 005 2836, **www.responsibletravel.com**

Travelroots, 020 8341 2262, **www.travelroots.com**

VOLUNTEER AND FUND-RAISING HOLIDAYS

The Adventure Company, 0870 794 1009, **www.adventurecompany.co.uk**

Biosphere Expeditions, 0870 446 0801, **www.biosphere-expeditions.org**

British Trust for Conservation Volunteers,
01302 572244, **www.btcv.org.uk**

Charity Challenge, 020 8557 0000,
www.charitychallenge.com

Coral Cay Conservation, 0870 750 0668,
www.coralcay.org

The Different Travel Company, 02380 669903,
www.different-travel.com

Discover Adventure, 01722 718444,
www.discoveradventure.com

The Earthwatch Institute, 01865 318838,
www.earthwatch.org

Global Vision International, 0870 608 8898,
www.gvi.co.uk

Go Differently, 01799 521950,
www.godifferently.com

Hands Up Holidays, 0800 783 3554,
www.handsupholidays.com

Imaginative Traveller, 0800 316 2717,
www.imaginative-traveller.com

i-to-i, 0800 011 1156,
www.i-to-i.com

National Trust Working Holidays, 0870 429 2429,
www.nationaltrust.org.uk/volunteering

North South Travel, 01245 608291,
www.northsouthtravel.co.uk

People and Places, 01795 535718,
www.travel-peopleandplaces.co.uk

Saga, 0800 096 0084,
www.saga.co.uk

Scientific Exploration Society, 01747 853353,
www.ses-explore.org

VSO, 020 8780 7200,
www.vso.org.uk

CAMPAIGNS AND ECOLOGICAL ADVICE

Animal welfare

Born Free, 01403 240170,
www.bornfree.org.uk

Friends of Conservation, 020 7603 5024,
www.foc-uk.com

International Fund for Animal Welfare,
020 7587 6700, **www.ifaw.org**

The Travel Foundation, 0117 927 3049,
www.thetravelfoundation.org.uk

Travel Operators for Tigers, 01285 643333,
www.toftiger.org

Whale and Dolphin Conservation Society,
0870 870 0027, **www.wdcs.org**

World Wide Fund for Nature,
01483 426444, **www.wwf-uk.org**

Climate care

Airport Watch,
www.airportwatch.org.uk

Atmosfair,
www.atmosfair.de

The Carbon Neutral Company, 0870 199 9988,
www.carbonneutral.com

Carbon Planet,
www.carbonplanet.com

Choose Climate,
http://chooseclimate.org/flying/

Climate Care, 01865 207000,
www.climatecare.org

CO2 Balance,
www.co2balance.com

EU Emissions Trading Scheme,
www.uketg.com

Flight Pledge,
www.flightpledge.org.uk

My Climate,
www.myclimate.co.uk

Pledge Against Airport Expansions,
www.airportpledge.org.uk

Stop Climate Chaos, 020 7324 4750,
www.stopclimatechaos.org

TerraPass,
www.terrapass.com

Conservation

Blue Flag beaches,
www.blueflag.org

Golf Environment Europe, 01620 850659,
www.golfenvironmenteurope.org

Friends of Conservation, 020 7603 5024,
www.foc-uk.com

Friends of the Earth, 0808 800 1111,
www.foe.co.uk

Green Coast Awards, 01646 681949,
www.keepwalestidy.org

Greenpeace, 020 7865 8100,
www.greenpeace.org.uk

Keep Scotland Beautiful,
www.keepscotlandbeautiful.org.

The Marine Conservation Society, 01989 566017,
www.goodbeachguide.co.uk

National Trust for Ireland,
www.cleancoastireland.org

The Scottish Golf Course Wildlife Group,
www.scottishgolf.com/environment

Seaside Awards, 01942 612618,
www.seasideawards.org.uk

Fair trade and treatment of workers

Brighter Futures,
www.brighterfutures.biz

Fair Trade in Tourism South Africa,
www.fairtourismsa.org.za

International Porter Protection Group (IPPG),
www.ippg.net

Tourism Concern "Sun, Sea, Sand and Sweatshops" campaign,
www.tourismconcern.org.uk/campaigns/ssss.html

Human rights

Amnesty International, 020 7033 1500,
www.amnesty.org.uk
The Burma Campaign UK, 020 7324 4710,
www.burmacampaign.org.uk
The Free Burma Coalition,
www.freeburmacoalition.org
Free Tibet Campaign, 020 7324 4605,
www.freetibet.org
Friends of Maldives, 01722 504330,
www.friendsofmaldives.org
Tourism Concern, 020 7133 3330,
www.tourismconcern.org.uk

Water

British Waterways,
www.waterscape.com
British Waterways London, 020 7985 7200,
www.britishwaterwayslondon.co.uk
Broads, 01603 610734,
www.broads-authority.gov.uk
Drifters Waterway Holidays, 0845 762 6252,
www.drifters.co.uk
Environment Agency,
www.environment-agency.gov.uk
Scottish Environmental Protection Agency,
www.sepa.org.uk
Surfers Against Sewage, 0845 458 3001,
www.sas.org.uk
Waterways Trust, 01452 318220,
www.thewaterwaystrust.co.uk
www.waterwaysholidaysuk.com

Crime

End Child Prostitution, Child Pornography and
Trafficking of Children for Sexual Purposes
(ECPAT), 020 7233 9887,
www.ecpat.org.uk; see also
www.child-safe.org.uk and www.thecode.org
Fair Trials Abroad, 01223 319009,
www.fairtrialsabroad.org
Prisoners Abroad, 020 7561 6820,
www.prisonersabroad.org.uk

Claiming compensation

Abta, 020 7637 2444,
www.abta.com
Air Transport Users' Council, 020 7240 6061,
www.auc.org.uk
Aito, 020 8744 9280,
www.aito.co.uk
England and Wales Court service,
www.courtservice.gov.uk
Scottish Court Service,
www.scotcourts.gov.uk
Holiday Travel Watch, 0121 747 8100,
www.holidaytravelwatch.co.uk

Emergency cash

Western Union, 0800 833833,
www.westernunion.co.uk
Travelex, 0870 240 5405,
www.travelex.co.uk
MoneyGram, 00800 8971 8971,
www.postoffice.co.uk
CPP, 0870 120 1251,
www.cpp.co.uk
Sentinel, 0800 414717,
www.sentinelcardprotection.com

House sitters

Absentia, 01279 777412,
www.home-and-pets.co.uk
Animal Aunts, 01730 821529,
www.animalaunts.co.uk
Home and Pet Care, 016974 78515,
www.homeandpetcare.co.uk
The Home Service, 0845 130 3100,
www.housesitters.co.uk
Homesitters, 01296 630730,
www.homesitters.co.uk
Minders Keepers, 01763 262102,
www.minders-keepers.co.uk
National Association of Registered Petsitters,
0870 350 0543, recorded info 0870 950 4030,
www.dogsit.com
Universal Aunts, 020 7738 8937,
www.universalaunts.co.uk

Mobile phones

easyMobile, 0845 612 4500,
www.easymobile.com
O2, 0870 521 4000,
www.o2.co.uk
Orange, 07973 100150,
www.orange.co.uk
T-Mobile, 0845 412 5000,
www.t-mobile.co.uk
Vodafone, 0800 068 6695,
www.vodafone.co.uk
Nokia phone, unlock it via
www.unlock123.com

SIM card services

0044, 0870 950 0044,
www.0044.co.uk
uk2abroad, 0870 922 0825,
www.uk2abroad.com
Gosim,
www.gosim.com
Sim4travel, 0870 126 4879,
www.sim4travel.co.uk

Phone cards

1st Phone Cards, 0845 123 5858,
www.1st-phonecards.co.uk
Planet Phone Cards, 0870 145 1016,
www.planetphonecards.com

Mobile tariffs and protection

Carphone Warehouse, 0800 925925,
www.carphonewarehouse.com
Cellhire, 0800 610610,
www.cellhire.co.uk .
eKit,
www.ekit.com
GSM World,
www.gsmworld.com
Office of Communications,
www.ofcom.org.uk/advice/mobile_abroad/
One Compare,
www.onecompare.com
Spinvox, 0870 033 7300,
www.spinvox.com
Steve Kropla's Help for World Travellers,
www.kropla.com

MONEY AND CREDIT CARDS

Foreign currency

American Express, 0870 600 1060,
www.americanexpress.co.uk
Barclays, 0845 600 8090,
www.barclays.co.uk
International Currency Exchange, 01455 897801,
www.currency-express.com
Marks & Spencer Money, 0870 600 3502,
www.marksandspencer.com/travelmoney

Nationwide, 0870 010 0719,
www.nationwide.co.uk
The Post Office, 0845 722 3344,
www.postoffice.co.uk
Thomas Cook, 0870 010 2913,
www.thomascook.com
Travelex, 0870 240 5405,
www.travelex.co.uk
TTT Moneycorp, 0800 393967,
www.ttt.co.uk

Credit and debit cards

www.cardwatch.org.uk
www.chipandpin.co.uk
www.maestrocard.com
www.mastercard.com
www.moneysupermarket.com
www.visaeurope.com

Pre-paid cash cards

American Express Traveller's Cheque Card, 0800
085 0023, www.americanexpress.co.uk/tcc
International Currency Exchange's Cash2Go card,
01296 380030, www.cash2go.com
Post Office, 0845 722 3344,
www.postoffice.co.uk
Travelex, 0870 240 5405,
www.travelex.co.uk
Western Union Travel Cash Card, 020 8535 7000,
www.wutcc.co.uk

TRAVEL INSURANCE

Association of British Insurers, 020 7216 7455,
www.abi.org.uk
Association of British Travel Agents,
020 7307 1907, www.abta.com
British Insurance Brokers Association,
0870 950 1790, www.biba.org.uk
Financial Ombudsman Service, 0845 080 1800,
www.financial-ombudsman.org.uk
Foreign & Commonwealth Office,
0845 850 2829, www.fco.gov.uk

Insurance price comparison sites

www.find.co.uk/insurance
www.gapyear.com/travelinsurance
www.insuresupermarket.com

Insurance companies

The AA, 0800 085 7240,
www.theaa.com
Accomplish, 0845 230 1082,
www.accomplishtravel.co.uk
Admiral, 0870 225 9122,
www.admiraltravelinsurance.com)
Age Concern, 0845 601 2234,
www.ageconcern.org.uk
American Express, 0800 028 7573,
www.americanexpress.co.uk

Asda 0845 300 7131,
 www.asdafinance.com
Boots, 0870 730 3344,
 www.boots.com
Bradford & Bingley, 0800 169 4078,
 www.bradford-bingley.co.uk
Brunsdon, 01452 623623,
 www.brunsdon.co.uk
Churchill Insurance, 0800 026 4050,
 www.churchill.com
CIS, 0845 746 4646,
 www.cis.co.uk
Club Direct, 0800 083 2466,
 www.clubdirect.com
Columbus Direct, 0870 033 9988,
 www.columbusdirect.com
Direct Line, 0845 246 8704,
 www.directline.com
Direct Travel Insurance, 0845 605 2500,
 www.direct-travel.co.uk
Dogtag, 0870 036 4824,
 www.dogtag.co.uk
E&L, 0870 402 2710,
 www.eandl.co.uk
Endsleigh, 0800 028 3571,
 www.endsleigh.co.uk
Essential Travel, 0870 343 0024,
 www.essentialtravel.co.uk
Esure, 0845 600 3950,
 www.esure.com
Extrasure, 0870 850 6090,
 www.extrasureonline.co.uk
Flexicover, 0879 990 9292,
 www.flexicover.com
Free Spirit, 0845 230 5000,
 www.free-spirit.com
Go Travel Insurance, 0870 421 1521,
 www.gotravelinsurance.co.uk
Golfplan, 0800 591834,
 www.golfplan.co.uk
GolfSafe, 020 8542 1116,
 www.golfsafe.net
Gosure, 0845 222 0020,
 www.gosure.com
Help the Aged, 0800 413180,
 www.helptheaged.org.uk
Insurancebookers,
 www.insurancebookers.com
Insure and Go, 0870 901 3674,
 www.insureandgo.com
J&M Insurance, 01992 566924,
 www.jmi.co.uk
Leading Edge, 0870 112 8099,
 www.leadedge.co.uk
Marks and Spencer Money, 0800 068 3918,
 www.marksandspencer.com
MediCover, 0870 735 3600,
 www.medi-cover.co.uk

MRL Insurance Direct, 0870 876 7677,
 www.mrlinsurance.co.uk
Nationwide, 0500 302016,
 www.nationwide.co.uk
NatWest, 0800 051 5401,
 www.natwest.com
Netcover Direct,
 www.netcoverdirect.com
Norwich Union Direct, 0800 121007,
 www.norwichuniondirect.co.uk
NW Brown, 0870 774 3760,
 www.freedominsure.co.uk
Orbis Insurance Services, 01424 220110,
 www.orbis-insure.co.uk
Photoguard, 02476 851030,
 www.photoguard.co.uk
Post Office, 0800 169 9999,
 www.postoffice.co.uk/travelinsurance
Preferential, 0870 600 7766,
 www.preferential.com
Primary Insurance, 0870 220 0634,
 www.primaryinsurance.co.uk
Prudential, 0800 300300,
 www.pru.co.uk
RAC, 0800 550055,
 www.rac.co.uk
RIAS, 0800 068 1655,
 www.rias.co.uk
Saga, 0800 056 5464,
 www.saga.co.uk
Sainsbury's Bank, 0845 300 3190,
 www.sainstravel.co.uk
Simple, 0870 444 3778,
 www.simpletravelinsurance.co.uk
Ski Club of Great Britain, 0870 075 9759,
 www.skiclub.co.uk
STA Travel, 0870 160 0599,
 www.statravel.co.uk
Swiftcover, 0870 484 0100,
 www.swiftcover.com
Travel Insurance Agency, 020 8446 5414,
 www.travelinsurers.com
Travel Insurance Web,
 www.travelinsuranceweb.com
Travelplan Direct, 0870 774 4177,
 www.travelplandirectinsurance.com
Travsure, 01635 860505,
 www.travsure.co.uk
Worldwide Travel Insurance Services,
 0870 112 8100, **www.worldwideinsure.com**

Travelling with pets

Dogs Away, 020 8441 9311,
 www.dogsaway.co.uk
Passports for Pets, 020 7589 6404,
 http://freespace.virgin.net/passports.forpets/
Pet Planet,
 www.petplanet.co.uk

Pet Travel Scheme, 0870 241 1710,
www.defra.gov.uk

Passports, customs and immigration

Convention on International Trade in Endangered
Species of Wild Fauna and Flora (CITES),
www.cites.org; CITES UK, www.ukcites.gov.uk
Customs & Excise, 0845 010 9000; +44 20 8929
0152 from outside UK, www.hmrc.gov.uk
Department for Environment, Food and Rural
Affairs (Defra), 0845 933 5577, +44 20 7238
6951 from outside the UK, www.defra.gov.uk
Department of Health,
www.dh.gov.uk/travellers
Direct Gov (Health),
www.direct.gov.uk.
European Health Insurance Card, 0845 605 0707,
www.ehic.org.uk
Foreign & Commonwealth Office, 0845 850 2829,
www.fco.gov.uk/knowbeforeyougo
Identity and Passport Service, 0870 521 0410,
www.ips.gov.uk

Visas

Gold Arrow, 0870 165 7412,
www.goldarrow.info
Thames Consular, 020 7494 4957, 020 8995 2492,
www.thamesconsular.com
Travcour, 020 7223 5295,
www.travcour.com
Trailfinders, 0845 058 5858,
www.trailfinders.co.uk
Visa Express, 0906 160 8472,
www.visaexpress.co.uk
The Visa Service, 0870 890 0185,
www.visaservice.co.uk

US visa information

www.usembassy.org.uk
www.dhs.gov/us-visit.
www.usembassy.org.uk/dhs/cbp/i94.html

HEALTH AND SAFETY

Equipment

Carbon Monoxide and Gas Safety Society,
www.co-gassafety.co.uk
Catch 22, 01942 511820,
www.catch22products.co.uk
IdentiKids, 0845 125 9539,
www.identifyme.co.uk
Lifesystems, 0118 981 1433,
www.lifesystems.co.uk
Teaching-aids At Low Cost, 01727 853869,
www.talcuk.org
TravelPharm, 01395 233771,
www.travelpharm.com
Young Explorers, 01789 414791,
www.youngexplorers.co.uk

First aid courses

British Red Cross, 0870 170 9222,
www.redcross.org.uk/firstaid
St John Ambulance, 0870 010 4950,
www.sja.org.uk

Health and hygiene information

CheckSafetyFirst,
www.checksafetyfirst.com
Royal Society for the Prevention of Accidents
(RoSPA), www.rospa.co.uk
Holiday Which?,
www.which.co.uk

Medical services

Blood Care Foundation,
01403 262652, www.bloodcare.org.uk
International Association for Medical Assistance
to Travellers, 001 716 754 4883, www.iamat.org
Medex, 01273 223002,
www.medexassist.com

Travel health advice

Bradt Guides,
www.bradtguides.com
Cancer Research UK,
www.cancerresearchuk.org
Center for Disease Control,
www.cdc.gov/travel
Fit for Travel,
www.fitfortravel.scot.nhs.uk
Foreign & Commonwealth Office,
www.fco.gov.uk/travel
International Society for Travel Medicine,
www.istm.org
Malaria Hot Spots,
www.malariahotspots.co.uk

National Travel Health Network and Centre,
www.nathnac.org
Net Doctor,
www.netdoctor.co.uk/travel/
Travel Health Online,
www.tripprep.com
World Health Organization,
www.who.int

Travel health clinics

E-med, 020 7806 4028,
www.e-med.co.uk
Fleet Street Clinic, 020 7353 5678,
www.travellers-health.info
Hospital for Tropical Diseases, London,
appointments 020 7388 9600, recorded,
country-specific advice , 020 7950 7799,
www.thehtd.org
Liverpool School of Tropical Medicine,
appointments 0151 708 9393, country-specific
and general travel health advice 0906 701 0095,
www.liv.ac.uk/lstm
Malaria Reference Laboratory, London,
0906 550 8908, **www.malaria-reference.co.uk**
Medical Advisory Services for Travellers,
0906 822 4100, **www.masta.org**
Nomad Travellers' Store and Medical Centre,
0906 863 3414, **www.nomadtravel.co.uk**
Trailfinders, 020 7938 3999,
www.trailfinders.com

Personal safety

Advice for women,
www.journeywoman.com
Australian government advice,
www.smarttraveller.gov.au
Canadian government advice,
www.voyage.gc.ca
Foreign & Commonwealth, 0845 850 2829,
www.fco.gov.uk/travel; www.gogapyear.com
Objective Travel Safety, 01788 899029,
www.objectivegapyear.com
PlanetWise, 0870 200 0220,
www.planetwise.net
Red 24, 020 8080 0220,
www.red24.info
The Suzy Lamplugh Trust, 020 7091 0014,
www.suzylamplugh.org
US government travel advice,
http://travel.state.gov

LIFESTYLE

GEAR AND EQUIPMENT

For clothes, luggage and travel accessories.

Active Travel Apparel (0845 450 6424,
www.activetravelapparel.com) sells a wide
range of travel gear
Antler (0161 762 5000,
www.antler.co.uk) for luggage
Berghaus (0191 516 5600,
www.berghaus.co.uk) makes clothing and
equipment
Bill Amberg (020 7727 3560,
www.billamberg.com) makes elegant,
masculine luggage
Blacks Outdoor Group (0800 056 0127,
www.blacks.co.uk) is a chain of shops selling a
wide range of equipment
Boots (**www.boots.com**) and other chemists sell
lots of useful travel gear, including ear plugs,
sunscreen, travel wash and mosquito repellent
Brasher Boot Company (0191 516 5770,
www.brasher.co.uk) sells the popular boot
Catch 22 (01942 511820,
www.catch22products.co.uk) offers gadgets
and travel gear
Columbia Sportswear (0118 922 0130,
www.columbia.com) makes a wide range of
clothes and equipment
Cotswold Outdoor (0870 442 7755,
www.cotswoldoutdoor.com) – huge range of
outdoor gear
Craghoppers (0870 220 6604,
www.craghoppers.co.uk) makes clothes and
gear for outdoor types
Delsey (020 8731 3530, **www.delsey.com**) for
luggage and travel accessories
Eagle Creek (**www.eaglecreek.com**) for bags,
rucksacks and packing aids
Edward Bates of Jermyn St (020 7734 2722,
www.bates-hats.co.uk) for hats that fit
Ellis Brigham Mountain Sport
(**www.ellis-brigham.com**) has mountaineering,
walking and winter sports gear
Field and Trek (0870 777 1071,
www.fieldandtrek.com), stores selling outdoor
gear
First Ascent (01629 580484,
www.firstascent.co.uk) is the UK distributor
for several specialist equipment lines, including
Platypus, Eagle Creek and Therm-A-Rest
Gerber (**www.gerberblades.com**) for knives
Itchy Feet (01225 442618, **www.itchyfeet.com**)
sells a wide range of equipment online or
through its shops in Bath and London

Jack Wolfskin (015394 35253,
www.jack-wolfskin.com), a German firm that
makes a wide range of outdoor gear
Karrimor (01254 893000, www.karrimor.com)
makes equipment including rucksacks
Kathmandu (www.kathmandu.co.uk) sells a wide
range of gear through its shops in Bristol and
London, but not online
Leatherman (01539 721032
www.leatherman.co.uk) for knives
Lowe Alpine (www.lowealpine.com) makes
clothing and equipment
Magellan's (0870 600 1601,
www.magellans.co.uk), the UK sales arm of
the US travel gear company
Maglite (www.maglite.com) makes hard-wearing
torches
Mandarina Duck (020 7495 8200,
www.mandarinaduck.com) for travel bags
Milletts (0800 389 5861, www.milletts.co.uk)
supplies outdoor gear through its high street
shops
Nomad Travel Stores (020 8889 7014,
www.nomadtravel.co.uk) sells a wide range
of equipment and clothing, and also has travel
health clinics for vaccinations and advice
The North Face (www.thenorthface.com) makes
a wide range of gear
Ortlieb (01539 625493, www.ortlieb.de),
waterproof bags and other gear
Outdoor Accessories (0870 382 5089,
www.outdooraccessories.co.uk) sells a wide
range of equipment online
Petzl (www.petzl.com) produces LED torches
Rohan (0870 601 2244, www.rohan.co.uk) makes
clothing for travellers
Safariquip (01433 620320,
www.safariquip.co.uk) sells travel and
expedition equipment, by mail order, online or
at its shop in Castleton, Derbyshire
Safe Skies (www.safeskies.locks.org), for TSA-
approved luggage locks
Samsonite (www.samsonite.com) for luggage
and accessories
Silva (01506 406277, www.silva.se) makes
excellent compasses
Snow + Rock (01483 445335,
www.snowandrock.com), a chain of outdoor
equipment shops
Teva (www.teva.com) for footwear and
accessories
Thaw (01668 283300, www.thawonline.co.uk),
outdoor clothes designed for women
Therm-a-Rest (www.thermarest.com) for
camping mats
Tilley (0800 374353, http://tilleyuk.com), hats
and other outdoor equipment

Travel Sentry (www.travelsentry.org) for TSA-
approved luggage locks
Travelling Light (0845 330 3777,
www.travellinglight.com) makes clothes for
travelling in hot climates
Tumi (0800 783 6570, www.tumi.com) for stylish
luggage
Vango (01475 746000, www.vango.co.uk) for
rucksacks, tents and other gear
Victorinox (www.victorinox.com) for classic
Swiss Army knives
Wenger (www.wenger-knife.ch) for classic Swiss
Army knives
Young Explorers (01789 414791,
www.youngexplorers.co.uk) – outdoor kit
for kids

FAMILY HOLIDAYS
General information
www.babygoes2.com
www.family-travel.co.uk
www.kidsintow.co.uk
www.takethefamily.com

Family holiday specialists
Most operators listed later in this directory offer
family holidays; this is a selection of specialists.

Club Med, 0845 367 6767,
www.clubmed.co.uk
Esprit, 01252 618300,
www.esprit-holidays.co.uk
Mark Warner, 0870 770 4227,
www.markwarner.co.uk
Neilson, 0870 333 3356,
www.neilson.com
Powder Byrne, 020 8246 5300,
www.powderbyrne.co.uk
Quo Vadis?, 01279 639600,
www.quovadistravel.co.uk
Scott Dunn, 020 8682 5010,
www.scottdunn.co.uk
Sunsail, 0870 777 0313,
www.sunsail.com/clubs

Family adventure specialists
The Adventure Company, 0870 794 1009,
www.adventurecompany.co.uk
Cox & Kings, 020 7873 5000,
www.coxandkings.co.uk
Dragoman, 01728 861133,
www.dragoman.com
Exodus, 0870 240 5550,
www.exodus.co.uk
Explore, 0870 333 4001,
www.explore.co.uk
Imaginative Traveller, 0800 316 2717,
www.imaginative-family.com

Walks Worldwide, 01524 242000,
   www.walksworldwide.com

UK activity holidays

Acorn Adventure, 0870 121 9950,
   www.acornadventure.co.uk
Adventure Activities Licensing Authority,
   02920 755715, www.aala.org.uk
The British Activity Holiday Association,
   020 8842 1292, www.baha.org.uk
Camp Beaumont, 0870 499 8787,
   www.campbeaumont.co.uk
EAC Activity Camps, 0845 113 0022,
   www.activitycamps.com
The Family Holiday Association, 020 7436 3304,
   www.familyholidayassociation.org.uk
PGL Adventure, 0870 055 1551, www.pgl.co.uk
Wickedly Wonderful, 07941 231168,
   www.wickedlywonderful.com

GAP–YEAR TRAVEL

Over the past few years, there has been an
explosion in the number of older travellers taking
career-break trips, and more recently we've seen
an increasing number of families taking gap years.
Currently, *Times Travel* is serialising the tales of a
London family with three children under ten who
are travelling the world for a year.

It takes passion, guts and determination to
organise a gap year or career break, whatever
your age or circumstances. Before you travel,
it's essential to think about both the trip itself
and your life back home. For many, particularly
younger people, a gap year consists of travelling
with no particular aim in mind other than to see
the world. I did that for several months in Asia,
and it was wonderful – you have time to see
places properly, even though you're on a budget.

But increasingly, long-term travellers want to
spend at least part of their trip on a project or
placement, such as teaching English, mapping
a forest or saving turtles. My gap year saw me
teaching music in a school in north India. As I
had been taken on as an English teacher, and
my music qualifications were limited to Grade V
Piano (failed), it came as a surprise to all of us,
and taught me plenty about thinking on my feet,
if nothing else.

Questions to ask include: will you, and the host
community, benefit from the project? What skills
will it give you? How much of the money you
must raise will help the project, rather than line
the pockets of the organisers? Are you properly
supported while you're in the field, and are
you insured? What about your personal safety,
especially if you decide to travel alone? (For
advice on this, *see* chapter 10.)

It's also essential to consider matters back home.

Should you rent out your house, ask for your
job to be kept open, sell your car? What about
pension contributions, insurance, applying for a
new job on your return? Use the listings here for
suggestions of the sort of trip you might take,
and consult "Further information", below, for
books and websites to help you make your choice
and tie up the practical ends.

Gap–year specialists

Africa & Asia Venture (01380 729009,
   www.aventure.co.uk) offers mostly teaching
   programmes for 18 to 24-year-olds in Africa,
   India and Mexico.
Africa Conservation Experience (0870 241 5816,
   www.conservationafrica.net) gives the
   opportunity to be involved in conservation in
   South Africa.
Blue Ventures (020 8341 9819,
   www.blueventures.org) works on marine
   projects in Madagascar, open to all ages.
British Trust for Conservation Volunteers
   (01302 572244, www.btcv.org.uk) offers
   conservation work in the UK and overseas.
BSES Expeditions (020 7591 3141,
   www.bses.org.uk) runs scientific expeditions to
   remote areas for 16 to 23-year-olds.
BUNAC (020 7251 3472, www.bunac.org)
   offers gap year and volunteer opportunities
   worldwide, including summer camp counselling
   in the USA.
Camp America (020 7581 7373,
   www.campamerica.co.uk) sends young people
   to work in summer camps across the USA.
Changing Worlds (01892 770000,
   www.changingworlds.co.uk) offers three- to
   six-month placements worldwide.
Community Service Volunteers (0800 374991,
   www.csv.org.uk) provides volunteer placements
   across the UK.
Coral Cay Conservation (0870 750 0668,
   www.coralcay.org) runs marine conservation
   projects worldwide for volunteers of all ages.
Earthwatch (01865 318838,
   www.earthwatch.org) runs research and
   conservation projects worldwide, offering work
   as scientists' assistants.
Frontier (020 7613 2422, www.frontier.ac.uk)
   runs conservation and development projects
   worldwide.
GAP Activity Projects (0118 959 4914,
   www.gap.org.uk) supplies voluntary
   placements in 27 countries worldwide for
   school leavers.
Gapguru (0800 032 3350, www.gapguru.com)
   runs projects across India.
Gap Sports (0870 837 9797, www.gapsports.com)
   offers sports and other projects worldwide, plus
   ski/snowboarder courses.

Global Vision International (0870 608 8898, **www.gvi.co.uk**) runs expeditions and conservation projects worldwide.

Greenforce (020 7470 8888, **www.greenforce.org**) runs marine and other conservation projects worldwide.

i-to-i (0800 011 1156, **www.i-to-i.com**) runs volunteer programmes from a week to six months, worldwide.

Inter-Cultural Youth Exchange (020 7681 0983, **www.icye.org.uk**), despite its name, offers volunteer opportunities to 18 to 70-year-olds worldwide.

International Voluntary Service (0131 226 6722, **www.ivs-gb.org.uk**) is a peace organisation running community projects worldwide.

The Leap (01672 519922, **www.theleap.co.uk**) runs volunteer projects worldwide for 18 to 60-year-olds.

Link Overseas Exchange (01382 203192, **www.linkoverseas.org.uk**) offers volunteer placements abroad for 17 to 25-year-olds.

Madventurer (0191 261 1996, **www.madventurer.com**) offers development projects and overland travel worldwide.

MondoChallenge (01604 858225, **www.mondochallenge.org**) runs development programmes in Africa, Asia and South America working and living with local people.

Outreach International (01458 274957, **www.outreachinternational.co.uk**) runs small community projects worldwide.

Outward Bound (0870 513 4227, **www.outwardbound.org**) runs a range of overseas training courses and expeditions.

Project Trust (01879 230444, **www.projecttrust.org.uk**) runs year-long volunteer programmes in 25 countries for school leavers.

Quest Overseas (01444 474744, **www.questoverseas.com**) offers voluntary projects in Africa and South America.

Raleigh International (020 7371 8585, **www.raleighinternational.org**) runs four, seven or ten-week volunteer programmes for young people worldwide.

Real Gap Experience (01892 516164, **www.realgap.co.uk**) offers gap year, volunteering and career break opportunities worldwide, mostly aimed at 18 to 26-year-olds. Its sister company Gap Year for Grown Ups (01892 701881, **www.gapyearforgrownups. co.uk**) offers opportunities for older travellers.

Students Partnership Worldwide (020 7222 0138, **www.spw.org**): young volunteers work on health and environment projects with young people in rural Africa and Asia.

Teaching and Projects Abroad (01903 708300, **www.teaching-abroad.co.uk**): volunteer projects, including teaching English and community work, worldwide.

Travellers Worldwide (01903 502595, **www.travellersworldwide.com**): volunteer projects in 16 countries, from two weeks to a year.

Trekforce (01444 474123, **www.trekforce.org.uk**) offers expeditions and projects in the rainforests of central America and south east Asia.

VentureCo Worldwide (01926 411122, **www.ventureco-worldwide.com**) offers expeditions and volunteer projects of up to 16 weeks.

Voluntary Service Overseas (020 8780 7200, **www.vso.org.uk**) is an international development charity for older volunteers, typically with two-year placements.

World Challenge (020 8728 7272, **www.world-challenge.co.uk**) offers gap placements worldwide of up to nine months.

Worldwide Opportunities on Organic Farms (01273 476286, **www.wwoof.org.uk**) offers work on farms in 43 countries.

Further information

Findagap, **www.findagap.com**

Gap Advice, **www.gapadvice.org**

Gap Work, **www.gapwork.com**

Gapyear, **www.gapyear.com**, run by the gap year-guru Tom Griffiths. Gap Year Directory, **www.gapyeardirectory.co.uk**

Gap Year Show (**www.gapyearshow.co.uk**) sponsored by *The Times*, will be held at Manchester's G-MEX on November 10-11, 2006, and London's ExCel on November 17-18, 2006.

The Year Out Group (01380 816696, **www.yearoutgroup.org**) is an association of 35 companies that offer gap year and volunteering trips. Its website has masses of useful information for anyone planning a trip.

Expedition Advisory Centre (020 7591 3030, **www.rgs.org/eac**), part of the Royal Geographical Society, offers support to those planning adventurous expeditions.

GAY AND LESBIAN TRAVELLERS

Many gay and lesbian holidaymakers are happy to book through mainstream companies, but it can be helpful to book with a specialist if you're looking for a particularly gay scene, or want some advice about how you will be received overseas.

Chris Wright of specialist operator Travelling

Pink explained that he'd heard of gay couples being sent to destinations such as Dubai and the Maldives because the tour operator did not know that homosexuality is illegal there. Some gay holiday companies, such as Respect Holidays, even refuse to take bookings for the United Arab Emirates (which includes Dubai) because of its illiberal attitude to homosexuality. Of course it's perfectly possible for gay travellers to visit these destinations, but open displays of affection will be frowned upon and gay travellers may feel uncomfortable there.

In late 2005, Civil Partnerships became legal in the UK, leading to a rise in the number of gay couples taking honeymoons. The Foreign & Commonwealth Office was even prompted to put out advice to gay travellers (see **www.fco.gov.uk**, click on travel advice, then travel checklists), and the FCO also indicates on the Country Guides on its website those destinations where attitudes to homosexuality are illiberal and where openly gay couples may encounter hostility.

Destinations where gay travellers should be wary when booking holidays include Jamaica – where homophobic incidents have even included the murder of one gay activist – parts of Africa and the Middle East, and parts of Russia and eastern Europe. Conversely, gays are particularly welcome in countries with liberal laws such as Canada, Spain, New Zealand, the UK and Hawaii. Iceland, Bali and Thailand are also welcoming, along with the traditional gay holiday favourites of Mykonos in Greece, Sydney, San Francisco and New York.

Holiday operators

Man Around (020 8902 7177, **www.manaround.com**) is a long-established operator of holidays for gay men.

Olivia (001 800 631 6277, **www.olivia.com**) is a US-based company offering dedicated cruises and resorts for lesbians.

Respect Holidays (0870 770 0169, **www.respect-holidays.co.uk**) offers gay holidays across Europe.

RSVP Vacations (07968 962882, **www.rsvpvacations.com**) offers gay cruises, many in the Caribbean, plus land-based tours.

Travelling Pink (020 8758 4737, **www.travellingpink.com**), part of summer sun operator Sunvil Holidays, offers that company's worldwide programme tailored to the requirements of gay clients.

Walking Women (0845 644 5335, **www.walkingwomen.co.uk**) offers walking holidays in the UK (many in the Lake District) and overseas for both lesbian and heterosexual customers.

Wild Rose (0117 957 4477, **www.wildroseholidays.co.uk**), like Walking Women, is not specifically targeted at the lesbian community; it offers a UK and Europe programme of mostly walking-based activity holidays for women.

Village Travel (0161 236 3007, **www.village-travel.co.uk**) is a Manchester-based travel agency serving the gay and lesbian community.

The International Gay and Lesbian Travel Association (**www.iglta.com**) is based in Florida and offers advice and information, including a directory of gay-friendly holiday operators, though its bias is towards the Americas.

HOLIDAYS FOR DISABLED TRAVELLERS

General information

Holiday Access Direct, **www.holidayaccessdirect.com**

Holidays for All, 01865 432877, **www.holidaysforall.org.uk**

Royal Association for Disability and Rehabilitation, Radar, 020 7250 3222, **www.radar.org.uk**

Tourism for All, 0845 124 9974, **www.tourismforall.org.uk**

All Go Here (**www.allgohere.com**) lists hotels in the UK that cater for disabled guests, and has an airline section that outlines the facilities for the disabled on some of the world's major carriers.

The site **www.everybody.co.uk/airline** lists access arrangements on the major airlines.

Open Doors Organization (**www.opendoorsnfp. org**) has useful advice for disabled travellers to America.

Many tour operator say cruise holidays are well geared up for disabled travellers, with American cruise companies thought to be particularly helpful. For contact details, see page 389.

Specialist operators

Access Travel, 01942 888844, **www.access-travel.co.uk**

Accessible Travel and Leisure, 01452 729739, **www.accessibletravel.co.uk**

Assistance Travel Service, 01708 863198, **www.assistedholidays.com**

Can Be Done, 020 8907 2400, **www.canbedone.co.uk**

Chalfont Line Holidays, 01895 459540, **www.chalfont-line.co.uk**

Enable Holidays, 0871 222 4939, **www.enableholidays.com**

UK specialists

3H Fund, 01892 547474, **www.3hfund.org.uk**

Action for Blind People, 020 7635 4800, **www.afbp.org**

Arthritis Care Hotels, 01865 432877,
www.arthritiscarehotels.org.uk
Break, 01263 822161, www.break-charity.org
British Ski Club for the Disabled, 01747 828515,
www.bscd.org.uk
Calvert Trust, 01598 763221,
www.calvert-trust.org.uk
Caravanning for the Disabled,
www.caravan-sitefinder.co.uk/features/
disabled/
Disaway Trust, 01323 640289,
www.disaway.co.uk
Grooms Holidays, 0845 658 4478,
www.groomsholidays.org.uk
Handicapped Aid Trust, 01253 796441
Holidays with Help, 020 8390 9752,
www.holidayswithhelp.org.uk
Jubilee Sailing Trust, 0870 443 5783,
www.jst.org.uk
Leonard Cheshire, 020 7802 8200,
www.leonard-cheshire.org
National Blind Childrens Society, 01278 764770,
www.nbcs.org.uk
Phab, Physically Disabled and Able Bodied, 020
8667 9443, www.phabengland.org.uk
Vitalise, formerly the Winged Fellowship Trust,
0845 345 1970, www.vitalise.org.uk

LUXURY TRAVEL SERVICES

Concierge services

Quintessentially (0870 850 8585,
www.quintessentially.com) offers personal
concierge services to members such as
organising private jets, yachts or booking the
best hotels and restaurants; from £750pa.
Blossom & Browne's Sycamore (020 8552 1231,
www.blossomandbrowne.co.uk) will collect
your suitcase full of dirty holiday clothes from
any London address and wash and dry clean it
for you.
First Luggage, 0845 270 0670,
www.firstluggage.com
Carry My Luggage, 0845 009 0362,
www.carrymyluggage.com
Both of these companies will organise luggage
transfer to save you carrying your bags on
holiday.

Private yacht brokers

Nigel Burgess, 020 7766 4300,
www.nigelburgess.com
Edmiston, 020 7495 5151,
www.edmistoncompany.com
Camper & Nicholsons, 020 7491 2950,
www.cnconnect.com
Cavendish White, 020 7381 7600,
www.cavendishwhite.com

Avolus (0845 450 1504, www.avolus.com)
allows you to buy blocks of limo, jet, yacht or
helicopter time.
The Whistlejacket Club (01756 799022,
www.thewhistlejacketclub.com) offers you
a fractional share in a 200ft yacht, starting at
£150,000 for ten days' exclusive use per year.
For private jets, see page 420. For luxury tour
operators, see page 416.

HOLIDAYS FOR SINGLE TRAVELLERS

Friendship Travel, 02894 462211,
www.friendshiptravel.com
Just You, 0800 915 8000,
www.justyou.co.uk
Just You, 0800 915 8000,
www.kindredspiritstravel.com
Kuoni, 01306 747008,
www.kuoni.co.uk/singles/
Saga, 0800 414444,
www.saga.co.uk
Solitair Holidays, 0845 123 5515,
www.solitairhols.co.uk
Solos Holidays, 0870 072 0700,
www.solosholidays.co.uk
Speedbreaks, 0845 838 2600,
www.speedbreaks.co.uk
Travel One, 0870 787 5414,
www.travelone.co.uk
www.companions2travel.co.uk
www.holiday41.co.uk
www.someone2travelwith.com
www.soulescape.com.
The Single Travellers Action Group, Church Lane,
Sharnbrook, Bedford MK44 1HR, or email
vivstag1@aol.com (annual subscription £12).
www.travel-companion.net
www.travellersconnected.com
www.wanderlust.co.uk

Single-parent holidays

See also Family Holidays, general advice and
information.
Family Travel,
www.family-travel.co.uk
Gingerbread, 0800 018 4318,
www.gingerbread.org.uk
Holiday Endeavour for Lone Parents,
01302 728791, www.helphols.co.uk
Mango, 01902 373410,
www.mangoholidays.co.uk
One Parent Families, 0800 018 5026
Single Parent Travel Club, 0870 241 6210
Small Families, 01767 650312,
www.smallfamilies.co.uk

PLANNING

GENERAL INFORMATION
Brochure Bank,
 www.brochurebank.co.uk
CIA World Factbook,
 www.cia.gov/cia/publications/factbook/index.html
Craigslist,
 www.craigslist.org
Foreign & Commonwealth Office,
 www.fco.gov.uk,
Holiday Wizard,
 www.holidaywizard.co.uk
Official Travel Guide,
 www.officialtravelguide.com
Online travel brochures,
 www.onlinetravelbrochures.com
Surf2Travel,
 www.surf2travel.com
World Heritage Sites,
 http://whc.unesco.org
World Travel Guide
 www.travel-guides.com

Weather
Metcheck,
 www.metcheck.com,
Times Online,
 www.timesonline.co.uk
Weather 2 Travel,
 www.weather2travel.com
Weather Online,
 www.weatheronline.co.uk

What's on
Bugbog,
 www.bugbog.com
Rough Guides,
 http://worldparty.roughguides.com
What's on When,
 www.whatsonwhen.com

Magazines and newsletters
Action Asia,
 www.actionasia.com
Asia and Away,
 www.asiaandaway.com
Business Traveller,
 www.businesstraveller.com
CNN Traveller,
 www.cnntraveller.com
Coast,
 www.coastmagazine.co.uk
Conde Nast Traveler,
 www.concierge.com/cntraveler

Conde Nast Traveller,
 www.cntraveller.com
Far Flung,
 www.farflungmagazine.com
The Great Outdoors,
 www.tgomagazine.co.uk
Harper's Bazaar,
 www.harpersandqueen.co.uk
Herald Tribune,
 www.iht.com
High Life magazine,
 www.ba.com
Hip Guide,
 www.hipguide.com
Holiday Which?,
 www.which.co.uk
I-escape,
 www.i-escape.com
Islands,
 www.islands.com
National Geographic,
 www.nationalgeographic.com
New York Times,
 www.nytimes.com
Outdoor Enthusiast,
 www.oe-mag.com
Responsible Travel,
 www.responsibletravel.com
Sunday Times Travel,
 www.sundaytimestravel.co.uk
Tatler,
 www.tatler.co.uk
Town & Country Travel,
 www.hearstmags.com
Travel & Leisure,
 www.travelandleisure.com
Travel Africa,
 www.travelafricamag.com
Travel Intelligence,
 www.travelintelligence.net
The Traveller,
 www.traveller.co.uk
Travel Lists,
 www.travel-lists.co.uk
Vanity Fair,
 www.vanityfair.co.uk
Wallpaper*,
 www.wallpaper.com
Wanderlust,
 www.wanderlust.co.uk
World Heritage Sites,
 http://whc.unesco.org

Destination reviews
www.holidaysuncovered.co.uk
www.holidaywatchdog.com
www.holiday-truth.com
www.tripadvisor.co.uk

www.trivago.co.uk
www.virgin.net/travel/resortfinder

Luxury destination reviews

You have to subscribe to several of these.
Andrew Harper's *Hideaway Report*,
 001 512 340 7850, **www.andrewharper.com**
The Gallivanter's Guide,
 www.gallivantersguide.com
LuxuryLink,
 www.luxurylink.com
Nota Bene, 0870 240 4089,
 www.nbreview.com
WOWtravel
 www.kiwicollection.com

TRAVEL SHOWS

The Times Presents Destinations, the Holiday and
 Travel Show, 0870 120 0332,
 www.destinationsshow.com
The Holiday & Travel Show,
 www.holidayshows.com
The Global Adventure Sports + Travel show,
 www.globalsnowshows.co.uk
The Daily Mail Ski and Snowboard Show,
 0870 590 0090, **www.dailymailskishow.co.uk**
The Daily Telegraph Adventure Travel and Sports
 Show, 0870 161 2122,
 www.adventureshow.co.uk
The Ordnance Survey Outdoors Show,
 0870 010 9086, **www.theoutdoorsshow.co.uk**
Dive Shows,
 www.diveshows.co.uk
Cycle Show, 0870 126 1795,
 www.cycleshow.co.uk
Spa Show, 0870 060 6090,
 www.spashow.co.uk
One Life Live, 0870 272 0001,
 www.onelifelive.co.uk
Accessible Holiday Show,
 www.accessibleholidayshow.co.uk
The Luxury Travel Fair, 0870 060 6090,
 www.luxurytravelfair.com

TRAVEL CLUBS

Globetrotters,
 www.globetrotters.co.uk
Royal Geographical Society, 020 7591 3000,
 www.rgs.org
South American Explorers' Club,
 www.saexplorers.org
The Travellers Club,
 020 7930 8688, **www.thetravellersclub.org.uk**
Wexas, 020 7589 3315, **www.wexas.com**

TOURIST BOARDS

The Association of National Tourist Office
Representatives (0870 241 9084,

www.antor.com) can put you in touch with
around 70 tourist offices based in the UK. The
Tourism Offices Worldwide Directory
(**www.towd.com**) is a guide to official tourist
information sources. Also *see* page 5.

GUIDEBOOK PUBLISHERS

The AA,
 www.theaa.com/bookshop
Alastair Sawday's Special Places to Stay,
 www.alastairsawday.co.uk
Armchair Traveller,
 www.hauspublishing.co.uk
Berlitz,
 www.berlitzpublishing.com
Blue Guides,
 www.blueguides.com
Bradt Guides,
 www.bradtguides.com
Bugbooks,
 www.bugbooks.com
Cadogan Guides,
 www.cadoganguides.com
Cicerone,
 www.cicerone.co.uk
Culture Smart Guides,
 www.culturesmartguides.co.uk
Discovery Guides,
 www.walking.demon.co.uk
Dorling Kindersley,
 http://uk.dk.com
The Economist,
 www.economist.com
Eland,
 www.travelbooks.co.uk
Fodor's,
 www.fodors.com
Footprint,
 www.footprintguides.com
Frommer's,
 www.frommers.com
Hedonists' Guides,
 www.ahedonistsguideto.com
In Your Pocket guides,
 www.inyourpocket.com
Insight Guides,
 www.insightguides.com
Let's Go,
 www.letsgo.com
Lonely Planet,
 www.lonelyplanet.com
Luxe City Guides,
 www.luxecityguides.com
Michelin,
 www.michelin.com
Moon Handbooks,
 www.moon.com
National Geographic,

www.nationalgeographic.com
Navigator Guides,
www.navigatorguides.com
Purple Guides,
www.thepurpleguide.com
Rother,
www.rother.de
Rough Guides,
www.roughguides.com
Sunflower,
www.sunflowerbooks.co.uk
Thomas Cook Publishing,
www.thomascookpublishing.com
Time Out,
www.timeout.com
Trailblazer,
www.trailblazer-guides.com
Vacation Work Publications,
www.vacationwork.co.uk

BUYING BOOKS AND MAPS

British Cartographic Society,
www.cartography.org.uk
Daunt Books, 020 7224 2295,
www.dauntbooks.co.uk
Greaves & Thomas, 01983 568555,
www.globemakers.com
Harvey Maps, 01786 841202,
www.harveymaps.co.uk
Latitude Maps and Globes, 01707 663090,
www.latitudemapsandglobes.co.uk
Maps International, 0800 038 6277,
www.mapsinternational.co.uk
Maps Worldwide, 0845 122 0559,
www.mapsworldwide.com
National Map Centre, 020 7222 2466,
www.mapsnmc.co.uk and
www.mapstore.co.uk
Ordnance Survey, 0845 200 2712,
www.ordnancesurvey.co.uk
Oriental and African Books,
01743 352575, www.africana.co.uk
Ramblers' Association, 020 7339 8500,
www.ramblers.org.uk/navigation
Stanfords Map and Travel Bookshop,
020 7836 1321, www.stanfords.co.uk
The Travel Bookshop, 020 7229 5260,
www.thetravelbookshop.co.uk

TOUR OPERATORS

MAINSTREAM TOUR OPERATORS

Most of the companies listed in this category have extensive holiday programmes to destinations worldwide. Their trips range from the cheapest bucket-and-spade bargains to upmarket, luxurious, once-in-a-lifetime breaks.

Many are members of the Federation of Tour Operators (www.fto.co.uk) whose website gives brief information about how the travel industry works in the UK, as well as a summary of what these holiday companies offer.

As I explained in chapter 4, many of these companies are "in bed" with travel agents and airlines: for example, the MyTravel group (www.mytravel.com) includes Airtours Holidays, Manos Holidays, the travel agent Going Places and MyTravel Airways, amongst other brands. It's useful to keep this in mind when consulting a travel agent, so you can be sure you are being offered a wide choice of trips.

Airtours Far & Away, 0870 608 1945
www.airtours.co.uk
Airtours Prestige, 0870 241 5369
www.airtours.co.uk
Airtours Summer Sun, 0870 608 1940
www.airtours.co.uk
Airtours Winter Sun, 0870 241 8900
www.airtours.co.uk
Archers Direct, 0870 460 3894,
www.archersdirect.co.uk
British Airways Holidays, 0870 243 4224,
www.baholidays.com
Club 18–30, 0870 752 0913,
www.club18-30.com
Cosmos, 0870 443 1823,
www.cosmosholidays.co.uk
Cresta, 0870 238 7711,
www.crestaholidays.co.uk
Crystal, 0870 402 0291,
www.crystalholidays.co.uk
Direct Holidays, 0870 242 2404,
www.directholidays.co.uk
Eclipse Direct, 0870 243 0638,
www.eclipsedirect.co.uk
First Choice, 0870 850 3928,
www.firstchoice.co.uk
Inghams, 020 8780 4400,
www.inghams.co.uk
Kuoni, 01306 742222,
www.kuoni.co.uk
Libra Holidays, 0870 242 2525,
www.libraholidays.co.uk
Manos Holidays, 0870 753 0530,
www.manos.co.uk

Neilson, 0870 333 3356,
  www.neilson.com
Olympic Holidays, 0870 429 4242,
  www.olympicholidays.com
Panorama Holidays, 0870 759 5595,
  www.panoramaholidays.co.uk
Sunstart, 0870 850 3928,
  www.firstchoice.co.uk
Thomson Summer Sun, Winter Sun, Platinum,
  Gold and Superfamily programmes,
  0870 242 6043, www.thomson.co.uk
Tradewinds, 0870 609 1340
  www.tradewinds.co.uk
Thomas Cook, JMC and Sunset, 0870 111 1111,
  www.thomascook.com
Thomas Cook Signature, 0870 443 4447,
  www.tcsignature.com
2wentys, 0870 020 2069,
  www.2wentys.co.uk
Virgin Holidays, 0870 220 2788,
  www.virginholidays.co.uk

SUMMER SUN OPERATORS

These companies concentrate mainly on the
Mediterranean. Also consult individual country
specialists, below.

Belleair Holidays (020 8785 3266,
  www.belleairholidays.com), for Malta, Gozo
  and Sicily.
Cachet Travel (020 8847 8700,
  www.cachet–travel.co.uk), Crete and Turkey,
  plus the Greek island of Samos, Madeira, the
  Canary Islands, the Azores and Brazil.
Cadogan (0800 082 1006,
  www.cadoganholidays.com), upmarket hotel-
  based holidays across the Med.
Castaways (01737 812255,
  www.castaways.co.uk), Madeira and Portugal,
  Majorca, Spain and France.
Chevron Air Holidays (0870 062 2292,
  www.chevron.co.uk), Malta and Gozo.
Classic Collection Holidays (01903 823088,
  www.classic–collection.co.uk), hotel-based
  holidays in Spain, Portugal, Italy and Cyprus.
Cricketer Holidays (01892 664242,
  www.brocktravel.co.uk): holidays across the
  Mediterranean, especially Spain, Portugal and
  North Cyprus, plus city breaks in the Baltics, and
  tours in Egypt, Morocco, Iceland, Poland and
  Cuba.
Freelance Holidays (01789 297705,
  www.freelance–holidays.co.uk), villas on
  Majorca, Crete and Sardinia.
French Affair (020 7381 8519,
  www.frenchaffair.com), mostly villas and some
  hotels across France; sister companies offer
  holidays in Spain, Portugal, Corsica, Romania,
  Croatia and South Africa.

Holiday Options (0870 013 0450,
  www.holidayoptions.co.uk), Croatia, Slovenia
  and Montenegro, plus Corsica, Sardinia and
  Sicily and the Cape Verde islands off the coast
  of Senegal.
Ilios Travel (0870 060 0607, www.iliostravel.com),
  upmarket villas in Italy (mostly Tuscany), Turkey,
  Spain and Madeira.
Inntravel (01653 617788, www.inntravel.co.uk),
  wide programme of gentle walking, cycling and
  cultural tours.
Keytel (020 7616 0300, www.keytel.co.uk) is the
  booking agent for paradors in Spain, Portuguese
  pousadas and Chateaux & Hotels de France.
Malta Direct (0845 365 3409,
  www.maltadirect.com), Malta.
The Mediterranean Experience (0870 499 0511,
  www.medexperience.co.uk), luxury
  holidays in the Med.
Perfect Places (0870 366 7567,
  www.perfectplacesholidays.co.uk): Spain,
  Portugal, France, Italy and Croatia.
Planos Holidays (01373 814200,
  www.planos.co.uk) specialises in the Greek
  island of Paxos, Andalusia in Spain, and Slovenia,
  and also has a Caribbean programme.
Prestige Holidays (01425 480400,
  www.prestigeholidays.co.uk), upmarket
  holidays in popular Mediterranean destinations,
  plus Madeira, the Canaries and Morocco.
Simply Travel (0870 166 4979,
  www.simplytravel.com), wide range of
  upmarket villas and classy hideaways.
Simpson Travel (0845 811 6500,
  www.simpsontravel.com), villas and other
  charming properties across the Mediterranean.
Sunspot Tours (01580 720295,
  www.sunspottours.com), Malta and Gozo, plus
  Cyprus, Madeira and Australia.
Travel Club of Upminster (01708 225000,
  www.travelclubofupminster.co.uk),
  Greece, Spain and Portugal.
Vintage Travel (01954 261431,
  www.vintagetravel.co.uk) offers villas with
  pools in quiet areas of Catalunya, Galicia,
  Andalusia and the Balearics in Spain, parts of
  southern France, Italy, Istria in Croatia and the
  Minho region of northern Portugal.
Voyages Ilena (020 7924 4440,
  www.voyagesilena.co.uk), villas with pools,
  cottages, and hotel-based holidays in Provence,
  Corsica and Sardinia.

WORLDWIDE OPERATORS

1st Class Holidays (0161 877 0433, **www.1stclassholidays.com**) tailor-makes holidays to Canada, Alaska, the USA and New Zealand.

Abercrombie & Kent (0845 070 0618, **www.abercrombiekent.co.uk**), for upmarket holidays with knowledgeable staff.

Aspire (0845 458 9455, **www.aspireholidays.co.uk**) offers upmarket holidays to more than 30 countries, including some by private jet.

Audley Travel (01869 276222, **www.audleytravel.com**), upmarket trips to destinations across Asia, Africa, Arabia, Australasia and Latin America.

Azure Luxury Hotel Collection (01244 322770, **www.azurecollection.com**), hotels and villas in the Caribbean, Indian Ocean, Dubai and the Middle East, South Africa, New York and Miami.

Bales Worldwide (0870 752 0780, **www.balesworldwide.com**), long-established family-run operator, escorted and tailor-made trips to more than 60 countries.

Black Tomato (020 7610 9008, **www.blacktomato.co.uk**), unusual, adventurous trips such as staying at the Burning Man festival in Nevada or watching elephant polo in Thailand.

British Airways Holidays (0870 243 4224, **www.baholidays.com**): upmarket holidays to popular destinations.

The Captain's Choice (020 8879 7705, **www.captainschoice.co.uk**); exclusive trips, often by privately chartered jumbo jet or in all-suite cruise ships.

Carrier (0161 491 7630, **www.carrier.co.uk**), luxury villa and hotel holidays.

Cleveland Collection (0845 450 5732, **www.clevelandcollection.co.uk**), tailor-made trips to Europe, Asia and the Far East.

Cox & Kings (020 7873 5000, **www.coxandkings.co.uk**), upmarket, cultural, group and tailor-made tours across Asia (especially India), Latin America, Africa and eastern Europe.

Elegant Resorts (01244 897000, **www.elegantresorts.co.uk**), one of the original luxury travel operators, with a large hotel and villa programme.

Exodus (0870 240 5550, **www.exodus.co.uk**), mostly escorted and active trips.

The Exploration Company (01993 822443, **www.explorationcompany.com**): upmarket, private safaris and tailor-made tours in Africa, the Indian Ocean islands, India and Nepal, and South America.

Explore (0870 333 4001, **www.explore.co.uk**), adventure and activity holidays in 130 countries.

Expressions Holidays (020 7433 2600, **www.expressionsholidays.co.uk**), upmarket holidays to hotels.

Exsus Travel (020 7292 5060, **www.exsus.com**), upmarket, adventurous, long-haul trips.

Far Frontiers (01285 850926, **www.farfrontiers.com**): adventurous itineraries to exotic destinations.

Fleewinter (020 7112 0019, **www.fleewinter.co.uk**), self-catering in South Africa, Tobago, Sri Lanka and Morocco.

Harlequin Luxury Worldwide Travel (01708 850300, **www.harlequinholidays.com**), upmarket holidays throughout the Caribbean, the Indian Ocean and Dubai, South Africa and Europe.

Hayes & Jarvis (0870 366 1636, **www.hayesandjarvis.co.uk**), wide choice of long-haul holidays.

Intrepid Travel (0800 917 6456, **www.intrepidtravel.com**), group trips, including some for families.

ITC Classics (01244 355527, **www.itcclassics.co.uk**), luxury specialist with expert service and an extensive programme.

Jewel in the Crown Holidays (01293 533338, **www.jewelholidays.com**), Goa, Kerala, Sri Lanka, Cambodia, Turkey and the Red Sea.

Kuoni (01306 742222, **www.kuoni.co.uk**), the UK's biggest long-haul specialist, with knowledgeable staff; escorted tours or tailor-made.

Lakes and Mountains Holidays (01329 844405, **www.lakes-mountains.co.uk**), holidays across the European Alps and Canada, including fly-drives, touring, walking, activity and wildlife trips.

Magic Globe (0870 011 0270, **www.magicglobe.com**), upmarket, tailor-made trips and safaris to five countries in southern Africa and five in South America.

Mosaic Holidays (020 8574 4000, **www.mosaicholidays.co.uk**), mostly hotel-based holidays in Turkey, North Cyprus, Egypt, Dubai, Sri Lanka and the Maldives; plus a specialist dive programme.

Nomadic Thoughts (020 7604 4408, **www.nomadicthoughts.com**), luxury tailor-made trips.

Odyssey Holidays (0870 429 5090, **www.odysseyholidays.com**), holidays to popular package destinations: Greece, Cyprus, Mexico, the Dominican Republic, The Gambia, Egypt and Goa.

Orient-Express (0845 077 2222, www.orient-express.com), luxury hotels and rail trips.

Original Travel (020 7978 7333, www.originaltravel.co.uk), adventurous short breaks.

Page & Moy (0870 833 4012, www.pageandmoy.com), escorted group trips, often by coach, as well as river and ocean cruises.

Peregor Travel (0845 345 0003, www.peregortravel.co.uk), tailor-made holidays.

Pettitts (01892 515966, www.pettitts.co.uk), India, plus the Far East, Morocco, Turkey and Ethiopia.

Premier Holidays (0870 889 0854, www.premierholidays.co.uk), North America and the Caribbean, southern Africa, India and the Indian Ocean, the Middle and Far East, plus the Isle of Man and the Channel Islands.

Quest Travel (0870 442 3542, www.questtravel.com) specialises in long-haul travel, especially to Australia, New Zealand and the South Pacific, and also to Asia, Africa and the Americas.

Regent Holidays (0117 921 1711, www.regent-holidays.co.uk): eastern Europe, the Baltics, Russia, Central Asia, Iceland and Greenland, Cuba, China, Indochina and North Korea.

Saga Holidays (0800 096 0089, www.sagaholidays.co.uk), for the over-50s, and their companions over 40.

Seasons in Style (01244 202000, www.seasonsinstyle.co.uk), luxury, tailor-made holidays to some of the world's best hotels, including golf, spa and skiing trips.

Somak (020 8423 3000, www.somak.co.uk), safaris, tours, beach and activity holidays in Africa, the Indian Ocean islands, India, Sri Lanka and the Middle East.

Sovereign (0870 366 1634, www.sovereign.com) features upmarket hotels in popular summer and winter sun destinations.

Steppes Travel (01285 885333, www.steppestravel.co.uk), tailor-made trips to the more exotic parts of Latin America, Africa and Asia.

Sunvil Holidays (020 8568 4499, www.sunvil.co.uk), Cyprus and Greece specialist plus destinations including Armenia, Italy, Portugal, the Azores, Latin America and quieter parts of the Caribbean.

Tailor-Made Travel (0845 456 8006, www.tailor-made.co.uk), individual itineraries to Australia, New Zealand and the Pacific, plus Canada, Africa and the Far East, and can fix round-the-world trips.

Thomson Worldwide (0870 160 7427, www.thomsonworldwide.co.uk), packages from the country's biggest tour operator.

Tim Best Travel (020 7591 0300, www.timbesttravel.co.uk), tailor-made, upmarket trips to destinations across Africa, Latin America and Australia.

Titan Travel (01293 422420, www.titanhitours.com), escorted tours.

Trailfinders (0845 050 5890, www.trailfinders.com), the travel agent, also packages its own holidays.

Travel City Direct (0870 950 8020, www.travelcitydirect.com), budget Florida and North America specialist, plus popular Mediterranean resorts.

Travelmood (0870 990 9900, www.travelmood.com), flights and holidays to long-haul destinations, plus diving and adventure programmes.

Travelsphere (0800 191418, www.travelsphere.co.uk), escorted journeys.

Tribes Travel (01728 685971, www.tribes.co.uk) offers mostly tailor-made trips to 13 countries, including Tanzania, Morocco, Peru and Nepal, and emphasises its ethical responsibilities towards local communities.

Tropical Locations (020 7229 9199, www.tropical-locations.com), upmarket tailor-made trips to Arabia, the Indian Ocean, the Far East, India, Africa and the Caribbean.

Turquoise Holidays (0870 443 4177, www.turquoiseholidays.co.uk), Africa, the Indian Ocean and Australasia.

Ultimate Travel Company (020 7386 4646, www.theultimatetravelcompany.co.uk), tailor-made and escorted tours to adventurous destinations.

Undiscovered Destinations (0191 206 4038, www.undiscovered-destinations.com) features unusual countries such as Bangladesh, Eritrea and Sao Tome.

Virgin Holidays (0870 220 2788, www.virginholidays.co.uk), good deals on destinations served by Virgin Atlantic.

Voyages Jules Verne (0845 166 7003, www.vjv.com), escorted tours.

Voyana (0871 271 5200, www.voyana.com), upmarket holidays and cruises.

Western & Oriental (0870 499 1111, www.westernoriental.com), luxury tailor-made holidays.

World Odyssey (01905 731373, www.world-odyssey.com), tailor-made trips throughout South America, Africa, the Indian sub-continent and the Middle East.

SPECIALIST TRAVEL AGENTS

These travel agents have experience in putting together complex and round-the-world trips.

Airline Network, 0870 700 0543,
  www.airline-network.co.uk
Flight Centre, 0800 587 0058,
  www.flightcentre.co.uk
STA Travel, 0870 163 0026,
  www.statravel.co.uk
Tailor-Made Travel, 0845 456 8006,
  www.tailor-made.co.uk
Trailfinders, 0845 058 5858,
  www.trailfinders.com
Travelbag, 0800 082 5000,
  www.travelbag.co.uk
Travelmood, 0870 066 0004,
  www.travelmood.com

Online travel agents

www.asda-travel.co.uk
www.cheapflights.co.uk
www.directholidays.co.uk
www.ebookers.co.uk
www.expedia.co.uk
www.flexibletrips.com
www.freshholidays.com
www.lastminute.com
www.lowcosthols.com
www.lowcostpackages.com
www.onlinetravel.com
www.opodo.co.uk

REGIONAL SPECIALISTS
Middle East

Also see "Worldwide"

Longwood Holidays (020 8418 2500,
  www.longwoodholidays.co.uk), Red Sea
  specialist, Israel, Egypt and Jordan
Magic Carpet Travel (01344 622832,
  www.magic-carpet-travel.com), small group
  and tailor-made journeys through Iran
Peltours (020 8371 5200,
  www.peltours.com), Egypt, including the Red
  Sea and Mediterranean coasts, Nile cruises; plus
  Romania
Persian Voyages (01306 885894,
  www.persianvoyages.com), Iran
Shaw Travel (01635 47055,
  www.shawtravel.co.uk), specialists in Oman
Superstar Holidays (020 7957 4300,
  www.superstar.co.uk), the holiday arm of El
  Al Israel Airlines; wide range of holidays across
  Israel
Wind, Sand & Stars (0870 757 1510,
  www.windsandstars.co.uk), started by offering
  journeys in southern Sinai, working with the
  local Bedouin tribespeople; also western Egypt,
  Sri Lanka and pilgrimage routes in Spain

Africa and the Indian Ocean

For the African Travel and Tourism Association,
  see **www.atta.co.uk**
See also "Worldwide", and the overlanding section
  of "Activity".
Aardvark Safaris (01980 849160,
  www.aardvarksafaris.com), upmarket tailor-
  made safaris and holidays across Africa, the
  Indian Ocean and Madagascar
African Safari Club (0845 345 0014,
  www.africansafariclub.com), beach and safari
  trips to Kenya, plus cruises around the Indian
  Ocean
Africa Travel Centre (0845 450 1520,
  www.africatravel.co.uk), can tailor-make tours
  across Africa and the Indian Ocean islands
Aim 4 Africa (0845 408 4541,
  www.aim4africa.com), Kenya and Tanzania
Arkno Tours (020 8855 6373, **www.arkno.com**),
  for Libya
Aspects of Tunisia (020 7836 4999,
  www.aspectsoftunisia.co.uk)
Beachcomber (01483 445610,
  www.beachcombertours.co.uk), Mauritius and
  the Seychelles, plus Dubai and South Africa
Bushbaby Travel (0870 850 9103,
  www.bushbabytravel.com), family holidays to
  South Africa and Mauritius
Cape Verde Travel (0845 270 2006,
  www.capeverdetravel.co.uk), trips to all nine of
  the West African archipelago's islands
Cedarberg African Travel (020 8898 8533,
  www.cedarbergtravel.com), tours, safaris and
  self-drive holidays in Africa and the Indian
  Ocean islands
Expert Africa (020 8232 9777,
  www.expertafrica.com), southern and eastern
  Africa, focusing on smaller lodges and more
  adventurous safaris
Farside Africa (0131 315 2464,
  www.farsideafrica.com), tailor-made holidays
  and safaris to eastern and southern Africa, the
  Indian Ocean islands, plus Gabon and Morocco
The Gambia Experience (0845 330 4567,
  www.gambia.co.uk), year-round trips to The
  Gambia and Senegal, including bird-watching,
  fishing and beach holidays
Gane & Marshall (020 8441 9592,
  www.ganeandmarshall.co.uk), extensive Africa
  programme, and also offers countries in South
  America
Hartley's Safaris (01673 861600,
  www.hartleys-safaris.co.uk) specialises in
  Botswana, plus southern Africa and Tanzania
J&C Voyageurs (01373 832111,
  www.jandcvoyageurs.com), safaris across
  southern Africa

Journeys by Design (01273 623790, www.journeysbydesign.co.uk), small, luxurious safaris in remote areas of mainstream safari destinations, plus Ethiopia

The Odyssey Experience (01242 224482, www.theodysseyexperience.co.uk), tailormade trips to Africa, the Indian Ocean and Arabia

Okavango Tours & Safaris (020 8343 3283, www.okavango.com) tailor makes safaris and other holidays to Africa and the Indian Ocean

Rainbow Tours (020 7226 1004, www.rainbowtours.co.uk), tailormade trips, honeymoons, safaris and family holidays to southern and eastern Africa, Madagascar and the Indian Ocean

Roxton Bailey Robinson Worldwide (01488 689700, www.rbrww.com), safaris, family and other trips across Africa, plus new Latin America division and fishing holidays worldwide

Safari Consultants (01787 228494, www.safari-consultants.co.uk), tailor-made safaris to eastern and southern Africa, the Indian Ocean islands and Nepal, with an emphasis on wildlife

Safari Drive (01488 71140, www.safaridrive.com), self-drive safaris in Zambia, Malawi, Namibia, Botswana, Kenya and Tanzania, and Oman

Tikalanka Tours (020 8802 3680, www.tikalanka.com), Sri Lanka and the Maldives

To Escape To (0871 711 5282, www.toescapeto.com), luxurious and unusual hideaways and hotels, safaris, beach, golf and other trips to South Africa, Zanzibar, Kenya, Botswana, Mozambique, Mauritius and the Seychelles

Travel Butlers (0845 838 2450, www.travelbutlers.com), trips for independent travellers in South Africa and Namibia, including safari guiding

Visions of Africa (0845 345 0065, www.visionsofafrica.co.uk), tailor-made trips to countries across southern Africa

Wild about Africa (020 8758 4717, www.wildaboutafrica.com); budget, small group tours of Namibia

The Americas

Also see "Worldwide"

North America

Affordable New York (001 212 533 4001, www.affordablenewyorkcity.com) for apartments

All America Holidays (0870 167 6676, www.allamericaholidays.com), tailor-made holidays across North and South America

America As You Like It (020 8742 8299, www.americaasyoulikeit.com) can book accommodation and organise fly-drives across America and Canada

America Options, 0845 345 1212, www.americaoptions.com

AmeriCan & Worldwide Travel (01892 511894, www.awwt.co.uk), self-drive, touring and ski trips in America and Canada

American Round-Up (01798 865946, www.americanroundup.com), ranching, riding, fishing and white-water rafting holidays in the USA and Canada

Bon Voyage (0800 316 0194, www.bon-voyage.co.uk), North America, the Caribbean plus Dubai

Complete North America, 0115 950 4555, www.completenorthamerica.com

Connections, 01494 473173, www.connectionsworldwide.co.uk

Cruise America (0870 514 3607, www.cruiseamerica.org.uk) hires motorhomes (known as recreational vehicles, or RVs) for self-driving tours in the USA and Canada

Florida Options, 0845 345 1212, www.floridavillaoptions.com

Frontier Travel (020 8776 8709, www.frontier-travel.co.uk), year-round holidays to Canada, including skiing, golf, wildlife and motorhome hire

Funway Holidays (0870 444 0770, www.funwayholidays.co.uk) specialises in Florida, and also offers Mexico and the Caribbean

Go Native America, 01924 840111, www.gonativeamerica.com

Go Visit America, 0870 499 9767, www.flywho.com

Hawaiian Holidays, 0870 350 7873, www.hawaiian-holidays.co.uk

Jetlife, 0870 787 5957, www.jetlife.co.uk

Jetsave Florida (0870 161 3400) and Jetsave Touring (0870 162 3500, www.jetsave.co.uk)

Just America, 01730 266588, www.justamerica.co.uk

New England Country Homes, 0870 192 1037, www.newenglandcountryhomes.co.uk

North America Travel Service, 0113 246 1466, www.northamericatravelservice.co.uk

North American Highways, 01902 851138, www.northamericanhighways.co.uk

North American Vacation Homes (01444 450034, www.usahomes.co.uk), for New York and Florida

Prestige Holidays (01425 480400, www.prestigeholidays.co.uk) has a specialist programme to Bermuda

Ranch America (01923 671831,
  www.ranchamerica.co.uk), ranch holidays
  across several US states and in Canada
Ranch Rider (01509 618811,
  www.ranchrider.com), ranch holidays across
  the western US and Canadian states
Statesavers (01364 644477,
  www.statesavers.com) for motorhome and
  other trips
Tauck Tours, 0800 961834,
  www.tauck.com
TrekAmerica (0870 444 8735,
  www.trekamerica.co.uk), small group
  adventure and activity holidays across North,
  Central and South America, Australia and New
  Zealand
United Vacations, 0870 606 6358,
  www.unitedvacations.co.uk
US Airtours, 0871 210 0500,
  www.usairtours.co.uk
Vacations Group (01582 469662,
  www.vacationsgroup.co.uk), holiday
  programmes in Florida, California, Carolina and
  New England.
Virgin Holidays, 0870 220 2788,
  www.virginholidays.co.uk

* Campers: try the National Parks Service
  (**www.nps.gov**) or Kampgrounds of America
  (**www.koa.com**).

Central and South America, including Antarctica

For a free guide to the region and to many of the
tour operators and airlines that go there, contact
the Latin American Travel Association (020 8715
2913, **www.lata.org**). For details of operators that
specialise in trips to Antarctica, and guidelines for
such visits, see the website of the International
Association of Antarctica Tour Operators
(**www.iaato.org**).

Abercrombie & Kent (0845 070 0614,
  www.abercrombiekent.co.uk), luxurious trips
  across Central America, the Caribbean and
  Antarctica, with dedicated offices in the region
Andean Trails (0131 467 7086,
  www.andeantrails.co.uk), active trips
  throughout the Andes, in Peru, Bolivia, Ecuador,
  Chile and Argentina
Audley Latin America (01869 276210,
  www.audleytravel.com), upmarket
  tailor-made trips
Austral Tours (020 7233 5384,
  www.latinamerica.co.uk), tailor-made trips and
  can source good value air fares to the region
Cathy Matos Mexican Tours (0870 890 0040,
  www.cathymatosmexico.co.uk) specialises in
  Mexico, Guatemala and Belize

Cazenove & Loyd (020 7384 2332,
  www.cazloyd.com) have knowledgeable staff
  who can arrange private itineraries across the
  region
Exsus (020 7292 5050, **www.exsus.com**),
  luxurious holidays across South America
Geodyssey (020 7281 7788,
  www.geodyssey.co.uk), Venezuela, Costa Rica,
  Trinidad and Tobago, Nicaragua and Ecuador
Journey Latin America (020 8747 8315,
  www.journeylatinamerica.co.uk), wide choice
  of individual and group tours across Central and
  South America, and also sells flights
Last Frontiers (01296 653000,
  www.lastfrontiers.com) tailor-makes tours
  throughout Central and South America,
  including Antarctica and the Galapagos Islands,
  and the Dutch Caribbean
Latin America Travel (0870 442 4241,
  www.latinamericatravel.co.uk) covers the
  region, with an emphasis on Brazil
Latin Odyssey (020 7610 6020,
  www.latinodyssey.com), tailor-made trips
  across the continent
Llama Travel (020 7263 3000,
  www.llamatravel.com), Peru specialist
New Worlds (020 8445 8444,
  www.newworlds.co.uk), Ecuador and the
  Galapagos, Costa Rica, Cuba, Peru, Chile
  and Bolivia
Preston Reid (01347 822235,
  www.prestonreid.com), tailor-made trips to
  South America, and Southern Africa
Pura Aventura (0845 225 5058,
  www.pura–aventura.com), activity holidays in
  several countries across Latin America,
  plus Spain
Scott Dunn Latin America (020 8682 5030,
  www.scottdunn.com), upmarket
  tailor-made trips
Select Latin America (020 7407 1478,
  www.selectlatinamerica.co.uk), holidays across
  the continent, including the Galapagos and
  Antarctica
South American Experience (020 7976 5511,
  www.southamericanexperience.co.uk), experts
  in arranging travel across the continent
Sunvil Latin America (020 8758 4774,
  www.sunvil.co.uk), small group and tailor-
  made trips to Costa Rica, Guatemala, Ecuador
  and Peru
Trips Worldwide (0117 311 4400,
  www.tripsworldwide.co.uk), tailor-made
  holidays in Latin America and the "alternative"
  Caribbean (such as Guadeloupe and Dominica)
Tucan Travel (020 8896 1600, **www.tucantravel.
  com**), adventurous and budget trips to Latin
  America

Veloso Tours (020 8762 0616, www.veloso.com) offers group and individual tours across many South and Central American countries

The Caribbean

Caribtours (020 7751 0660, www.caribtours.co.uk), wide choice of Caribbean islands and Bermuda

Complete Caribbean (01423 531031, www.completecaribbean.co.uk) features 100-plus hotels across 30 Caribbean islands plus Bermuda

Interchange (020 8681 3612, www.interchange.uk.com), Cuba specialist

Just Grenada, 01373 814214, www.justgrenada.co.uk

Just Tobago, 01373 814234, www.justtobago.co.uk

Tropic Breeze (01752 873377, www.tropicbreeze.co.uk), tailor-made trips to many of the Caribbean islands, plus the Maldives

Voyager World Travel (01580 766222, www.voyagercuba.co.uk), Cuba specialist

Asia

Also see "Worldwide"

Far East Gateways (0161 437 4371, www.gateways.co.uk), tailor-made Asia specialist which also offers Africa and the Indian Ocean

Gecko Travel (02392 258859, www.geckotravel.com), south east Asia, particularly Thailand and Indochina, group tours and tailor-made itineraries

Hinterland Travel (01883 743584, www.hinterlandtravel.com) specialises in unlikely destinations – the Kurdistan region of northern Iraq, Afghanistan and Kashmir

Silverbird (020 8875 9090, www.silverbird.co.uk) specialises in tailor-made trips across Asia, particularly the Far East – China, Indochina, Malaysia, Indonesia, Thailand – plus India and Australia

China and the Far East

CTS Horizons (020 7836 9911, www.ctshorizons.com), China specialist, offering tailor-made and group trips, plus other long-haul destinations

Koryo Tours (00 86 10 6416 7544, www.koryogroup.com), North Korea

Panoramic Journeys (01608 811183, www.panoramicjourneys.com), Mongolia

Sanya China Travel (01256 863030, www.sanyachinatravel.com), tours throughout China, but especially to Sanya, a tropical coastal resort

Tell Tale Travel (020 7659 5432, www.telltaletravel.co.uk), new Thailand specialist offering cultural tours

Travel Indochina (01865 268940, www.travelindochina.co.uk), small group tours in Indochina, China and India

Wendy Wu Tours (0870 343 0386, www.wendywutours.co.uk), China and Indochina

Indian subcontinent

Ampersand (020 7723 4336, www.ampersandtravel.com) for India, Bhutan and Sri Lanka

Blue Poppy Tours & Treks (020 7700 3084, www.bluepoppybhutan.com), specialises in Bhutan

Colours of India (020 8343 3446, www.colours-of-india.com), luxury India specialist

Cox & Kings (020 7873 5000, www.coxandkings.co.uk), expert staff and long experience in India

Goaway (0870 890 7800, www.goaway.co.uk), Goa and Kerala

Greaves Travel (020 7487 5687, www.greavesindia.com), knowledgeable India specialist which offers top-end tailor-made trips

Jewel in the Crown Holidays (01293 533338, www.jewelholidays.com), Goa, Kerala, Sri Lanka plus motorbike tours of India on Enfield bikes

Lazydays in Goa, 01202 484257, www.lazydays.co.uk

Mahout (020 7373 7121, www.mahoutuk.com), expert advice on India's historic hotels

Pettitts (01892 515966, www.pettitts.co.uk), India specialists

Royal Expeditions (020 8150 6158, www.royalexpeditions.com), based in India, has an extensive selection of holidays

Trans Indus (020 8566 2729, www.transindus.com), tailormade and escorted small group tours to India, plus Sri Lanka, Nepal, Indochina

TravelPak (07961 169045, www.travelpak.co.uk) specialises in Pakistan

Australasia

These operators feature Australia, New Zealand and the Pacific Islands; also see "Worldwide".

All Ways Pacific, 01494 432747, www.all-ways.co.uk

Austravel, 0870 166 2020, www.austravel.com

Bridge & Wickers, 020 7483 6555 www.bridgeandwickers.com

Continental Europe

Croatia

Adriatic Holidays, 01865 516577,
    www.adriaticholidaysonline.com
Adriatica, 020 7183 0437,
    www.adriatica.net
Balkan Holidays, 0845 130 1114,
    www.balkanholidays.co.uk
Bond Tours, 01372 745300,
    www.bondtours.com
Bosmere Travel, 01473 834094,
    www.bosmeretravel.co.uk
Croatia for Travellers, 020 7226 4460,
    www.croatiafortravellers.co.uk
Croatia Gems, 0871 855 1031,
    www.croatiagems.com
Croatian Affair, 020 7385 7111,
    www.croatianaffair.com
Dalmation Destinations, 020 7730 8007,
    www.dalmatiandestinations.com
Hidden Croatia, 0871 208 0075,
    www.hiddencroatia.com
Holiday Options, 0870 013 0450,
    www.holidayoptions.co.uk
MyCroatia, 0118 961 1554,
    www.mycroatia.co.uk
Sail Croatia, 020 7751 9988,
    www.sailcroatia.net

France

The Association of British Tour Operators to
France (**www.abtof.org.uk**) lists operators to
France and holiday ideas. There are also many
operators to France in the "camping" section,
below, page 416.

Allez France, 0845 330 2056,
    www.allezfrance.com
Alternative Aquitaine, 0870 609 2845,
    www.alternative-aquitaine.com
Balfour France, 020 8878 9955,
    www.balfourfrance.com
Belle France, 0870 405 4056,
    www.bellefrance.co.uk
Bonnes Vacances, 0870 760 7074,
    www.bvdirect.co.uk
Bowhills, 0870 235 2727,
    www.bowhills.co.uk
Brittany Travel, 0845 230 1380,
    www.brittanytravel.com
Chez Nous, 0870 238 5963,
    www.cheznous.com
Corsican Places, 0845 330 2059,
    www.corsica.co.uk
Direct Corsica, **www.directcorsica.com**
Dominique's Villas, 020 7738 8772.
    www.dominiquesvillas.co.uk
France Afloat, 0870 011 0538,
    www.franceafloat.com

French Affair, 020 7381 8519,
    www.frenchaffair.com
French Country Cottages, 0870 078 1500,
    www.french-country-cottages.co.uk
French Country Cruises, 01572 821330,
    www.frenchcountrycruises.com
French Life, 0870 336 7105,
    www.frenchlife.co.uk
French Travel Service, 0870 241 4243,
    www.f-t-s.co.uk
Gascony Secret, 01284 827253,
    www.gascony-secret.com
Gites: book online at
    www.gites-de-france.fr
Holiday in France, 01225 310623,
    www.holidayinfrance.co.uk
Individual France, 0870 078 0189,
    www.individualfrance.com
Just France, 020 8780 4480,
    www.justfrance.co.uk
Lagrange Holidays, 020 7371 6111,
    www.lagrange-holidays.co.uk
Normandie Vacances, 0845 230 5130,
    www.normandy-holidays.co.uk
Owners in France, 0870 556 1475,
    www.ownersinfrance.com
Pierre et Vacances, 0870 026 7144,
    www.pierreetvacances.com
Pure France, 0871 288 4198,
    www.purefrance.com
Real Provence, 01491 413660,
    www.real-provence.com
Susan Paradise, 01395 597759,
    www.susanparadise.co.uk
VFB Holidays, 01242 240310,
    www.vfbholidays.co.uk
Voyages Ilena, 020 7924 4440,
    www.voyagesilena.co.uk

Greece and Cyprus

Amathus Holidays, 0870 251 4920,
    www.amathusholidays.co.uk
Argo Holidays, 0870 066 7070,
    www.argoholidays.com
Best of Greece, 0870 442 2442,
    www.bestofgreece.co.uk
Catherine Secker's Crete, 020 8460 8022,
    www.catherine-secker-crete.co.uk
Cretan Ambience, 020 7553 6959,
    www.cretanambience.com
Cyprus Paradise, 020 8343 8888,
    www.cyprusparadise.com
Direct Greece, 0870 191 9244,
    www.directgreece.co.uk
Filoxenia, 01653 617755,
    www.filoxenia.co.uk
Greek Island Sailing, 0118 970 1259,
    www.greekislandsailing.co.uk

Greek Islands Club, 020 8568 4499,
  www.greekislandsclub.com
Greek Options, 0870 241 8668,
  www.greekoptions.co.uk
Greek Sun Holidays, 01732 740317,
  www.greeksun.co.uk
Hidden Greece, 020 8758 4707,
  www.hidden-greece.co.uk
Houses of Pelion, 0870 199 9191,
  www.pelion.co.uk
Ionian Island Holidays, 020 8459 0777,
  www.ionianislandholidays.com
Island Wandering, 0870 777 9944,
  www.islandwandering.com
Islands of Greece, 0845 675 2600,
  www.islands-of-greece.co.uk
Kosmar, 0871 700 0747,
  www.kosmar.co.uk
Laskarina Holidays, 01444 880380,
  www.laskarina.co.uk
Meltemi Travel, 0845 458 0350,
  www.meltemi-travel.co.uk
Olympic Holidays, 0870 429 4141,
  www.olympicholidays.com
Planet Holidays, 0870 066 0909,
  www.planet-holidays.net
Planos Holidays, 01373 814200,
  www.planos.co.uk
Pure Crete, 020 8760 0879,
  www.pure-crete.com
Sunvil Holidays, 020 8568 4499,
  www.sunvil.co.uk
Travel a la Carte, 01635 201250,
  www.travelalacarte.co.uk
Travelux Holidays, 01580 765000,
  www.traveluxgreece.co.uk

* Visitors who plan an island-hopping trip around
  Greece should pack the annually updated guide
  Greek Island Hopping by Frewin Poffley (Thomas
  Cook Publishing, £12.99;
  www.greekislandhopping.com).

Italy

Association of British Travel Organisers to Italy,
  www.italiantouristboard.co.uk/abtoi.html
Bellini Travel, 020 7602 7602,
  www.bellinitravel.com
Bridgewater, 0161 787 8587,
  www.bridgewater-travel.co.uk
Carefree Italy, 0870 330 3133,
  www.carefree-italy.com
Citalia, 0870 909 7555,
  www.citalia.com
Costa Smeralda Holidays, 020 7493 8303,
  www.costasmeralda-holidays.com
Cottages to Castles, 01622 775217,
  www.cottagestocastles.com
Cuendet, 0800 085 7732,
  www.cuendet.com

Dolce Vita Villas, 020 7436 0426,
  www.dolcevitavillas.com
Fine Art Travel, 020 7437 8553,
  www.finearttravel.co.uk
Hello Italy, 01483 419964,
  www.helloit.co.uk
Invitation To Tuscany, 020 8600 2522,
  www.invitationtotuscany.com
Italia nel Mondo, 020 7828 9171,
  www.thesicilianexperience.co.uk
The Italian Connection, 01424 728900,
  www.italian-connection.co.uk
Italian Journeys, 020 7373 8058,
  www.italianjourneys.com
Just Sardinia, 01202 484858,
  www.justsardinia.co.uk
Long Travel, 01694 722367,
  www.long-travel.co.uk
Real Holidays, 020 7359 3938,
  www.realholidays.co.uk
Secret Marche, 00 39 0733 281445,
  www.secretmarche.com
Solemar, 020 8891 1294,
  www.solemar.co.uk
Summer's Leases, 0845 230 2223,
  www.summersleases.com
Think Sicily, 020 7377 8518,
  www.thinksicily.com
To Tuscany, 020 7193 7782,
  www.to-tuscany.co.uk
Traditional Tuscany, 01553 810003,
  www.traditionaltuscany.co.uk
Tuscan Enterprises, 020 7286 5278,
  www.tuscanenterprise.it
Tuscan Holidays, 015394 31120,
  www.tuscanholidays.co.uk
Tuscany Now, 020 7684 8884,
  www.tuscanynow.com
Venetian Apartments, 020 8878 1130,
  www.venice-rentals.com
Veronica Tomasso Cotgrove, 020 7267 2423,
  www.vtcitaly.com

Northern and Eastern Europe

Balkan Holidays (0845 130 1114,
  www.balkanholidays.co.uk), Bulgaria, Croatia,
  Slovenia, Serbia, Montenegro and Romania
Balkan Tours (02890 246795, **www.balkan.co.uk**)
  operates to Bulgaria from Belfast and Dublin
Baltic Holidays (0870 757 9233,
  www.balticholidays.com) specialises in the
  three Baltic states of Lithuania, Latvia and
  Estonia
Baltic Travel Company (0870 753 7747,
  www.baltictravelcompany.com), Lithuania,
  Latvia and Estonia
Baltics and Beyond (0845 094 2125,
  www.balticsandbeyond.com), for the Baltic
  states plus Kaliningrad and Belarus

Canterbury Travel (0845 125 2752,
  www.santa-holidays.com), Lapland specialist,
  including visits to Santa
Dertour (0870 403 5442,
  www.dertour.co.uk), Germany
Discover the World (01737 218800,
  www.discover-the-world.co.uk), Scandinavia
  and the Arctic regions, plus Antarctica
Emagine (0870 902 5399,
  www.emagine-travel.co.uk), Scandinavia
  specialist
Exeter International (020 8956 2756,
  www.exeterinternational.co.uk), Russia,
  central Europe, eastern Europe and
  the near east
Fjord Line (0870 143 9669,
  www.fjordline.co.uk), Norway
Iceland Holidays, 01773 853300,
  www.icelandholidays.com
Icelandair Holidays, 0870 787 4020,
  www.icelandair.co.uk
Just Slovenia, 01373 814230,
  www.justslovenia.co.uk
Moswin's Germany, 0870 062 5040,
  www.moswin.com
Romanian Affair, 020 7835 5766,
  www.romanianaffair.com
The Russia Experience, 020 8566 8846,
  www.trans-siberian.co.uk
Scantours (020 7554 3530,
  www.scantours.co.uk), Scandinavia, Iceland,
  Russia and the Baltic states
Simplicity Austria, 01706 360888,
  www.simplicityaustria.co.uk
Slovakian Travel, 01282 692650,
  www.slovakiantravel.co.uk
Specialised Tours (01342 712785,
  www.specialisedtours.com), Scandinavia and
  the Baltic states
Transylvania Uncovered, 0845 300 0247,
  www.beyondtheforest.com

Spain and Portugal

Many companies listed here feature both
countries on the Iberian peninsula; I have also
listed separately a handful of Portugal specialists,
below.

Andalucian Adventures, 01453 834137,
  www.andalucian-adventures.co.uk
Astbury Formentera, 01642 210163,
  www.formentera.co.uk
Balearic Agrotourism Association,
  00 34 971 721508, **www.topfincas.com**
Barwell Leisure, 0870 049 3095,
  www.barwell.co.uk
Casas Cantabricas, 01223 328721,
  www.casas.co.uk

EHS Travel, 01993 700600,
  www.ehstravel.co.uk
Mallorca Farmhouses, 0118 947 3001,
  www.mfh.co.uk
Mundi Color Holidays, 020 7828 6021,
  www.mundicolor.co.uk
PCI Holidays, 0845 130 1440,
  www.pci-holidays.com
Pyrenean Experience, 0121 711 3428,
  www.pyreneanexperience.com
Real Ronda, 01275 464225,
  www.real-ronda.com
Spain and Portugal Affair, 020 7385 8127,
  www.spanishaffair.com
Step in Time Tours, 0870 199 8788,
  www.muslimspain.com
Stowaway Travel, 0845 230 1212,
  www.stowawaytravel.co.uk
Surf Spain, 01691 648514,
  www.surfspain.co.uk
Travel Club of Upminster, 01708 225000,
  www.travelclubofupminster.co.uk
Travellers Way, 01527 559000,
  www.travellersway.co.uk
Try Holidays, 0870 754 4545,
  www.tryholidays.co.uk
Vintage Travel, 0845 344 0460,
  www.vintagetravel.co.uk

Portugal

Affinity Villas, 01428 727277,
  www.affinityvillas.com
Archipelago Azores, 017687 75672,
  www.azoreschoice.com
Caravela, 0870 443 8181,
  www.caravela.co.uk
Destination Portugal, 01993 773269,
  www.destination-portugal.co.uk
Light Blue Travel, 01223 568904,
  www.lightbluetravel.co.uk
Portugala, 020 8444 1857,
  www.portugala.com
Pousadas de Portugal (00 351 218 442001,
  www.pousadas.pt), bookable through Keytel,
  020 7616 0300, **www.keytel.co.uk**
The Villa Agency, 01273 747811,
  www.thevillaagency.co.uk

Turkey and northern Cyprus

Alternative Travel & Holidays, 0870 041 1448,
  www.alternativeturkey.com
Anatolian Sky Holidays, 0870 850 4040,
  www.anatolian-sky.com
Blue Cruise, 020 8968 7770,
  www.bluecruise.co.uk
DayDreams, 020 7637 8921,
  www.daydreams-travel.com
Elixir Holidays, 020 7722 2288,
  www.elixirholidays.com

Exclusive Escapes, 020 8605 3500,
www.hiddenturkey.com
IAH Holidays, 0870 027 2921,
www.iah-holidays.co.uk
Metak Holidays, 020 8290 9292,
www.metakholidays.co.uk
Mosaic Holidays, 020 8574 4000,
www.mosaicholidays.co.uk
Savile Tours, 020 7923 3230,
www.saviletours.com
Tussock Cruising, 020 8510 9292,
www.tussockcruising.com
Undiscovered Turkey, 0845 330 2064,
www.undiscoveredturkey.co.uk

Camping in Europe

Most operators in this section offer large, ready-erected tents, or mobile homes, on organised campsites with plenty of activities and childcare laid on. They operate predominantly in France, with some of them offering other European destinations too.

Alan Rogers Travel Service, 0870 405 4055,
www.alanrogers.com
Brittany Ferries, 0870 556 1600,
www.brittanyferries.com
Camping Life, 0870 197 1964,
www.campinglife.co.uk
Canvas Holidays, 0870 192 1159,
www.canvasholidays.co.uk
Carisma, 01923 284235,
www.carisma.co.uk
Club Cantabrica, 01727 866177,
www.cantabrica.co.uk
Eurocamp, 0870 366 7552,
www.eurocamp.co.uk
Fleur Holidays, 0870 750 2121,
www.fleur-holidays.com
French Freedom Holidays, 01724 282303,
www.french-freedom.co.uk
Ian Mearns Holidays, 01993 822655,
www.ianmearnsholidays.co.uk
Keycamp, 0870 700 0123,
www.keycamp.co.uk
Matthews Holidays, 01483 285213,
www.matthewsfrance.co.uk
Sandpiper Holidays, 01746 785123,
www.sandpiperhols.co.uk
Select France, 01865 331350,
www.selectfrance.co.uk
Siblu, 0870 242 7777,
www.siblu.com
Thomson Al Fresco, 0870 166 0366,
www.thomsonalfresco.co.uk
Ugogo, 0870 366 7606,
www.ugogo.co.uk
Vacansoleil, 0870 077 8779,
www.vacansoleil.co.uk

Venue Holidays, 01233 629950,
www.venueholidays.co.uk
Yelloh! Village Holidays, 00 800 8873 9739,
www.yellohvillageholidays.com

Book a pitch

For owners of tents, caravans and motorhomes to book pitches and Channel crossings:

The Camping and Caravanning Club,
0845 131 7631,
www.campingandcaravanningclub.co.uk
Eurocamp Independent, 0870 366 7572,
www.eurocampindependent.co.uk
Select Sites, 01873 859876,
www.select-site.com
Sites Abroad, 0870 904 0030,
www.sitesabroad.co.uk
Vacansoleil, 0870 077 8779,
www.vacansoleil.co.uk

Short breaks and city breaks

Cities Direct, 0870 442 1820,
www.citiesdirect.co.uk
Contempo Hotels, 0870 300 0400,
www.contempohotels.com
Cresta, 0870 238 7711,
www.crestaholidays.co.uk
Great Escapes, 0845 330 2057,
www.greatescapes.co.uk
Kirker Holidays, 0870 112 3333,
www.kirkerholidays.com
Leger Holidays, 0845 458 5599,
www.legerbreaks.info
McKinlay Kidd, 0870 760 6027,
www.seescotlanddifferently.co.uk
Original Travel, 020 7978 7333,
www.originaltravel.co.uk
Osprey Holidays, 0845 310 3031,
www.ospreyholidays.com
Short Breaks by Air, 0870 027 6010,
www.shortbreaksbyair.com
Thomas Cook Signature Cities, 0870 443 4434,
www.tcsignature.com
Thomson Cities and Short Breaks, 0870 606 1476,
www.thomsoncities.co.uk
Travel Editions, 020 7251 0045,
www.traveleditions.co.uk
Webweekends, 0870 745 8808,
www.webweekends.co.uk

LUXURY TRAVEL

Many of the tour operators in this directory offer luxury trips: here is a selection of specialists.

Abercrombie & Kent, 0845 070 0610,
www.abercrombiekent.co.uk
Azure Luxury Hotel Collection, 01244 322770,
www.azurecollection.com

The Captain's Choice, 020 8879 7705,
  www.captainschoice.co.uk
Carrier, 01625 547000,
  www.carrier.co.uk
Cazenove & Loyd, 020 7384 2332,
  www.cazloyd.com
Contempo Hotels, 0870 300 0400,
  www.contempohotels.com
Cox & Kings, 020 7873 5000,
  www.coxandkings.co.uk
Elegant Resorts, 01244 897555,
  www.elegantresorts.co.uk
ITC Classics, 01244 355400,
  www.itcclassics.co.uk
Kuoni World Class, 01306 747001,
  www.kuoni.co.uk
Latitude, 0870 443 4483,
  www.latitude-online.co.uk
Powder Byrne, 020 8246 5300,
  www.powderbyrne.com
Scott Dunn, 020 8682 5006,
  www.scottdunn.com
Seasons in Style, 01244 202000,
  www.seasonsinstyle.co.uk

Bespoke luxury travel consultants

Earth,
  www.earthlondon.com
Lanza & Baucina, 020 7738 2222,
  www.lanzabaucina.com
Luxury Explorer,
  www.luxuryexplorer.com
The Private Travel Company, 020 7751 0990,
  www.theprivatetravelcompany.co.uk

Specialists with insider knowledge

Ampersand (020 7723 4336,
  www.ampersandtravel.com) has good
  contacts in India and Sri Lanka.
Bellini Travel (020 7602 7602,
  www.bellinitravel.com) specialises in
  Italy for connoisseurs.
Descent International (020 7384 3854,
  www.descent.co.uk) offers high-end
  ski chalets in the Alps.
Exeter International (020 8956 2756,
  www.exeterinternational.co.uk)
  specialises in Russia and Eastern Europe.
Fine Art Travel (020 7437 8553,
  www.finearttravel.co.uk) offers private
  tours to Italy.
I-Escape (020 7652 4625,
  www.i-escape.com) hunts out imaginative
  boutique hotels worldwide.
Journeys by Design (01273 623790,
  www.journeysbydesign.co.uk) is a
  knowledgeable Africa specialist.

Kirker Holidays (0870 112 3333,
  www.kirkerholidays.com) is a short-break and
  European cultural specialist.
Mahout (020 7373 7121, **www.mahoutuk.com**) is
  knowledgeable about India's hotels.
Robin Pope Safaris (00 260 6246090,
  www.robinpopesafaris.net) offers safaris in
  Zambia with highly experienced guides.
Steppes Travel (01285 651010,
  www.steppestravel.co.uk) specialises in
  off-the-beaten-track parts of Asia, Africa
  and South America.
Villazzo (020 8123 3375, **www.villazzo.com**)
  offers ultra-luxurious, serviced villas.
Wilderness Australia (020 7373 7121,
  www.wildernessaustralia.com.au) offers
  tailor-made safaris in the Australian outback.

REGULATORY BODIES FOR BONDED HOLIDAYS

Association of Bonded Travel Organisers Trust,
  www.abtot.com
Association of British Travel Agents,
  020 7307 1907, **www.abta.com**
Association of Independent Tour Operators,
  020 8744 9280, **www.aito.co.uk**
Bonded Coach Holidays, 020 7240 3131,
  www.bondedcoachholidays.co.uk
Federation of Tour Operators,
  www.fto.co.uk
Passenger Shipping Association, 020 7436 2449,
  www.the-psa.co.uk
Travel Trust Association, 0870 889 0577,
  www.traveltrust.co.uk

TRANSPORT

Scheduled airlines

Adria Airways (020 7734 4630,
www.adria-airways.com) Slovenia
Aeroflot (020 7355 2233,
www.aeroflot.co.uk) Russia
Air Baltic,
www.airbaltic.com
Air Canada, 0871 220 1111,
www.aircanada.com
Air China, 020 7744 0800,
www.air-china.co.uk
Air France, 0870 142 4343,
www.airfrance.com/uk
Air India, 020 8745 1111,
www.airindia.com
Air Jamaica, 020 8570 7999,
www.airjamaica.com
Air Malta, 0845 607 3710,
www.airmalta.com
Air Mauritius, 020 7434 4375,
www.airmauritius.com
Air Namibia, 020 7960 6743,
www.airnamibia.com
Air New Zealand, 020 8600 7600,
www.airnz.co.uk
Air Seychelles, 01293 596655,
www.airseychelles.co.uk
Air Zimbabwe, 020 7399 3600,
www.airzim.co.zw
Alaska Airlines, 01992 441517,
www.alaskaair.com
Alitalia, 0870 544 8259,
www.alitalia.co.uk
American Airlines, 0845 778 9789,
www.americanairlines.co.uk
ANA – All Nippon Airways, 0870 837 8866,
www.ana.co.uk
Aurigny Air Services (0871 871 0717,
www.aurigny.com), Channel Islands
Austrian Airlines, 0870 124 2625,
www.austrianairlines.co.uk
Avianca (0845 838 7941,
www.avianca.co.uk), Colombia
bmi, 0870 607 0555, www.flybmi.com
British Airways, 0870 850 9850,
www.ba.com
British Mediterranean (0870 850 9850,
www.flybmed.com), Middle East and
Central Asia
BWIA West Indies Airways, 0870 499 2942,
www.bwee.co.uk
Cathay Pacific Airways, 020 8834 8888,
www.cathaypacific.com

China Airlines, 020 7436 9001,
www.china-airlines.com
City Jet (00 353 1 870 0100, www.cityjet.com),
connects London City and Dublin
Croatia Airlines, 020 8563 0022,
www.croatiaairlines.hr
CSA Czech Airlines, 0870 444 3747,
www.csa.cz/en
Cyprus Airways, 020 8359 1333,
www.cyprusairways.com
Delta (020 7932 8300, www.delta.com),
US-based carrier
Eastern Airways (0870 366 9100,
www.easternairways.com), services across the
UK linking many smaller airports
Egyptair, 020 7734 2864,
www.egyptair.com.eg
El Al Israel Airlines, 020 7957 4100,
www.elal.co.uk
Emirates (020 7808 0033,
www.emirates.com), based in Dubai
EOS Airlines (0800 019 6468,
www.eosairlines.com), first-class only airline
between Stansted and New York
Estonian Air, 020 7333 0197,
www.estonian-air.ee
Ethiopian Airlines, 020 8987 9086,
www.flyethiopian.com
Etihad (0870 241 7121, www.etihadairways.com),
based in Abu Dhabi
EuroManx (0870 787 7879,
www.euromanx.com) links the Isle of Man
with UK airports
EVA Airways (020 7380 8308, www.evaair.com),
based in Taiwan
Flywho (0870 112 2767, www.flywho.com)
flies between Birmingham and Florida
GB Airways (0870 850 9850, www.ba.com),
destinations across the Mediterranean
Liat (001 268 480 5601, www.fly-liat.com),
Caribbean inter-island airline
Loganair (0870 850 9850,
www.loganair.co.uk), Scotland
Lot Polish Airlines, 0845 601 0949,
www.lot.com
Lufthansa German Airlines, 0870 837 7747,
www.lufthansa.co.uk
Malaysia Airlines, 0870 607 9090,
www.malaysiaairlines.com
Malev Hungarian Airlines, 0870 909 0588,
www.malev.com
Maxjet Airways (0800 023 4300,
www.maxjet.com), all-business-class airline
from Stansted to the US
Mexicana, 0870 890 0040,
www.mexicana.com
Middle East Airlines (020 7467 8000,
www.mea.com.lb), based in Lebanon

Northwest Airlines (0870 507 4074,
www.nwa.com), US carrier
Olympic Airlines (0870 606 0460,
www.olympicairlines.com), Greece
Pakistan International Airlines, 0800 587 1023,
www.piac.com.pk
PGA Portugalia Airlines
(**www.flypga.com**), Portugal
Qantas Airways (0845 774 7767
www.qantas.co.uk), Australia
Qatar Airways, 020 7896 3636,
www.qatarairways.com
Royal Air Maroc (020 7307 5800,
www.royalairmaroc.com), Morocco
Royal Brunei Airlines, 020 7584 6660,
www.bruneiair.com
Royal Jordanian, 020 7878 6300,
www.rja.com.jo
SAA (South African Airways), 0870 747 1111,
www.flysaa.com
Saudi Arabian Airlines, 020 7798 9890,
www.saudiairlines.com
Scandinavian Airlines, 0870 607 2772,
www.flysas.com
ScotAirways 0870 606 0707,
www.scotairways.com
Singapore Airlines, 0844 800 2380,
www.singaporeair.co.uk
SN Brussels Airlines, 0870 735 2345,
www.flysn.co.uk
Sri Lankan Airlines, 020 8538 2001,
www.srilankan.aero
Swiss, 0845 601 0956,
www.swiss.com
Syrian Air, 020 7493 2851,
www.syriaair.com
TAP Air Portugal, 0845 601 0932,
www.flytap.com
Thai Airways International, 0870 606 0911,
www.thaiair.com
Tunisair, 020 7437 6236,
www.tunisair.com
Turkish Airlines, 020 7766 9300,
www.turkishairlines.com
Ukraine International Airlines, 01293 596609,
www.flyuia.com
United Airlines, 0845 844 4777,
www.unitedairlines.co.uk
Virgin Atlantic Airways, 0870 380 2007,
www.virgin-atlantic.com
VLM Airlines, 0871 666 5050,
www.flyvlm.com

Budget airlines

Aer Arann (0800 587 2324,
www.skyroad.com), based in the Republic
of Ireland, offers domestic, UK and France
connections.

Air Berlin (0870 738 8880, **www.airberlin.com**),
based in Germany, is one of the largest budget
carriers with a network of routes across Europe,
and flies into five UK airports.
Air Scotland (0870 850 0958,
www.air-scotland.com) is a small Scottish
airline operating to five Spanish destinations
plus Athens.
Air Southwest (0870 241 8202,
www.airsouthwest.com) is a Plymouth-based
airline with a network of UK routes plus Dublin.
Atlas Blue (**www.atlas-blue.com**), a subsidiary of
Moroccan national carrier Royal Air Maroc, flies
from Marrakesh to Gatwick and other European
destinations.
BA Connect (0870 850 9850, **www.ba.com**) is
British Airways' version of a budget airline,
offering short-haul routes to Europe from
regional UK airports.
Bmibaby (0871 224 0224, **www.bmibaby.com**),
a subsidiary of bmi, is one of the UK's largest
budget airlines, with flights out of 18 regional
UK airports to destinations across Europe.
Centralwings (00 48 22 558 0045,
www.centralwings.com), an arm of Polish
carrier LOT, operates out of three UK airports to
seven in Poland, and across Europe.
easyJet (0905 821 0905, 65p/min,
www.easyjet.com) has several major hubs and
hundreds of routes across Europe, and is testing
the business model by adding farther-flung
destinations such as Marrakesh and Istanbul.
Flybe (0871 700 0535, **www.flybe.com**), formerly
British European, flies out of 21 UK airports to
destinations across Europe.
FlyGlobespan (0870 556 1522,
www.flyglobespan.com), a Scottish airline,
flies out of Edinburgh, Glasgow and Stansted to
cities across Europe.
FlyMe (00 46 770 790790, **www.flyme.com**); this
Swedish-based airline connects Gothenburg
with Stansted and other European destinations.
Germanwings (0870 252 1250,
www.germanwings.com) is a large German
budget carrier which connects four UK airports
with four across Germany.
Hapag-Lloyd Express (0870 606 0519,
www.hlx.com), part of the same group as
Thomson Holidays, is a German airline and
connects various UK and German cities.
Helvetic (020 7026 3464, **www.helvetic.com**) is
a Swiss airline that flies out of Zurich to Luton
and a host of other European destinations.
Iceland Express (0870 240 5600,
www.icelandexpress.com) links Stansted and
Reykjavik.
Jet2 (0871 226 1737, **www.jet2.com**) is a UK-
based airline with more than 50 routes out of
seven UK airports.

Meridiana (0845 355 5588,
  www.meridiana.it): an Italian airline that flies
  from Gatwick to Florence and Olbia, on Sardinia,
  and other routes, mostly within Italy.
Monarch Scheduled (0870 040 5040,
  www.flymonarch.com) has long been known
  as a charter carrier. It also has a scheduled
  operation which uses a budget business model,
  flying from various UK airports to sunshine
  destinations in Spain and Portugal.
Niki (0870 738 8880, www.flyniki.com), based in
  Austria, links Stansted and Vienna; it is named
  after its owner, Niki Lauda.
Norwegian Air Shuttle (00 47 21 490015,
  www.norwegian.no) flies between Oslo and
  Stansted, and Manchester and Bergen.
Ryanair (0871 246 0000, www.ryanair.com), the
  largest budget airline in Europe, has hundreds
  of connections from 22 UK airports.
SkyEurope (0905 722 2747, 25p/min,
  www.skyeurope.com) operates between
  airports in the UK and the Czech Republic,
  Hungary, Slovakia and Poland.
Sterling (0870 787 8038, www.sterlingticket.
  com) is a Danish airline that flies into Gatwick
  and Edinburgh from Copenhagen, Billund, Oslo
  and Helsinki.
Thomsonfly (0870 190 0737,
  www.thomsonfly.com), part of the TUI group
  that also owns Thomson Holidays, operates
  from a large number of UK airports to sunshine
  destinations across the Mediterranean; it also
  operates as a charter airline.
Transavia (020 7365 4997,
  www.transavia.com) connects Stansted
  with Rotterdam, and Glasgow Prestwick with
  Amsterdam.
Wizz Air (00 48 22 351 9499, www.wizzair.com)
  operates from Luton, Liverpool and Glasgow
  Prestwick to destinations across Central and
  Eastern Europe.
Zoom Airlines (0870 240 0055,
  www.flyzoom.com) flies between five UK
  airports and eight Canadian cities.

Charter airlines

Air Transat, 0870 556 1522,
  www.airtransat.co.uk
Astraeus, 01293 819800,
  www.flyastraeus.com
Excel Airways, 0870 169 0169,
  www.xl.com
First Choice Airways, 0870 757 2757,
  www.firstchoice.co.uk
Flyjet, 01293 602000,
  www.fly-jet.com
Monarch, 0870 458 2861,
  www.flymonarch.com

MyTravel, 0870 241 5333,
  www.mytravel.com
Thomas Cook Airlines, 0870 758 0204,
  www.thomascookairlines.co.uk
Thomsonfly, 02476 282828,
  www.thomsonfly.com

Private jet contacts

Aspire Holidays, 0845 345 9095,
  www.aspireholidays.co.uk
Bombardier Skyjet International, 020 8538 0225,
  www.skyjetinternational.com
Bookajet, 0870 458 3384,
  www.bookajet.com
Club 328, 02380 629800,
  www.club328.com
Hannington Aviation, 01242 251799,
  www.hanningtonaviation.co.uk
Jeffersons, 0870 850 8181,
  www.jeffersons.com
Kuoni World Class, 01306 747001,
  www.kuoni.co.uk/worldclass
London Air Charter Centre, 020 8460 7755,
  www.london-aircharter.com
Lufthansa Private Jet, 00 49 18 0299 3300,
  www.lufthansa-private-jet.com
Marquis Jet, 020 7590 5110,
  www.marquisjet.com
NetJetsEurope, 020 7590 5120,
  www.netjetseurope.com
Scholefield, Turnbull and Partners, 01344 628181,
  www.stptravel.com/luxury

Consumer information

Air Transport Users' Council (AUC),
  020 7240 6061, www.auc.org.uk
Civil Aviation Authority (CAA), 020 7453 6430,
  www.atol.org.uk
Office of Fair Trading,
  www.oft.gov.uk.

Buying a flight

www.airline-network.co.uk
www.avro.co.uk
www.deckchair.com
www.dial-a-flight.com
www.ebookers.com
www.expedia.co.uk
www.flightline.co.uk
www.flightsavers.co.uk
www.freedomflights.co.uk
www.lastminute.com
www.opodo.co.uk
www.skydeals.co.uk
www.trailfinders.com
www.travelocity.co.uk
www.travelrepublic.co.uk
www.travelselect.com

Price comparison websites

www.allcheckin.com
www.cheapflights.co.uk
www.moneysavingexpert.com/flightchecker
www.shermanstravel.co.uk
www.sidestep.com
www.skyscanner.net
www.travelfusion.com
www.traveljungle.com
www.travelsupermarket.com

Flight, planning and airport information

www.airlinequality.com.
www.airsafe.com
www.airtrek.com
www.dohop.com
www.flightmapping.com
www.flightontime.info.
www.seatguru.com
Aviation Health Institute, 01865 715999,
   www.aviation-health.org
The Official Airlines Guide,
   www.oag.com

Airport lounges

Many tour operators and travel agents can book lounges for you, or book direct with the airport.

APH, 0870 733 0515,
   www.aph.com
BCP, 0870 013 4542,
   www.bcponline.co.uk
Executive Lounges, 0161 490 5735,
   www.executivelounges.com
Holiday Extras, 0870 844 4186,
   www.holidayextras.co.uk
Lounge Pass, 020 8253 5146,
   www.loungepass.com
Priority Pass, 020 8680 1338
   www.prioritypass.com
Regency Premier Lounges, 01205 761176

Airport parking

Airparks, 0870 844 2384,
   www.airparks.co.uk
Airport Car Parking,
   www.airport-car-parking.com
APH, 0870 733 0515, www.aph.com
BAA, 0870 000 1000,
   www.baa.com
BCP, 0870 013 4580,
   www.bcponline.co.uk
Chauffeured Parking Services, 0870 411 1118,
   www.parkwithcps.com
Compare Airport Parking,
   www.compare-airport-parking.co.uk
Eparking, 01279 666060,
   www.eparking.uk.com

FHR, 0870 745 6377, www.fhr-net.co.uk
Happy Parking, 0870 844 2389,
   www.happyparking.com
Help Me Park, 0870 300 6009,
   www.help-me-park.com
Holiday Extras, 0870 844 4186,
   www.holidayextras.co.uk
MBW Valet Park, 020 8759 5252,
   www.mbwvaletparking.com
NCP Flight Path, 0800 128128,
   www.ncp.co.uk
Park and Save,
   www.parkandsave.co.uk
Parking Express, 0871 222 0222,
   www.parkingexpress.co.uk
PAS Gatwick, 0870 242 4670,
   www.parkinggatwick.com
Pink Elephant, 0870 060 7071,
   www.pinkelephantparking.com
Purple Parking, 0845 450 0808,
   www.purpleparking.com
Q-Park, 0870 013 4781,
   www.q-park.co.uk

Baggage tracking services

GlobalBagtag, 0870 765 7280,
   www.globalbagtag.com
Holiday Care,
   www.holiday-care.co.uk
i-TRAK, 0870 127 0002,
   www.i-trak.com
Yellowtag,
   www.yellowtag.com

Fear of flying courses

Aviatours, 01252 793280,
   www.aviatours.co.uk
Flying Without Fear, 01423 714900,
   www.flyingwithoutfear.info
Also see www.askthepilot.com

Travelling to UK airports

Countrywide

National Express, 0870 5757747,
   www.nationalexpress.com
National Rail enquiries, 0845 748 4950,
   www.nationalrail.co.uk

London

Heathrow Connect, 0845 678 6975,
   www.heathrowconnect.com
Heathrow Express, 0845 600 1515,
   www.heathrowexpress.com
Gatwick Express, 0845 600 1515,
   www.gatwickexpress.com
Stansted Express, 0845 600 7245,
   www.stanstedexpress.com

Thameslink line, 0845 748 4950,
www.thameslink.co.uk
The Piccadilly line, London Underground,
020 7222 1234, **www.tfl.gov.uk**

RAIL TRAVEL
Travelling by train (Europe)
European Rail Guide,
www.europeanrailguide.com
Eurostar, 0870 518 6186,
www.eurostar.co.uk
Eurotunnel, 0870 535 3535,
www.eurotunnel.com
International rail links,
www.hacon.de/hafas_e/www.shtml
Inter Rail,
www.interrailnet.com
Seat 61,
www.seat61.com

Booking direct
France
SNCF,
www.voyages-sncf.com
TGV,
www.tgv.co.uk
Thalys,
www.thalys.com

Germany
Cross-Europe night trains,
www.nachtzug.de
German Railways, 0870 243 5363,
www.bahn.co.uk

Italy
Trenitalia,
www.trenitalia.com
Trenok, **www.trenok.com** offers low-cost
services (in Italian only)
www.italiarail.co.uk

Spain
Elipsos, international overnight services,
www.elipsos.com
Renfe train service,
www.renfe.es

Rail agents
European Rail, 020 7387 0444,
www.europeanrail.com
Freedom Rail, 0870 757 9898,
www.freedomrail.com
Rail Pass Direct, 0870 084 1413,
www.railpassdirect.co.uk
RailBookers, 0870 458 9080,
www.railbookers.com
RailChoice, 0870 165 7300,
www.railchoice.co.uk

RailEurope, 0870 584 8848,
www.raileurope.co.uk
SD Enterprises, 020 8903 3411,
www.indiarail.co.uk
Simply Rail, 0870 084 1414,
www.simplyrail.com
The TrainLine, 0870 084 1417,
www.internationaltrainline.com
Trainseurope, 0871 700 7722,
www.trainseurope.co.uk

Motorail
French Motorail, 0870 241 5415,
www.raileurope.co.uk
Railsavers, 0870 750 7070,
www.railsavers.com

Classic train journeys
Blue Train, South Africa,
www.bluetrain.co.za
The Ghan, Australia,
www.railaustralia.com.au
Glacier Express, Switzerland,
www.glacierexpress.ch
Palace on Wheels, India,
www.palaceonwheels.net
Rocky Mountaineer, Canada,
www.rockymountaineer.com
Royal Scotsman, UK,
www.royalscotsman.com

Rail holiday operators
Cresta, 0870 238 7711,
www.crestaholidays.co.uk
Enthusiast Holidays, 020 8699 3654,
www.enthusiasthols.com
eRail, 020 7387 0444,
www.erail.co.uk
Ffestiniog Travel, 01766 512400,
www.festtravel.co.uk
French Travel Service, 0870 241 4243,
www.f-t-s.co.uk
Great Rail Journeys, 01904 521900,
www.greatrail.com
On the Go Tours, 020 7371 1113,
www.onthegotours.com
Orient-Express, 0845 077 2222,
www.orient-express.com
Railtrail, 01538 382323,
www.railtrail.co.uk
Regent Holidays, 0870 499 0911,
www.regent-holidays.co.uk
Vodkatrain, 020 8877 7650,
www.vodkatrain.com

Rail and sail

Dutchflyer, 0870 545 5455,
www.dutchflyer.co.uk
SailRail, 0845 075 5755,
www.sailrail.co.uk

COACH TRAVEL
Coach holiday operators

Archers Direct, 0845 600 1910,
www.archersdirect.co.uk
Coachtrips.com, 020 8450 5354,
www.coachtrips.com
Consort Travel, 0845 345 0300,
www.consorttravel.com
Cosmos Tourama, 0800 083 9837,
www.cosmostourama.co.uk
David Urquhart Travel, 0845 700 0400,
www.davidurquharttravel.co.uk
Eurolines, 0870 580 8080,
www.eurolines.co.uk
Insight Vacations, 01475 741203,
www.insightvacations.com
Leger Holidays, 0800 018 9898,
www.legerbreaks.com
Page & Moy, 0870 833 4012,
www.pageandmoy.com
Saga, 0800 096 0089,
www.saga.co.uk
Thomas Cook Tours, 0870 443 4436,
www.thomascooktours.com
Titan HiTours, 01293 455345,
www.titanhitours.co.uk
WA Shearings, 01942 824824,
www.washearings.com

FERRIES
You can book ferry tickets through your travel
agent, direct with the ferry companies listed
below, or through these specialist agencies that
offer tickets from a variety of ferry lines.

Ferry agents

Cheap4Ferries, 0870 111 0634,
www.cheap4ferries.co.uk
Direct Ferries, 0871 222 3312,
www.directferries.com
Eurodrive, 0870 442 2440,
www.eurodrive.co.uk
Ferry Booker, 0870 442 2418,
www.ferrybooker.com
Ferry Savers, 0870 990 8492,
www.ferrysavers.com
The Passenger Shipping Association,
www.sailanddrive.com

Ferry companies
You can book ferry tickets through your travel
agent, direct with the ferry companies listed
below, or through these specialist agencies that
offer tickets from a variety of ferry lines.

Acciona Trasmediterranea (0871 720 6445,
www.atferries.com); since May 2006 this
Spanish operation has linked Portsmouth and
Bilbao.
Brittany Ferries (0870 536 0360
www.brittanyferries.co.uk) dominates the
western channel, offering both conventional
ferry and high-speed seacat services from
Portsmouth, Poole and Plymouth to Cherbourg,
Caen, Roscoff, St Malo and Santander.
Caledonian MacBrayne (Calmac) (0870 565 0000,
www.calmac.co.uk) provides a lifeline service
with 30 vessels going between 22 islands and
four peninsulas in the west of Scotland.
Condor Ferries (0845 345 2000
www.condorferries.com) links Portsmouth,
Poole and Weymouth to St Malo and the
Channel Islands, and Cherbourg in summer,
using three fast ferries and a conventional ferry.
DFDS Seaways (0870 252 0524,
www.dfdsseaways.co.uk) operates from
Harwich to Esbjerg in Denmark, and from
Newcastle to Kristiansand in Norway,
Gothenburg in Sweden, and Amsterdam.
Fjord Line (0870 143 9669, www.fjordline.co.uk)
operates a service from Newcastle to Bergen,
Haugesund and Stavanger in Norway.
Hoverspeed (0870 524 0241,
www.hoverspeed.com) operates high-speed
catamarans on the Dover-Calais route, out of
dedicated ports, which it claims helps to offer
a speedy turnaround. Crossings take less than
an hour.
Irish Ferries (0870 517 1717,
www.irishferries.com) goes from Dublin to
Holyhead and Rosslare to Pembroke. On the
Dublin-Holyhead route it offers a catamaran
service, plus the giant *Ulysses*, the world's
largest ferry, which takes 1,342 cars and 2,000
passengers over 12 decks. It also runs a service
from Rosslare to Cherbourg and Roscoff.
Isle of Man Steam Packet Company (0870 552
3523, www.steam-packet.com); operating
since 1830, it offers a conventional ferry service
from Douglas to Heysham year-round, plus fast
craft services to Liverpool, Belfast and Dublin
in summer.
Norfolkline (0870 870 1020,
www.norfolkline.com) is the only ferry
operator on the Dover-Dunkirk route, offering
ten sailings each day, taking two hours. It also
offers Irish Sea crossings, linking Birkenhead
and Heysham with Belfast and Dublin (0870 600
4321, www.norsemerchant.com).

Northlink Ferries (0845 600 0449,
   www.northlinkferries.co.uk) links Aberdeen
   and Scrabster to Orkney and Shetland.
P&O Ferries (0870 520 2020,
   www.poferries.com) offers three routes:
   Dover-Calais, Hull-Rotterdam/Zeebrugge, and
   Portsmouth-Bilbao. It has a branch of Langan's
   Brasserie on each ferry and on the *Pride of
   Bilbao*, operating to Spain, a wildlife officer
   helps passengers to spot whales and dolphins in
   the Bay of Biscay.
P&O Irish Sea (0870 242 4777,
   www.poirishsea.com) offers ferry services
   between Dublin and Liverpool, Larne and Troon
   and Larne and Cairnryan.
Red Funnel (0870 444 8898,
   www.redfunnel.co.uk) serves the Isle of Wight,
   operating three car ferries from Southampton
   to East Cowes, and four high speed passenger-
   only ferries from Southampton to West Cowes.
SeaFrance (0870 571 1711, www.seafrance.com)
   is the only French operator on the Dover-Calais
   route, where it operates four vessels including
   its flagships, the new *SeaFrance Rodin* and
   SeaFrance Berlioz, which both take up to 1,900
   people and 700 cars. These ferries take 70
   minutes, the two older ferries take 90 minutes,
   and there are 15 daily crossings in all.
Speedferries (0870 220 0570,
   www.speedferries.com) offers 55-minute
   crossings between Dover's Eastern Docks and
   Boulogne on a Speedcat catamaran, all year
   round.
Stena Line (0870 570 7070, www.stenaline.co.uk)
   offers a mixture of conventional and high-speed
   ferries from Harwich to the Hook of Holland,
   Larne to Fleetwood, Belfast to Stranraer, Dublin
   to Holyhead, Dun Laoghaire to Holyhead and,
   in summer, Rosslare to Fishguard, a route they
   have plied for 100 years in 2006.
Superfast Ferries (www.superfast.com) operates a
   daily overnight 18-hour service between Rosyth
   in Scotland and Zeebrugge in Belgium.
Swansea Cork Ferries (01792 456116,
   www.swansea-cork.ie) unsurprisingly links
   Swansea and Cork, using one conventional
   car ferry which takes ten hours to make the
   crossing.
TransEuropa (01843 595522,
   www.transeuropaferries.co.uk) offers car
   ferries (no foot passengers) between Ramsgate
   and Ostend in Belgium.
Transmanche Ferries (0800 917 1201,
   www.transmancheferries.com) offers a four-
   hour crossing from Newhaven to Dieppe, the
   only operator on this route since Hoverspeed
   abandoned it in 2005.

Wightlink (0870 582 7744 www.wightlink.co.uk)
   serves the Isle of Wight, with car and passenger
   services from Portsmouth to Fishbourne and
   Lymington to Yarmouth, plus a passenger-only
   fastcat service from Portsmouth to Ryde.

DRIVING OVERSEAS
General contacts
The British Vehicle Rental And Leasing
   Association, www.bvrla.co.uk
Driver and Vehicle Licensing Agency (DVLA),
   0870 240 0009, www.dvla.gov.uk
Euro Consumer, www.euroconsumer.org.uk
Insurance4carhire.com, 020 7012 6300,
   www.insurance4carhire.com

Breakdown cover
The AA, 0800 444500,
   www.theaa.com
Direct Line, 0845 246 8704,
   www.directline.com
Europ Assistance, 0870 737 5720,
   www.europ-assistance.co.uk
Green Flag Motoring Assistance, 0800 400638,
   www.greenflag.co.uk
The RAC, 0800 550055,
   www.rac.co.uk

Car hire firms
Alamo, 0870 400 4562,
   www.alamo.co.uk
Avis, 0870 010 0287,
   www.avis.co.uk
Autodriveaway, USA,
   www.autodriveaway.com
Budget, 0870 156 5656,
   www.budget.co.uk
Europcar, 0870 607 5000,
   www.europcar.co.uk
Hertz, 0870 848 4848,
   www.hertz.co.uk
National, 0870 400 4560,
   www.nationalcar.co.uk
Sixt, 0870 156 7567,
   www.e-sixt.co.uk

Car hire brokers
Car Hire Warehouse, 01233 500464,
   www.carhirewarehouse.com
Carrentals.co.uk, 0845 225 0845,
   www.carrentals.co.uk
easyCar, 0906 333 3333, 60p/min,
   www.easycar.com
Holiday Autos, 0870 400 0000,
   www.holidayautos.co.uk
OnAirport, 0870 902 8021,
   www.onairportcarhire.com
Suncars, 0870 500 5566,
   www.suncars.com

UK HOLIDAYS

Tourist boards

England: 0845 456 3456,
www.enjoyengland.com
Scotland: 0845 225 5121,
www.visitscotland.com
Wales: 0870 830 0301,
www.visitwales.com
Northern Ireland: 02890 246609,
www.discovernorthernireland.com

UK activities

Active Breaks, 0845 330 8584,
www.active-breaks.com
Association of British Riding Schools,
01736 369440, www.abrs-info.org
British Activity Holiday Association,
020 8842 1292, www.baha.org.uk
British Gliding Association, 0116 253 1051,
www.gliding.co.uk
British Hang Gliding and Paragliding Association,
0870 870 6490, www.bhpa.co.uk
British Horse Society, 0870 120 2244,
www.bhs.org.uk
British Orienteering Federation, 01629 734042,
www.britishorienteering.org.uk
Disability Sport England, 0161 953 2499,
www.disabilitysport.org.uk
Factivities, 0870 777 3567,
www.factivities.co.uk, directory of outdoor
pursuits across the UK
Snowsport England, 0121 501 2314,
www.snowsportengland.org.uk
Sport England, 0845 850 8508,
www.sportengland.org
UK Skydiving, 0800 111 6880,
www.ukskydiving.co.uk
VisitBritain,
www.visitbritain.com/getactive

Heritage and culture

Association of Leading Visitor Attractions,
www.alva.org.uk
British Resorts Association,
www.britishresorts.co.uk
Cadw, the Welsh Assembly's environment body,
www.cadw.wales.gov.uk
Churches Conservation Trust, 020 7213 0660,
www.visitchurches.org.uk
England's World Heritage Sites, 020 7211 6000,
www.ukworldheritage.org.uk
English Heritage, 0870 333 1182,
www.english-heritage.org.uk
Hidden England,
www.hiddenengland.org

Historic Houses Association, 020 7259 5688,
www.hha.org.uk
Historic Royal Palaces,
www.hrp.org.uk
Historic Scotland, 0131 668 8600,
www.historic-scotland.gov.uk
National Trust, 0870 458 4000,
www.nationaltrust.org.uk
Royal Horticultural Society,
020 7834 4333, www.rhs.org.uk
The Royal Collection,
www.royalcollection.org.uk
The Treasure Houses of England,
www.treasurehouses.co.uk
UK Heritage Railways,
www.heritagerailways.com

Nature activities and conservation

Association of National Park Authorities,
www.anpa.gov.uk
British Trust for Conservation Volunteers,
01302 572244, www.btcv.org
The Campaign to Protect Rural England,
020 7981 2800, www.cpre.org.uk
Countryside Alliance, 020 7840 9200,
www.countryside-alliance.org
English Nature, 01733 455100,
www.english-nature.org.uk
Field Studies Council, 0845 345 4071,
www.field-studies-council.org
Forestry Commission, 01223 314546,
www.forestry.gov.uk
National Association for Areas of Outstanding
Natural Beauty, 01451 862007,
www.aonb.org.uk
National Trust, 0870 458 4000,
www.nationaltrust.org.uk
National Trust Working Holidays, 0870 429 2429,
www.nationaltrust.org.uk/volunteering
National Trust for Scotland, 0131 243 9300,
www.nts.org.uk
Royal Society for the Protection of Birds,
01767 680551, www.rspb.org.uk
Scottish Natural Heritage, 0131 447 4784,
www.snh.org.uk
The Wildfowl and Wetlands Trust, 01453 891900,
www.wwt.org.uk
The Wildlife Trusts, 0870 036 7711,
www.wildlifetrusts.org
Woodland Trust, 01476 581135,
www.woodland-trust.org.uk

Food and drink

British Food Fortnight,
www.britishfoodfortnight.co.uk
English Wine Producers,
www.englishwineproducers.com
Farm Retail Association,
www.farmshopping.com

Food from Britain,
  www.regionalfoodanddrink.com
Great Little Places, 01686 668030,
  www.little-places.co.uk
National Association of Farmers' Markets,
  www.farmersmarkets.net
The Pembrokeshire Food Guide, 0870 510 3103,
  www.visitpembrokeshire.com
The Taste District, 015394 44444,
  www.golakes.co.uk
The Tastes of Lincolnshire,
  www.tastesoflincolnshire.com
Trencherman's Guide, 0870 442 0880,
  www.indulgesouthwest.co.uk
VisitBritain,
  www.visitbritain.com/taste
Welsh Rarebits, 01686 668030,
  www.rarebits.co.uk

Public transport in the UK

Megabus, 0900 160 0900, premium rate,
  www.megabus.com
National Express, 0870 580 8080,
  www.nationalexpress.com
National Rail, 0845 748 4950
  www.nationalrail.co.uk
Q Jump, www.qjump.co.uk
The Train Line,
  www.thetrainline.com
Train Taxi,
  www.traintaxi.co.uk
Transport Direct,
  www.transportdirect.com
Travel Line, 0870 608 2608,
  www.traveline.org.uk

UK HOTELS AND HOTEL GROUPS

Abode,
  www.abodehotels.co.uk
Alias Hotels,
  www.aliashotels.com
Apex Hotels,
  www.apexhotels.co.uk
Best Loved Hotels, 020 8962 9555,
  www.bestlovedhotels.com
Best Western, 0845 456 7050,
  www.bestwestern.co.uk
Bridgehouse Hotels, 0870 333 9124,
  www.bridgehousehotels.com
Britain's Finest, 01488 684321,
  www.britainsfinest.co.uk
Center Parcs, 0870 067 3030,
  www.centerparcs.co.uk
Chic Treats, 0870 458 6392,
  www.chictreats.co.uk
City Inn,
  www.cityinn.com

De Vere Hotels and Resorts, 0870 111 0516,
  www.devere.co.uk
Elite Hotels, 020 7495 8801,
  www.elitehotels.co.uk
The Eton Collection,
  www.theetoncollection.com
Exclusive Hotels,
  www.exclusivehotels.co.uk
Fine Individual Hotels,
  www.fihotels.co.uk
Firmdale Hotels,
  www.firmdalehotels.com
Great Inns of Britain, 01423 770152,
  www.greatinns.co.uk
Great Little Places, 01686 668030,
  www.little-places.co.uk
Hand Picked Hotels, 0845 458 0901,
  www.handpicked.co.uk
Historic House Hotels,
  www.historichousehotels.com
Hotel du Vin,
  www.hotelduvin.com
Ireland's Blue Book, 00 353 1 676 9914,
  www.irelands-blue-book.ie
Les Routiers,
  www.routiers.co.uk
Macdonald Hotels and Resorts, 0870 830 4812,
  www.macdonaldhotels.co.uk
Malmaison,
  www.malmaison.com
Manor House Hotels, 00 353 1 295 8900,
  www.manorhousehotels.com
Marston Hotels, 0845 130 0700,
  www.marstonhotels.com
Niche Hotels,
  www.nichehotels.com
Paramount Hotels, 0870 168 8833,
  www.paramount-hotels.com
Pride of Britain Hotels, 0800 089 3929,
  www.prideofbritainhotels.com
Q Hotels,
  www.qhotels.co.uk
Shire Hotels, 01282 414141,
  www.shirehotels.com
Von Essen hotel group, 01761 240121,
  www.vonessenhotels.co.uk
Warner Breaks, 0870 264 0263,
  www.warnerbreaks.co.uk
Welsh Rarebits, 01686 668030,
  www.rarebits.co.uk

BUDGET ACCOMMODATION
B&B agencies

At Home in London, 020 8748 1943,
  www.athomeinlondon.co.uk
Bed & Breakfast and Homestay Association,
  020 7385 9922, www.bbha.org.uk

Distinctly Different, 01225 866842,
www.distinctlydifferent.co.uk
Unique Home Stays, 01637 881942,
www.uniquehomestays.com
Uptown Reservations, 020 7937 2001,
www.uptownres.co.uk
Wolsey Lodges, 01473 822058,
www.wolseylodges.com

Budget hotels
Dakota, 0870 442 2727,
www.dakotahotels.co.uk
Days Inn, 0800 028 0400,
www.daysinn.co.uk
easyHotel, **www.easyhotel.com**
Etap, **www.etaphotel.com**
Express by Holiday Inn, 0870 400 8143,
www.hiexpress.co.uk
Ibis,
www.ibishotel.com
Premier Travel Inn, 0870 242 8000,
www.premiertravelinn.com
Travelodge, 0870 085 0950,
www.travelodge.co.uk

Pod hotels
easyhotel,
www.easyhotel.com
Formule 1,
www.hotelformule1.com
Nitenite, 0845 890 9099,
www.nitenite.com
Yotel,
www.yotel.com

Hostels
An Oige, Irish Youth Hostel Association,
00 353 1 830 4555, **www.anoige.ie**
The Generator, 020 7388 7666,
www.generatorhostels.com
Hostelling International Northern Ireland,
02890 324733, **www.hini.org.uk**
Piccadilly Backpackers, 020 7434 9009,
www.piccadillyhotel.net
Scottish Youth Hostels Association,
0870 155 3255, **www.syha.org.uk**
St Christopher's Inns, 020 7407 1856,
www.st-christophers.co.uk
The YMCA,
www.ymca.org.uk
The Youth Hostels Association, 0870 770 8868,
www.yha.org.uk

COTTAGE RENTAL AGENCIES
Some of the biggest UK agencies are now part
of the Holiday Cottages Group, which is owned
by American travel giant Cendant. Its buying
power gives it some authority, the ability to

impose standards, and help if things go wrong.
These brands are within it and are combined on
its website **www.cottages4you.co.uk**, which is a
good place to look for late deals.

Blakes, 0870 078 1300,
www.blakes-cottages.co.uk
Country Holidays, 0870 197 6895,
www.country-holidays.co.uk
English Country Cottages, 0870 197 6890,
www.english-country-cottages.co.uk
Welcome Cottages, 0870 336 7770,
www.welcomecottages.com

Other agencies that offer cottages across the UK
include:

The Big Domain (01326 240028,
www.thebigdomain.com) specialises in large
properties; its sister company
www.thelittledomain.com offers cottages
for two.
The Cottage Collection (01603 724809,
www.the-cottage-collection.co.uk) has 500
properties for rent across the UK.
Cottage Line (**www.cottageline.com**) combines
the offerings of 11 regional specialists, making
nearly 2,000 self-catering homes throughout
England, Wales and Scotland available through
this website.
Cottage Net (**www.cottagenet.co.uk**) claims to
be the largest rental database for Britain and
Ireland, with more than 25,000 holiday
cottages on offer.
Hoseasons (0870 534 2342
www.hoseasons.co.uk) offers cottages, holiday
parks and boating holidays in the UK, Ireland
and Europe, with nearly 2,000 properties in the
UK and Ireland.
Premier Cottages (01271 336050,
www.premiercottages.co.uk) is a marketing
association which offers around 900 four and
five-star properties across the UK; you book
direct with the owners.
Special Escapes: The guidebook company Alastair
Sawday offers Special Escapes
(**www.special-escapes.co.uk**), a directory of
140 inspected self-catering properties "with
personality" in the UK.
The Youth Hostels Association runs a Rent-a-
Hostel scheme (**www.rentahostel.com**).

Historic, upmarket, fabulous
Blandings (020 7947 3290,
www.blandings.co.uk) offers top-notch rental
properties, often large houses, and regularly
caters for films stars and MPs.
English Heritage (0870 333 1187,
www.english-heritage.org.uk/
holidaycottages) released six of its historic

properties, including Dover Castle and Osborne House on the Isle of Wight, for rental for the first time in 2006.

Landmark Trust (01628 825925, www.landmarktrust.org.uk) restores derelict buildings and rents them to holidaymakers to pay for their restoration; it has 183 properties on its books, most in the UK but with a handful in Italy and the USA.

Loyd & Townsend-Rose (01573 229797, www.ltr.co.uk) offers Scottish castles and manor houses to rent, most for exclusive use and starting at around £20,000-£25,000 per week.

National Trust Cottages (0870 458 4422, www.nationaltrustcottages.co.uk) offers for rent 320 properties across England, Wales and Northern Ireland.

National Trust for Scotland (0131 243 9331, www.nts.org.uk) has around 50 properties to rent across Scotland.

Rural Retreats (01386 701177, www.ruralretreats.co.uk) offers more than 400 high-end properties in Scotland, England and Wales; it acts as the agent for Trinity House, renting out former lighthouse-keepers' cottages at a dozen lighthouses.

Stately Holiday Homes (01638 674749, www.statelyholidayhomes.co.uk) offers 70 luxury cottages and apartments across the UK and Ireland, typically in the grounds of stately or historic houses.

Vivat Trust Holidays (0845 090 0194, www.vivat.org.uk); similar to, but much smaller than, Landmark Trust, Vivat also restores historic buildings and rents them out.

UK regional cottage agencies

Cumbria

Cumbrian Cottages, 01228 599960, www.cumbrian-cottages.co.uk
Heart of the Lakes, 015394 32321, www.heartofthelakes.co.uk
Lakeland Cottage Company, 0870 442 5814, www.lakelandcottagecompany.com
Lakelovers, 01539 488855, www.lakelovers.co.uk

Northern England

Dales Holiday Cottages, 0870 909 9500/5, www.dales-holiday-cottages.com
Northumbria Byways, 016977 46777, www.northumbria-byways.com
Northumbria Coast and Country Cottages, 01665 830783, www.northumbria-cottages.co.uk
Peak Cottages, 0114 262 0777, www.peakcottages.com

Shoreline Cottages, 0113 244 8410, www.shoreline-cottages.com
Yorkshire Cottages, 01228 406701, www.yorkshire-cottages.info

West Country

Blue Chip Vacations, 01803 855282, www.bluechipvacations.com
Classic Cottages, 01326 555555, www.classiccottages.co.uk
Cornish Cottage Holidays, 01326 573808, www.cornishcottageholidays.co.uk
Cornish Traditional Cottages, 01208 821666, www.corncott.com
Dorset Coastal Cottages, 01305 854454, www.dorsetcoastalcottages.com
Helpful Holidays, 01647 433593, www.helpfulholidays.com
Marsden's Cottage Holidays, 01271 813777, www.marsdens.co.uk
Powell's Cottage Holidays, 0800 378771, www.powells.co.uk
Southwest Holiday Cottages, 01752 260711, www.southwestholidaycottages.com
The Thatched Cottage Company, 01395 567676, www.thethatchedcottagecompany.co.uk
Toad Hall Cottages, 01548 853089, www.toadhallcottages.com
West Cornwall Cottage Holidays, 01736 368575, www.westcornwallcottageholidays.com

Southern England and East Anglia

Big House Holidays, 01394 412305, www.bighouseholidays.co.uk
Cottage in the Country, 0870 027 5930, www.cottageinthecountry.co.uk
Great Escape Holiday Company, 01485 518717, www.thegreatescapeholiday.co.uk
Hideaways, 01747 828170, www.hideaways.co.uk
Norfolk Country Cottages, 01603 871872, www.norfolkcottages.co.uk
Norfolk Countryside Cottages, 01263 713133, www.holiday-cottage-norfolk.co.uk
Suffolk Cottage Holidays, 01394 412304, www.suffolkcottageholidays.com
Suffolk Secrets, 01502 722717, www.suffolk-secrets.co.uk

Scotland

Cottages and Castles, 01463 226990, www.cottagesandcastles.co.uk
Discover Scotland, 01556 504030, www.discoverscotland.net
Ecosse Unique, 01835 822277, www.unique-cottages.co.uk
Hamster Cottages, 01764 685400, www.hamstercottages.co.uk

Large Holiday Houses, 01381 610496,
www.lhhscotland.com
Little Holiday Houses,
www.littleholidayhouses.com
Mackays' Agency, 0870 429 5359,
www.mackays-self-catering.co.uk
Scottish Country Cottages, 0870 787 4715,
www.scottish-country-cottages.co.uk
Scotts Castle Holidays, 01208 821341,
www.scottscastles.com

Also in Scotland are operators that offer upmarket outdoor activity holidays, such as shooting and fishing, for individuals or groups, including the following:

CKD Galbraith, 01738 451600,
www.sportinglets.co.uk
George Goldsmith, 0131 476 6500,
www.georgegoldsmith.com
Loyd & Townsend-Rose, 01573 229797,
www.ltr.co.uk
Roxton Bailey Robinson, 01488 689700,
www.rbrww.com

Wales

Brecon Beacons Holiday Cottages, 01874 676446,
www.breconcottages.com
Coast and Country Holidays, 01239 881297,
www.welsh-cottages.co.uk
Coastal Cottages of Pembrokeshire,
01437 765765, **www.coastalcottages.co.uk**
Menai Holiday Cottages, 01248 717135,
www.menaiholidays.co.uk
North Wales Holiday Cottages and Farmhouses,
0870 755 9888,
www.northwalesholidaycottages.co.uk
Quality Cottages, 0800 169 2256,
www.qualitycottages.co.uk
Wales Cottage Holidays, 01686 628200,
www.wales-holidays.co.uk

Ireland

The Hidden Ireland, 00 353 98 66650,
www.hiddenireland.com
Irish Country Cottages, 0870 078 1600,
www.irish-country-cottages.co.uk
Rural Cottage Holidays, 02890 441535,
www.ruralcottageholidays.com
Shamrock Cottages, 01823 660126,
www.shamrockcottages.co.uk

CARAVANNING

The Caravan Club, 0800 521161,
www.caravanclub.co.uk
The Camping and Caravanning Club, 0845 130
7631, **www.campingandcaravanningclub.co.uk**
Camping and Caravanning UK, 0115 877 4477,
http://camping.uk-directory.com

National Caravan Council, 01252 318251,
www.nationalcaravan.co.uk
Caravan camping sites,
www.caravancampingsites.co.uk

FARM STAYS

Farm Stay UK, 01271 336141,
www.farmstayuk.co.uk
Farm and Cottage Holidays, 01237 479146,
www.farmcott.co.uk
Cartwheel, 01392 877842,
www.cartwheel.org.uk
National Farm Attractions Network,
01536 513397, **www.farmattractions.net**

Index